Early International Praise for *The Forgotten Revolution*

"*The Forgotten Revolution* should be required reading for anyone engaged in the struggle against the fortune hunters who derive their profits by destroying the ability of working men and women to distinguish illusion from reality."

Valério Arcary, a leading voice of the Brazilian labour movement, Emeritus Professor of History of the Federal Institute of São Paulo (FSP), author of numerous critically acclaimed books, including *O Martelo da História* (2016).

"This is the first book in any language to tell the true story of what happened in Hungary in 1919 and under the counterrevolutions that followed, including the current one under Viktor Orbán's leadership."

András Bíró, born in Bulgaria to Hungarian-Serbian parents, writer and civil rights activist, winner of the Right Livelihood Award for his defense of the environment, minority rights, poverty alleviation, and the promotion of civil society at grassroots level in post-communist Hungary.

"This volume sheds new light on the Councils' Republic in Hungary, including the important parts played by women and women's organisations in the plebeian revolt that shook bourgeois order in Central Europe for an exhilarating moment in 1919. A welcome addition to the literature on the lost revolutions of 1918-23."

Gareth Dale, Senior Lecturer in politics and history at Brunel University, London, whose writings have been translated into several languages, including the definitive biography, *Karl Polanyi: A Life on the Left* (2017).

"Obscured for more than a century, the true story of a people's heroic and spontaneous seizure of power is vividly displayed in this important book that illuminates the direct democratic character of the 1919 Hungarian Republic of Councils. *The Forgotten Revolution* reminds us that 'working men and women are fully entitled to be lead actors on the center stage of modern history.'"

George Katsiaficas, Professor of Humanities (ret) Wentworth Institute of Technology, Boston, global authority on "people power", author of 14 books including the American Political Science Association's Michael Harrington book award winner, *The Subversion of Politics* (2001) and *The Global Imagination of 1968* (2018).

"These essays offer a new compass for exploring the policy universe of the revolutionary states of the modern and post-modern world. They present a paradigmatic shift in our view of 'People Power.' A fresh voice in the public debate on the road forward from Dead End Capitalism and the perils of global warming."

Ilan Ziv, Israeli born filmmaker, director of *Srebrenica* (Silver Nymph and International Jury prize, Monte Carlo Television Festival); *Human bombs* (special mention, Prix Europa, Berlin International Film Festival); *The Junction* (Best Documentary, Haifa International Film Festival) and many others including *Capitalism; People Power;* and *Tango of Slaves*.

THE FORGOTTEN REVOLUTION

THE 1919 HUNGARIAN REPUBLIC OF COUNCILS

András B. Göllner, ed.

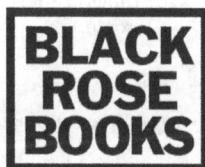

BLACK ROSE BOOKS

Montreal • Chicago • London

Black Rose Books No. UU413

Cover designed by Tina Carlisi.
Cover image by Mihály Biró (*Munkások! Polgarok*! ["Workers! Citizens!"], 1912).
Typesetting by Associes libres Design.

Library and Archives Canada Cataloguing in Publication

Title: The forgotten revolution : the 1919 Hungarian Republic of Councils.
Other titles: Forgotten revolution (2022)
Names: Göllner, András B., 1944- editor.
Description: Edited by András B. Göllner.
Identifiers: Canadiana (print) 20200209000 | Canadiana (ebook) 20200209019 | ISBN 9781551647173 (hardcover) | ISBN 9781551647159 (softcover) | ISBN 9781551647197 (PDF)
Subjects: LCSH: Hungary—History—Revolution, 1918-1919. | LCSH: Hungary—Politics and government—1918-1945. | LCSH: Communism—Hungary—History—20th century. | LCSH: Budapest (Hungary)—History—1872-1945.
Classification: LCC DB955.7 .F67 2020 | DDC 943.905/1—dc23

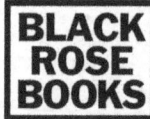

BLACK ROSE BOOKS

C.P. 35788 Succ. Léo Pariseau
Montréal, QC H2X 0A4
CANADA
www.blackrosebooks.com

ORDERING INFORMATION

USA/INTERNATIONAL	CANADA	UK/EUROPE
University of Chicago Press	University of Toronto Press	Central Books
Chicago Distribution Center	5201 Dufferin Street	Freshwater Road
11030 South Langley Avenue	Toronto, ON	Dagenham
Chicago IL 60628	M3H 5T8	RM8 1RX
(800) 621-2736 (USA)	1-800-565-9523	+44 20 8525 8800
(773) 702-7000 (International)	utpbooks@utpress.utoronto.ca	contactus@centralbooks.com
orders@press.uchicago.edu		

CONTENTS

Acknowledgments x

Preface xx

Introduction: When the Impossible Becomes Inevitable 1
Raquel Varela and András B. Göllner

1. The Roots and Antecedents of the 1919 Hungarian Republic 32
   of Councils
   Péter Csunderlik

2. Workers' Councils and Revolution: The German Example 68
   Marie Josée Lavallée

3. Workers' Councils and the 1919 Hungarian Commune 92
   Lajos Csoma

4. Exploring the Public Policy Universe of the 1919 120
   Hungarian Republic of Councils
   András B. Göllner

5. Working Women and the 1919 Commune
   Part I: Introducing Magda Aranyossi 157
   Susan Zimmermann

   Part II. The Impact of the 1917 Russian Revolution and the 1919 166
   Republic of Councils on the Working Women's Movement in Hungary
   Magda Aranyossi

6. Vienna and Budapest After WWI: A Tale of Two Cities 179
   Kari Polanyi Levitt

7. The Exiled Voice of the 1919 Commune 184
   Christopher Adam

8. The Rhapsody of the Permanent Counterrevolution 204
   in Hungary
   András B. Göllner

   Conclusion — And 1956: Coda 243
   Dimitrios Roussopoulos

   Index 245

   Bibliography 252

   Contributors 271

This book is dedicated to the memory and celebration of Ilona Duczynska,
the woman who, at the age of 20, lit the fuse of the 1918–1919 revolutions in Hungary and devoted her entire life to help liberate the oppressed, the forcefully silenced and wilfully mislead citizens of the world regardless of their nationality, race, colour or faith.

A SHARED VISION

None of the principles on which men claim to rule and
hold other men in subjection to them, are strictly right.

—Aristotle

Without clarity in aim, a political vision of a revolutionary state, there can be
no victory over tyranny and oppression… Poles apart, power and respect for
humanity are essential for the achievement of a revolutionary vision…
Respect for humanity involves direct democracy, which puts into practice its
intrinsic design—the antibodies on bureaucratic structures, the spontaneous
initiatives in all walks of public life… There is no longer a "center" a "great
model" of the revolutionary state following the gruesome tragedy of
Stalinism and the hesitant and contradictory return to sanity… The model of a
new kind of state, one that correctly handles the dichotomy of power and
respect for humanity, is yet to be worked out… It is for the revolutionary to
search for the synthesis of these opposites. For to exercise power is
unavoidable, and to practice respect for humanity, is an inalienable duty…
With the less dogmatic national and social liberation movements, this
historical task is recognized from the first as valid and legitimate…
The trend is toward autonomy, direct democracy, plurality
of forms, spontaneous initiatives in all walks of public life.

—Ilona Duczynska

I shit on all the revolutionary vanguards of this planet!… During the cold war,
Capitalism created a military horror: the neutron bomb, a weapon that
destroys life while leaving buildings intact… Its newest wonder is the
financial bomb. Unlike those dropped on Hiroshima and Nagasaki, this new
bomb not only destroys the polis, but imposes death, terror, and misery on all
those who live there. Neoliberalism and globalization destroys the material
basis of sovereignty, in order to reconstruct the nation-state according to a
single model. We are in a planetary war, of the worst and cruelest kind,
waged against all of humanity and if humanity wants to survive and improve,
its only hope resides in those pockets where the excluded, the left-for-dead,
the 'disposable' reside… We teach our children, that the world is where
words are born, that there are as many words as there are colours and they
should speak with the truth, that is to say, speak with their hearts.

—Subcomandante Marcos

ACKNOWLEDGMENTS

I AM INDEBTED TO many for not only inspiring me to undertake this project but helping me to bring it to fruition. I've chosen to give thanks and recognition to them not according to some rank order but in the manner I was taught to play jazz on the tenor saxophone by Tom Levitt, the grandson of Ilona Duczynska and Karl Polanyi, key players themselves in the drama that is the focus of this book.[1]

I am convinced that the challenge of putting this book together would not have been taken up by me or pursued with the determination and concentrated attention it deserves had I not been prompted and urged on to do so by Dimitrios Roussopoulos, the founding publisher of Black Rose Books in Montréal. One day, what seems like centuries before something called Covid-19 had changed our lives forever, I went to talk with him about a book he recently published on the 1917 Russian Revolution.[2] Somehow our conversation turned to the 1919 Hungarian Republic of Councils, and the role played by workers' councils in that short-lived Republic. We shared the view that the 1919 Budapest Commune was a critical but long neglected early attempt by working men and women to take direct control of their lives, that it was in some ways a prototype, a primordial genetic seedling that others would try to improve upon in many other parts of the world, most recently in Rojava, Northern Syria (thanks to the followers of Apo[3]). We agreed that a combination of neglect and wilful distortion by historians from all sides of the political spectrum, had badly tarnished the reputation of this enterprise, the wall of ignorance surrounding it had become as impenetrable as those thorn bushes that entombed Sleeping Beauty for a century. It was time for a fresh approach, a new take on this long-neglected part of our past. Dimitrios knew of my work and current engagement in writing a book on Ilona Duczynska, the woman who lit the fuse of the 1918–1919 revolutions in Hungary. He suggested I put together a proposal for his editorial board on the 1919 Republic of Councils and that is where this all began. He is the spiritual father of this collection and I am deeply grateful for his confidence in my ability to put his idea into practice.

Though the idea for this volume rests on his shoulders, my own interest in the revolutionary events of 1918–1919 in Hungary, goes back much further in time and space than that conversation I had a couple of years ago with Dimitrios

Roussopoulos in Montréal. He would be the first to agree: I needed very little prompting to engage in this backward glance, this voyage of discovery into a long neglected, long distorted territory of our past. Clearly, I must acknowledge the influence of those who turned my attention towards this period of world history and kept my focus on it throughout the preceding decades.

My first encounter with this "relic in our attic"—the 1919 Budapest Commune —was straight forward. It happened in my home, during my early teens in the late 1950s after my parents fled Hungary and we were granted refugee status and given a path to citizenship in Canada. This may appear maudlin to some, but I feel a never fading gratitude to my parents for yanking me off a path that seemed like a dead end to me by the time I finished my first three years of elementary schooling in Hungary. They rescued me and provided me with an environment where I could fearlessly explore the haphazard frontiers of my curiosity throughout my life. My parents, educated upper middle-class professionals prior to fleeing their homeland, joined the ranks of the millions of manual labourers upon arriving in Canada in 1956. My father worked on a garbage truck, cleaned hockey arenas, my mother cleaned houses. They taught me to respect all those who shared their station in life.

I should be careful not to create a false impression: A confrontation with the 1919 Budapest Commune is not at all an unusual occurrence for anyone who was born in Hungary after March 21, 1919. One cannot avoid bumping into this milepost in his or her country's past and remain indifferent to it. What made me perk up my ears was that virtually everyone I turned to for some insights about those events, including my parents, would become very agitated, and complain profusely of the bad taste left in their mouths by the object of my curiosity. My curiosity was further stimulated by the absence of any semblance of agreement among those I consulted just what the taste is that irritates them so badly.

For the benefit of those readers, who were not born in Hungary I owe a brief explanation. For the past 100 years, the story of the 1919 Commune had been spoon-fed to succeeding generations of Hungarians, including mine, as a horror show. Not only the extreme right, but most Hungarian democrats, liberals, and conservatives look upon it as one of the darkest, most shameful moments in their country's 1,000-year long history. To them, the 1919 Commune was a period of unrestrained 'Red Terror', an assassination attempt on Hungary's national character, a time when 'the Left' (led by 'immigrant Jews') went on the rampage and attempted to destroy the country's 1000 year long Christian-National *identity*.

Many on the Left in Hungary look on this event to this day as a badly botched effort by their comrades a 100 years earlier. They, along with most of the Left worldwide are upset that the inexperience, the recklessness of Béla Kun and his 'Lenin Boys' in Hungary had given a permanent black eye to anyone who seeks to promote the virtues of socialism anywhere in the world. (Even such a sterling historian as Eric Hobsbawm cannot restrain himself from piling on the Hungarian 'Left' by suggesting in his introduction to Ilona Duczynska's book on the Austrian civil war, that Austria's avoidance of the dire straights that befell the Hungarian working classes after WWI was primarily due to the superiority of Austria's Marxists.[4] No wonder Ilona Duczynska would spend virtually her entire book dispossessing us of that false impression.)

I carried my own negative images in my head about the apparent failures of the Hungarian proletariat in 1919 until I was close to thirty. It was only near the end of my doctoral studies in Political-Economy at the London School of Economics in the mid-1970s before I began to hear anything other than scorn or guilty admissions of failure about the 1919 Republic of Councils from anyone. I consider myself blessed, and incredibly fortunate that the first to pull the wool back from my eyes about the 1919 Republic of Councils was non other than Ilona Duczynska, the woman who at age 20, lit the fuse of the 1918–1919 rebellions in Budapest with the torch she carried from the Zimmerwald Movement's headquarters in Zurich, Switzerland to the Hungarian capital in April 1917. If anyone, she knew fine well what this rebellion was about. Because my indebtedness to her runs so deep, I would like to address it more, than in a cursory fashion.

Ilona and I gravitated towards each other as if pulled by some kind of mysterious string when I was in my late twenties and she was in her late seventies. We had some mutual friends in Hungary and had heard of each other through 'the grape-vine' during the early 1970s. Ilona was living in Pickering, Ontario by then. I was a Canadian-Hungarian graduate student in London, England. (As I alluded to earlier, I left Hungary as a child, in 1956, and came of age, as they say, in Montréal.) Both of us were travelling to Hungary from our respective outposts in the 'New World' in pursuit of our curiosity about the world we had left behind. I would meet with her finally in 1975, when I returned to Canada to begin my academic career, first in Ottawa then in Montréal. (The person who introduced us was a mutual friend—László Rajk Jr.[5]) During the last three years of her life, Ilona would often visit with me in Montréal, and we would spend long evenings talking about 1919—her role in those events, and her views of the long term impact of those events on members of the so called "Budapest School of Political Economy". Ilona had heard second hand of my work on the ideas and efforts of this group of economists to design a new socialist economic mechanism for their country, which at that time was still part of the Soviet empire. (Any effort to tamper with the Soviet model of socialism at that time was a highly dangerous maneuver and could easily land one in prison or in permanent exile. One had to be careful about what one said about these matters publicly.) For Ilona, and she assured me that she reflected her late husband, Karl Polanyi's views (Polanyi passed away in 1964), the roots of the latest economic reforms in Hungary—the New Economic Mechanism (NEM) of 1968—stemmed from the seeds sown by her generation back in 1919. She told me that the success of this new, post WWII reform generation in Hungary was her last hope for the kind of synthesis between power and humanism she spoke of in her book, *Workers in Arms*, from which I reproduced a passage inside the front-cover of these essays.

Ilona was deeply interested in what I knew of those reforms that she had pinned her hopes on, and I was curious about what she knew of the original seedlings. We developed a relationship that was based on mutual trust and respect. As a reflection of this mutual trust, she asked me to edit the draft of her first public admission—after 60 years of silence—to a conspiracy she undertook with the Hungarian anarcho-syndicalist Ervin Szabó (a cousin of Karl Polanyi), to assassinate the war-time prime minister of Hungary, Count István Tisza in May 1917. She concocted this plot with the help of Szabó, to spark a revolution in Hungary against the war, and to overthrow the old order. She talked to me about this plot even before she showed me the manuscript she was working on, during one of our late-night conversations at my home. She recounted how she was on her way to the PM's office in May 1917, pistol in her pocket to do the job, when she heard from passersby that the Prime Minister had just resigned. She recounted the deep psychological impact this aborted encounter left on her mind and how it affected her subsequent actions in Budapest leading up to the critical events of 1918–19.[6] I am forever beholden to Ilona Duczynska for eliminating the cobwebs from my mind about the 1919 Commune and for the confidence she placed in me before her passing.

At this point I would also like to acknowledge the help of three people from a small circle of friends Ilona would categorize as her "political grandchildren" in Hungary: young people she saw as rebels worthy of her support. The first on this list is the aforementioned László Rajk Jr, then Miklós Haraszti, and György Dalos. Each of them sat through lengthy interviews with me and shared their experiences and insights that were invaluable to me in this project and during my composition of my stand-alone portrait of Duczynska.

Obviously, I cannot do justice here to the hundreds of historians, fellow students, teachers who sustained my interest in the 1919 Hungarian Commune. I can only single out a few that stand above the rest. First on *this* list is Teresa Rakowska Harmstone, one of my professors and my thesis advisor at Carleton University in Ottawa where I earned a Master's Degree in International Relations and Political Science. Teresa became my first true mentor after I stumbled my way towards her to Carleton University from my rather undistinguished earlier performance 'at bat' as an honours undergraduate student in Montréal. I am certain that I would never have made it to second base, or joined the ranks of academia, had I not had the good fortune of catching her attention. She was the one who gave me the self-confidence to pursue my interest in the struggles of working men and women in Central Europe to build socialism with a human face. She and another teacher at Carleton University, the Czech dissident academic Radoslav Seluczky, were instrumental in sparking my early interest in the challenges of workers' self-management.[7] This initial spark was given even more oxygen when I began to pursue my doctoral studies in political economy at the London School of Economics under the guidance of Peter J. Wiles and my external advisor, Wlodzimierz Brus (the latter was teaching at Oxford University at the time). I also benefitted greatly from conversations during this time with Sir Nicholas Kaldor, who was teaching at Cambridge. Kaldor himself was a key participant in the development of the Hungarian Social Democratic Party's 3 Year Economic Plan in 1947 and played a key role in rebuilding Hungary's post-WWII economy. He was intimately familiar with the thinking of those Hungarian economists who would eventually constitute the Budapest School of Political Economy. I am grateful for the time he spent with me and for sharing his insights about the pre-WWII, socialist roots of Hungary's post-Stalinist economic reforms. Of these scholars I owe my greatest gratitude to the late Peter J. Wiles for his inspiration, for the patience and sympathy, the masterful and always critical guidance as I tried to penetrate the mysteries of those reforms that Ilona could "die for".

I must also say thanks, somewhat obliquely, to another one of my professors at the London School of Economics, Leonard Schapiro, for raising the question to which this book is my answer. When I was a participant in one of his seminars, Schapiro was the uncontested giant of the British school of Kremlinology. While acknowledging his immense knowledge of the internal machinations of the Communist Party of the Soviet Union, I was generally unhappy with his one-dimensional portrayal of political life under one-party rule in Central Europe and dared to suggest in one of his seminars that the working men and women of the country where I have just come back from—Hungary—are not playing dead, but actually have fire in their bellies. I dared to suggest to him and to others in the room at the time, that the Kremlinologists' totalitarian image of life under one party rule is limiting our ability to see the trees from the forest.[8] Schapiro looked me up and down as if he was inspecting the troops in the colonies (I wasn't a regular in his seminar, he could spot that I was a North American from my accent) and glared at me through his thick, bushy eyebrows and asked me in a rather condescending tone: "Pray tell, who are these working men and women of yours?" I was at a bit of a loss for words at the time, especially since one of those workers, my friend Miklós Haraszti had just been given an 8-year suspended sentence in

Budapest for writing about being a worker in a workers' state.[9] I was afraid of uttering anything publicly that may put him or my own pending journey to Budapest at risk (Ilona Duczynska had a lot to do with Haraszti's sentence being suspended). This book then is a belated reply to Leonard Schapiro and to anyone who is interested to know who are "these working men and women of mine" in Hungary.

And now in a more rapid order: Dimitrios Roussopoulos gave me carte blanche to find the best people I could to produce a volume he and his colleagues at Black Rose Books could be proud of as one of their signature publications celebrating 50 years in publishing. When I began to put together my "ensemble" for this publication I was immediately struck by an asymmetry in the notes left behind by the composers and the conductors who preceded me. Anyone who immerses herself/himself in the historical interpretations of the 1919 Commune cannot avoid being struck by the persistence and durability of its lopsided "gender profile". The number of studies, memoirs, reflections produced by men vastly outnumber those written by women. Not surprisingly, this lopsided profile had cast a long, patriarchal shadow on its subject. What role did working-women play in the 1919 "Dictatorship of the Proletariat" in Hungary? What kind of policies, civil or political rights were gained by or fought for by Hungarian women during this time, and what have historians written or said about all of this during the past century? During my review of the scholarly literature on the 1919 Republic of Councils, I was struck by how little attention had been paid to these important questions during the preceding 100 years.

It is not an exaggeration to say, that neither before nor after the end of state-socialism in Hungary in 1990 had any historian studied the Hungarian Republic of Councils systematically with a focus on women or from a gender history perspective. Most recently, the work of Emily Gioielli in Hungary and Judit Szapor in Montréal had begun to fill this gap. (I am grateful to the latter, for reassuring me that my efforts to redress the gender imbalance is not in vain.[10]) To sum up: Compiling a new take on the 1919 Commune, in which yet again, all the contributors are men, was out of the question. To achieve the balance I wanted, I sought advice not only from colleagues in Canada, but from several female scholars in Hungary and Austria who are specialists on early 20th century European history. I would like to say thank you to all of them briefly, and in alphabetical order: Eszter Bartha, Dóra Czeferner, Eleonóra Gera, Veronika Helfert, Tímea Jablonczay, Zsuzsanna B. Kádár, Andrea Pető, Susan Zimmermann. Their responses enabled me to achieve not only gender parity in numbers but helped me to do so in a manner that greatly enhanced the harmony and sound fidelity of our performance.

This then explains, briefly, why five of the 10 contributors to this volume are women, but it does not explain why I chose a manuscript on the role of women in the 1919 Republic of Council that was written 65 years ago. For this decision I owe a deep debt of gratitude to Professor Susan Zimmermann, one of the Hungarian historians whose opinion and help I sought. She is the one who suggested that I look at a long dormant and neglected piece of early scholarship, that may serve as a good opening to this topic both as a historical study and as a historical document. The study she sent my way was written by Magda Aranyossi (the aunt of the celebrated novelist Péter Nádas, as I learned during my correspondence with Professor Zimmermann) who, along with Ilona Duczynska, was in the thick of the 1919 events as a young 23-year-old activist. I shared Professor Zimmerman's enthusiasm about this manuscript after I read it and decided to translate significant portions of it for inclusion in this collection. I am also deeply grateful to Professor Zimmerman for preparing an original and highly poignant introduction to Magda Aranyossi for our book that sheds important new light not only on Aranyossi, on the relationship between Péter Nádas and his aunt, but on the current impediments to research on this important area thanks to the machinations of Viktor Orbán's autocratic government.

In addition to the female scholars I consulted with during the selection of my 'ensemble', I also consulted with a number of 'male referees' who were of great help to me during this phase of the project: Professors András Bozóki and Attila Melegh proved to be great "talent scouts". I owe them a special thanks for helping me to put together my ensemble. Their 'recommendations' proved to be not only great individual performers but were a pleasure to work with. And this leads me directly to my team, the scholars who responded positively to my call for an original piece of research that would become part of this collection. It is their professionalism, dedication to excellence, and to upholding the highest standards of empirical verifiability that provides the backbone of this book. I consider myself fortunate to have had the opportunity to work with them and to learn from them. Though I am most appreciative of all their effort, I would like to single out two of my contributors for special appreciation. One is Professor Kari Polanyi Levitt, the person I have known the longest among the contributors to this book, the other is Professor Marie Josée Lavallée, who was the last to join my ensemble.

I have already alluded to my relationship with Professor Polanyi-Levitt's son Tom and expanded upon my relationship with her late mother Ilona Duczynska. Kari and I have been not only academic colleagues in Montréal, but friends for many decades, and neighbors for the last eight years. After we became neighbors in 2013, we decided to form our own two person "intellectual salon"—informal meetings, alternating between her place and mine, to discuss matters of mutual intellectual curiosity over a bottle of wine (and one or two cigarettes until we both stopped this reckless behavior). It was at one of these early sessions that she asked me if I would consider writing a biography of her late mother, Ilona. I did not require an introduction from someone before asking her to consider writing a piece for this book. Of all the contributors to this collection, she is the only one I had to tell to stop putting more time and effort into polishing her manuscript. She pleaded with me for a bit more time so she could do some "additional research on Otto Bauer and Austro-Marxism"—this after suffering a stroke, that kept her mind as sharp as a razor, but greatly limited her mobility and her ability to speak. I in turn pleaded with her for a bit more time until I finish this book, before sending my manuscript about her mother to a publisher. I'm forever grateful to Kari Polanyi Levitt for all that she taught me over the years, for patiently submitting to my priorities, and last but not least for the great personal effort she made to upholding her commitment to providing me with a brilliant manuscript on *"Vienna and Budapest: A Tale of Two Cities".*

Professor Marie-Josée Lavallée was the last to join my ensemble but was singularly helpful to me from the moment that she joined this collective enterprise. She had less time than any of the other members of my team to prepare her submission, and in spite of this, she managed to provide me with an original piece of research that added a most valuable dimension to this collection. She was not only generous with sharing her ideas but helped me with editing and critically evaluating some of the other texts, including mine. I am most grateful to her for her generous and attentive help.

I would like to also acknowledge the helpful assistance of the Department of Political Science, the School of Community and Public Affairs, and the Karl Polanyi Institute of Political Economy at Concordia University for supporting a colloquium on April 16, 2019 to discuss some of the themes and ideas that would form part of this book. I'm grateful to my friend and colleague, Professor Daniel Salée for helping to organize and moderate this colloquium and would like to also thank Professor Margie Mendel the Director of Concordia University's Karl Polanyi Institute and Ana Gomez for their helpful assistance and participation. Throughout this project and during my research on Ilona Duczynska, I benefitted immensely from my access to the Duczynska-Polanyi archives held at Concordia University and from the generous and attentive help of the custodian of those papers, the aforementioned Ana Gomez.

This is also the place where I would like to express my appreciation to the American Hungarian Educators Association and to the Hungarian Studies Association of Canada for enabling me to present and test some of my ideas pertaining to the 1919 Republic of Councils at their annual conferences in Pittsburgh and Vancouver in April and June 2019.

Finally, I owe a huge thank you to those who participated in the actual production of this book, the editors, and assistants at Black Rose Books, in particular Clara Swan Kennedy, Nathan McDonnell, and none more so than Jason Toney, who helped me hugely in putting this text into its final shape. He was an indispensable help and friendship from the beginning to the very end of this project.

It goes without saying—those who inspired and helped me to execute my project carry no burden of responsibility for any of its shortcomings. That remains entirely my own.

NOTES

1 Tom Levitt works and plays in Montréal. He is the Founder of Montréal's *Institute of Saxophone Metaphysics* (which I had the pleasure of serving for a while as Secretary General). For two of Levitt's works that I'm indebted to, please see *The Leak Light Speaks: Saxophone Purchase, Assessment, Set up, Repair, Overhaul, Customization, and Reflections* (Montréal, QC: Create Space, 2015). Also, *Karate as Calligraphy: The Budo Revival in Shotokan* (Montréal, QC: Create Space, 2016).

2 Emma Goldman, Alexander Berkman, and Ida Mett, *1917: Revolution in Russia and Its Aftermath* (Montréal, QC: Black Rose Books, 2019).

3 On the Kurdish Freedom Movement please see Thoman Jeffery Miley, *Your Freedom and Mine: Abdullah Öcalan and the Kurdish Question in Erdgan's Turkey* (Montréal, QC: Black Rose Books, 2018).

4 E.J.Hobsbawm. "Introduction" in Ilona Duczynska, *Workers in Arms* (New York, NY: Monthly Review Press, 1978), 15–27.

5 László Rajk *senior* was a top ranking member of the underground Communist Party in Hungary from the late 1930s. He was a veteran of the Spanish civil war, and became the minister of Interior in Hungary after WWII, faithfully carrying out the Bolsheviks' "salami tactics" against their political opponents (which included hundreds if not thousands of innocent citizens including some veterans of the 1919 Commune). Once the Hungarian Bolsheviks succeeded in gaining full power in Hungary in 1948, they arrested their comrade, László Rajk for allegedly moonlighting as an agent for the CIA, the Vatican, the Yugoslav communists, etc. They also arrested Rajk's wife Julia, all as part of their "Stalinist" recipe to incite fear and to innoculate the general public against any attempt to rebel. Rajk Sr was horribly tortured and broken in captivity. He became the central figure in the most infamous post WWII show trial in Central Europe, before he was executed on trumped up charges and burried in an unmarked grave. His son, László jr, who was born just months prior to his father's arest in 1949 was placed in a state orphanage, given a new name, István Kovács. Rajk Jr would only be reunited with his real mother after the death of Joseph Stalin in the Soviet Union, and after the Hungarian Bolsheviks admitted publicly the injustice committed against his father. Rajk Sr was ceremoniously reburried by the Hungarian State on October 6th 1956. Hundreds of thousands of ordinary citizens of Budapest paid their last respects in the streets of Budapest to this Communist victim of Stalinism in Hungary. The turn-out was the dress-rehearsal for the 1956 Hungarian Revolution, that broke out two weeks later on October 23 and was put down by Soviet troops on November 4 1956. László Rajk Jr. became one of the leading dissidents against one party rule in Hungary during the mid-1970s and was a close friend and devotee of Ilona Duczynska. He is the godfather of my first born, Adam Leith Göllner. László served in Hungary's parliament for a short period after 1990, and became an internationally respected set designer, artistic director of over 100 films, including *The Son of Saul*, that won the Academy Award for the best foreign film in 2016. For a brief synopsis, please see my own portrait: "The Son of Rajk in Montréal". *The Hungarian Free Press*. November 16, 2016. For a video of his presentation in Montréal on "Art and the Holocaust" here <http://hungarianfreepress.com/2016/11/16/the-son-of-rajk-in-montréal-video/>. László Rajk's posthumous autobiography based on a series of interviews with András Mink provides a fuller picture; see László Rajk, András Mink and Judit Rajk, *A tér tágassága: életútinterjú* (The Expanse of Space: Life inteview) (Budapest: Magvető, 2019).

6   I kept to this day my editorial notes, and the piece of paper on which Ilona scribbled, in her inimitable tiny scrawl, her request that I should not share with anyone her manuscript before it is published. For the published Hungarian text of this admission, please see Ilona Duczynska, "A cselekvés boldogtalan szerelmese" (The Unhappy Lover of Action). *Valóság* no 5. (1978). For a first English translation of a significant portion of this admission please see my forthcoming portrait. András B. Göllner, *Ilona: Portrait of a Rebel.*

7   There is no doubt in my mind: Teresa possessed the key that turned me on and kept me running as a scholar. She remained a lasting inspiration and friend till her passing in Poland in January, 2017. After retiring from Carleton University in 1995, she moved back to her homeland, and became the Director of the Strategic Studies Program at Collegium Civitas in Warsaw. I managed to get away from the neo-fascist revival in Central Europe by 2010. Teresa tried to return from the one that began to grip Poland by then as well, but she was considerably older than me and could not get it together. She died in Poland, but asked the executors of her will to burry her ashes next to her parents in Ottawa.

8   I was familiar by then with the powerful grip workers' councils had on the imagination of working men and women in Hungary, and the fearless efforts of a group of political economists in Hungary to keep the embers of the 1918–1919 and 1956 revolutions alive. I read the first works of Bill Lomax, I had met Miklós Haraszti by then. I had first-hand knowledge of his persecution, and the role Ilona Duczynska played in keeping him out of prison. I also knew of his account of factory life in so-called socialist Hungary.

9   The English version of Haraszti's banned manuscript would be released on May 1st, 1978 and with the help of Ilona Duczynska. See: Miklós Haraszti, *A Worker in a Worker's State: Piece-Rates in Hungary* (Harmondsworth: Penguin Books, 1977).

10   Judit Szapor. "Women's Activism, Gender Politics and the 1919 Hungarian Commune" Presentation to a Symposium at Concordia University on the 1919 Hungarian Commune (April 16, 2019).

András B. Göllner

THIS BOOK IS A critical reassessment of a long forgotten but monumental rebellion that occurred one hundred years ago on the territory of the by now extinct Austro-Hungarian Empire which was one of the world's most powerful Empires at the start of the 20th century. This rebellion by the Empire's subjects— millions of working men and women—had not been treated kindly by historians over the past century for fear that full disclosure of its true dimensions may spark a repeat performance on a global scale and bring both capitalism and socialism as we know them to their knees.[1] Before we cut to the chase, it's imperative that we remove our blindfolds—the proverbial wool which Orpheus had taught his followers thousands of years ago to never allow anyone to pull over their eyes, especially not at the start of their journey into the unknown.[2]

Were it not so out of place, or misleading, it would have been tempting for us to follow the precedents set by mainstream Western historiography, especially its Hungarian variant, and allegorize the performance of Hungary's long exploited working classes on history's central stage along the lines of a fairy tale, known to people in the English speaking part of the world as *Sleeping Beauty*.[3] The heroine of that well known fairy tale is the victim of a curse that put her to sleep for 100 years, until Prince Charming came along and woke her from her deep, catatonic slumber with a kiss.[4] Purists tend to bristle at the romanticised version of this medieval lore that made it to Hollywood and the Disney Studios, thanks to the Grimm brothers (no, not the Kochs, stupid!).[5] Hungarian feminists would also rightfully object to attempts at casting Hungary's women's movement in such light.

According to the original, and long forgotten 12th century version of this fairy tale, Prince Charming was not so charming after all. Instead of waking the sleeping beauty with a kiss, he pulled down his lederhosen, and impregnated her as she lay prostrate and unconscious on her bed. Once he finished with her, he slipped out the back door and went back to his wife without feeling any sense of remorse for violating his defenseless, innocent young victim (not to mention, his transgressions against one of his God's Ten Commandments or his sacred marriage vows). The missionary position of the original sinner became canonized in the annals of folklore. The Italian poet, Giambattista Basile (1575–1632), would reframe the marauding prince's perverse act as "the gathering of the first fruits of love" (sic). But there are even more surprising parts that are missing from the original *score*. According to the first and authentic version of the tale, the sleeping beauty slept through the act of rape, the labour pains that followed nine months later, as well as the difficulties of giving birth to twins (two bouncing baby boys). She only woke when one of the hungry little bastards began sucking on her finger and removed the flax seed that pricked her and put her to sleep a hundred years earlier. Obviously, she had a lot of catching up to do. And so do we.[6]

Whichever version of *Sleeping Beauty* one prefers, the sanitized or the *coursé*, it is hard not to see a similarity between how storytellers handle the misfortunes of Sleeping Beauty over time and how historians depict the misfortunes of the world's common people in their accounts of human progress through time and space. Most of the *raconteurs* of the 1919 Hungarian Republic of Councils appear to be labouring under the same archetypal spell as those historians of "Western civilization", who depict the centuries long rape of the world lying outside the West's back-yard as "white man's burden".[7] Some burden, quite some fairy tale..

I came to this project with the desire to end this highly popular, but fairy-tale approach to the depiction of the role working men and women play in either Hungarian or in world history. The introduction to this book provides what my colleague, Raquel Varela and I believe is an unequivocal and universal argument for a paradigm-shift.[8] The chapters that follow, provide the empirically verifiable evidence that sustains what Kant described in the preface to the second edition of his *Critique of Pure Reason* (1871) as a "revolution in our way of thinking" ("*Revolution der Denkart*") about historical change.

Since views are highly divided about the identity, the spirit, the motivation and performance of the leading actors in the 1919 Republic of Councils, it's important to remove any ambiguity about our *ensemble's* "revolutionary" perspective or approach to this controversial historical event. Our protagonists are those working men and women of Hungary who have had enough by March 1919 of the abuses they were subjected to for generations. We portray them as men and women who wanted to take control of their lives and of the political-economic processes that governed who got what, when, and how in their communities. We argue that they were moved to raise their fists by the same inextinguishable revolutionary spirit at the end of WWI as the people who lit up the night sky above Paris at the end of the 18th century, extolling the virtues of *Liberté, Égalité, Fraternité*. We see the 1919 generation in Hungary as the spiritual brothers and sisters of those men and women who formulated those 12 demands in Budapest in March 1848 that included calls for an end to the privileged treatment of the nobility and the enslavement of that country's commoners. The 1919 Hungarian Commune was fuelled by the same spirit as the one that fueled the Paris

Commune of 1871. We believe that Hungary's agricultural and industrial workers took the teachings of Jesus to their hearts and they justifiably felt betrayed by those who ruled Hungary in His name by the time WWI was over in 1918.

Make no mistake about it: Our protagonists were angry, and resentful about what their unelected leaders, such as Count István Tisza had put them through with the blessing of their priests and their churches.[9] The drama we are about to raise the curtain on is not about a people, out for a Sunday picnic, happy within its skin, at peace with its past, present or future. Before the rulers of Europe had rushed their "herds" out to the killing fields to be slaughtered by the tens of millions in a war they pitched to their people as "The War to End All Wars", Hungary's working men and women were already bleeding from far too many wounds not of their own making. Years before the start of the hostilities in 1914, more than a million Hungarians fled overseas, to the industrial heartland of America, to the Canadian prairies, because of the inhuman, unsustainable way they were forced to exist back home "on the farm". Had Orwell been writing at the time, he may well have called Austria-Hungary Europe's largest Animal Farm. One of Orwell's conservative countryman, a member of Britain's upper crust who was known for his disdain of "the Left", Britain's wartime Prime Minister, Lloyd George said it all: "Hungary has the worst system of landholding in Europe. The peasants there are as oppressed as they were in the Middle Ages. There are few countries in the world so much in need of a revolution as Hungary".[10]

But let us stop this practice of turning to Europe's parliamentarians for advice on what's really happening or needed by the common people living east of London, Paris, Berlin and Rome. This book gives Hungarians a chance to speak for themselves. (Péter Csunderlik's opening chapter of this book will fully reveal the pressures that blew the lid off Hungary's "Chernobyl" in 1919—the country's socially irresponsible and dangerous system of deciding who got what, when and how.) Let us summarize the views of a group of non-partisan Hungarian patriots—as objective observants of their political system before and during WWI as one could possibly find. It is for their verifiable patriotism, reasonable, and peaceful behavior that the reigning Hapsburg ruler, Charles IV was willing to listen to them just before the roof fell in on his empire.

The Monarchy is not only unwilling to satisfy the just demands of its subject peoples but is incapable of doing so. It is unprepared to either grant democratic liberties or the right of peoples to self-determination; it is a feudal and militarist organization, forcing itself upon many millions of unwilling subjects... it is based on a foolish policy which imagines that a people kept in the darkness of ignorance will not realize its degraded condition... exploitation of women and children is favoured almost by medieval and ruthlessly enforced conditions of labour, heedless of the worker's family life, educational needs or human dignity.[11]

After losing over a million of their loved ones who fled overseas before WWI,[12] Hungarians would lose another million of their relatives who would perish in a losing war that had just ended when the authors of those words in the previous paragraph met with their King, and Emperor. Hundreds of thousands among the survivors from the war were now back from the battle-field, many of them suffering from permanent disabilities, racked by various infectious diseases and facing starvation and unemployment.[13] Hungary's working men and women were hungry, cold and exhausted, without the slightest hope whatsoever for a better future for themselves or for their children. Their country was overrun by marauding troops from the neighborhood, out for revenge. The Great Imperialist powers held a knife to their throats, barring their access to the basic amenities of life until they would agree to play dead and give away their dreams and their country. What *these* wretched of the earth wanted was nothing more than the right to control their own lives. They wanted their habitat to be economically sustainable and governed according to universally accepted norms of justice, and constitutionalism. (Their concept of equality under the law did not apply to their oppressors, those who had pulled the wool over their eyes for generations, keeping them ignorant and fearful of thinking for themselves.) Socialism was the only item on the menu that promised to give them what they wanted. They went for it in 1919 and a hundred years later, they are still treated as "red terrorist" for daring to be human.

The world has come a long way since that first attempt at the changing of the guard in Paris in 1789. The "Congress of Vienna" in 1814 made a valiant effort to put the spirit of the revolution back in the bottle and keep Europe's aristocracy in power. It did not reckon with the fact that the revolutionary spirit of the common people is immortal. The flames of the revolution may die down, they may appear extinguished for long periods of time, only to roar back to life, catching the firemen off guard, and burning a path towards a place that promises justice, equality under the law and an ecologically sustainable future for the exploited and hopelessly misled underclass.

Those scholars who kindly consented to my request to contribute a chapter to this book on the 1919 Hungarian Republic of Councils do not look upon Hungary's working men and women as zombies, asleep at the wheel, cursed by some bad omen from which they can only be roused by a romantic kiss from a Prince or by a little bastard they have no recollection of conceiving. Every one of us know that working men and women may feign sleep while being violated, but they suffer terribly throughout such ordeals. We know that the inaction, or passivity of the victims of rape are not to be heralded as signs of consent, but as reflections of the victims' inability to resist due to the wool over their eyes, the hood placed over their heads, the hand on their mouths the dagger at their throats and the desire to live through the ordeal. This book is a tribute to the immortality of the revolutionary spirit against all forms of oppression and deceit, especially against those which specialize in limiting the ability of working men and women to recognize the reality of their exploitation, the identity of their exploiter. Our book condemns rather than applauds the 'pain killers' used by the exploiters to reduce their victims' suffering just so they can prolong their own pleasures at their victims' expense.

This book then is a call to arms like the one on its cover, against those who are destroying the boundary between illusion and reality and are preventing humanity from traveling towards an ecologically sustainable future along the path of justice and equal rights under the law. Ultimately, this book is dedicated to ensuring that working men and women do not forget what was done to them in 1919, and time and time again afterwards, not only in Hungary but in many other parts of the world to this day, and not infrequently under the label of socialism.

NOTES

1   This is how a member of the American delegation at the Paris Peace Conference of 1919 put it diplomatically: "if the troubles in Hungary spread, they'll make waste paper of our conventions". Quoted by Margaret MacMillan in. Margaret MacMillan, *Paris 1919 Six Months That Changed the World* (London: Murray, 2019), 257.

2   For further guidance on this manoeuvre, please consult W K C.Guthrie, *Orpheus and Greek Religion: a Study of the Orphic Movement* (Princeton, NJ: Princeton University Press, 1993). (Originally published in London by Methuen in 1952)

3   The name Hungarian storytellers have given to their sleeping beauty is *Rózsika* a more endearing version of her English name, *Rose* or the German *Rosamund*

4   The identity of Prince Charming according to the story-tellers on the left is non-other than Karl Marx, (1818–1883) or better still, Vladimir Ilych Lenin (1870–1924). It's their "kisses"—their revolutionary tracts—that enabled the downtrodden masses to finally see the light.

5   Apologies for this bastardization of James Carville's celebrated outburst—"it's the economy, stupid"—to fellow workers on Bill Clinton's 1992 Presidential election ampaign, when they were at a loss as to which fairy tale to use for the purpose of maximizing electoral support for their candidate. As for the Koch Brothers—they are the hidden financial backers of the American story-tellers today that portray the destruction of the planet as a charitable activity and celebrate the artificial blond bomber in the White House as a very stable genius. (See: Jane Mayer, *Dark Money: The Hidden History of the Billionaires Behind the Rise of the Radical Right* (New York: Anchor Books, a division of Penguin Random House LLC, 2017); also Philip Rucker and Carol Leonnig, *A Very Stable Genius: Donald J. Trump's Testing of America* (New York, NY: Penguin Books, 2020).

6   The precise authorship of the first version of *Sleeping Beauty* is unknown. Its origin predates Gutenberg's printing press and is considered to be from the mid-12th century as part of a larger body of orally transmitted narrative commonly referred to as *Le Roman de Perceforest*. It first appears in print in Paris in 1528, as *La Tres Elegante Delicieux Melliflue et Tres Plaisante Hystoire du Tres Noble Roy Perceforest*. The first Italian language version of *Perceforest* appeared in 1531, A Spanish translation is also known to exist from that time. An 800-page partially abridged English

translation appeared in 2011 (see A Bryant, *Perceforest Reader: Selected Episodes From Perceforest: the Prehistory of King Arthur's Britain* (Woodbridge: Boydell and Brewer Limited, 2012). Giambattista Basile's version of Sleeping Beauty was part of a larger body of work—*Pentamerone*—published in 1634 after the author's passing. He called his version of this story, *Sun, Moon and Talia*. The Grimm Brothers worked from Basile's version and published theirs in 1812 and reflect the transition from agrarian to industrial production. In Basile's version, Sleeping Beauty is pricked by a flaxseed, in Grimms' fairy tale the culprit is a spindle. The Grimms and Walt Disney are silent, of course, about the "prick" that raped Talia while she lay unconscious in her bed in the 12th century.

7   The best, perhaps most elegant recent "cover-up" of Western civilization's perversities is Niall Ferguson, *Civilization: the West and the Rest* (London: Penguin Books, 2018).

8   On the concept and dynamics of paradigm shifts please consult Thomas S. Kuhn, *The Structure of Scientific Revolutions* (Chicago, IL: University of Chicago Press, 1970).

9   Though he may disagree, our position largely coincides with that which Miklós Gáspár Tamás voiced recently in a not unrelated context in present-day Hungary: *"We're not here to drum up support for the violence committed by the poor—even if we understand them. We just want them to be free, and to diminish their suffering"*. <<https://merce.hu/2018/05/14/tgm-a-kopkodesrol/>.

10   Quoted in Margaret MacMillan. op.cit. 257–8.

11   This passage from the Hungarian social scientists' brief to Charles IV is a short segment from the one that is fully reproduced in Oscar Jászi's *Revolution and Counterrevolution in Hungary* (London: P.S. King and Sons Ltd, 1924), 5–13.

12   Please remember, this was a time prior to the existence of Facebook, Instagram, live chat, e-mail, and other apps that keep people connected today. This was well before trans Atlantic flights and travel by the lower classes was a possibility. The dispossessed, illiterate and exploited workers and peasants who went abroad were lost to their loving relatives forever.

13   For the record: World War I was started by the tormentors of the Austro-Hungarian empire's commoners for no other reason than to punish a small country on the periphery of their empire—Serbia—because one of its sons, a poor 19-year-old Bosnian-Serb by the name of Gavrilo Princip, assassinated the heir to the Austro-Hungarian throne, Archduke Franz Ferdinand and his wife, Sophie, in the city of Sarajevo on June 28, 1914. (Sarajevo was the capital of Bosnia and Herzegovina, and one of the holdings of the Austro-Hungarian Empire at the time. The Kings and Princes of Serbia long considered this Austro-Hungarian colony as part of their holdings. The Empire that treated its working men and women like commodities rather than as human beings, wanted to make a point, and wilfully sacrificed a significant part of its "herd" in a losing effort to retain its exclusive privileges. It would take many more decades and the loss of hundreds of thousands of innocent lives before the citizens of Sarajevo and its surroundings would be allowed to finally govern themselves in 1995, free of Serbian or Austro-Hungarian dictat.)

When the Impossible Becomes Inevitable: The 1919 Hungarian Republic of Councils in a Global Historical Perspective

Raquel Varela and András B. Göllner

The Gathering Storm

THE AWARENESS THAT working men and women have a decisive role to play in history emerges in Europe during the second half of the 19th century and asserts itself with spectacular, revolutionary fervor at the beginning of the 20th. The revolutions of 1848 had already energized France and Germany's workers, but it was the Paris Commune of 1871 that vividly demonstrated for the first time how a non-proprietary class could stand on its own feet, seize power, and make a go of it. As we enter the 20th century, "working men—and to a lesser extent—working women begin to make their presence felt in the public arenas of most European countries".[1] The gathering storm is evident from the first Russian revolution of 1905, followed quickly by the anarchist revolt of Barcelona in 1909. (The latter would be crushed by "the bosses" but live on in the memories of millions as "that tragic week".)

The first decade and a half of the 20th century is witness to a rising tide of labour unrest and strikes in France, Germany, Italy, and England, as well as in North America. There are 500 industrial conflicts in France alone between 1900 and 1915. From its founding in Chicago in 1905, the Industrial Workers of the World—commonly known as the "Wobblies"—would become a powerful voice for working men and women in America. The Winnipeg General Strike in May-June 1919 brought capitalism to its knees for over a month in Canada's third-largest city, leaving an unforgettable impact on that country's political landscape. In Italy, a Russian born 23-year old doctoral student, Angelica Balabanoff, would begin to organize immigrant textile workers into a formidable revolutionary force in 1900. By 1915 she would head the Secretariat of the Zimmerwald Movement, which included such luminaries of the international labour movement as Vladimir Ilych

Lenin, Leon Trotsky, Karl Liebknecht, Rosa Luxemburg, Henriette Roland-Holst, and Clara Zetkin.[2]

England was also rocked by an unprecedented wave of strikes in 1911. In Germany, 1 million workers took part in the strikes that swept through that country during 1912. By 1914, union membership in Britain and Germany rose to 2 million—roughly 30% of the labour force. By the fall of the Portuguese monarchy in October 1910, workers' presses in that country exhibited a historically unprecedented burst of vigour as hundreds of new publications saw the light of day, extolling the virtues of politically active working men and women. The French Socialist Party—first constituted as the French Section of the International, to highlight the party's internationalist origin, garnered one and a half million votes in the 1914 French national elections. It is as an emissary of Angelica Balabanoff and the Zimmerwald Movement's International Socialist Commission, that a 20-year-old Austro-Hungarian engineering student, Ilona Duczynska (the wife-to-be of Karl Polanyi), goes from Zurich to Hungary, to make contact with the leaders of the Hungarian labour movement in 1917 and lights the fuse of the 1918–1819 revolutions in that country.[3]

As we enter the "roaring twenties" of the 21st century, we cannot and must not continue to deny that capitalism and the inevitable crises that followed in its wake are in a cause-and-effect relationship with the worldwide proliferation of political and social revolutions throughout the 20th century. The prognostications of that 19th-century thinker, Karl Marx, who saw the proletariat as the newest actor on the stage of history may be questioned on many fronts, but he is right on the money in *The Communist Manifesto*,[4] where he tells us that capitalism will give birth to the greatest number of revolutions and counterrevolutions in the whole of human history.[5]

Here is a partial listing: The Boxer Rebellion in China 1899–1901, Russia 1905, Catalonia 1909, Portugal 1910, Mexico 1910, Ireland 1916, Russia again in 1917, Spain 1917–1920, Italy 1919–1920, Hungary 1918–1919, Germany 1918–1923, China 1927, Austria 1934, Spain 1934–36, Indonesia 1946–49, China 1949, Bolivia 1952, the German Democratic Republic 1953, Poland, Hungary 1956, Cuba 1959, all the anti-Colonial revolutions—most importantly Algeria, Indochina, Vietnam—Prague 1968, Italy 1969, Chile 1970–73, Portugal 1974, Nicaragua 1979 Iran 1979, followed by Solidarnos in Poland, the collapse of the Berlin Wall and with it, the Soviet Empire in 1990 and then The Arab Spring that would provide its bitter harvest in Syria, Egypt and elsewhere as the 20th century closes. And who could forget the Zapatistas of Mexico, the Tupamaros of Uruguay, or the Kurdish Freedom Movement of Abdullah Öcalan and its permanent social revolution dedicated among others to local self-governance, religious and gender equality for working men and women in, of all places, the war, and sectarian torn regions of the Middle East.[6]

Perhaps no one has captured more clearly the excitement of the masses as they get onto the centre stage of history during the initial decades of the 20th century than Mayakovsky, that most unpredictable and thunderous of Russian poets, in his Order No. 2 to the Army of the Arts: "There are no more gaping fools waiting for the word of the 'master'".[7] Another great poet, Árpád Tóth in Hungary, would pen his vision of the 'new order':

A towering, blood-coloured and naked body rises.
Legs spread as wide as the planet,
His earth-shaking growl resonates
From the Red East towards the pale West He bellows,
"I have come!
The Red God has arrived"[8]

While the essential feature of the revolutionary process during the 20th century is the entry of common people onto the stage of world history, it would be a great mistake to ascribe this phenomenon to a sudden attentiveness by the largely illiterate masses to the philosophers of revolution such as Karl Marx, or to the gentle poets quoted above. The great upheavals did not follow a carefully choreographed script or preordained plan for social transformation. Without exception, they were all, and none more so than the one in Hungary in 1919, the result of a bitter, collective recognition, that the leading actors on the stage of history had blown their parts and that "the old regimes can no longer be tolerated".[9] (For the analysis in the case of Hungary please turn to the opening chapter of this book by Péter Csunderlik). It is changing mass consciousness, "the rapid, intense and passionate psychological changes of the pre-revolutionary classes",[10] the recognition that what is good for the stock markets of the world is not good for the workers of the world, that provided the revolutionary tide of the 20th century with its impulse, drive, and its inexhaustible energy.

If we accept that capitalism (and its colonial, imperial manifestations) was the primary irritant that propelled waves of working men and women to rush the centre stage of history throughout the world during the late 19th and 20th centuries, we cannot avoid asking ourselves the obvious question at the beginning of the 21st: What now? Has the umbilical connection between capitalism and the desire of working men and women to take matters into their own hands been permanently severed as we begin our move into the age of artificial intelligence? Better still, has capitalism been pushed aside by the rise of the information age, the drastic reduction in the marginal cost of information? Will this phenomenon divest capitalism of its central irritants so that it can no longer make working men and women feel peripheral and therefore rebellious?[11] Is the electoral victory in America of a Wall Street billionaire in 2016 and his seeming popularity with non-college-educated blue-collar workers a sign of a new-found and lasting social peace between labour and capital throughout the world? Will cyber-capitalism prove to be more or less successful at containing its externalities, its socially disruptive side effects than its 20th-century version? Highly unlikely.[12]

Rather than retreating from its prized position as the key to the "wealth of nations", capitalism is simply transforming itself as we are entering the "Roaring Twenties" of the 21st century. It is shedding its previous skin and replacing it with a new cyber veneer that is better suited for the information age. While the global financial crisis of 2008 let a lot of the steam out of the pressure cooker, the past decade has not been able to hide the distasteful odour, the bitter taste of its repetitive servings to the working men and women of the planet. Rather than changing the menu, digital capitalism has chosen to focus on altering our senses, our feelings about it. By developing techniques to limit our abilities to distinguish fact from fiction, illusion from reality, its newest innovations seek to disguise the dish on our platter and to immunize us against that which is revolting. This strategy, like many before it, will not produce more than temporary relief.

The bond which unites the authors of this introduction with those who have contributed their thoughts to this volume is the belief and conviction that working men and women are fully entitled to shape their destinies, to be the lead actors on the centre stage of modern history. Our commitment to the values of constitutional governance based on the principles of justice and ecologically sustainable economic development does not frighten us from examining episodes where working men and women turn to the path of political or social revolution to achieve those objectives. Our only concern, like that of the great French intellectual, Michel Foucault, is to maintain a critical stance vis-à-vis all forms of power and authority, including those wielded in the name of the proletariat, and to assess them all in terms of their adherence to the principles of justice, equality for all under the law, and ecologically sustainable economic development.[13]

Political vs Social Revolutions

How can we make any sense of those "hurricanes" 100 years ago that swept working men and women in two of the great empires of the world—the Russian and the Austro-Hungarian—to the centre stage of history? Lest we forget: The Austro-Hungarian Empire was one of the major global powers at the start of WWI. Territorially it was second only to the Russian Empire. It was the third most populous empire after Russia and Germany, respectively. Though it was the "breadbasket" of Europe, it possessed the fourth-largest machine-building industry of the world, after the United States, Germany, and the United Kingdom.

To help us organize our thoughts—to see the forest from the trees—Charles Tilly uses the concept of "dual power" as the central defining element of revolutionary phenomenon.[14] In his study of the Russian revolution, in which he played such a decisive role, Leon Trotsky highlighted not two but three elements that characterize a situation as revolutionary: The arrival of millions of mobilized workers on the scene, the attraction of the intermediate sectors of society by the organizations and methods of struggle manifested by the working classes, and a national crisis. A revolutionary situation, in other words, would be a political process characterized by the emergence of vast sectors of the population (workers and middle classes) that alter the relationship of power between social classes within a framework of national crisis (decay). Trotsky will later add to his conceptualization of the "perfect revolutionary storm" the presence of a revolutionary party.[15]

In his investigation of 20th-century revolutions, the historian and political activist Valério Arcary proposes yet another framework. He suggests that we should distinguish between two types of working-class revolutions, "political revolutions", and "social revolutions".[16] In the former, political power changes hands; in the latter, economic power—ownership and control over the means of production—becomes the focus of attention for working men and women. Applying Arcary's dichotomy to Russia, the February Revolution of 1917 is seen as a political revolution, the one in October, a social revolution. Similarly, the so-called "Chrysanthemum Revolution" of Hungary at the end of October 1918 is seen as a political revolution, while the one on March 21st, 1919, is a social revolution.

The authors featured in this book come at their subject matter from different directions, but all are in agreement: the 1919 Hungarian Republic of Councils was a social revolution: This is what distinguishes it above all from its 1918 relative, this is what makes it a blood relative of the 1956 revolution, where once again, workers councils came to play such a heroic but long-forgotten role.

On hindsight, most of the 20th-century revolutions were "February revolutions"—revolutions that changed political regimes—rather than "October revolutions" that displaced the market's universal control over human destinies.[17]

To sum up: There were a few cases where workers' councils played an important role in the tumultuous revolutionary events of the 20th century. But in most of these cases (e.g. in Germany in 1918 as we shall see from the chapter by Marie-Josée Lavallée), the affected workers did not aspire to or achieve control over the production and distribution of goods and services on a societal scale. In the few places where the revolution eliminated the private ownership of the means of production—such as Hungary in 1919, or in 1956, when it stood against its return—the class struggle receded and gave way to new forms of hierarchy; or, in isolated cases, scarcity incompatible with socialism, as was the case in Cuba.

Arcary argues that "the revolutionary processes that triumphed and went to expropriation (Yugoslavia, Albania, China, Korea, Vietnam, Cuba) contradicted three predictions of classical Marxism: 1. The proletariat was not the ruling social subject, these were agrarian revolutions, with strong peasant protagonists; 2. They did not give rise to pluralist self-organization or direct democracy. Dualist territorial power structure based on revolutionary armies or militarily centralized guerrilla groups gave way to one-party dictatorial regimes; 3. Instead of pursuing an internationalist posture, they all morphed into an intensely nationalistic stance except for the Cuban revolution in its earlier years".[18] Arcary goes on to argue, however, that irrespective of the direction of revolutionary change, the reforms undertaken by capitalism over the past century—the Keynesian innovations, the New Deal, the Welfare State—can only be understood in the context of the revolutionary challenges posed to capitalism by the social forces unleashed by its self-generated internal contradictions: "Only when they were seriously threatened by revolutionary danger—as by the Paris Commune and by the two revolutionary waves following the October Revolution in Russia—did the capitalists agree to compromise. The historical project of capitalist reform has failed again and again and again".[19] Arcary's conclusion about the impact of capitalism on the wealth of nations is vividly illustrated by the following equation: 1% of the world's population today has the same wealth as the remaining 99%.[20] But more on this later.

Questions about why so many tropical storms do not develop into full-fledged hurricanes and die out after reaching landfall can be more easily answered than ones that wonder why so many political revolutions do not develop into social revolutions. The explanation developed by Karl Marx stressed the importance of objective, measurable variables—the characteristics of a society's economic system, the sources of that society's wealth, the relative weight of industry in the GNP, its level of maturity, the size and resolve of the industrial working class to take matters into its own hands, etc. On Marx's 'weather map', industrially advanced capitalism provides the most favourable conditions for the transformation of political storms into social revolutions. According to his forecast, the storm that replaced Feudalism and put the bourgeoisie into power cannot sustain itself: The further it moves along its path, the more precarious, and unstable it becomes. It carries within itself the seeds of its destruction. It sweeps up a new set of elements—the industrial proletariat, the working men and women of the factories, the exploited wage earners—who will rise and put an end to the cyclical destructiveness produced by the private ownership of the means of production.

While Lenin developed his own explanation by 1916 about how an agrarian setting can host an anti-capitalist social revolution,[21] he often reminded us in his assessments of the revolution that he led in Russia that: "It is a great misfortune that the honour of starting the first socialist revolution has fallen to the most backward people in Europe".[22] Many would share his views later, though not necessarily for the same reasons that compelled Lenin to utter the politically incorrect words above about the quality of Russia's pre-revolutionary human resources. Whatever we may think of Lenin's political language, it is a fact: At the beginning of the 20th century, Russia was a semi-feudal agrarian society rather than an industrially advanced, mature capitalist enclave ready to burst at the seams by the force of the bitter divide between her proletariat and her bourgeoisie. The share of the country's wealth that came from agriculture far outweighed that which came from industry. What is more, the total agricultural output in Russia was almost 33% less than Germany's and almost 25% less than England's.[23] Writing about the post-1917 Russian civil war, one of the leaders of the Communist International, Victor Serge, recalls that it was not the 14 foreign armies or the strength of the Russian bourgeoisie that demoralized them the most, but the "typhus and the famine".[24]

Ultimately, it was a Hungarian political economist, Karl Polanyi, who fled to North America via Vienna and London after the collapse of the 1919 Budapest Commune, who provided the first and still most persuasive correction to Marx's weather map.[25] As Robert Kuttner, an astute reader of Polanyi reminded us recently: "The great prophet of how market forces taken to an extreme destroy both democracy and a functioning economy was not Karl Marx but Karl Polanyi. Marx expected the crisis of capitalism to end in universal worker-revolt and communism. Polanyi, with nearly a century more history to draw on, appreciated that the greater likelihood was fascism".[26] The most recent signs from Putin's Russia, from Trump's America, from Viktor Orbán's Hungary, from Austria and Italy and other parts of Europe suggest that the storms ahead of us are more likely to follow Polanyi's weather pattern than the one plotted by that arch-nemesis of capitalism, Karl Marx.

A Brief Message from the Sponsors of Universal Capitalism[27]

We are told by the sponsors of universal capitalism that the historic defeat of the British Labour Party at the polls on the 100th anniversary of the 1919 Budapest Commune is a harbinger of things to come. They tell us that "the Left" is on the run worldwide, the Socialist Party of Hungary is on the verge of extinction. This is how Steve Bannon, a former high-powered Wall Street executive, who served as chief strategist of Donald Trump's 2016 electoral victory summarized the sponsors' pitch well before the start of the 2020 election campaign in America:

"We'll govern for 50 years. The Democrats have lost sight of what the world's about. The media has no fucking idea what's going on".[28]

The sponsors of capitalism tell us, and can prove it with numbers when pressed, that there are more capitalist cars (systems or models) on the political-economic highways of the world than socialist ones because "more people want them (stupid)".[29] The reason why more people want the capitalist model is equally simple: It makes people feel better than the socialist vehicle. They add that it's this unbeatable feature of capitalism that makes millions of migrants rush towards the shores of Western Europe and North America. Capitalism has outlasted all the models that identify themselves as socialist, especially those archaic ones in Central and Eastern Europe that called themselves the dictatorship of the proletariat way back when.

The sponsors of universal capitalism can call on an inexhaustible supply of empirically verifiable survey data which shows that even the working classes consider the capitalist model to be more fun to ride in than the socialist brand. They close by telling us that whatever its alleged flaws, capitalism offers far more freedom of choice to its passengers, causes far less pain to keep on the road than socialism. Unlike the latter, it can repair itself when it falters. It is the ideal mode of transport for any human with a brain bigger than a walnut.

This is how Donald Trump's first Ambassador to the UN, the two-term governor of South Carolina, Nikki Haley, recently summarized the central message of universal capitalism's sponsors in America for members of The Hudson Institute, one of America's most influential Think Tanks: "The American system is capitalism. Period". She admonished those who are "flirting with socialism" in the following manner: "Though the Founders never used the word, they gave us capitalism because capitalism is another word for freedom. And it springs from America's most cherished ideals. Some conservatives have turned against the market system. They tell us America needs a different kind of capitalism. A hyphenated capitalism. They want to give government more power to make more decisions for business and workers. They differ from socialists only in degree. They advocate in effect government 'industrial policy', socialism's essential ingredient".[30]

The sponsors of capitalism are not stupid, though they are often portrayed as such by their socialist opponents. They mean business. Hayley may well prove Bannon right and lead cyber-capitalism's storytellers to victory by becoming America's first female President in 2024. Their tailor-made messaging does the trick especially with those who have trouble distinguishing illusion from reality, facts from fiction, and are angry about being left behind by forces they cannot comprehend.

Those among the middle classes and the intelligentsia who want a more detailed, more sophisticated version of the universal capitalist sales pitch than the one Nikki Hayley pitches above are told that capitalism is a better "model" than socialism because it is powered by the most efficient political-economic engine of human progress ever invented. This engine, we're told, is propelled by a 'natural' hence inexhaustible fuel—the desire for personal wealth. That desire, we are told, is as natural as the air we breathe. Any attempt to shut it down is contrary to "the laws of nature".

The sponsors of capitalism claim that their engine of choice comes with an automatic override that shields it against human frailty or tampering. It is driven by an unseen hand that cannot be blinded by those who portray the accumulation of wealth as a sin. The beauty of the beast resides in its ability to determine who gets what, when and how in society by responding to commodity price signals— first and foremost to the factor prices of land, labour, and money—and by harnessing the currents of supply and demand on local, national, and international markets. It is an engine that comes off the assembly line perfectly balanced and is always in pursuit of equilibrium after it's turned on, especially when left to its own devices. The sponsors tell us to just sit back, go with "the flow" and buy shares on the stock market in order not to be left behind.[31]

In the latest ads for capitalism, the market is portrayed as an adjunct of artificial intelligence, therefore it must be listened to and obeyed by those who want to succeed. We are told that any political attempts to interfere with the capitalist engine's automatic mechanisms—attempts to interfere with the markets' price-setting mechanisms, to manipulate supply or demand, to offer an alternative route, pick winners and losers, or to nationalize some of its privately-owned stands no less—will produce sub-optimal performance, will hinder rather than promote human progress and make us all as unhappy and side-tracked as the working men and women of the Soviet Union and Hungary were under Bolshevik rule decades earlier. Haven't we heard what a horrid mess that Hungarian Commune produced on the Blue Danube in 1919? Haven't we heard of the "Red Terror" its leaders resorted to in order to get their way accepted by the misguided masses during those tragic days? Haven't we heard of the bloody suppression of the 1956 Hungarian "Freedom Fighters" by the Soviet Union, by those "Lenin-Boys" who sponsored the first bloody mess in Budapest in 1919? Do we really want to make refugees out of our children and grandchildren in America as well?

Those who are still doubtful of the superiority of the capitalist engine of progress are instructed to look at the engine that drives the so-called "socialist" economy of China along its "Silk Road" to success. The reason why the Chinese economy is so robust, our sponsors tell us, is plain to see: its engine of progress is a carbon copy of the one that made America great. Even Donald Trump calls it a rip-off, the intellectual property of capitalism. [32]

We are told by the sponsors of universal capitalism that the ability of the Chinese model to outperform its American prototype, is a function of the following seven refinements:

1. The value settings for labour, money and land on the Chinese model are set at artificially lower levels than on the American model, therefore it is cheaper to run and is more competitive on international markets. This is why, for example, the most highly valued American company, Apple, manufactures most of its products in China.

2. Investment costs into the Chinese model's modernization are much lower than for the original American prototype because the Chinese developers rely on stolen (i.e. free) intellectual property. This gives the Chinese model an unbeatable competitive edge over its American relative.

3. The regulatory burden on the Chinese model is much lower or lighter than on the American prototype. The Communist leadership's greater tolerance of its engine's 'externalities' (its informational asymmetries, its environmental harmfulness, its assault on human and civil rights, etc.) reduces its operating costs, increases its comparative advantages on global markets.

4. The Chinese 'copy-cat' operates on a huge Asian market, enjoying unparalleled economies of scale which enable it to work with lower marginal costs and prices.

5. Unlike the Western capitalist engine of progress, the Chinese model is vertically and horizontally integrated: the state controls its input and output valves and can keep an eye on everything. "Surveillance capitalism"[33] in the West is years behind China. This provides the driver of the Chinese engine far greater freedom to by-pass traffic jams and other hindrances in its way. (It is somewhat amusing how this particular feature of the Chinese model is portrayed as an advantage, whereas, anyone advocating the same approach in America would most likely have an ice-pick planted in his or her skull by Nikki Haley, that gentle Senator Mitt Romney, or Laura Ingraham over at Fox.)

6. The Chinese model is a relatively recent arrival on the global markets—its final refinements took place only recently, well after Mao's disastrous Cultural Revolution ended in 1976. The American model is well over 150 years old— ok, 90 if we count back to Roosevelt's New Deal. Compared to those

numbers, the Chinese prototype is virtually new. It was only rolled out and at first very tentatively by Deng Xiaoping in 1978. It is only now starting to experience the first inevitable signs of the law of diminishing returns.

7. Finally, the Chinese leadership protects its engine by the enforcement of much stricter labour laws, the banning of workers' councils, independent unions, collective bargaining, and working-class dissent. This political stewardship is yet another source of the Chinese prototype's competitive economic edge.

It is clear that the advocates of universal capitalism are imbued with a love/hate relationship towards China's remarkable engine of progress. On the one hand, they complain bitterly about its 'socialist' modifications, on the other they would love to have a free hand to reengineer theirs in the same fashion.

The closing argument of the sponsors of universal capitalism usually consists of the following amalgam. There is no alternative to capitalism for anyone who is sane and values life, liberty, and the pursuit of happiness. Social revolutions like the one in Russia in 1917 or Hungary in 1919 must apply Jacobin-like terror, go to the Gulag, pass through the Nazi concentration camps before they are finally rescued by an army of Chicago trained shock-therapists or by clones generated by the Milton Friedman school of political-economic thought. Those who insist on calling themselves socialists, speak of revolution, and want to discard the engine that made America great, are not only fools but un-American. They are enemies of the people, enemies of freedom itself. If they stick to their guns, they will spark a civil war wherever they go, and produce the same horror show that rocked Russia and Hungary 100 years ago, leaving the people of those distant lands not only poorer but unfree.[34]

Back to Reality

This brief rejoinder to the sponsors of capitalism is not driven by the desire to establish the superiority of systems that claim to be socialist but by the need to establish that capitalism grossly undervalues the truth and when left to its own devices it produces unjust, unconstitutional, and unsustainable outcomes. And nowhere is this more apparent in Europe today than in Hungary, where that country's fortune hunters have chosen to portray the 1919 Hungarian Republic of Councils as that country's darkest moment in history.

Most of those who, for whatever reason, still insist on calling themselves socialists never deny that capitalism is a huge step forward from Feudalism in the relentless march of human history. By breaking down the barriers of the closed feudal or semi-feudal systems that preceded it, capitalism in Western and Eastern

Europe, in North America and elsewhere, allowed the introduction of competition, the internal market, and wage labour, propelling the greatest leap in the development of humanity's ever-productive forces.[35] While recognizing capitalism's achievements, socialists insist, and rightly so, on not only speaking out but defending themselves and their fellow human beings against capitalism's failures. Whatever we may think of it, it is not the failure of socialism but of capitalism that produced the 1919 Hungarian Republic of Councils as we shall see from the opening chapter of this book.

This rejoinder then does not deny the persuasiveness of capitalism's marketing pitch. On the surface, there are even some grains of truth sprinkled among its bombast. Capitalism has indeed undergone a dizzying number of changes prior to its current metamorphosis of which the most important was the growth of the capitalist state, the imposition of public interventions into the mechanisms of local, national, and international markets.[36] A brief summary will suffice.

The transformation of capitalism after the Russian and Hungarian revolutions and the rise of fascism began with the abandonment of Say's Law (Say's fantasy would be more appropriate) in the early 1930s and the emergence of Keynesian principles of national economic management. It gathered considerable steam after WWII not only via transfers of productive assets from private into public ownership, but through a wide array of macro and microeconomic interventions as well as fiscal and monetary innovations through public spending and regulatory, tax, and monetary policies. Suffice it to say, the state plays a larger rather than a smaller role in the capitalist economy today than it did before WWII.[37] The question is—who are the primary beneficiaries of this expansion? Has capitalism become socially just? Has it chosen an ecologically sustainable path to the future, where equality for all before the law is the rule rather than the exception? The answer to those questions is a resounding no.

We must begin our rejoinder by stating that the face of the past 150 years has been permanently disfigured by the consequences of four major depressions, every one of them directly related to the reigning political establishments' reliance on that capitalist "engine of progress" so persuasively promoted to this day by its sponsors.

The first major depression—the one in 1870—already showed signs of capitalism's limited shelf life, its propensity to run out of gas: "By giving birth to an absolute surplus of capital without objective conditions to feedback into the valorization circuit, the burning of wealth becomes its metabolic imperative".[38] War and barbarism, production for destruction is the main and ultimately self-destructive feature of the gathering capitalist cyclone. The Paris Commune of 1871 was the first emphatic 'No' on this "Road to Hell" or what another Austrian-

American Harvard economist, Joseph A. Schumpeter would euphemistically call "creative destructiveness".[39]

To be sure, the first consequences of the carnage on the road travelled by European capitalism were conveniently "off-shored" onto the colonies. During the last decades of the 19th century, and the first decade of the 20th, 10 million Indigenous peoples would perish in the Congo alone because of King Leopold's quest for personal profits in Africa.[40] A similar pattern of behaviour—all in the name of God, Civilization, "White Man's Burden" and the laws that governed "The Wealth of Nations" as laid down by that decent Scottish moral philosopher, Adam Smith—would be exhibited by the major Imperial powers in all the far-flung corners of the world, in Asia, Africa, the Middle East, and Latin America. In North America, hundreds of Indigenous civilizations (First Nations) would be wiped out by the westward trek of the white fortune hunters from Europe and the viruses they carried with them into the New World.[41] By 1914, the only refuge for the ordinary passengers in this European-made capitalist vehicle were in the muddy, blood-soaked trenches of World War I. Close to 100 million perished because of this first big, albeit avoidable, meltdown.

The carnage produced by the first depression was repeated with even greater vehemence 10 years on the heels of the second depression that started in August 1929. The Second World War was punctuated by two mushroom clouds over Hiroshima and Nagasaki, which wiped out hundreds of thousands in the flash of an eye. The two capitalist depressions that led to two world wars in the space of 25 years resulted in the death of close to 200 million people during the first 50 years of the 20th century. "Liquidation of value"—the destruction of wealth—becomes the only path towards resuming the process of capitalist accumulation.[42] The relative prosperity of the West during the second half of the 20th century was built on a century of wanton destruction that preceded it. (The effect of the 2020–2021 "burn-off" is impossible to estimate at the time this manuscript is being written.)

The destruction produced by Europe's capitalist enthusiasts in the colonies would leave much deeper psychological scars than those left on the face of the imperial centres and would take a far longer time to heal as Frantz Fanon would show in his classic study[43] and as events in the Middle East and Africa to this day demonstrate. Anyone who still thinks that the earlier wars in Korea, Indochina, the Middle-East, Vietnam, then later in Iraq, Afghanistan, 9/11, the Syrian disaster, the rise of ISIS, the plight of the Kurds, the Palestinians, the perilous state of Israel, the current conflict between Iran and America, the war between Saudi Arabia and Yemen, the violence in Africa, parts of Central and South America, the tens of millions of dead, mutilated, starving are independent of the blind greed of the former Imperialist powers or of America's willingness to take out a second mortgage on that blind selfishness is dreaming in technicolour. As Chris Harman reminds us, imperialism is not just a stage in history in which disputes over colonies rise to the surface. Imperialism is "a system whose logic was total militarization and total war, despite the social devastation it causes".[44]

The third depression produced by capitalism came in 1970–73 with the end of Bretton Woods and the fourth in 2008 when massive state intervention was required to rescue the world's largest banks and industries from a catastrophe of global proportions produced by the uncontrolled greed and deceptive behaviour of the market-players on Wall Street such as Lehman Brothers. The 2008 crash produced a real wage drop of 25% in the US and 30–40% in the south of Europe and vastly increased the riches of the wealthy everywhere.[45] It destroyed not only the accumulated savings of tens of millions, but robbed hundreds of millions of wage earners of their opportunities for a better future, to be better educated, to be better prepared for the cataclysmic changes hastened by the arrival of artificial intelligence, world-wide climate change, and the migration of tens of millions from the paths of war, exploitation and destruction during the first half of the 21st century.

A long-standing but now highly popular myth propagated by the sponsors of universal capitalism is the one that portrays capitalism and democracy as peas in a pod, inseparable from each other like Siamese twins. Where capitalism goes, democracy follows. If capitalism dies, so does freedom and liberty. By this logic, the critics of capitalism are enemies of democracy "enemies of the people". Though Western "civilization" has promoted this belief in its civic education programs, in its school systems, in its privately-owned media outlets, for at least a century, it is now at peak popularity at its global headquarters in America and within the hundreds of university economic departments, media outlets, think-tanks, and policy-institutes funded annually by the donor billionaire classmates of the Koch brothers, the Mercers in America.[46] And yet, when we take a closer look at the relationship between capitalism and democracy, the reality couldn't be further from this idyllic image of their cohabitation. Instead of a marriage made in heaven, the relationship has been hell for both parties for much of the past 200 years. The two systems have behaved like cats and dogs toward each other. Instead of opening its arms to democracy, capitalism has fought tooth and nail against the latter's slightest advances. A few examples will suffice.

We have already alluded to capitalism's assistance in the subjugation of the Indigenous populations of the Americas along with its profiteering from slavery. The captains of American capitalism did not bat an eye at the civil and human rights abuses directed at black folks in America till the early 1960s. It only eased up under duress. Western capitalism profited immensely from the oppression of hundreds of millions in the colonies well into the second half of the 20th century.

It is that brutal "off-shore" exploitation that made Britain, France, Spain, Holland, Portugal, Germany, Austria, etc. "great" and allowed their capitalist leaders to let up a bit on their domestic workers when they threatened to rush the stage during the first half of the 20th century. Capitalism flourished in Nazi Germany, Fascist Italy, South Africa under Apartheid and does even better in Putin's Russia, Orbán's Hungary, or under the Saudi Arabian human meat-grinder, Mohammed bin Salman—autocrats who were all treated as heroes by the White House under Trump right until his last days in office.[47]

The fact is that the relationship between capitalism and democracy is not a relationship of the heart. It is an enforced marriage, from which capitalism has wanted to extricate itself from day one. Ever since the couple has been together the relationship has been punctuated by frequent and bitter public scandals often spilling into violence and abuse. This "antipathy" of capitalism towards democracy, and the irrefutable evidence of capitalism's propensity to go to bed with a wide assortment of authoritarian regimes, including the Nazis in Germany, should cause us considerable concern as we enter the information age. What is at the base of this behaviour, this often-unrepressed antagonism?[48]

Contrary to the claims of its earliest apologist, Adam Smith, (the moral philosopher who Nikki Haley would most likely dismiss as a socialist if she bothered to read his treatise), contrary to its many sponsors over the years, and to the teachings of classical and neo-liberal economists today, capitalism tends to produce outcomes not on the basis of perfect information, but on the basis of information asymmetry (a technical term for deception). Instead of producing outcomes that are in alignment with the truth, and our Judeo-Christian ethics, it produces moral hazards for those who climb aboard and put their lives and those of their loved ones into its hands.[49] Apart from its ability to create great wealth for some nations (mostly at others' expense) and enrich some people (mostly at others' expense), this engine is the source of the most spectacular crashes the world has ever seen. So where does all this leave us in 2021, at the start of another "Roaring Twenties?"

By the beginning of the 21st century, universal capitalism has produced, once again, the greatest concentration of wealth in the hands of the fewest number of people. (See our earlier notes on this and the UN's latest report on global inequality.)[50] Today, 200 fortune hunters and their families control more than half of the resources produced worldwide by more than 3 billion actively working men, women, and children. According to the Institute for Policy Studies, in America, the country that is the global headquarters of universal capitalism, the country's three richest individuals—Bill Gates, Warren Buffett, and Jeff Bezos—collectively hold more wealth than the bottom 50% of the domestic population, a total of 160 million people or 63 million American households.[51] Hungary is no exception to this deformation. Social mobility in that country registered the sharpest decline, the growth rate in the number of working poor the sharpest increase, in all of Europe, under the stewardship of Donald Trump's best friend in Central Europe—Viktor Orbán.[52]

It is the capitalist system's unforgettable and recurring crashes, its reluctance to embrace "Lady Liberty", its proven and frequent propensity to cheat on her, its devil may care approach to sleeping with every harlot in the neighbourhood, and not caring about the spread of the deadly viruses that behaviour produces that causes us concern. It is capitalism's undeniable, empirically verifiable, systemic propensity to lend a helping hand to the enemies of social justice, constitutional governance and sustainable development, its systemic hindrance of working men's and women's access to the centre stage of history that is the source of the revolutionary turmoil and violence we have witnessed during the previous century. Like it or not—capitalism is revolting. Until it can demonstrate evidence of its ability to heal itself, it will continue to revolt millions who are sucked into its tendentially manipulative, asymmetric information orbit. Until it divests itself of its pathological propensity to deceive, to lie, to blur the line separating illusion from reality, it will invite rebellion from those who want to live in ecologically sustainable communities governed according to the principles of social justice and equal rights for all under the law.

Where have all the Socialist Flowers Gone?

The biggest flower of them all, the *Great October Revolution of 1917* in Russia, the one that inspired so many of the early revolutions in the 20th century, including Hungary's 1919 Commune, succumbed to the Stalinist Thermidor in 1928. By then, the USSR had a lower GDP than before the start of WWI in 1914. The destruction caused by the World War, followed by the Civil War, the sanctions against the Bolsheviks by the Imperial Powers, the trade blockade, the military invasions combined with the Bolshevik leadership's inexperience with and suspicion of participatory democracy as an appropriate instrument of governance, produced a disastrous cumulative effect on the fragile Soviet economy. Workers' revolutions in Germany, France, Italy, Austria-Hungary, and in places where productive capacity could have been redirected to the heartland of the world revolutionary movement may have stopped the bleeding in Russia. In their absence, the dictatorship of a minority—the Communist Party bureaucracy—took control of the USSR's scarce resources and treated itself to the kind of privileges that George Orwell so masterfully caricatured as the triumph of the pigs on Animal Farm.

Rather than pursuing the path of freedom and justice under the law, and ecologically sustainable economic development, the Bolsheviks took the working men and women of the Soviet Union on a ride in the opposite direction after 1928 and used the label of socialism to conceal their betrayal from Soviet citizens and the world at large for most of the 20th century. That betrayal has left a destructive, radioactive footprint on our global perception of socialism not unlike the one left on the Ukrainian countryside by the meltdown of the Chernobyl Nuclear Power Plant in April 1986. The Bolsheviks' 1928 betrayal of the revolution would permanently poison the socialist well for those working men and women who wanted to quench their thirst for justice, equal treatment before the law, and sustainable economic development. Nowhere is this poisonous after-effect more evident than in America where anti-socialist scare mongering has become as common as apple pie.

Lenin foresaw the destruction that would follow if Stalin would succeed him as the head of his Party. After his passing in 1924, his warnings were hidden from the comrades on Stalin's orders. In Victor Serge's brutal expression, Lenin's and Trotsky's party was shot dead when Stalin came to power in 1928. After 1928, and under the leadership of Stalin, many of the leaders of the 1917 October Revolution were rebranded as "enemies of the people" and executed or sent to the Gulag to experience a slower, more painful death in the permafrost. Those who did not die from the lack of food and the cold in Siberia, such as Karl Radek, Ilona Duczynska's colourful mentor during the Second World Congress of the Comintern in 1920, were beaten to death in the camps run by the Bolsheviks' secret police, the dreaded NKVD. Stalin's forced collectivization drive resulted in the mass starvation and extermination of millions of impoverished and overworked peasants. He introduced forced labour in industry and the militarization of society. Under the dictatorship of Stalin's security forces, the head of the political police replaced the head of the workers' commission as the most important authority in the workplace. In 1928, women, who have made the greatest leap of emancipation with the Russian revolution, were once again thrust into slavery at home and in their places of work. This is the time when the prohibition of abortion is reintroduced, and the number of freely available daycare centres is drastically reduced in the Soviet Union. The Molotov-Ribbentrop Pact and the ensuing gang-rape of Poland by the Nazis and the Soviet Red Army in 1939 would dispel any illusions about who was sleeping with whom on the international stage. That ice-pick planted in the skull of Leon Trotsky in Mexico in 1940, on the orders of Stalin, was the period at the end of the Great October Revolution's death sentence.

For some champions of the oppressed, such as Fanny Kaplan, who spent eleven years in Siberia doing hard labour under the last Tsar, or such early allies of the Bolsheviks as Rosa Luxemburg, Angelica Balabanoff (one of Duczynska's early mentors) or Emma Goldman, the affinity fraud played on the workers of the world by the Russian Bolsheviks started much earlier than 1928. According to

Luxemburg, whose brutal murder in January 1919 was orchestrated by the leaders of the German Social Democratic Party, the betrayal started with Lenin's reformulation of Marx's original ideas and his insistence on submerging the will of the working class to the dictates of the Communist Party's self-appointed leadership. In her 1904 essay "Organizational Questions of Russian Social Democracy" Luxemburg makes clear the fundamental difference between her basic democratic position and Lenin's ultra-centralistic party concept. "The mistakes that are made ... by a truly revolutionary workers' movement are, historically speaking, immeasurably more fruitful and more valuable than the infallibility of the best possible 'Central Committee'".[53] In her 1918 manuscript on "The Russian Revolution" she makes her position even clearer. For her, the dictatorship of the proletariat should be "the work of the class and not of a little leading minority in the name of the class—that is, it must proceed step-by-step out of the active participation of the masses [...]".[54] She says that "The whole mass of the people must take part, otherwise socialism will be decreed from behind a few official desks, by a dozen intellectuals. Public control is indispensable, otherwise, the exchange of experiences remains only with the closed circles of the officials of the regime. Corruption becomes inevitable".[55] She categorically rejects "the use of terror in so wide an extent by the Soviet government" and warns against its use as a model to be followed by the international proletariat.[56] She concludes by proclaiming that the freedom of the press, of free association and assemblage are essentials for the "rule of the broad mass of the people".[57] If only Béla Kun and Tibor Szamuely had listened in Hungary.[58]

The Leninist prescription that infuriated Luxemburg would be tightened by Stalin after Lenin's death. Stalin would proclaim at Lenin's funeral[59] and elaborate on this in his celebrated pamphlet on linguistics[60] that the leading role of the Party elite is fully warranted, Luxemburg be damned, because, "We Communists are special people, we are made of special material".

Ilona Duczynska, the woman who lit the fuse of the 1918–1919 Hungarian revolutions saw the writing on the wall very early on. She left her high-powered position in Béla Kun's Commissariat scarcely a month after her appointment and moved back to Switzerland. There, she took up an insignificant low-level position in the Swiss labour movement under a false name. She saw what happened to Angelica Balabanoff after she met her in Moscow during the summer of 1920. She saw where the revolution was heading in Russia as well and asked to be sent back to Vienna. By early 1922, she was kicked out of the exiled Hungarian Communist Party under Lenin's watch because she refused to buy into those 21 points that were forced upon all members of the Third International at its Second World Congress. She was branded as a "Luxemburgian": a "sin" as András B. Göllner argues in Chapter 4, most of the Hungarian Communists were equally "guilty" of during those revolutionary days in Budapest a couple of years earlier and none more so than their chief ideologue, György Lukács.

According to Fanny Kaplan, the Bolshevik betrayal came in July 1918, when Lenin ordered the bloody liquidation of the Socialist Revolutionary Party (commonly known as the SRs).[61] This frail, visually impaired working-class woman, Fanny, had seen enough. She decided to take matters into her own hands by taking a shot at Lenin at the end of August 1918. Within days, and without trial, she would be shot in the back of the head on the orders of Lenin's security chief, Yaakov Sverdlov. Her body would be stuffed into a barrel and set on fire near the walls of the Kremlin in the Alexander Gardens. Some claim that Lenin's wife, Krupskaya, wept when she heard what they did to the woman who tried to take her husband's life. True or not, her tears cannot erase the fact that habeas corpus died in the Soviet Union under Lenin's rather than Stalin's rule, the reign of terror unleashed by the Cheka, which claimed hundreds of thousands of innocent victims before Lenin's death was not introduced by Stalin. It became official Soviet policy on September 3, 1918. (For a discussion of terror in the Hungarian Republic of Councils see Chapter 4.)

According to the aforementioned Angelica Balabanoff, one of Lenin's closest associates in Zurich (some say they were lovers for a while in Switzerland), the cause of the international labour movement was dealt a lethal blow weeks before the launch of the Hungarian Republic of Councils, when Lenin used her to hoodwink delegates to the opening Congress of the Third International during March 2–6, 1919.[62] Though Kun didn't attend the founding session of the Comintern (he was in prison along with his top colleagues in Budapest) Balabanoff had met him in 1918 when they were both in Moscow. She was repulsed by Kun and thought that the "political love-affair" between Lenin and Kun was a recipe for a disaster.[63]

Emma Goldman, Alexander Berkman, Ida Mett, lifelong champions of working men and women, would place the date of the Great October Revolution's betrayal to 1921, when the sailors of Kronstadt, many of them heroes of the 1917 revolution, would be massacred for raising their voices in protest against the unjust, unsustainable, lawless actions of Lenin's Bolsheviks.[64]

As we shall see from the ensuing chapters, events in Hungary after the October 1918 "Chrysanthemum Revolution" took a somewhat different path than Russia's October Revolution, but the result was still the same. The flowers of the revolution wilted there as well, and much faster than in the Soviet Union. The 1919 Hungarian Republic of Councils was already dead when the Imperialist powers unleashed their "pitbull", Admiral Nicholas Horthy, on the Hungarian working class in November 1919. As the last chapter of this book shows, the post-1919 counter-revolution just passed its 100th anniversary.

The Rise of a New Defeatism on the Left

By the time this book is going to press, the sponsors of universal capitalism will most likely have increased their already significant marketing edge in the race to win the hearts and minds of working men and women around the world with their posturing as the only job creators who matter. At capitalism's global headquarters in America, the word "socialism" is used as if it is an infectious disease. During the four years of the Trump administration, more anti-labour laws and regulations were passed in America than during the entire post-WWII era.[65] The forces on "The Left" appear to be as powerless to stop this as they were in keeping Stalin, Hitler, Mussolini, Salazar, Franco, and other autocrats out of power during the first half of the 20th century. When Bernie fessed up to being a democratic socialist during the Democratic Party's leadership race in 2020, he had nowhere to go but down. Militancy on the part of workers in America is seen as a dangerously disruptive barrier to economic progress, law and order, and good governance. When tens of millions of angry and abused American workers swarm around Trump's Twitter feed like bees around a honeycomb, when they are whipped into the kind of frenzy the world witnessed on January 6, 2021, we come face-to-face with not only the challenge but the failure of the American Left. When the mainstream Conservative Press in America and half of the US Congress can get away with depicting three elderly liberal politicians (Joe Biden, Chuck Schumer, and Nancy Pelosi) as "Dangerous Communist Radicals" on a mission to destroy the American working class on behalf of big business, we come face-to-face with the efficacy of the political language of cyber-capitalism in the age of virtual reality.

As we move from the centre towards the peripheries of universal capitalism, the situation is no better. The organizational strength of the global labour movement is at its historically lowest level since the triumphant years of fascism (the current rate of unionization in the world is below 7%). Countries that advertise themselves as followers of Marx (China, Cuba, North Korea, Vietnam) have banned independent labour unions and workers' councils many decades ago. Virtually all the states that were once ruled by the Bolsheviks are ruled by criminal gangs (headed by former Bolsheviks who have successfully mastered the political language of cyber-capitalism). They are all, without exception, keen participants in universal capitalism's global supply chain and none more so than Hungary's Orbán.

By 2020, the European Union (EU) has become more of a question mark than an affirmation of its values and its unique "European social model". The growing inequalities in opportunities, incomes, and rights over its territory have undermined the faith of many in the EU's ability to create a commonly shared identity for its working men and women. The ability of the Orbán government to successfully defraud Europe's taxpayers of hundreds of billions of Euros for its own enrichment and profit while denying Hungarian working men and women their basic rights to justice, the rule of law, and ecologically sustainable economic development under the EU charter is but one, albeit irrefutable, piece of evidence of this failure. (The other side of this devalued coin is the 3% support in polls in Hungary for the only political party that dares to call itself socialist.)

The exit of Britain from the European Union is almost entirely due to this failure of the EU to deliver on its promises to the citizens of that country. The other side of the coin in Britain is the unparalleled scale of the British Labour Party's rejection by working men and women in that country's last national elections.

Defeatism is not a new but a recurring phenomenon on the Left.[66] We saw it rise in Hungary after the leaders of the 1919 Republic of Council took the last train out of Budapest for the safety of Vienna on August 1st, 1919. It is similar to the defeatism that emerged elsewhere—in Tokyo, Berlin, Rome, Lisbon, Madrid and Vienna—as the collusion between capitalism and various types of author-itarianism went on a deadly rampage during the first half of the 20th century or when Stalinism and its subsequent mutations poisoned the well for socialism the world over.

What is the cause of this recurring defeatism on the Left? What is behind the 21st century's climate of defeatism as capitalism sheds its old skin and replaces it with a new, digital veneer that destroys the ability of working men and women everywhere to see through its artificial, misleading façade?[67]

Part of the new "fear of flying" is the inevitable result of universal capitalism's successful hold on the imagination of working men and women—the gatekeeping, agenda setting, framing and priming advantages that accrue to it from its ownership of the principal networks of mass and social media.[68] The impact of changes in communications technologies on the human mind are also playing a major role in this process as Canada's greatest communications theoreticians, Harold Innes and Marshall McLuhan had shown many decades ago.[69] The other part of this asymmetry stems from a source that writers on "The Left" often overlook—the superior messaging skills of the opinion leaders employed by the advocates of universal capitalism.[70] Addressing fully the defeatism fuelled by this information asymmetry alone could fill an entire book. We merely mention it here, en passant, as a critical factor to address if we are to overcome our "fear of flying" over the territory of cyber-capitalism.[71]

The ability of the sponsors of digital or cyber-capitalism to not only hide from the view of the working classes the roots of their discontent, to depoliticize them, to hinder their access to the voting booths, to successfully temper their desire to be leading actors on the central stage of history, and to put their fate instead into the hands of an Artificial Blond Bomber (aka Donald Trump) is enough to demoralize anyone with a clear vision onto the past and onto the dangerous path that lies ahead for humanity and its ill-informed inhabitants. The popularity and profitability of the syndicated radio networks and television channels in America that add fuel to the global fortune hunters' fire just make the taste of the pill one must swallow ever more bitter.

Passion and disappointment are not our best allies in confronting the newest mutation of the capitalist virus.[72] "Physician, heal thyself" may sound like a cheap slogan, but it is perhaps the most effective and simple medication. Where does one begin?

We have already touched on this during our reflections on Rosa Luxemburg's and Balabanoff's disagreements with Lenin. Defeat invariably is the result of a loss of direct connection, and engagement with those whose lives matter—the people who are on the receiving end of the fortune hunters' unabated, self-serving, and often fraudulent pursuit of privilege, primacy, or profits. It is the disconnect with the people whose lives matter, the disconnect of the Party leadership with the workers', peasants', and soldiers' councils that led to the collapse of the 1919 Republic of Councils. There is an expression in the world of football that says it all and much better than any revolutionary tract: Never take your eyes off the ball.

If only Hannah Arendt and her followers had been aware of this dictum. They correctly identified the undeniable similarity between Stalin's and Hitler's regimes: Both were totalitarian dictatorships hell-bent on destroying the common people's ability to distinguish fact from fiction, illusion from reality.[73] What they failed to recognize and inform us about was that Hitler's dictatorship and our liberal democracies share the same "ball": both possess a common capitalist DNA. Hitler's rise to uncontested levels of political authority in Germany was made possible by the initial and enthusiastic support of the captains of German industry and finance. The same was true in the case of Mussolini's Italy, Salazar's Portugal, Franco's Spain, the Fascists of Austria, or in Horthy's Hungary. The enthusiastic support of the German "billionaire class" for the politically untried housepainter is not at all unlike the enthusiasm shown by Wall Street for the "pussy grabbing" reality television star and bankruptcy artist, Donald J. Trump in America.[74] Hungary's current autocratic ruler is a similar ballplayer. Like Trump, he is supported not only by his corrupt corporate oligarchy but by the entire armada of multinational corporations in Hungary, as well as by the EU's central bankers, because he delivers for universal capitalism. Chapter 8 of this book provides a vivid overview of where that delivery left Hungary's working men and women by 2021.

Confronting the contribution of intellectuals on the Left with the current wave of defeatism is as important as keeping one's eyes on the ball. A brief self-reflection is clearly in order. According to Jim Wolfreys, it is no coincidence that some of the intellectuals who made the greatest theoretical contributions to the neo-liberal renaissance (the new philosophers) are all disappointed, embittered members of the May '68 generation. Defeat is often the moving force of defeatism. Wolfreys claims that the '68 Generation lost its faith in the transformative potential of politics. Its intellectual leaders became the carriers of a historical pessimism born of political defeat, all are the victims of a political unhappiness that resentment and fear generate in the aftermath of defeat.[75]

The late American intellectual, Ellen Meiksins Wood, also spoke about an "intellectual retreat" in the face of the evident successes of the billionaire class:

> We live in curious times. Just when left-wing intellectuals in the West have the rare opportunity to do something useful, if not really historical, they— or a large portion of them—are in full retreat. Just as reformers in the Soviet Union and Eastern Europe look to Western capitalism for paradigms of economic and political success, many of us seem to abdicate the traditional role of the Western left as a critic of capitalism. Just when more than ever we need a Karl Marx that reveals the inner workings of the capitalist system, or a Friedrich Engels that exposes ugly reality 'on the ground', what we have is an army of 'post-Marxists' whose primary function is, apparently, to conceptually dispel the problem of capitalism.[76]

Frustration is the breeding ground for the defeatism that is so evident everywhere. Frustration is the magnet that draws many into linguistic bubbles that are yet again as impenetrable to the oppressed, as far removed from their daily concerns and curiosity, as the far side of the moon.

Has the revolutionary fervor of the 20th century finally succumbed to capitalism's formidable transformative powers? Will Polanyi be proven right? Must Fascism descend upon us once again and perhaps with greater universal force than it did a century ago? Is Covid-19 the signal for the start of the post-modern Dark Ages? What can we learn and apply from the experiences of those long-forgotten social revolutions a hundred years ago as we are taken into the uncharted territories of artificial reality in the 21st century where those who speak truth to power are silenced, dismissed, and disdained and those who are in power have no respect for the truth?

Lessons from the Forgotten Social Revolutions

What kind of seeds did the working men and women of those long-forgotten social revolutions in Russia or Hungary sow? What kind of harvest would those seeds have produced, had those who planted them were allowed to care freely and peacefully for their gardens?

We know that the political soil of those countries was filled with a wide variety of seeds spilt by the hands of those who had recently clashed over them. In both countries, the seeds of capitalism, liberalism, the old monarchy, semi-feudal conservatism, a social-democratic bourgeois democracy, a Leninist- Stalinist Bolshevik Party dictatorship lay next to yet another variety—an entirely new, untried, no-name brand that grew out of the aspirations, dreams, the inextinguishable revolutionary spirit of the exploited peasantry, the proletariat, and a significant segment of those other wage earners who cross class lines in all societies in smaller or larger numbers at critical historical moments. This new seed promised to guard them all and the world against all forms of destructive human behaviour. These new seeds promised to ensure that the production and distribution of goods and services in Hungary, for example, would no longer be exclusively for the benefit of the nobility or the affluent upper-middle-class or a self-appointed Bolshevik party elite, but would be governed by constitutionally guaranteed principles of justice, equity, and sustainability under the direct supervision of the labouring classes themselves—through their locally organized and run councils, on which men and women would be represented equally. Those new but untested, unbranded, unharvested seeds of the Russian and Hungarian Revolutions are still available to humanity wherever the need, the demand arises for them. It has been planted, for example, time and time again by the followers of Apo, in what is now the inhospitable, infertile political soil of Northern Syria. As one of the custodians of this seedling proclaimed recently:

> This is a revolution which aspires to *ecological sustainability*, even in the midst of all-out war. These four features—direct democracy against the state, women's liberation, multicultural accommodation, and social ecology —together distinguish the revolution in Rojava, lending credence to the claims of those who see it as rekindling an emancipatory flame several times submerged but never fully extinguished—with radical-democratic, revolutionary precedents which can be found, for example, in the Paris Commune, in the Hungarian Republic of Councils, and in the Spanish revolution.[77]

On March 21, 1919, a name had to be found for this new seedling—the dictatorship of the proletariat appeared to be acceptable to most everyone in Budapest and the surrounding countryside, populated by millions of landless, illiterate, and exploited agricultural labourers. Can anyone blame Béla Kun for thinking, that there is no reason to build capitalism in Hungary, when not a gunshot was heard in its defence? What turned the 1919 Republic of Councils into a monumental event was the spontaneity, the ingenuity, the heroism of the working men and women of Hungary to do what their brothers and sisters in Germany, France, England and throughout Western Europe were unable to do so: to organize themselves into local councils to take charge of their lives, their communities, their gardens as it were, and try to make a go of it. It was this noble, almost majestic behaviour that triggered the initial and large number of crossovers to the revolution from the Hungarian bourgeoisie, from the world of arts and letters, from the universities, from the intelligentsia. Even a small scattering of noblemen and aristocrats were swept away by the spirit of this revolution during its first promising moments. It was its proven, clearly observable ability to sweep so many away with its intoxicating, liberating magic that is the source of the counter-revolutionary anger directed against it from all sides of the ideological divide for the past 100 years. It is this infectious quality of the 1919 Hungarian Republic of Councils that scared the daylights out of the imperialist powers in Versailles that we reported on at the beginning of our introduction. This is why the truth about the 1919 Republic of Councils is so irritating, so frightening to the current authoritarian rulers of Hungary and why they spend so much of their energies repressing it.

It is the promise of a new seed that would be resistant to the exploitation of working men and women by the affluent classes or by those who professed to know better what is in the common peoples' interest that made the 1919 Republic of Councils so unforgettable to those who look upon it with open eyes. Was the 1919 Budapest Commune simply one of the dozens of failed attempts to replace capitalism with socialism? Hardly so.

The working men and women of Russia in 1917, in Hungary in 1919, had no idea whatsoever what the term socialism meant other than something that's the opposite of capitalism. Those who heard of the term socialism hoped that it would be something for the better, a state of being where they would no longer be exploited by the fortune hunters. By 1990, most people on the former territory of the Soviet Empire had even less of an idea of what socialism meant, other than the bad taste it left in many of their mouths after swallowing the daily lies and breathing in the noxious fumes produced under its label for decades.

One of the "take-aways" from the 1919 Hungarian Republic of Councils—a take-away that has been falsified for generations—is that it owes its initial success to its Kropotkian, Luxemburgian, Pannekoekian, rather than Leninist roots. Peter Kenez is right to remind us: "Bela Kun had little understanding of Leninist ideology and the theoreticians [László Rudas or György Lukács in particular] had not yet freed themselves from their Western European Revolutionary Socialist background... The Hungarian Communists' concept of the Party was more Luxemburgian than Leninist" [78]

The spectacular flare-up in Budapest in 1919 may never have happened if the woman who lit its fuse, and many around her, had not listened to Rosa Luxemburg, Angelica Balabanoff, Anton Pannekoek, Ervin Batthány or Ervin

Szabó and learned to speak the language of those whose lives mattered.[79] The sparkplugs of the Budapest Commune embraced the people, rather than the party that spoke in the people's name. Duczynska and her comrades went out to the factories of Csepel on the outskirts of the Hungarian capital, sat down with the toughest shop-stewards of the Hungarian labour-movement to make sure they were on the same page with them. It was their solidarity, direct connection with the hearts and minds of the people whose lives mattered that brought tens of thousands out into the streets of Budapest on November 25, 1917, to set the fire that blossomed into the social revolution of 1919 in Hungary.

As we have stated earlier, and as this book shows, it was the disconnect between the party's political leadership of the dictatorship of the proletariat and the people whose lives mattered that caused the revolution to fail. (In his first telegram to Lenin from Vienna after he fled Budapest, Kun would blame the working men and women of Hungary for the collapse of their tragic, heroic undertaking. It showed how far he had moved away from the lives of those that mattered.)

Contrary to the rhetoric directed against them, the objectives of the "common people" in Hungary in 1919 had been remarkably modest, and consistent with the ones enunciated by that Greek intellectual labourer, Aristotle: they wanted an ecologically sustainable communal life for themselves and their children, where the principles of justice and equality before the law are constitutionally enshrined. They and generations of common people around the world wanted and want to this day nothing more, nothing less than what they are entitled to: To be actors rather than props in a play about who gets what, when and how in their communities. The task of the intellectual worker is to help working men and women to find the path they are drawn to and to help them to stay on it without being lured into painful traps along the way by competing fortune hunters who specialize in various forms of affinity-fraud to get what they want from their victims.

As we look back on the 1919 Hungarian Republic of Councils, the one thing we can say about it with any degree of certainty is this: It was not a freak storm, but part of a global 'weather pattern' and it did not end when Béla Kun and his comrades boarded the last train out of Budapest for Vienna on August 1st, 1919. It only came to a temporary halt when the Imperialist great powers sent their caretaker into Budapest on November 16, 1919, and told the spontaneously constituted workers', peasants', and soldiers' councils of Hungary where to get off. The latter would be back at it for a while in 1945, and even more spectacularly in 1956. They may well be back at it yet again. The spirit of the workers' revolution has been made immortal not by the theoreticians of socialism, but by the practitioners of capitalism.

As we can see from the last chapter of this book, Hungary's workers' rebellions in 1919 and 1956 did not end well. That unhappy ending would be repeated many times over in different parts of the world. If there is a single message to this book it is this: *The 1919 Republic of Councils was not a failure of socialism but of capitalism.* If world history can be of any guidance to us, it is this: The revolutionary spirit of working men and women is immortal, it cannot be destroyed, the counterrevolution is the source of its destruction. It will be overcome.

NOTES

1 Dick Geary, *European Labour Politics From 1900 to the Depression* (New Jersey, NJ: Atlantic Highlands, 1991), 1.

2 See: Horst Lademacher, *Die Zimmerwalder Bewegung: Protokolle Und Korrespondenz* (The Hague, 1967). Robert Craig Nation, *War on War: Lenin, the Zimmerwald Left, and the Origins of Communist Internationalism* (Chicago, IL: Haymarket Books, 2009). Maria Lafont, *The Strange Comrade Balabanoff: the Life of a Communist Rebel* (Jefferson, NC: McFarland & Company, Inc., Publishers, 2016).

3 Márta Tömöry, "Duczynska Ilona feljegyzései az 1918-as januári sztrájk előzményeiről". (Recollections of Ilona Duczynska on the events leading up to the January 1918 General Strike). *Történelmi Szemle, no 1-2. (1958).* Also: András B. Göllner, *Ilona: Portrait of a Rebel* (forthcoming, 2022).

4 Karl Marx et al., *Manifesto Do Partido Comunista* (Lisboa: Edições Avante!, 1975).

5 Valério Arcary and Grícoli Iokoi Zilda Márcia, *As Esquinas Perigosas Da história: Um Estudo Sobre a história Dos Conceitos De época, situação e Crise revolucionária No Debate Marxista* [Dangerous Corners of History—Revolutionary Situations in a Marxist Perspective] (São Paulo, 2000).

6 Thomas Jeffery Miley, *Your Freedom and Mine: Abdullah Ocalan and the Kurdish Question in Erdogan's Turkey* (Montréal, QC: Black Rose Books, 2018).

7 Vladimir Maiakóvsky, *Poemas,* (Poems) (São Paulo: Perspectiva, 2017), 93.

8 Árpád Tóth, *Az új Isten* (The New God). *Nyugat* (Budapest. April 1, 1919). Translated from Hungarian by András B. Göllner.

9 Leon Trotsky, *História Da Revolução Russa* (Sao Paulo: Sundermann, 2007), 10.

10 *Ibid.*

11 The best known, most sophisticated theory of post-capitalism is by Paul Mason, *Postcapitalism: A Guide to Our Future* (London: Allen Lane, 2015). The best criticism of Mason's thesis is by Christian Fuchs "Henryk Grossman 2.0: A Critique of Paul Mason's Book *Post Capitalism: A Guide to Our Future*" in *TrippleC,* (April 12, 2016).

12 The American political commentator Paul Street is of course perfectly right to warn us: *Don't blame the Trump presidency on the white proletariat. The real responsibility for this epically transgressive administration—headed by an individual Noam Chomsky rightly describes as "the most dangerous criminal in human history"—lies with the billionaire class.* "Trump's Real Base is the Ruling Class", in *Truthdig* (March 3, 2020).

13 On Foucault's position see Michel Foucault, *"Face aux gouvernements, les droits de l'Homme",* quoted in James Miller, *The Passion of Michel Foucault* (New York, NY: Simon and Schuster, 1993), 316. Also, Michel Foucault. *Discourse and Truth: the Problematization of parrhesia* (Foucault.info: Digital Archive, 1985).

14 Charles Tilly, *Las Revoluciones Europeas, 1492–1992* (Barcelona: Crítica, 1995), 26–27.

15 Trotsky 2007, *op. cit.* as well as Leon Trotsky, Luma Nichol *The Permanent Revolution & Results and Prospects* (Seattle, WA: Red Letter Press, 2010).

16 Arcary 2000, *op. cit.*

17 *Ibid.,* 104.

18   *Ibid.*, 98.

19   Valério Arcary, *O Encontro da Revolução com a História* (São Paulo: Sundermann, 2006), 296.

20   "1% of global population owns same wealth as remaining 99%, says study", *BBC News*, 18 January 2016. For a more detailed discussion, see: Thomas Piketty , *Capital in the Twenty-First Century* (Cambridge, MA: The Belknap Press of Harvard University Press, 2017).

21   Vladimir Ilyich Lenin, *Imperialism: the Highest Stage of Capitalism a Popular Outline* (London: Pluto Press, 1996). (First published in 1916).

22   Rosa Luxemburg, Isabel Loureiro, and Stefan Fornos Klein, *Textos Escolhidos* (São Paulo: Editora Unesp, 2011), 17.

23   Robert O. Paxton, *Europe in the Twentieth Century* (Orlando, FL: Harcourt, 1997), 11.

24   Victor Serge, *Ofício de Revolucionário* (Rio de Janeiro: Moraes Editora), 108.

25   Karl Polanyi, *The Great Transformation* (Boston, MA: The Beacon Press, 1957). Polanyi taught at Columbia University, but his wife Ilona Duczynska was denied entry into the US from 1947 on, because of her unwillingness to lie to American border control about how she feels about capitalism, or what she did in the past on behalf of working men and women in Central Europe. This is how the couple's home base came to be in Canada—Pickering, Ontario. Polanyi commuted from there to his job at Columbia until his retirement. Ilona and Karl's only child, Kari Polanyi Levitt (one of the contributors to this book), and their grandchildren live in Montréal, Canada.

26   Robert Kuttner, "The Man from Red Vienna," *New York Review of Books* (December 21, 2017).

27   Karl Polanyi was the first to use the term "universal capitalism" to describe the political-economic system that had led to the Great Depression of the 1930s and World War II; see "Universal Capitalism or Regional Planning," *The London Quarterly of World Affairs* 10, no. 3, (1945), 86-91.

28   Michael Wolff, *The Hollywood Reporter* (November 18, 2016). The crooked conspiracy theorist's prophecy would be proven wrong by the Democrats in the 2020 Presidential election. Bannon escaped prosecution as a consequence of the Presidential pardon given to him by Trump on his last day in office.

29   *"It's the economy, stupid"* is a phrase attributed to James Carville, a political strategist in Bill Clinton's successful 1992 presidential campaign against incumbent George H. W. Bush. His phrase was directed at Clinton's campaign workers, exhorting them to focus on their target audiences' economic fears and aspirations. It is that singular focus that got Clinton into the White House in 1992.

30   See, George F. Will's account of Nikki Haley's performance on The Hudson Institute's stage in the paper owned by the third wealthiest Americans; Jeff Bezos. George F. Will, "Nikki Haley picks a worthy fight," *The Washington Post*, March 8, 2020, A23. Will of course is one of the favoured scribes of the fortune hunters that put Trump into the White House; see Jane Mayer, *Dark Money: The Hidden History of the Billionaires Behind the Rise of the Radical Right* (New York, NY: Anchor Books, a division of Penguin Random House LLC, 2017), 145.

31   On "Flow Theory" please turn to the work of Mihály Csikszentmihályi, an internationally celebrated Hungarian-American social psychologist sponsor of universal capitalism from the University of Chicago. (See: Mihaly Csikszentmihalyi, *Flow: The Psychology of Optimal Experience* (New York, NY: Harper and Row, 2009). "Flow", for Csikszentmihályi is an ideal state of mind, in which people are so involved in an activity that nothing else seems to matter to them, not even black lives, or the truth. The American psychologist was given two of Hungary's highest state honors following Orbán's electoral victories in 2010 and 2014 (the Szécheny Prize in 2011 and The Grand Cross Order of Merit of the Republic of Hungary in 2014.) He is credited for helping the Hungarian autocrat to hold Hungary's working men and women back from the centre of that country political stage by making them think nothing of it.

32   For an interesting recent critique of the Chinese model from a Leftist perspectiv see: Annamarie Artner. "Can China Lead the Change of the World?" *Third World Quarterly* (August 4, 2020). Strangely enough, by the summer of 2021, she had changed her tune, and came to look at the Chinese Communist Party's approach as a fitting alternative to universal capitalism. (In a letter dated April 24, 2021 addressed to the Double Movement Group of the Hungarian Karl Polanyi Center, she wrote: *"I have become convinced that China's road is a (if not "the") feasible one for getting rid of the capitalist nightmare and transforming the society, step by step, for a socialist one"*

33 On the concept of "surveillance capitalism" see Shoshana Zuboff, *The Age of Surveillance Capitalism: The Fight for a Human Future at the New Frontier of Power* (New York, NY: Public Affairs, 2020).

34 For the earliest scholarly version of the above ad, please turn to Polanyi's Austrian nemesis Ludwig von Mises, *Socialism: An Economic and Sociological Analysis* (London: Jonathan Cape, 1936). And the book written by von Mises' Austrian devotee, Friedrich Hayek, *The Road to Serfdom* (Chicago, IL: University of Chicago Press, 1944). The two Austrian immigrants to America are the founding fathers of the so-called "Chicago School of Economics", which is the intellectual bastion for the sponsors of universal capitalism.

35 E. J. Hobsbawm, *A Era Do Capital 1848-1875* (Rio de Janeiro: Paz e Terra, 2009). And E. J. Hobsbwam, *A Era do Império (The Age of Empire: 1875–1914)* (Lisboa: Presença, 1990).

36 This is the "double-movement" Polanyi talks about in *The Great Transformation* as well. op.cit.

37 The champions of capitalism tend to explain this expansion of the state into market domains as a subjective phenomenon, the product of a shift in our values, the product of a new, adversarial counterculture that can be countervailed because of its subjective nature. This view led to the rise of Reaganomics and Thatcherism. For a brief analysis of the *objective* forces behind the growth of the state under capitalism see András B. Göllner, *Social Change and Corporate Strategy* (Stamford: IAP, 1983), 51-82.

38 Osvaldo Coggiola, *As Grandes Depressões* (São Paulo: Alameda, 2009), 10–11.

39 See Jospeh Schumpeter, *Capitalism, Socialism and Democracy*, 2nd ed. (Santa Clarita, CA: Impact Books, 2014).

40 See Adam Hochschild, *King Leopold's Ghost: A Story of Horror, Greed, Terror and Heroism in Colonial Africa* (Boston, MA: Mariner Books, 1998).

41 See Francis Jennings, *The Invasion of America* (New York, NY: W.W. Norton and Co., 1975).

42 Coggiola, *op. cit.*, pp.10–11.

43 Frantz Fanon, *The Wretched of the Earth* (New York, NY: Grove Press, 1961).

44 Chris Harman *A People's History of the World* (London and Sidney: Bookmarks, 1999), 409.

45 Michael Roberts, *The Long Depression* (Chicago, IL: Haymarket Books, 2016).

46 For a brilliant investigative analysis of the destructive power of this class of fortune-hunters behind the Republican Party in America, see: Jane Mayer, *op.cit.,*

47 See Ben Hubbard, *MBS: The Rise to power of Mohammed bin Salman* (New York, NY: Tim Dugan Books, 2020).

48 For a thoughtful discussion; see Robert Kuttner, *Can Democracy Survive Global Capitalism?* (New York, NY: W.W. Norton and Co., 2018). For the United Nation's latest report on the threat posed to democracy globally by universal capitalism's breakneck pursuit of inequality please see the UN's 2020 *World Social Report*, published by the *UN* Department of Economic and Social Affairs (DESA), January 21, 2020.

49 *Information asymmetry* is a term that is part of the vocabulary of information economics. In this context, it means that the parties in an economic interaction have different information in their hands about the nature of their "deal"—one party has more or better information than the other. In the lexicon of information economics, *moral hazard* occurs when one person takes more risks because someone else bears the burden of those risks. Herein lies the key to the behaviour of Lehman Brothers and the crisis they produced for hundreds of millions of working men and women around the world in 2008. The economists who finally discovered this aspect of the capitalist engine's behaviour—George Akerlof, Robert Stiglitz, Michael Spence—were awarded the Nobel Prize for Economics in 2001; see Joseph E. Stiglitz,"Information and the Change in the Paradigm in Economics," Nobel Prize Lecture, Stockholm, December 8, 2001.

50 *World Social Report 2020: Inequality in a Rapidly Changing World / Department of Economic and Social Affairs* (New York: United Nations, 2020).

51 See Noah Kirsch's report in *Forbes*, November 9, 2017.

52 For the Orbán government's betrayal of Hungary's working men and women please turn to Chapter 8.

53 Peter Hudis and Kevin B. Anderson eds., *The Rosa Luxemburg Reader* (Monthly Review Press: New York, NY, 2004),250-265.

54   *Ibid.* p.308.

55   *Ibid.* p.306.

56   *Ibid.* pp.306, 309.

57   *Ibid.* p.304.

58   Tibor Szamuely, one of the champions of the use of "terror" during the Hungarian Republic of Councils, and Kun's chief Bolshevik opponent was in Berlin during the German Revolution, and left Berlin for Budapest in January 1919 just before the murder of Rosa Luxemburg, disgusted with her and her unwillingness to follow the Russian Bolshevik's brutal, bureaucratic, terroristic approach. For more details on this see Chapter 4.

59   Moscow, *Pravda*, January 30, 1924.

60   J.V. Stalin, *Marxism and Problems of Linguistics* (Foreign Languages Press: Peking, 1972).

61   Unbeknown to Duczynska, the close bond between Lenin and Béla Kun was cemented in July 1918, while the bullets were flying around the Kremlin between the defenders of the Bolsheviks and the SRs. Duczynska recalls asking Bukharin and Radek in Moscow in 1920 what all those bullet holes were doing in the walls of the Kremlin, but they just laughed and brushed it off. She did not know, that Béla Kun, and a handful of other Hungarian POWs in Russia like Tibor Szamuely, or her immediate colleague in Kun's Commissariat, Ernő Pór all fought with guns to liberate Lenin and the other Bolshevik leaders who were barricaded inside their Kremlin offices by the SRs in July 1918. When all this was going down Ilona was shut off from the world, imprisoned and facing a military trial for her own clandestine revolutionary activities in Hungary.

62   Hungarian accounts of the date of the founding Congress frequently place it at a time subsequent to the launch of the Hungarian Republic of Councils. The Congress took place during the first week of March, 1919.

63   See Angelica Balabanoff, *My Life as a Rebel* (New York, NY: Harper & Brothers, 1938), 224. And Angelica Balabanoff, *Impressions of Lenin* (Ann Arbor, MI: University of Michigan Press, 1964).

64   See Emma Goldman, Alexander Berkman *et al.* *1917: Revolution in Russia and its Aftermath* (Montréal, QC: Black Rose Books, 2018).

65   See The Center for American Progress Action Fund's report dated January 26, 2018, *President Trump's Policies are Hurting American Workers*. Also, Steven Greenhouse, *The Worker's Friend? Here is How Trump has Waged his War on Workers* (Washington, DC: The American Prospect, August 30, 2019).

66   For an excellent survey of the ""defeatism" that affected Hungary's left prior to the 1919 Republic of Councils see Péter Csunderlik. "Variációk a "defaitizmusra": Az I. világháború és a Galilei Kör "antimilitarista" tevékenysége galileista memoárokban. (Variations on Defeatism: WWI and the Anti-Militaristic Activities of the Galilei Circle in the Memoirs of its Members). *Kommentár*. no 2. (2014), 33-52.

67   Chris Hedges provided an excellent journalistic overview of this viral spread in America a decade ago in *The Empire of Illusion* (New York, NY: Alfred A. Knopf, 2009).

68   See Edward S. Herman and Noam Chomsky, *Manufacturing Consent: The Political Economy of the Mass Media* (New York, NY: Pantheon, 1988). And Paul Nesbitt-Larking, *Politics, Society and the Media*, 2nd ed. (Toronto, ON: Broadview Press, 2007), 315-349.

69   See Harold A. Innis, *Empire and Communications* (Toronto, ON: Dundurn Press, 2007). And Marshall McLuhan, *Understanding Media: The Extensions of Man* (London: Routledge, 1964). Studies into the destructive impact of modern social media and digital communications technologies on our minds, on the ability of working men's and women's ability to distinguish illusion from reality are only just beginning to surface.

70   A good introduction to this latter subject is the work of American communications theorist, George Lakoff, e.g., *Moral Politics. How Liberals and Conservatives Think* (Chicago, IL: University of Chicago Press, 2002); *Metaphors We Live By* (Chicago, IL: University of Chicago Press, 2003). And *Don't Think of an Elephant* (White River Junction, VT: Chelsea Green Publishing, 2014).

71   A key variable that is central to this equation, requires a book by itself rather than a footnote: the recurring unpreparadnes of the Left "to run with the ball" so working men and women end up winning rather than losing at the end of the match.. György Lukács would himself admit as much

after it was game over for him in Hungary in August, 1919 (for details please turn to András Göllner's chapter 4).

72 For a good discussion of capitalism and the 2020 Coronavirus pandemic please see Radhika Desai, "The Unexpected Reckoning: Coronavirus and Capitalism," *Canadian Dimension,* (March 17, 2020). For the blindness to the affinity fraud working men and women are being subjected to throughout the world by Stalinists and most recently by the Chinese Communist Party via the use of cyber-communications technologies developed by capitalism, see the "Manifesto" championed by Radhika Desai, her husband, Alan Freeman and their Geopolitical Economy Research Group at the University of Manitoba, September, 2021. For a common sense, easy to comprehend argument of the perilous state of universal capitalism even before the coronavirus pandemic hit; see Steven Pearlstein, "A market Crash was Coming Even Before the Coronavirus," *The Washington Post* (March 10, 2020), A24.

73 Hanna Arendt, *The Origins of Totalitarianism*, 2nd ed. (New York, NY: Meridian Books, 1958).

74 For a partial listing of his financial backers see Jane Mayer's *Dark Money*. Op.cit.

75 Jim Wolfreys, "The Centre Cannot Hold: Fascism, the Left and the Crisis of French Politics" *international Socialism*, (Summer 2002).

76   Ellen Meiksins Wood, *The Retreat from Class* (London: Verso, 1999).

77 Thomas Jeffrey Miley, *Rojava Betrayed*. (Manuscript, April, 2020).

78 See Peter Kenez, *Coalition Politics in the Hungarian Soviet Republic* in Andrew C. Janos and William B. Slottman eds., *Revolution in Perspective* (Berkeley, CA: University of California Press, 1971), 70-71.

79 Perhaps one of the best summaries or syntheses of Balabanoff's approach to pulling the wool back from the eyes of the ill-informed, deceived proletariat, is by Richard W. Wilkie, "The Marxian Rhetoric of Angelica Balabanoff," *Quarterly Journal of Speech* 60, no 4 (1974), 450-458. See also: Bertram D. Wolfe, "Balabanoff and V.I. Lenin: The Opposing Poles of the Socialist Movement Against War," *The Antioch Review* 24, no. 2 (1964), 223–236.

CHAPTER 1

The Roots and Antecedents of the 1919 Hungarian Republic of Councils

Péter Csunderlik

ON A CLOUDY MARCH 21, 1919, the citizens of Hungary's capital awoke to find thousands of leaflets blowing in the wind along Budapest's main thoroughfares. The strange-looking leaflet carried a message addressed "To All". Throughout the city, groups of people could be seen huddled over them, pushing and shoving each other, trying to get a better view, straining to listen to those who were reading them out loud. As soon as someone was finished with it, others grabbed at the leaflet—they were passed in great haste from hand to hand, like some forbidden fruit or contraband. Those who had read or heard its contents began to run off in all directions, and in a state of high excitement, shouting to others on their way. The news of the event taking place that morning spread like a wildfire throughout the city and then to the outlying towns and villages of Hungary. Most of the people reacted to this leaflet the way a drowning man would react to a lifejacket being thrown his way in the middle of a raging sea.

The leaflet addressed to all contained a message from a hitherto unheard-of political body—the *Revolutionary Governing Council* (RGC). It claimed to speak on behalf of a new political party—one so new it did not yet have a commonly agreed-upon name. It was created the night before through a secret merger between two parties that had been at each other's throats during the previous months. One party to this merger was the Hungarian Social Democratic Party (HSDP)—a Party that was for decades the Party of the Hungarian Trade Union movement, a party that had almost half of the cabinet portfolios in the government that resigned the day before. The other partner in this merger was the Hungarian Communist Party (HCP), which was only created a few months earlier, had no parliamentary representation, possessed rather limited roots within the Hungarian labour movement, and whose leaders were under arrest until the night before.

The leaflet blowing around in the streets of the war-weary Hungarian capital proclaimed the end of the Hungarian People's Republic, which was set up only a few months earlier, following the so-called *"Őszirózsás Forradalom"* ("Chrysanthemum Revolution") of October 31, 1918—a highly popular uprising, which declared Hungary's independence from Austria, put an end to the Monarchy and initiated a Republican, parliamentary path to democratic governance in Hungary. The leaflet being passed from hand to hand declared that the Hungarian proletariat had seized control and replaced the People's Republic with the Republic of Councils.

March 21, 1919, marks the beginning of a heroic revolutionary experiment in Hungary that is known under a variety of names: The Budapest Commune, the Hungarian Republic of Councils, the Hungarian Soviet Republic. The counterrevolutionary forces that succeeded this four-month long revolutionary experiment on August 1, 1919, refer to this period as the low point, the nadir, of Hungarian national history. According to Miklós Horthy (1868–1957), the man who eventually took over the country after the Dictatorship of the Proletariat collapsed on August 1, 1919, the preceding four months constituted an utterly shameful period in the nation's 1,000-year history, a period, when Budapest *"got dressed up in red rags"*.

Who was this man, Horthy, who rode into Budapest on the back of a white stallion after the collapse of the Commune to berate the citizens of "the sinful city" and unleash a "White Terror" that would claim a significant number of lives throughout Hungary during the first year of his reign? He was the last Admiral of the puny Mediterranean navy of Hungary, when Hungary was still part of the Austro-Hungarian Empire. He came from a well to do family and respected order, discipline, and obedience. He would give his life to defend the privileges enjoyed by his class, church, and empire, but as a high-ranking officer, he was part of the Austro-Hungarian war machine that was responsible for the death of tens of thousands of Entente soldiers in the European war zone. In other words, he was swept to power in Budapest after August 1, 1919, by the same Entente powers he had fought against only a few months earlier. He owed his succession to the pledge he made to his former enemies: he would submit to their dictates, safeguard the imperial interests of the Great Powers in Hungary, and return his country to the global Capitalist fold.

As Hungary's Regent, Horthy put an end to the Dictatorship of the Proletariat. He restored the Monarchy, the privileges of Hungary's propertied classes, and abandoned all of the progressive reform initiatives of his predecessors, including the introduction of the universal franchise, secret ballot, and land reform. Instead of building a just, constitutional, and fully independent democracy, he wilfully and enthusiastically delivered Hungary into Hitler's and Mussolini's imperialistic arms. Hungary's troops fought alongside the Nazis until the very last days of

WWII. Horthy's regime lasted 25 years. By the end, over a million Hungarians had lost their lives under the most gruesome circumstances—600,000 of whom were Jews who were deported to the gas chambers of Auschwitz under Horthy's watch.

It's only after 1949, that Hungarian historians would begin to speak with some degree of honesty about those 133 days that started in Budapest on March 21, 1919, and they did so rather tentatively at first. Joseph Stalin, the man who ordered the murder of virtually all the leaders of the 1919 Hungarian Commune after they fled to Moscow for their safety, was still calling the shots in the Soviet Union and Hungary became part of his Empire after 1945. It's only after Stalin's death, from the mid-1950s on, that some voices would begin to refer to those 133 days in 1919 as perhaps the most interesting and tragic days of Hungarian and European history.[1] Why did the Hungarian Republic of Councils come into existence?[2] How could a dictatorship of the proletariat be proclaimed in a country that was a semi-feudal, agricultural backwater of Europe, albeit, with some pockets of rapid industrial development around Budapest? That March 21 manifesto blown by the wind along the streets of Budapest pretty much told the truth when it stated the following:

> It was the complete collapse of the bourgeoisie and the failure of the earlier coalition governments that forced Hungary's workers and peasants to take this final step. Capitalist production has come to a standstill in our country. From now on, Hungary's workers and peasants refuse to serve as the slaves of finance capital and for the large landowners. Only socialism and communism can save this country from the anarchy of total collapse.
>
> We realize, that we launch this revolution under international circumstances that can only be described as catastrophic. The Paris Peace Conference has decided to place almost the entire territory of our country under military occupation. The Entente treats the current lines of occupation as the country's final post-war borders. Consequently, our capital's access to food, and fuel is cut off. Our ability to feed our citizens or to heat our homes is denied. Under these circumstances, we have no other recourse than to give power to the people, to declare the dictatorship of the proletariat, and let the proletariat and our poor agrarian labourers seize power and govern themselves.[3]

The motivation behind the establishment of the Hungarian Republic of Councils and its widespread initial popularity can only be understood within the historical context of the period following World War I. By 1919, most Hungarians were convinced that the catastrophe of World War I was the death knell of Global

Capitalism and the only way forward would be along the path of Socialism. This was the view not only of the most influential student organization of Hungary, the Galilei Circle,[4] or those within the labour movement, but also of many conservative politicians, such as Count Albert Apponyi (1846–1933). It is an empirically verifiable historical fact that Socialism was broadly embraced in Hungary by the end of WWI by the widest spectrum of Hungarian society. Socialism's allure in Hungary was not the monopoly of left-wing intellectuals, the working classes, or the landless peasantry. The aristocratic leader of the Hungarian delegation sent to the Paris Peace Treaty wrote: "returning to the old system is out of the question. We are part of the great socialist world revolution, and what we experience is only the local part of this world process".[5]

It is this widely embraced mood of the era that explains how the world-famous Marxist philosopher György Lukács (1885–1971), the son of a millionaire financier, could turn from a bourgeois philosopher rejecting violent means into the chief ideologist of the Dictatorship of the Proletariat, and how he would come to openly support the use of force by the winter of 1918–1919. It is this widespread allure of Socialism at the end of WWI that explains why the darling of the Hungarian Right in the 1930s and 1940s, Dezső Szabó (1879–1945), could serve as a 'Prophet of Communism' in 1919. We should not forget the bourgeois writer Sándor Márai (1900–1989), the author of the best-selling *Embers*, who was also an inspired communist around the age of eighteen when he launched the Circle of Anti-Nationalist Communist Writers and Activists.

This is how that well-known liberal-conservative Hungarian writer Tamás Kóbor (1867–1942) reflected upon the proclamation of the Hungarian Republic of Councils: "This was a last desperate act by the crew of a steamship that was blown off course, without food and without coal, after it came face to face with the incompetence of its commanding officers".[6]

The despair in Hungary in 1919 was triggered by the 'collapse' of a 'bourgeois world', which many had believed to be everlasting and indestructible. The reference to 'the incompetence of the commanding officers' above reflected a consensus: the ruling political establishment was unable to get the country back on its feet after a disastrous war. The country was prostrate, felled by an apparently insurmountable socio-economic crisis. Her once proud and healthy body was being torn to pieces like a dead carcass by vultures and hyenas that took her for dead.

To understand the depth of despair that produced the Budapest Commune we should reflect upon the dramatic lines of Árpád Tóth (1886–1928) who would become known later on as an apolitical impressionist poet. He too was mesmerized by the 'Red God' in 1919 as were so many others, including Hungary's greatest poster artist of the time, Mihály Bíró, whose remarkable poster (reproduced on the cover of this book) captured the spirit of Tóth's poem *The New God* (*Az Új Isten*), written just days after the start of the Commune and published in the April 1, 1919, issue of the journal *Nyugat*, (*The West*), a journal that was not the house organ of the working class but that of Hungary's progressive, liberal intellectuals.

It is a new God addressing you now, People!
He was given birth by the soil of this earth
The soil, that's soaked in blood.
That bitter, thick, blood that was spilled everywhere,
Has now congealed upon this aching land.
A towering, blood coloured, naked body rises.
Legs spread as wide as the planet,
His earth-shaking growl resonates
From the Red East towards the pale West He bellows,
"I have come!
The Red God has arrived"
(Translation: András B. Göllner)

Faith in the strength of the 'Red God' also explains why even many of the conservative-nationalist army officers of the Austro-Hungarian Monarchy sided with the internationalist Commune at the end of the War. (The future military elite of the counterrevolutionary Horthy Era would be staffed by these very same officers, after they deserted the Red Army of the Hungarian Republic of Councils in August 1919.) Back in March, many of them were also convinced that their bleeding Republic, the newly formed Dictatorship of the Proletariat, would be protected by the "New God" from "the East".

The Councils that rose, as if by magic, from the ashes of the war, an entire nation were united in their belief that the mighty Red Army of the Soviet Union would help put an end to the violation of Hungary's territories by the Entente after Hungary had signed in good faith the armistice that ended WWI on November 11, 1918. The single unshaken belief which united the Left, the Right, and the Centre in Hungary in March 1919 was this: The Russian Red Army would countervail the Republic's humiliating betrayal by "The West". Soviet troops would put an end to the *sparagmo*, the unilateral military dismemberment of Hungary by the Entente encouraged neighbouring troops from Czechoslovakia, Romania, and Serbia and save the newly formed Republic of Councils from destruction and set the brutalized country on the path to sustainable economic development, social justice, and the rule of law.

Most of the citizens of Budapest immediately understood and agreed with the message of that leaflet from the Revolutionary Governing Council which was cluttering the streets of the capital on March 21, 1919. They accepted its argument that the Dictatorship of the Proletariat was necessitated by the successive failures and incompetence of the "previous coalition government". Most agreed with its main thesis: the leading politicians of the Károlyi government were unable to face up to the difficult challenges after they were catapulted into power by the Chrysanthemum Revolution of October 1918: The collapse of the bourgeois government was inevitable.

If we want to know why the leaders of the largest opposition party in the land, the Social Democratic Party of Hungary, with a long and proud history behind it, would join forces with the newest kid on the bloc—the few months old Communist Party of Hungary that has been at its throat ever since it came into existence—we need to go beyond the conflicts and struggles that engulfed the government of Count Mihály Károlyi after it was swept into power by the Chrysanthemum Revolution on October 31, 1918. To rediscover and understand the long forgotten 1919 Hungarian Republic of Councils, we must go all the way back to the birth of the Hungarian Labour Movement at the end of the 19th century and to a period when this movement first began to flex its muscles at the beginning of the twentieth.

The Hungarian Labour Movement and Socio-Political Tensions in Dualist Hungary

It can never be emphasized often enough: from its earliest days on, the Hungarian labour movement followed the German rather than the Russian path to Socialism. Its leaders were inspired by the ideas of Ferdinand Lassalle, Eduard Bernstein, and Karl Kautsky. (It wasn't until 1917 that the name of Lenin became known in Hungary. Even György Lukács hadn't met his works and only became familiar with them *after* he became the leading ideologist of the Hungarian Communist Party in 1919, and *after* the fall of the dictatorship of the proletariat on August 1, 1919.)

The Hungarian Social Democratic Party was founded in 1890. Although organizational antecedents had already existed before, greeting letters to its inaugural congress were sent by Friedrich Engels himself and Wilhelm Liebknecht.[7] The initial and overarching political aim of the HSDP was deter-mined by the Second International, which set out objectives for social democratic parties throughout Europe at the time. Instead of engaging in revolutionary takeovers, the goal of these parties was to become mass parties and to gain power through parliamentary means. This indeed was the HSDP's own 1903 program, which was based verbatim on the Erfurt Program of the Social Democratic Party of Germany (SDPG). The Hungarian Social Democrats demanded the right to vote for every citizen over the age of twenty and wanted to use parliament as their instrument for curtailing the oppressive power of the propertied classes in industry and agriculture. Their demands included suffrage regardless of gender, secret ballots, local elections, and, most importantly, elections to be held on public holidays to hinder the efforts of employers in restricting their employees from exercising their democratic rights.

The HSDP became a mass party relatively quickly even though the number of industrial workers in Hungary was low, except for Budapest and a small handful of industrial towns in the countryside. Becoming a mass party was helped by the growing network of the Hungarian trade unions from the end of the 19th century onwards. Union membership granted automatic HSDP membership. The subscribers to the party newspaper *Népszava* (People's Voice) were considered 'Socialists' from the paper's first issue on April 1, 1905. The first editor of *Népszava*, the moderate Ernő Garami (1876–1935),[8] was the leader of the HSDP at this time. Women workers had their own paper called *Nőmunkás* (Woman Worker) from 1905. Its editor was Mariska Gárdos (1885–1973). She was the first president of the Hungarian Women Workers' Society, established in 1903.[9] The HSDP also had its own theoretical journal called *Socialism* from 1906 onwards which carried longer essays and discourses. This was also edited by top HSDP leaders like Ernő Garami and Zsigmond Kunfi (1879–1929). Marxist ideas were also published in popularized format by the *Worker's Library* series, this too under the Party's editorial supervision.

By the beginning of the 20th century, a whole new workers' counterculture came into existence in Hungary. The movement had its own printing presses, publications, literature, matinees, and celebrations, the most important celebration was on the first of May each year. The sounds of this new counterculture, its protestations against injustice stirred up the towns and the countryside alike. Its pamphlets and leaflets caused great consternation among the ruling political establishment that consisted of a small but powerful aristocratic core and a much more numerous nobility—titled and untitled, the latter commonly referred to as the gentry.

Hungary was not an ethnically homogenous Kingdom prior to, or at the turn of, the 20th century. At the start of the 20th century, little over half of the population was *not* of Hungarian ethnicity. In the capital, Hungarian was a minority language. This explains why apart from *Népszava*, several HSDP papers were also published in minority languages, like the *Volksstimme*, that targeted members of the German-speaking Hungarian community. During the age of Dualism—the term commonly used for the Austro-Hungarian Monarchy or

Empire that came into being in 1867 and lasted until 1918—the highest share of Hungarian speakers ever recorded in Greater Hungary was in 1910. Even then, and following decades of strenuous efforts by a series of nationalist governments to "convert" the non-ethnic minorities in the country to Hungarian, Hungarians constituted only 54.5% of the total population. The second-largest ethnic group in Hungary was Romanian with 16%, followed by Slovaks and Germans with 10.7% and 10.4% respectively.[10]

While the 'red monster', as considered by the right-wing, or 'red giant' according to the left, experienced a growth spurt during the first decade of the 20th century, the HSDP would not be able to gain a seat in Hungary's parliament until 1918 because of the country's archaic electoral laws and restricted franchise. Only 5–6% of the Hungarian population had the right to vote at the beginning of the 20th century. (Although changes were made to this restrictive electoral law in 1913 and 1918, elections were not held based on the new law because of World War I.)

Social Democrats were often referred to as "good for nothing aliens" by the ruling conservative establishment on account of their devotion to their 'blood red flag', their internationalism, their multi-ethnic composition and their affinity for Hungary's industrial workers. In his leaflet called *Patriotism and Internationalism*, published in 1903, Ernő Garami wrote the following response to this disparaging portrayal:

> The People of our country today are homeless. They are depicted, sadly, as good for nothing aliens by those who rule over them. It is those who call themselves patriots and disparage our people today, who made our people homeless—and they did so in the name of the homeland. The international Social Democratic movement is the only defender of those who are trampled on and crushed underfoot, and are forced to suffer these false accusations. We shall always defend our people and our country from those who made us homeless![11]

It should be pointed out that until Social Democrats entered the political scene in 1890, political parties in Hungary were more like gentlemen's clubs, unstructured, ephemeral, and somewhat unruly gatherings engaged in passionate debates and countless duels. It was the birth of the Social Democratic Party and its rule-based structures that gave voice to Hungary's workers and enabled the organization of mass strikes in some of the towns and cities of Hungary. Its early successes served as an example and a catalyst for the competing parties to set their own houses in order. The Social Democrats achieved some early successes even though they did not hold any seats in Hungary's Parliament. They fought to introduce worker's insurance and new measures to improve working conditions, but their fight for general and secret suffrage failed.[12]

As we have alluded to above, from the late 19th to early 20th century onward the demand for democratic electoral reforms, and full suffrage was one of the top items on the public policy agenda of the Dualist period in Hungary. It was closely followed by demands for land reforms and the just demands of Hungary's ethnic minorities for greater human and civil rights. These pressures, however, were usually pushed onto the back seat by the recurring demands of various nationalist-conservative political forces inside Hungary who showed no interest in the concerns of the common people and were only interested in pushing agendas that would gain some advantages for the Hungarian nobility at the expense of the Hapsburgs.

The more radical elements of the nationalist-conservative forces were kept in check by the constitutional arrangements of the Austro-Hungarian Monarchy. Only the Hapsburg Emperor could decide who would become the Prime Minister (PM) of Hungary, and the Emperor would only appoint someone to this post who was loyal to the throne (Franz Joseph I followed by Charles I—the latter was known as Charles IV in Hungary). The Hungarian nationalists, represented by the Independence Party managed to win only one election during the Dualist era against the machinations and electoral frauds of the pro-monarchist aristocratic forces loyal to Vienna.[13] Once in power, the Independence Party would back away from enacting its promises and occupied itself with what many would dismiss as empty sloganeering.[14]

While the Hapsburgs kept the lid on the Austro-Hungarian Empire, the pressures for change and modernization in Hungary as well as Austria were steadily rising and came from a variety of sources. In Hungary, there were increasing pressures from within the middle-class for more radical social policies. Spearheaded by Oszkár Jászi (1875–1957) and a growing circle of middle-class intellectuals, this "radical" group wanted to replace "catchword politics" by what they called "scientific politics". Centred primarily in the Hungarian capital, this progressive intellectual movement called for the opening of windows, a movement for free speech and for fearless analyses of Hungary's socio-economic conditions in order to put an end to "the Empire of Illusions" and to set the country on the path to social justice, the rule of law, and sustainable economic development. Jászi's followers established the journal *Huszadik Század* (Twentieth Century) in 1899 and the Society for Social Sciences in 1900, that served together as the key platforms for the dissemination of their reformist ideas.[15] Jászi and his circle criticized what they believed to be a 'feudal' Hungary that failed to keep in step with the times. They promoted a Western-style, liberal, 'bourgeois' societal model by pursuing an anticlerical education policy, a tolerant nationality policy based on mutual cooperation between the various ethnic minorities. They also advocated radical land reforms, such as the elimination of the large estates by distributing their lands to millions of landless peasants who lived in abject poverty and misery. (The concentration of arable land in the hands of the Catholic Church and a few rich families was one of the most significant socio-economic problems of Hungary at the turn of the century.)

There were also growing numbers of agrarian socialist movements demanding land distribution from 1890 onwards, first in Southeast Hungary, then in the *Viharsarok* (The Stormy Corner), and finally on parts of the Great Hungarian Plain. Harvesters' strikes were spreading quickly throughout Hungary before WWI, reaching their zenith between 1905 and 1907. Agrarian socialist movements were 'active' manifestations of the tensions caused by the desire for land by Hungary's country folk. The other manifestation of this pressure was the 'passive' emigration wave. 1.3 million Hungarians left their homeland between 1871 and 1913, mostly for North America. Tens of thousands ended up on the Canadian prairies. The climax of this giant emigration wave was between 1905 and 1907 (1908 brought a temporary decrease followed by increasing return migration).[16]

The ruling political establishment of Hungary had no desire to promote land reform, electoral reform, or the promotion of greater minority rights because it had a vested interest in the maintenance of the status quo. Leading members of the Christian-Conservative political class during the late Dualist period, such as István Tisza (1861–1918), considered the great landowners and their organizational forces the guarantee, that the integrity of historical Hungary will survive the pressures for change. Tisza, Hungary's powerful Prime Minister between 1903–1905 and 1913–1917, pursued a double-barrelled political aim: He resisted demands for the expansion of the franchise to the common people and to Hungary's ethnic minorities[17] in order to protect not only the vested interests of the nobility, but the territories amassed over the centuries by a succession of royals (most of whom were not even Hungarians, but well connected foreign aristocrats, who would help Hungary's nobility to extend their territorial ambitions and prerogatives in Central Europe).

No wonder that the HSDP—the strongest and most organized party within Hungary—that wanted to realize its demands through popular representation, couldn't get any representatives into Parliament until 1918. From a membership of only 55 thousand in 1916, the membership of the HSDP rose to 215 thousand by 1917 and skyrocketed to 721 thousand by December 31, 1918.[18] The rising popularity of the HSDP was due to the following pledge: it promised to end injustice, improve the living standards of the common people who had to carry an unfair and increasingly unbearable burden for a senseless war, and to allow ordinary citizens a greater say into who gets what, when, and how in Hungary.[19]

Though the HSDP had no parliamentary representation until after WWI, its voice could be less and less ignored. Towards the end of WWI there were increasingly frequent meetings between its leaders and those who represented power in Hungary's parliament. Móric Eszterházy (1881–1960), the successor of István Tisza, went to the editorial offices of *Népszava* in the summer of 1917 to inform the social democrats of his plans. By the end, the HSDP's leaders were even invited to negotiate with the Hapsburg Emperor, who did double duty for Hungary's nobility as Hungary's King Charles the IV.[20]

The Origins of the Hungarian Council Movement and *The Chrysanthemum Revolution* of 1918

As we have seen above, by 1917 the party that was the exclusive representative of the Hungarian working classes, the HSDP, was given increasing access to the deliberations of the political elite, though not via actual parliamentary representation. The Bolshevik takeover in Russia in November 1917, however, greatly radicalized Hungary's working classes. They began to look at those who cooperated with the political elite as representatives of the state rather than the proletariat. For a growing number of workers, the only way around this predicament, and what many of them interpreted as a "sell-out" by the HSDP was to organize councils of their own from the ground up and to by-pass the HSDP and the Trade Union bureaucracy that was its affiliate. A growing number of workers came to the view that the Councils—also known as the Soviets—were more effective vehicles for the expression of their interests than the HSDP. Dezső Bokányi (1871–1943), one of the leaders of the HSDP was one of the first among the Party high brass to express sensitivity to this new trend after the giant and seemingly "spontaneous" workers' protest of Budapest on November 25, 1917. This "spontaneous" protest was in fact set in motion by a small activist cell organized by Ilona Duczynska who had no ties at all to the HSDP leadership, and in fact avoided that leadership like the plague on the advice of her political mentor, Ervin Szabó (See: András B. Göllner, *Ilona: Portrait of a Rebel*, 2022):

> We need to confront the following reality: There are workers', soldiers' and peasants' councils in Russia. (…) We could also form a Council that could be expanded to wield enormous power, a Council that could act by uniting all of the forces who want to act.[21]

Councils started being established in Hungary's factories one after the other and spread like a wild-fire in the fall of 1917. In the capital, a spontaneous movement began for the establishment of a city-wide Workers' Council at the end of 1917.

Plans were also set in motion to assemble a future National Workers' Council that would serve as an umbrella organization for the growing number of councils in the towns and countryside. These new councils played a leading role in organizing the general strike of January 1918. Hungary's workers were following the example set by Austria's proletariat who were in step with their comrades in Germany. Though they were not the creative force behind the January 1918 General Strike, the HSDP leadership quickly stepped in to call it off by pleading on behalf of the government and arguing that the government had promised them a reform package in line with the strikers' demands. More radical elements of the Hungarian labour movement would, however, continue to raise the pressure and would not be satisfied anymore by mere promises. They continued to organize ever more protest actions throughout 1918. When the police fired upon a demonstration organized by the workers' council of the giant railway manufacturing factory on June 20, 1918, the incident set off a massive strike action in which hundreds of thousands participated.

Parallel with the growing industrial unrest, anti-war sentiments were also rapidly rising by the end of 1917. The government stepped in by laying the blame for the anti-war protests on the shoulders of a radical student organization, the Galilei Circle, in January 1918. The leaders of this anti-militarist conspiracy—Ilona Duczynska (1897–1978) and Tivadar Sugár (1897–1938)—were arrested and imprisoned along with a handful of their associates. The authorities were, however, unable to find any trace of the critical role played by these young revolutionary activists in radicalizing the shop-stewards, and workshop representatives in the factories around Budapest. The Budapest police force was increasingly powerless against the antics of this group that did not play by the rules. The Galileists reopened the doors of their common room and a group of workers and soldiers freed Duczynska, Sugár and their comrades from their prison cells on October 31, 1918.[22]

Widespread public desire for an end to the war in Hungary is the main reason why the aristocrat, Count Mihály Károlyi (1875–1955), one of Hungary's biggest landholders, who was an opponent of the war and perhaps the most popular opposition leader in Hungary's Parliament, came to power on October 31, 1918, on the back of the Chrysanthemum Revolution. (The reason why this revolution is associated with this flower—or its relative the Astor—is simple. All Saints Day comes at the end of fall. These fall flowers are in great abundance throughout the Hungarian capital during this time of the year. To this day, they are the flowers of choice hundreds of thousands of city dwellers take out to the capital's cemeteries to decorate the graves of their beloved. On October 31, tens of thousands of soldiers milling about the capital took off their Austro-Hungarian military insignia, and replaced them with Chrysanthemums, signalling the end of their commitment to the Empire and to the war and to demonstrate their solidarity with the citizens of Budapest.

Károlyi was a colourful aristocratic politician. He was super rich, flamboyant, drove fast cars, and gambled away fortunes playing cards in the casinos of Budapest and Europe's capitals without losing a step. (As a member of parliament, he once spent a whole night in his downtown palace duelling with the country's war-time prime-minister, István Tisza, over some misunderstanding.) But Károlyi also had another side that most of his aristocratic colleagues did not: He had a brain and a social conscience. Károlyi was a well-educated progressive in tune with the times, committed to social reforms, and to ending the war. In spite of his riches, he possessed some empathy for the wretched of the earth. He began to prepare his quest for the country's leadership before WWI, by pushing for closer collabouration with France and Russia rather than following every step taken by Austria-Germany. As one of the wealthiest landowners of Hungary, he first bought a newspaper that would propagate his views. He then resigned his membership in the largest opposition party in 1916 to create his own party, commonly known as the Károlyi Party. He wanted to promote rapprochement with the Great Powers and to further the peace process.[23] To achieve his goals, he gathered around him a group of left-leaning and radical intellectuals, led by Oszkár Jászi. By the fall of 1918, most people in Hungary were of the view that Károlyi would be someone who could bring an honourable peace to the country because of his assumed Entente connections. After Bulgaria had stepped back from the war on September 29, 1918, the immanent victory of the Entente powers became obvious to most but a handful of die-hard nationalists in Hungary. This also raised Károlyi's chances of becoming the country's next leader.

The collapse of Hungary's political house of cards began on October 17, 1918. The country's hard-line, war-time Prime Minister, István Tisza, who resigned in May but retained his parliamentary seat, stood up in Parliament that day and conceded to his nemesis Károlyi. He admitted that the game he started was over: The Central Powers had lost the war to the Entente. The disintegration of the "old order" began almost immediately. From here on out, workers and soldiers would refuse to obey their superiors and the poorest peasants began to occupy the large privately owned estates in order to satisfy their thirst for landownership and their desire to be treated as humans by a nobility that had treated them not much better than farm animals for centuries.[24]

From the People's Republic to the Hungarian Republic of Councils

The collapse that followed after Tisza's concession on October 17, 1918, obliterated not only the Austro-Hungarian Monarchy but the former Hungarian political elite as well. People fell in behind a hastily organized new political entity on October 25, 1918, that went by the name of the Hungarian National Council, which gathered into its fold, from inside and outside of the Hungarian Parliament, all those who demanded an end to the war and thoroughgoing social, economic, and political reforms. In spite of the establishment of this broad political coalition, the old parliamentary establishment and its aristocratic base would make one last-ditch effort to maintain its exclusive privileges. On October 30, in response to the demands from Hungary's conservative politicians, the Hapsburg emperor, Charles, appointed János Hadik (1863–1933) as Hungary's Prime Minister. This last desperate effort by the Hapsburgs and their loyal Hungarian followers to maintain the status quo proved to be a miserable failure.

It's estimated that by April of 1918, the number of army deserters trying to make ends meet in the Hungarian capital had risen to fifty thousand. The size of this largely homeless and angry mass of men rapidly increased during the ensuing months as a brutal and fruitless war extracted thousands of new casualties as well as deserters who flocked to the Hungarian capital each month. Their anger grew with no end in sight to the senseless fighting on the battlefields and due to the widespread suffering produced by an utterly senseless imperial war. Enraged veterans returning from the battlefront swelled the rising revolutionary tide in Hungary. Apart from the 'quitters' and the regular returnees from the battlefront—who had kept their weapons—there were also more than thirty thousand armed workers in the city by the fall because they simply helped themselves to the weapons stockpiled in the city's central armoury.[25]

As the war effort worsened and conditions in Budapest deteriorated, the government appointed a tough military man, Géza Lukachich (1865–1943) as military commander of the city. His task was to restore law and order to an increasingly lawless and restless capital. Lukachich had been on the front lines of the war prior to his new appointment. He earned a reputation on the battlefront as a ruthless and cruel disciplinarian. He seemed like the best weapon at the government's disposal for crushing the revolution that threatened to sweep the old, aristocratic order away at any moment. The prelude to the collapse came on October 28 and is commonly referred to in Hungary as "The Battle of the Chain Bridge". Lukachich ordered his men to attack a large group of demonstrators on this historical bridge that connects the two sides of the capital, Buda and Pest. In the ensuing battle, his men killed four demonstrators and wounded another 50 or 60. This Battle of the Chain Bridge proved to be the proverbial "straw that broke the camel's back".

During the night of October 29, the new Prime Minister János Hadik, ordered the city's military commander, Lukachich, along with the city's police chief, to meet with him privately at his home. He wanted to be briefed by them about the "breaking news": that many members of the city's police forces had come out in support of the newly formed Hungarian National Council, now holed up downtown at the Hotel Astoria. The police chief and Lukachich reassured the PM that this should not be cause for panic. They told the Emperor's new Hungarian PM that during the coming days, they would restore full order in the Hungarian capital, Vienna can go back to sleep. Lukachich admitted to his naiveté in his autobiography published a few years later and in the following manner:

> I was overconfident. I made the same mistake as the police chief during the early morning hours of October 30, when, at his personal request, we appraised the PM about the situation in Budapest. Despite my previous unfavourable experiences, I did not believe that discipline among my men had become so loose, that it would completely collapse 24 hours later.[26]

The collapse of military discipline and mass desertion was only part of the tottering government's problem. The revolutionary fervour had by now swept up many of the citizens of Budapest as well and not just the industrial workers or those who came back brutalized and destitute from the battlefront. The city's switchboard operators, consisting of many hundreds of poorly paid and exploited women had already shown their militancy during the strikes at the end of 1917. By October 1918, they would refuse to put up with any further abuse. According to the memoirs of one of the switchboard operators, Mrs. Rezső Mehringer, they listened in on the secret conversations of the city's military commander, Lukachich, on October 30 and 31, 1918, and refused to forward his commands to his officers to attack the headquarters of the Hungarian National Council.[27]

The fact of the matter is, that by October 30, even the National Council had lost control over the events coming to the fore in the Hungarian capital. Oszkár Jászi provides us with one of the best accounts of the days immediately prior to the Chrysanthemum Revolution of October 31:

> Revolutions are born, not made. In these feverish days of October, I realised, as never before, the irresistible force of mass movements towards social change and the impotence in the face of them of all those who wish to deliberately guide and control these mass movements... What happened in Budapest was almost always the opposite of what the intellectual general staff of the revolution had planned or proposed... Argument and persuasion, the careful weighing of data, the logical design and strict execution of plans, the considered distribution of functions, and other rational accompaniments of political action in normal times, stopped short as though under an enchanter's wand: In their place, a mysterious magnetic field rose from

within society, attracting the masses to themselves with merciless violence and subjecting to their influence the vast bulk of so-called independent opinion.[28]

Lukachich did not understand these magnetic forces. His forces surrounded the Hotel Astoria on the evening of October 30, but as soon as they did so, his men left their posts and joined the revolution. Their example was followed by members of the next detachment that Lukachich sent out to arrest those who had deserted their commanders an hour earlier. After these two consecutive fiascos—insubordination, desertion—and the sabotage of his lines of telecommunication by the women of Budapest's central switchboard operators, Lukachich had no option than to report to the Hapsburg Emperor, that he sees no hope for carrying out his orders. After Lukachich, the PM, János Hadik, also had a short conversation with the Emperor. He suggested to Charles, that he should appoint Mihály Károlyi as Prime Minister. In the evening of October 31, the Emperor did as he was told: he appointed the Count Károlyi as his prime minister and the appointment was publicly announced to the revolutionary crowd. With this, the revolution triumphed. When Lukachich was pressed much later on why he failed to arrest the "high command" of the revolution holed up in the Hotel Astoria, and thereby nip the revolution in the bud, he could only offer the following explanation: "The reason for this is simple: There was no firing squad at my disposal. The firing squad refused to follow my orders".[29]

It should be acknowledged that The Soldiers' Council of Budapest played perhaps the most important part in the victory of the revolution of October 30–31.[30] It was a spontaneous military organization, created independently from all of the political parties of Hungary at the time. Its membership consisted mainly of deserters—officers and ordinary soldiers—who left the battlefront disgusted by the carnage. They were joined by some who could be also described as political adventurers. If anyone called the shots in the streets of Budapest on October 30–31, it was this party—a politically neutral military organization composed of men who felt most directly the ravages of the war and the ruinous consequences of the ancient regime's policies. (The members of this Council elected Tivadar Sugár, Ilona Duczynska's 21-year-old lover and co-conspirator as their Vice-President, as soon as the two young revolutionaries were freed from their prison cells by the men of this Council.)

Some would suggest later that the murder of the wartime PM, István Tisza, in his home a few days after October 31 was the work of soldiers belonging to this particular Council. This has never been proven decisively.[31] According to Jászi, the murder of István Tisza was inevitable. He was seen by virtually everyone as the man who led Hungary into a senseless war and had to pay for his act with his life. In Jászi's view, Béla Kún would have met the same fate after the collapse of the 1919 Hungarian Republic of Councils had he not fled to safety to Austria, along with virtually the entire Revolutionary Governing Council, the night before the collapse of August 1, 1919. The head of the new revolutionary government, Mihály Károlyi sent a wreath to the funeral of his nemesis István Tisza with the epigraph "to my greatest political opponent". In his memoirs written after Károlyi himself was swept away by the revolutionary tide of 1918–1919, Károlyi would proclaim that "The cowardly murder of Tisza in his home was the first and only bloodstain on the honour of our October Revolution".[32]

The Chrysanthemum Revolution of October 31 produced a popular coalition government in Hungary, one that began to govern with broad public support, and with the highest of hopes placed in its leader, Count Mihály Károlyi, for the reasons we have outlined earlier. Besides members from the opposition bourgeois parties, a number of HSDP members were to join Károlyi's government as well. The diversity of the Károlyi government, however, carried within it the seeds of its eventual destruction. It tried to unite forces that represented irreconcilable opposites: bourgeois promoters of capitalism were sitting at the same cabinet table with left-wing internationalists and those who wanted to see an end to the private ownership of the means of production and wanted to pursue a socialist, rather than a capitalist path to the future.[33]

Károlyi's government from the very beginning confronted the HSDP with a huge dilemma. How could they participate in an enterprise that was, after all, engaged in the construction of a bourgeois liberal democracy, based on capitalism and the private ownership of the means of production, when their own party platform explicitly called for the replacement of the Capitalist path with a Socialist one? The HSDP's top leader at this time, Ernő Garami, was fully aware of this fundamental contradiction and was reluctant to join Károlyi's forces. He only agreed to join the coalition after prolonged and personal pleading from the Count himself, who argued that this was a time for national unity and national reconciliation, not for partisan politics.

Participation in Károlyi's coalition government meant, in practice, that the HSDP was forced into suspending the class struggle in order to consolidate the political power of the newly reconstituted Capitalist State. Its own daily, *Népszava*, became the voice of reason and national unity, advocating the need for everyone to return to their places of work, and begin the task of post-war reconstruction. The Party's top ideologue, Zsigmond Kunfi (1879–1929), welcomed the temporary suspension of the class struggle in a speech that created a huge controversy inside as well as outside of the government: "we only need to step back and join the governing forces for six weeks in order to create peace and democracy".[34]

The hoped-for calm did not last much longer than a raised eyebrow. (Kunfi committed suicide in exile, in 1929.) The HSDP's predicament was greatly exacerbated when some of its followers refused to suspend the class struggle, whereupon the Károlyi government took harsh and repressive measures against them. There were numerous cases in the countryside where landless and starving peasants took the law into their hands by looting the castles of the aristocrats or seizing the land of the nobility. The repressive brutality of the government, as in the case of the bombing raid over the village of Facsád (now a part of Romania) is an illustration of the double-bind the Social Democrats had fallen into by lining up behind the Count. The continuing membership of the HSDP in the government greatly undermined the party's legitimacy with its own revolutionary base. While the HSDP possessed only one cabinet post in the first Károlyi Government—namely the Ministry of Foreign Trade, headed by its leader, Ernő Garami—the government's harsh new measures left the entire party tainted. The toleration of harsh measures such as return to work legislation, the persecution of the peasants who were unhappy with the lack of progress with land reform, the protection of the landowners' interests over those of the landless agrarian labourers, and the government's inability to gain a handle over the economic crisis, were interpreted as a betrayal of the lower classes by a party that was supposed to be their champion.

In the midst of the rising discontent, the moderate Garami continued to plead for more time. He argued, that the Hungarian bourgeoisie had not exhausted its contradictions, it was not yet ready to be toppled. Although the HSDP was the only organized mass party of the country in the autumn of 1918, with a trade union base of seven hundred thousand members, Garami did not think the Hungarian working class was strong enough to seize the reins of power. As he wrote in his memoirs: "It is impossible for Hungary to enter Socialism from a feudal base, and by turning our back on the important improvements the bourgeois stage of development can bring us on the eventual road to a working class-driven Socialism".[35]

It is important to underline in this introductory chapter that in Hungary the bourgeois-democratic movement had only a few short months to attempt any kind of post-feudal consolidation or development. The catastrophic economic consequences of the war, the panic and disarray caused by the foreign occupation of her territories, the collapse of the Austro-Hungarian Empire and the secessionist ambitions of ethnic minorities on her territory, and, last but not least, the disastrous impact of the Spanish Influenza epidemic on the heels of the country's countless other troubles was far too much to handle even under the best of circumstances.

It is not the failure to construct cogent transition plans for the future that we need to fault the Károlyi government with. There were, in fact, numerous such plans in hand, some crafted even before the start of WWI. Groups such as the Society for the Social Sciences or the Galilei Circle had numerous alternatives for a "New Hungary" after the war. All of those plans went up in smoke after the collapse of the old order. The tragedy of the Chrysanthemum Revolution and the much-maligned Károlyi government is that it had to improvise under catastrophic circumstances and in an environment that was impossible to control. The Károlyi government inherited a century of unsolved challenges needing immediate action, while a tornado was sweeping through its headquarters. This is not to suggest, that the Károlyi government was doing as well as it could have under the circumstances. It was obviously not up to meeting its challenges. It compounded its own difficulties by its own, self-generated mistakes.

One of the criticisms levelled against the Károlyi government by those who claim 20/20 vision on hindsight is its failure to defend the country's territorial integrity against the marauding armies of the small and recently formed successor states, and its naïve trusting in the goodwill of the Entente Powers, that Hungary fought against during the war. Upon serious examination, Károlyi's 'naiveté', and his 'blind trust' of the Entente is more of a myth than reality. The Entente's hostility to his government was obvious to Károlyi and his colleagues on the day they were sworn into office. They did not suffer from any illusions. One of the first acts of the new government was to unveil its territorial protection program. It was not the lack of attention to this demand that Károlyi should be faulted for but the failure to recognize that the military challenge was impossible to meet. Maintaining Hungary's territorial integrity by military force was not a feasible option after having lost the war. In vain did the Károlyi government insist on this by its slogan "No! No! Never!" words which are falsely attributed to the irredentist far right that came to power after Károlyi was long gone.

Károlyi was quick to fire his incompetent, alcoholic, and neurotic Minister of Defense, Béla Linder (1876–1962), after he declared that "I never want to see another soldier again!" His successor, Albert Bartha (1877–1960) made a valiant attempt at the beginning of November 1918 to re-build the Hungarian army that disintegrated with the war. This effort, however, ran into a powerful resistance by the former members of Hungary's armed forces and by Hungary's civilian population. Hungary's citizens were sick of fighting by the end of 1918. They simply wanted peace.[36] Even if Bartha had been able to organize a fighting force from the ranks of the utterly beaten former Army, Hungary could not have withstood the simultaneous attack from the North by the Czechs, the Romanians from the East and the French supported Serbs from the South. Instead of coming to the aid of the Republic, Admiral Horthy and his men in the south chose to hobnob with the French. The final collapse of the Red Army of the Hungarian Republic of Councils during the summer of 1919 had fully demonstrated that a "military" solution was nothing but a pipedream. Although the Hungarian Red Army did chalk up some initial successes, it could not sustain its early momentum. Hungary was bleeding to death from a lost war. It was blockaded from all sides and opposed by all the Great Powers. Her neighbour to the West (Austria) was in no shape to lend a helping hand. Each of her three remaining neighbours chose this time to take revenge and punish the country for the self-serving, repressive, chauvinistic policies pursued by its former aristocratic leaders. Hungary did not have a single military ally in the world. Its faith in the Soviet Red Army never materialized.[37]

It is easy to be wise on hindsight, but the Károlyi government should have given up on its quest to maintain the country's territorial integrity against insurmountable odds. Instead of this unobtainable objective, it should have focused its limited resources on stabilizing the newly proclaimed republic by quickly announcing and holding nationwide popular elections. The republican form of government provided Hungary with a great opportunity, especially from a diplomatic stand-point. The holding of immediate elections under the universal franchise would have enabled the Károlyi government to vividly demonstrate to the outside world that the 'New Hungary' that's pleading for peace is completely different from the warring 'Old' one. By focusing on such a step, the country may have been able to achieve more favourable responses at the bargaining table with the Entente powers in Paris. The decision of the Károlyi government to appoint a feminist Rózsa Bédy-Schwimmer (1877–1948) as its Swiss ambassador—even though Swiss women had no suffrage yet—also fit the strategy of emphasizing the progressive and democratic nature of this "New Hungary".[38] But let us return to the first steps of the Chrysanthemum Revolution.

The old parliament had been dissolved and legislative power was put in the hands of an expanded National Council until the new democratic parliament would meet. This 'Great National Council' declared what it labelled as "the people's most important resolution"—the establishment of the Hungarian People's Republic. It called upon Károlyi to form a government and immediately introduce suffrage legislation and land reforms in order to solve the desperate existential conditions of Hungary's peasantry. Hungary became a 'People's Republic' on November 16, 1918 (the First Austrian Republic was proclaimed on November 12 in Vienna, the Czechoslovak Republic on November 14 in Prague).[39]

The most important demand of the HSDP for general, secret and equal suffrage regardless of gender for all citizens over the age of twenty was only partially realized after the bourgeois-democratic revolution of 1918. Only women over the age of 24 who could read and write were given the franchise by the Károlyi government, while all men over the age of 21 were given the right to vote. In spite of this gender inequality, the elections were continuously postponed on the grounds that larger and larger parts of the country fell into the hands of French, Czech, Serb, and Romanian troops. The Károlyi regime never managed to hold a free and nation-wide parliamentary election. The first post-war elections in Hungary took place under the dictatorship of the proletariat in April 1919, and these were council, rather than parliamentary elections. All men and women over 18 got the right to vote—only 'reactionaries' and former 'exploiters' were denied this right. Exploiters were defined as people who lived off the work of others and did not themselves work. The clergy and wealthy peasants were also denied the right to vote. While these new restrictions shut out a lot of people from the franchise, the April 1919 election had the largest participation rate in the country's entire history—more than two million people cast a valid ballot.

In its manifesto regarding land issues, published on October 8, 1918, and before the end of the war, the HSDP declared itself to be in favour of "a thoroughgoing agrarian reform".[40] After joining the Károlyi government, the Party sharpened its focus. It demanded the complete expropriation of medium and large estates and the redistribution of these lands to the landless peasants and the introduction of cooperative mechanisms to sustain the viability of the many small-scale farms that were to emerge as a result of land re-distribution. The National Council passed a land reform act in February 1919—The People's Act No. XVIII—which stipulated that no landowner can possess more than 500 acres. The law also stated, that

> ...the location of the 500 acres each landowner was to retain from his former landholdings should be chosen by the landowner at his own volition in order to ensure the most effective use of his remaining resources. What he could not do is to choose his remaining 500 acres in a manner that would be detrimental to village life, and to local community development.[41]

These were the conditions applied to the landholdings of even the Catholic Church, which was the single largest landholder in the country at that time. Where the needs of the local municipalities required it, even estates between 200 and 500 acres could be redistributed.

To secure the support of the peasantry for the new land-reform law, the Károlyi government-mandated one of the country's most popular novelist of the time, Zsigmond Móricz, to popularize this policy in a pamphlet called *The Small Catechism of the Land Reform*. Móricz, who was as far from being a Socialist or a Communist, as one could ever be, was effusive in his praise of the new land-reform:

> We have now the first legislation in our hands since the rulers of the House of Árpád, which gives to the people rather than takes things from them!

This land law is the first law that gives something to the poorest rather than empty their pockets.[42]

Gyula Krúdy, another well-known conservative literary icon went as far as to write, that a 'second Hungarian Conquest' is in the making as a consequence of the new law. He proclaimed this on February 28, 1919, in a place called Kápolna, where Count Mihály Károlyi, the country's President and one of the largest landholders in the country kicked off the land redistribution campaign by giving away all but 500 acres of his own lands. (No one could foretell that Károlyi would be running for his life just three weeks after his momentous gesture.)

The Land Reform Act championed by the HSDP proved to be a failure. Implementation was constantly hindered. Károlyi's estate was the only one which was redistributed before the First Republic collapsed on March 21, 1919. (The Hungarian Republic of Council took an entirely different approach to land reform from the Károlyi regime. The Social Democrats leading the People's Commissariat for Agriculture after March 21 simply nationalized the large agricultural estates rather than divide them into privately held plots. With that single move, the Republic of Councils managed to alienate the vast majority of Hungary's landless and poverty-stricken peasantry. But we are getting ahead of ourselves.)

As the bourgeois support of the Károlyi government decreased on account of the absence of any tangible successes vis á vis the Entente in foreign policy, or in getting the country back on its feet, the popularity of the HSDP began to increase initially. In response to their growing popularity, the HSDP began to demand a greater say in the affairs of the state and to demand more portfolios in the government than the single one given to them by Károlyi at the outset. By the middle of January 1919, there were five social democrats in Prime Minister Berinkey's cabinet, after Károlyi resigned as PM in order to take over as President of "The People's Republic".

Paradoxically, as the HSDP increased its representation in the bourgeois governments after the Chrysanthemum Revolution, its early popularity began to dissipate, especially among the industrial working classes, who began to gravitate towards a newly formed Communist Party that pushed for more radical changes than the Social Democrats. A growing number of factory workers, soldiers, and disabled war veterans began to argue that the HSDP leadership had been co-opted by the bourgeoisie and the more opportunistic members of the nobility that managed to remain in positions of authority in many parts of the country. More and more would come to argue that the HSDP betrayed the working class by reneging on its promises to the exploited classes in return for parliamentary portfolios and political perks.

The Hungarian Communist Party and the Peoples' Republic

By the summer of 1918, and parallel with the changes in Hungary, the Russian Bolsheviks were far advanced with their plans for the promotion of revolutionary changes in Germany and the rapidly disintegrating Austro-Hungarian Empire. The foundations of these plans were laid out in a memorandum by the Secretariat of the Zimmerwald Movement in March 1917, just before Lenin left Zurich by train for St. Petersburg. It was Ilona Duczynska's job to deliver a copy of this Memorandum from Angelica Balabanoff to the workers of Vienna and Budapest in April 1917. To accelerate the implementation of their revolutionary plans for Hungary, the Russian Bolsheviks enrolled hundreds of Hungarian prisoners of war in Russia into crash courses in Bolshevik revolutionary tactics. The first batch of graduates, between 40 and 50 activists, were already released into Hungary by the summer of 1918. (The number of those former prisoners who were not actually trained to engage in revolutionary action but who were simply 'infected' by the spirit of the Russian revolution, was far larger than those who were recruited and trained as Bolshevik change agents.)

The leading figure among the "Hungarian Bolshevik Graduates" was a former Hungarian Social Democrat, Béla Kun (1886–1938), a man from the Transylvanian part of Hungary who was hardly known in the HSDP's headquarters in Budapest prior to going to the battlefront in Russia. Kun quickly distinguished himself in Siberia as a super-fan of Bolshevik theory and practice and was moved up to the Russian capital with some of the top members of his "graduating class" from Tomsk (e.g. Ferenc Münnich, and Ernő Pór). In Moscow, Kun made a strong personal impression on Lenin with his fierce loyalty and no holds barred, fighting spirit. Kun and Pór were both involved in the fight against the Left Socialist Revolutionaries (the so-called SRs) who broke with the Bolsheviks, whose troops surrounded the Kremlin early in July 1918, before being beaten back by troops loyal to the Kremlin. (It was a former SR member, Fanny Kaplan, who would shoot Lenin on August 30, that same year.)

The most visible sign of Béla Kun's 'anointment' by Lenin came when he published an article, with Lenin's approval, in the Russian Communist Party's daily, *Pravda*, in October 1918. In this article, Kun announced that he was breaking with the Hungarian Social Democratic Party. *Been there, done that.* He declared that the time has come for creating a Hungarian Communist Party *inside* Hungary. Here is an excerpt from that article:

> History has gone into labour in Hungary. But instead of the cry of revolution, all we can hear from there are the cries of a woman in labour. These are in fact the cries of a Social Democratic Party that promises everything to everyone just to get rid of her pain... Comrades! This is not how a class

party, a party of the working class should behave! This is how a depraved woman of the streets behaves, by promising favours to anyone that comes her way. The HSDP has ceased to be the party of the urban proletariat, the party of the industrial workers, and of the rural poor. The time has arrived for the creation of a genuine working class party, a revolutionary communist party in Hungary that will overthrow the Hungarian bourgeoisie and the opportunistic social democrats at the same time.[43]

To be sure: a Hungarian section of the Russian Bolshevik Party had already been formed with Lenin's blessings in Moscow under Béla Kun's leadership in March of 1918. (There were other nationalities represented within this party-federation apart from the Hungarian one headed by Kun.) After consultations with Lenin, the leaders of this Hungarian Bolshevik group were secretly sent across enemy lines into Hungary at the beginning of November 1918, just days after the outbreak of the Chrysanthemum Revolution. Their job was straight forward: Set up the Communist Party of Hungary in Budapest along Bolshevik lines, take the lead in overthrowing the Károlyi regime, and establish the dictatorship of the proletariat. The entire enterprise was Soviet managed and financed via money transfers from Moscow using the networks of the International Red Cross.

After Kun was sent back to Hungary in November 1918, his position at the head of this Soviet trained Hungarian Bolshevik group in Moscow was taken over by a rather shady character, Endre Rudnyánszky. The latter would be the only representative of the Hungarian Communist Party, at the founding Congress of the Third International in Moscow on March 6, 1919. (Note: This first Congress of the Third International took place barely two weeks before the start of the Hungarian Republic of Councils. The reason why no one was present at the launch of the Third International from the top brass of the HCP was simple: the entire HCP leadership was in prison in Budapest at the time. Only Rudnyánszky, a man with no connections to the Hungarian labour movement was on hand in Moscow to assist Lenin in pulling the wool over the eyes of the international labour movement at this Moscow conference. Angelica Balabanoff, the first Secretary of the Third International provides an authentic, first-hand account of how Lenin mislead the workers of the world in order to legitimize the Bolshevik approach as the only legitimate path to Socialism (Balabanoff, 1968).

A few initial words about Béla Kun's character. He was, to put it mildly, a rather contradictory figure of history, and not just because he was sentimentally attached to his homeland as an internationalist, or because he admired aristocrats in spite of being a communist. Though he was tough as nails, he could not stop himself from crying under stressful situations. His critics tend to dismiss him as the devil incarnate and ridicule his public crying fits that were often followed by attacks of nausea and projectile vomiting. His occasional crying and vomiting fits were not due to drug addiction or alcoholism, but to an injury he suffered on the battlefront. Those who knew him well would disclose that it was as an antidote against these horrible and embarrassing seizures that Kun was incessantly sucking on candies. (A 1979 biography of Kun by the Hungarian historian György Borsányi, which the Hungarian Communist authorities banned for its honest portrayal of the man is highly recommended. It became available in English translation only in 1993, after the collapse of the Soviet Empire and one-party rule in Hungary.)[44]

The story of Kun's adventurous return from Moscow to Hungary early in November 1918 is also surrounded by numerous mythologies. The journey through enemy lines was first recounted by an ex-Communist and later anti-Communist propagandist György Nánássy in his booklet published in 1919 called "Why did I leave the Hungarian Communist party?"[45] The "homecoming" story was also confirmed by other Communist politicians, for example by a high-ranking comrade of Kun, Ferenc Münnich (1886–1967), who was a prisoner of war in Tomsk alongside Kun and made the trip back to Hungary at the side of Kun, along with a few other reliable comrades. Münnich played a significant role in the Revolutionary Governing Council then later in the Spanish Civil war. He survived the executions in Moscow during Stalin's reign of terror, because unbeknown to most of his Hungarian comrades, he was a high-ranking officer of the Soviet secret police, the NKVD.[46] Let us return to the establishment of the Hungarian Communist Party in November 1918, and its behaviour during the short-lived People's Republic between November 16, 1918, and March 21, 1919.

After a harrowing journey through enemy lines, befitting a spy-novel, Béla Kun and his friends arrived in Budapest on November 17, 1918. They were greeted by a well-organized but small group of revolutionaries who constituted the so-called 2nd generation ("*második garnitúra*") of revolutionary leaders after Duczynska, Sugár, and others were arrested in January 1918. Most prominent among this 2nd generation were Ernő Seidler and Ottó Korvin. Korvin (1894–1919) was a high-ranking bank official, an aspiring poet, and a superb revolutionary organizer by night. Ilona Duczynska gave Korvin the keys to the locker at the Budapest railway station where she hid the mobile printing press used by her revolutionary group before she was arrested in January 1918. Korvin would become chief of the political police during the dictatorship of the proletariat not because of his affinity for this kind of work, but because of his superior organizational capabilities. (He was in fact at constant loggerheads with the lawless and brutal machinations of those that engineered the so-called "Red Terror" during the first months of the Republic of Councils.) Korvin chose not to escape to Austria after the collapse of the Commune with Kun and the other

Commissars. He was arrested, horribly tortured, and then executed during the White Terror. (In his last will and testament, written during the night before his execution, Korvin asked that no one should commit any acts of violence after his execution or take revenge on his murderers.)

The formal launch of the Hungarian Communist Party (HPC) took place one week after Kun's arrival to Budapest, on November 24, 1918, and in an apartment that Ilona Duczynska occupied at first in the 2nd district before she gave it back to its proprietors, József Kelen (younger brother of Korvin and one of the Commissar of the 1919 Commune), and his wife, Jolán Kelen (1891–1979). Duczynska did not attend the launch of the HCP, because she was ordered to bed suffering from tuberculosis and Spanish influenza.[47]

The Russian trained Bolsheviks who set up the HCP managed to quickly attract the support of numerous disenchanted social democrats, radical young intellectuals, and former Galileists who were all dissatisfied with the opportunistic politics of the HSDP. (Many of these early radical supporters were devotees of the legendary anarcho-syndicalist Ervin Szabó who only passed away a few months before the Chrysanthemum Revolution and who advised all his followers to bypass the bureaucratic and unprincipled leadership of the HSDP. Szabó was not a follower of Lenin and cautioned his followers from following the Bolshevik's path. Some listened to his warnings, others ignored him.) The comrades returning from Russia were looked up to, because it was known that they enjoyed the support and confidence of Lenin and the Soviet Bolshevik leaders who were, after all, the only ones with revolutionary leadership experience. It was natural for everyone to defer to the authority of Béla Kun, who none of them knew very well and found rather odd.

In a short while, German-trained Marxist philosopher György Lukács, who was well known by then for his radical views, asked to be admitted into the HCP. Lukács let it be known in a polemical article that he had a moral dilemma with Bolshevism. Up to that point, he, like so many others, looked to the German Labour Movement for guidance and example. He could not wholeheartedly embrace the use of terror, violence, the dictatorship of the proletariat. At first, Lukács tried to press upon his new comrades that good cannot be achieved by "bad" means, freedom cannot be reached through oppression: "We cannot lie our way to the truth". After a while, he rejected his views in an essay entitled "Tactics and Ethics". In this, he came to the conclusion that a third path to Socialism and the liberation of humanity does not exist. Anyone who rejects, on ethical grounds, the use of force during the construction of Socialism will ensure nothing but the triumph of Capitalist exploitation and will thereby assist in the organization of yet another imperialistic world war. Lukács was aware that the use of terror is deplorable, but along with tens of thousands of his generation, he was also convinced that Communism is the only alternative to the 'inhumanity', the dead-end that Capitalism inevitably produces. (To this day, the work that best captures the spirit of those days in Budapest—the excitement, the uncertainty, the ferment, the mistaken fantasies, the desires and hopes of this intellectual generation—is a novel written by Ervin Sinkó [1898–1967], *The Optimists*. Sinkó lived through and participated in the events that led to the rise and fall of the Budapest Commune. He knew personally the main actors in that heroic tragedy that took place 100 years ago.)[48]

The HCP had one overarching strategy after November 24, 1918: Attack! It mercilessly opposed every step of the Károlyi government at every turn and all those who supported those policies. As we have shown earlier, after some initial hesitation, the HSDP joined the new governing coalition after the Chrysanthemum Revolution and publicly suspended the class struggle in Hungary, in order to enable the Hungarian bourgeoisie to transform the country's semi-feudal, agrarian base, rebuild the war-torn economy, and provide a better foundation for a parliamentary transition to Socialism. The HCP categorically rejected this approach. It argued that the Hungarian workers and peasants had suffered long enough: their suffering should not be prolonged by delaying the arrival of Socialism. It is not the proletariat's job to help build a nest for the bourgeoisie and to nurture its young. Its job is to destroy that nest, eliminate the class-based exploitation of labour by establishing the dictatorship of the proletariat. As we have shown earlier, the Károlyi regime's inability to deliver tangible results on its promises—a just peace, land reform, national elections based on universal franchise—and the HSDP's increasing identification with Károlyi's Presidency seriously eroded the HSDP's working-class support. Tens of thousands would switch over to the HCP, and agree with Béla Kun and his men, that the HSDP had sold out the Hungarian working class by joining the bourgeoisie and must therefore be rejected along with its partner, the Károlyi regime.

The virulently anti-government daily of the newly established HCP, the *Vörös Újság* (Red News), first published in December 1918, was the bullhorn for this sentiment as soon as it hit the stands. Its tone was fiery and uncompromising. It rejected dialogue with the Károlyi government and argued for its forceful replacement. It relentlessly pressed home its message: the only way ahead is through the dictatorship of the proletariat. The HCP did not look at the government as its opponent or competitor, but as its enemy. It dismissed the government's ministers as "lackeys" or "bastards" that do not deserve any mercy. At a time of severe paper shortages, *Vörös Újság* would bypass the rationing and acquire its supplies through illegal channels, and bribe the printers to get its issues unto the streets. As one of the Party members at that time, József Lengyel (1896–

1975), would write in a book published in Moscow in 1932 under the title *Visegrádi utca* (Visegrád Street, the location of the HCP headquarters), the headquarters of the Party and its newspaper was like a military outpost: it contained a veritable arsenal of weapons and explosives. The HCP did not come to praise the People's Republic, but to bury it.[49]

The HSDP's house organ, *Népszava*, valiantly fought back, dismissing the HCP's frontal assault on its ranks as an assault on the People's Revolution, accusing the Communists of undermining the achievements of the revolution and for promoting divisiveness at a time when Hungary needed unity above all to get back on its feet from a disastrous war. Their reposts were less and less effective because neither the Károlyi government nor the Berinkey one formed in January 1919 could provide a solution to the crisis facing Hungary. Under these circumstances, the popularity of the HCP rapidly accelerated. The new party quickly became the sole and genuine representative of the working class and of the angry veterans that returned from the battlefield and congregated in the capital by the tens of thousands, without work, often without a roof over their heads, hungry, uncared for, and freezing in unheated shelters and run-down tenement buildings. The events followed each other in rapid succession.

On January 28, 1919, Béla Kun unleashed the party's most popular initiative to date: He declared that not only officers but also non-commissioned officers leaving military service should be given an allowance of 5,400 Hungarian *korona*. '5400' became a lucky number for the communists, a number sewed on the flags of the demonstrators who flooded the streets of the capital with increasing frequency and frenzy.

In response to the relentless and increasingly violent pressure from the left, the HSDP ministers decided they'd had enough. They decided to follow the examples of their colleagues in Germany, Friedrich Ebert and Gustav Noske, who used the troops of the right-wing militias to finish off their radical left-wing opponents.[50] After the appointment of Mihály Károlyi to the presidency, the newly established Berinkey government availed itself of its constitutionally granted right to defend the People's Republic. The opportunity was given by a violent demonstration organized by the Communists in front of the HSDP's daily, the *Népszava*, on February 20 during which a number of policemen lost their lives in the HCP organized scuffles. The government pinned the blame for the violence on the Communist leaders and arrested all of them the next day and once they were incarcerated. The police took full revenge on the prisoners for the death of their colleagues. They almost beat Béla Kun to death in his cell, thereby making a martyr out of him once the news of his beating hit the streets. (One of the correspondents of the biggest tabloid in the city—*Az Est* [The Evening

Standard]—managed to get an interview with Kun after his beating and ran the story as a headline the following day.)

The brutal beating of the HCP leader triggered enormous interest throughout the country. Hundreds of thousands of people who read the story repeated the legendary answer of Béla Kun to the reporter, who asked him if he knew the identity of the men who nearly beat him to death: "It's not important who they are. They are ordinary people who have been misled, and deceived. I wish them no harm".[51] The HCP could not have wished for better publicity in its wildest dreams. The numbers of its sympathisers skyrocketed. It continued its organization of anti-government actions, lead now by leaders of its "shadow" Central Committee, who were elected previously as a precaution. With an upsurge of anti-government agitation, the relentless military encroachment on her territory by the armies of three of her neighbours, the blockade and ultimatum of the Entente—the so-called Vix Memorandum of March 20, 1919—President Károlyi dismissed his PM and turned to the HSDP to form a new government.

When he took this step, Károlyi had no idea that the leaders of the HSDP and the imprisoned leaders of the HCP had just met in the greatest of secrecy, and decided to bury the hatchet by uniting their parties. He was as surprised to hear, like everyone else, that these bitter rivals created a new party of unity—the name of which would be decided later—in order to put an end to the People's Republic and his own Presidency and put the country on an entirely new path. Károlyi learned from the flyers swept along the streets on March 21, 1919, that it was game over for the Chrysanthemum Revolution. He learned just like all the early morning commuters in Budapest that day that the People's Republic and the parliamentary path to Socialism was over. Henceforth, Hungary was a republic of councils whose mission would be the construction of Socialism via the dictatorship of the proletariat.

The procedures used for bypassing Károlyi were simple: the architects of the HSDP and HCP merger convinced the President's Secretary, Pál Kéri (1882–1961), to draft a resignation statement by the President and to forge his signature onto the document while the President slept during the night of March 20. By the time Károlyi woke up next morning and realized what had happened, the dictatorship of the proletariat had already been proclaimed by the newly merged party that called itself the Hungarian Socialist Party (HSP).[52] This temporary name was only changed three months later to The Party of the Socialist-Communist Workers of Hungary (PSCWH). By this time, the initial enthusiasm with those who announced the dictatorship of the proletariat had largely dissipated. Ernő Garami, the most important figure in the history of Hungarian social democracy, did not even join the united party. He simply did not want to be a member of a party that eliminated the word—democratic—from its name.

He left the country, along with Oszkár Jászi and Mihály Károlyi, as fast as he could once they realized that their presence would not be tolerated by the Bolsheviks on the path to Socialism.

The hundreds of thousands who became members of various Councils throughout Hungary during the preceding years had also heard the news like Károlyi—second hand, from fliers sweeping through the streets of Budapest and from reading the afternoon tabloids. Their reactions, like most people, was hopeful and positive. Disgruntled supporters of the largest opposition party, the HSDP, welcomed the changes as a sign that their leaders have finally come to their senses and had stopped their unprincipled wheeling and dealing behind the people's back. This feeling would be shared, at first, by millions of poor and landless agricultural labourers in the countryside as well. It is safe to say that even a majority of the country's bourgeoisie and conservative-nationalist strata supported the announcement of the Commune. It filled them as well with hope and excitement that perhaps this last-ditch effort may get their country moving towards a just peace settlement. That with a friend to the East, Russia, the assault by Hungary's neighbours might be beaten back and the country may finally embark on the path of social justice, the rule of law, and sustainable development. The best-known Hungarian catchphrase of today was unknown in 1919: this broadly based 1919 national coalition of optimists had not heard that hope is always the last one to die.

The architects of the dictatorship of the proletariat in Hungary were convinced that the world revolution was just around the corner and the events in Russia were the true signs of things to come throughout the world. They believed that, as a consequence of their own desperate but heroic actions, Hungary would find itself among the winners instead of the losers once the dust settled over Europe during the years ahead. Some, such as Zsigmond Kunfi, one of the prominent leaders of the HSDP, were possessed by a more existential, Kierkegaardian view of their undertaking: "This was our leap of death into the unknown!"[53]

Let there be no mistake about this: Although Hungary's second post-WWI revolution in 1919 was clearly a Russian inspired initiative, it owes its early successes first and foremost to the leadership skills and organizational talents of the Hungarian communists themselves. Béla Kun was nobody's fool. He did everything as skilfully and as thoroughly as Lenin would have done so during the first three months of the Hungarian Republic of Councils. It was only during the last month of the Commune that he would step out of line and begin to innovate and follow his own head. But by then this *leap of death* was into the last stages of its descent, its ending was no longer in doubt by those who understood the structures of tragedy.

What was the Hungarian Republic of Councils?

In an oft quotes essay, Béla Kun offered the following interpretation of the state structure that's based on Councils or Soviets, as follows:

> "It is only the unlimited power of the proletariat, their dictatorship that can fully guarantee the success of the transition to Socialism... The "Soviets", or councils of the workers and peasants, are the pillars, the form and structure of the dictatorship of the proletariat. They are the levers, the tools with which the authority of the workers and peasants is exercised".[54]

The executive arm, or the government of the Hungarian Republic of Councils, was known as the Revolutionary Governing Council (RGC). At first, it was divided into 13 portfolios, or ministries, that were headed by 16 men, of whom only two were Communist Party members (Béla Kun, International Relations, and Károly Vántus [1879–1927] who was one of the four commissars in charge of Agriculture). 14 of the 16 Commissars of the initial RGC in other words, were former HSDP members, as was the 17th, *ex officio* member, the President of the RGC, Sándor Garbai (1879–1947).

Everyone knew, inside and outside of this executive structure, however, that the person who wielded *de facto* power within the RGC was not the President of the RGC, but Béla Kun by virtue of his close relationship with V.I. Lenin and to Hungary's last hope—the Soviet Union. (The secret pact that was worked out by the HSDP and the HCP the night before March 21 stipulated that each Commissar would have a deputy and that the deputy could not be from the same Party as the lead Commissar. What the HCP lost in chief Commissariat posts, it regained at Deputy levels. Within a month, Deputy Commissars were raised to the same level of authority as their chiefs.)

Following the collapse of the Commune, and to this day, critics of the Commune would persist in their efforts to discredit the RGC, by arguing that it consisted of a group of untrained, unprofessional, blood-thirsty ideologues. Most are dismissed as professional revolutionaries, hot-headed trade-unionists, peasants, "proles", or journalists who just came off the construction site, the assembly line, or from one of the farms in the outback. A good example of this kind of character assassination is the case of Sándor Garbai, the President of the RGC. Even today, and in some academic journals, he is dismissed as merely a "brick-layer from Kiskunhalas", when in fact, Garbai only worked as a brick-layer for a very short time during his teenage years. By 1903 Garbai was the President of the Hungarian National Federation of Construction Workers. By 1907 he was the President of the National Workers' Insurance Fund and a respected member of the HSDP. Reading the accounts written about him one would think he showed up to the RGC's first cabinet meeting wearing a brick-layer's apron, with a trowel in one hand and the Communist Manifesto in the other.

Contrary to the widespread falsehoods propagated about its makeup over the past century, and in its historical context, the RGC could best be described as a technocratic-intellectual ensemble (which may already provide us with a clue as to why it lost the support of the proletariat and the peasantry in very quick order). Nearly half of its members were what could best be described as intellectuals: five were practising and respected lawyers, six were high-ranking, white-collar professionals. There were two medical doctors and two engineers among the Commissars, along with four well-known, serious journalists, and three teachers whose claim to fame stemmed not from their ideological fervour but their work as reformers in the field of higher education. Of those in the RGC who had a trade union background, only one worked for a short time at the start of their career as a physical labourer. In its social or professional makeup, if not in its policies, the RGC would be indistinguishable from any modern-day parliamentary democracy today in Europe or North America.[55]

There is another widespread myth about the 1919 Hungarian Republic of Councils that persists to this day. Since 61% of the members of the Revolutionary Governing Council were of Jewish origin, the dictatorship of the proletariat has often been portrayed by its opponents as a "Jewish Dictatorship".[56] The first thing to note with respect to this "myth"—which had served for almost a century as one of the pillars of anti-Semitism in Hungary—is that the so-called Jewish commissars were all atheists, assimilated internationalists, and did not possess a Jewish identity as such. The presence of a large number of Jews within the Hungarian labour movement cannot be explained by the conspiracy theory of Judeo-Bolshevism.[57] The cause of this phenomenon was due to the fact that Jews in this part of the world, in spite of the liberalization of the anti-Jewish laws in 1895, were still experiencing considerable discrimination based on their religion and ethnic origins. Participation in an international movement was a natural avenue for many among the Jewish community who wanted to use this route not only to escape national discriminatory practices but to participate in the events shaping the future of their national and international communities. Far from wanting to destroy "Christian civilization" these men and women went to the barricades to restore the Judaeo-Christian foundations and values of their civilization, values that stressed social-justice, sustainability, frugality, equality between men and women, respect for others, and an end to the exploitation of the down-and-out.

Hindsight enables us to declare with a fairly high degree of confidence that if Hungary had not fallen into such a deep abyss in 1919, if the circumstances under which the citizens of this country found themselves in had not been as hopeless as they were, the Revolutionary Governing Council that covered the streets of Budapest with a flyer heralding the dictatorship of the proletariat, would not have been so wholeheartedly embraced by the people of Budapest. The fact is, however, that by that fateful day, the intensity of the pain stemming from the post-war collapse and the sense of hopelessness it produced was unprecedented in modern Hungarian history. It is this unprecedented historical situation that compelled the citizens of Hungary—the proletariat, the landless peasants, tens of thousands of students, artists, intellectuals, displaced war veterans, many members of the bourgeoisie and even segments of the aristocracy, and nobility—to try something they had never tried before: they agreed that their only defense against "the total anarchy of the collapse" was "Socialism-Communism". This was, in short, a natural reaction by people who are pushed to the brink.

NOTES

1   About the remembrance of the Hungarian Soviet Republic: Péter Apor, *Az elképzelt köztársaság. A Magyarországi Tanácsköztársaság utóélete, 1945–1989* [A visioned republic. The afterlife of the Hungarian Soviel Republic, 1945–1989], (Budapest: MTA BTK Történettudományi Intézet, 2014). In English: Péter Apor, *Fabricating Authenticity in Soviet Hungary: The Afterlife of the First Hungarian Soviet Republic in the Age of State Socialism* (Londo: Anthem Press), 2015. resp. Péter Csunderlik, *A "vörös farsangtól" a "vörös tatárjárásig". A Tanácsköztársaság a korai Horthy-korszak pamflet- és visszaemlékezés-irodalmában* [From the 'red carnival' to the 'red invasion'. The Hungarian Soviet Republic in the pamphlet and remembrance literature of the early Horthy Era]. (Budapest: Napvilág, 2019).

2   The most complete adaptation of the history of the Hungarian Commune until today: Tibor Hajdu, *A Magyarországi Tanácsköztársaság* [The Hungarian Soviet Republic], (Budapest: Kossuth, 1969). A shortened version of the work has been published in English, *Tibor Hajdu: The Hungarian Soviet Republic*. (Budapest: Akadémiai Kiadó, 1979).

3   For the full text of the declaration see: Sándorné Gábor, Tibor Hajdu and Gizella Szabó (eds.), *A magyar munkásmozgalom történetének válogatott dokumentumai. Hatodik kötet. A Magyar Tanácsköztársaság 1919. március 21.–1919. augusztus 1. Első rész. 1919. március 21. 1919. június 11.* (Budapest: Kossuth, 1959), 3–4.

4   About the history of the left-wing radical student circle established in 1908, whose first leader was Károly Polányi, and in which later Ilona Duczynska played an important role between 1917–1919 cf. Csunderlik Péter, *Radikálisok, szabadgondolkodók, ateisták. A Galilei Kör (1908–1919) története* [Radicals, freethinkers, atheists: The history of the Galilei Circle (1908–1919)], (Budapest: Napvilág, 2017). About the life of Károly Polányi cf. Gareth Dale, *Karl Polanyi: A Life on the Left*, (New York, NY: Columbia University Press, 2016).

5   György Litván (ed.), *Károlyi Mihály levelezése. I. kötet. 1905–1920* [The Correspondence of Mihály Károlyi. I. kötet. 1905–1920], (Budapest, Akadémiai, 1978), 357.

6   Tamás Kóbor, *A bolsevismusról a bolsevismus alatt* [About bolshevism during the Bolshevism], (Budapest: Franklin Társulat, 1919), 52.

7   The works of Edit S. Vincze and Tibor Erényi give an insight into the beginning of the Hungarian labour movement and its situation at the beginning of the 20th century: Edit S. Vincze, *Az útkeresés évtizedei. Tanulmányok a magyarországi munkásmozgalom történetéből, 1868–1898* [Decades of pathfinding. Essays from the history of the Hungarian labour movements, 1868–1898], (Budapest: Gondolat Könyvkiadó, 1977). resp. Tibor Erényi, *Szocializmus a századelőn. Tanulmányok a magyarországi munkásmozgalom történetéből* [Socialism at the beginning of the 20th century. Essays from the history of the Hungarian labour movements, 1868–1898], (Budapest: Kossuth Könyvkiadó, 1979). A short English synopsis: Rudolf L. Tőkés, *Béla Kun and the Hungarian Soviet Republic. The Origins and Role of the Communist Party of Hungary in the Revolutions of 1918–1919*, (New York-Washington: Frederick A. Praeger, 1967), 1–23.

8   The memoirs and biography of Garami: Ernő Garami, *Forrongó Magyarország. Emlékezések és tanulságok* [Seething Hungary. Recollections and lessons,] (Budapest, Primusz Kiadó, 1989). resp. Lajos Varga, *Garami Ernő. Politikai életrajz* [Ernő Garami. A political biography], (Budapest: Napvilág, 1996).

9   The recollections of Gárdos: Mariska Gárdos, *Százarcú élet* [Hundred-faced life]. (Budapest: Szépirodalmi Könyvkiadó, 1975). About women's movements at the beginning of the 20th century cf. Judith Szapor, *Hungarian Women's Activism in the Wake of the First World War. From Rights to Revanche*, (London–New York: Bloomsbury, 2018), 15–34.

10   About the ethnic relations and problems of the Austro-Hungarian Empire- including Hungary cf. Oscar Jászi, *The Dissolution of the Habsburg Monarchy*, (Chicago, IL: Chicago University Press, 1929).

11   Ernő Garami, *Hazafiság és nemzetköziség* [Patriotism and internationalism], (Budapest: *Népszava*, 1975), 38–39, 44.

12   István Schlett, *A szociáldemokrácia és a magyar társadalom 1914-ig* [Social Democracy and the Hungarian society until 1914]. (Budapest: Gondolat, 1982).

13   About the election machinations of the Dualism cf. András Gerő, *The Hungarian Parliament, 1867–1918. The Mirage of Power*, (Highland Lakes, NJ: East European Monographs, 1997).

14   A short synopsis of the situation of Hungary in the Austro-Hungarian Empire: Joseph Held, The Heritage of the Past: Hungary before World War I. In: Iván Völgyes ed., *Hungary in Revolution, 1918–1919. Nine essays*, (Lincoln, NB: University of Nebraska Press, 1971), 1–9. Furthermore cf. the introduction of the synopsis of Ignác Romsics: Ignác Romsics, *Hungary in the Twentieth Century*, (Budapest: Corvina–Osiris, 1999).

15   About Jászi: György Litván: *A Twentieth-Century Prophet: Oszkár Jászi, 1875–1957*, (Budapest: CEU Press, 2006). About the periodical *Huszadik Század*: Attila Pók, *A magyarországi radikális demokrata ideológia kialakulása. A "Huszadik Század" társadalomszemlélete (1900–1907)* [The formation of the Hungarian radical democrat ideology. Social attitude of Huszadik Század (1900–1907)], (Budapest: Akadémiai Kiadó, 1990).

16   About the agrarian socialist movements: Péter Hanák: "Az agrárszocialista mozgalom mentalitása és szimbólumai" [The mentality and symbols of the agrarian socialist movements]. In: Péter Hanák, *A Kert és a Műhely* [The Garden and the Workshop], (Budapest: Gondolat Kiadó, 1988), 204–221. As for the problematic of emigration: Julianna Puskás, *From Hungary to the United States, 1880–1914* (Budapest: Akadémiai Kiadó, 1982).

17   About István Tisza: Gábor Vermes, *The Liberal Vision and Conservative Statecraft of a Magyar Nationalist* (New York, NY: Columbia University Press, 1985).

18   György Borsányi, *Októbertől márciusig. Polgári demokrácia Magyarországon, 1918* [From October till March. Bourgeois democracy in Hungary, 1918] (Budapest: Kossuth, 1988), 113. Synopsis of the history of the Hungarian social democracy during World War I: Lajos Varga, *Háború, forradalom, szociáldemokrácia Magyarországon, 1914. július–1919. március* [War, revolution, social democracy in Hungary, July 1914–March 1919] (Budapest: Napvilág, 2010).

19   On the hinterland situation of Hungary during World War I cf Péter Bihari, *Lövészárkok a hátországban. Középosztály, zsidókérdés, antiszemitizmus az első világháború Magyarországán* [Trenches in the hinterland. Middle class, Jewish question, antisemitism in Hungary during World War I] (Budapest: Napvilág, 2008).

20   About the political events in Hungary during World War I.: István Deák, "The Decline and Fall of Habsburg Hungary, 1914–1918." In: Iván Völgyes ed., *Hungary in Revolution, 1918–1919*, 10–30.

21   Tibor Hajdu, *Tanácsok Magyarországon 1918–1919-ben* [Councils in Hungary in 1918–1919] (Budapest: Kossuth, 1958), 7.

22   Csunderlik Péter, *Radikálisok, szabadgondolkodók, ateisták* [Radicals, freethinkers, atheists]: 325–332.

23   About Mihály Károlyi: Hajdu Tibor, *Ki volt Károlyi Mihály?* [Who was Mihály Károlyi?] (Budapest: Napvilág, 2012).

24   Pál Hatos, *Az elátkozott köztárasság. Az 1918-as összeomlás és az őszirózsás forradalom története* [The doomed republic. The history of the collapse of 1918 and the Aster revolution] (Budapest: Jaffa, 2018), 19–142.

25   György Borsányi, *Októbertől márciusig. Polgári demokrácia Magyarországon, 1918* [From October till March. Bourgeois democracy in Hungary, 1918], (Budapest: Kossuth, 1988), 77.

26 Eor the memoirs of Lukachich cf. Géza Lukachich, *Magyarország megcsonkításának okai* [On the reasons for mutilating Hungary], (Budapest, NYUKOSZ, [1932]), 114. On the role of the Budapest police in the revolutions of 1918–1919 cf. Károly Dietz, *Októbertől—augusztusig. Emlékirataim* [From October till August. My memoirs]. Budapest, Rácz Vilmos Könyvkiadóvállalata, 1920.

27 Rezsőné Mehringer: "A telefonkezelők a forradalomban" [Telephone operators in the revolution]. In: Ernőné Lányi (ed.), *Nagy idők tanúi emlékeznek, 1918–1919* [Witnesses of great times remember, 1918–1919], (Budapest: Kossuth, 1959), 64–72.

28 Oszkár Jászi, *Magyar kálvária—magyar föltámadás. A két forradalom értelme, jelentősége és tanulságai* [Hungarian calvary—Hungarian resurrection—the meaning, importance and lesson of the two revolutions] (Budapest: Magyar Hírlap Könyvek, 1989), 33.

29 Géza Lukachich, *Magyarország megcsonkításának okairól* [On the reasons for mutilating Hungary], 136.

30 László Bús Fekete, *Katona-forradalmárok* [Soldier revolutionists], (Budapest: "Phőnix" Könyv- és Lapkiadó Vállalat, 1918).

31 Ferenc Pölöskei, *A rejtélyes Tisza-gyilkosság* [The mysterious Tisza-assassination], (Budapest: Helikon, 1988).

32 Mihály Károlyi, *Hit, illúziók nélkül* [Faith without illusions], (Budapest: Európa Könyvkiadó, 1982), 131. The memoir of Károlyi was originally published in London, in 1956: Mihály Károlyi, *Faith Without Illusion. Memoirs*, (London: J. Cape, 1956).

33 On the Aster revolution and the struggles of political parties cf Tibor Hajdu, *Az 1918-as polgári demokratikus forradalom* [The bourgeois democratic revolution of 1918] (Budapest, Kossuth, 1968). See also: Gyula Mérei, *A magyar októberi forradalom és a polgári pártok* [The Hungarian October revolution and bourgeois parties] (Budapest, Akadémiai Kiadó, 1969). The party programs are presented by: Jenő Erdély, *Mit akarnak? Károlyi pártja, a szociáldemokraták, radikálisok, keresztény szocialisták, földművelők, bolsevikiek? Az összes magyar politikai pártok programmja és szervezete* [What do they want? The party of Károlyi, the social democrats, radicals, christian socialists, farmers, bolsheviks? A complete guide to the program and organization of Hungarian political parties], (Budapest, Benkő Gyula könyvkereskedése, 1919).

34 Köztársaságot követelünk! A népkormány tagjai a Nemzeti Tanács kezébe tették le az esküt [We demand a republic! Members of the People's Government take the oath in the National Council], *Népszava*, (November 2, 1918), 3.

35 Ernő Garami, *Forrongó Magyarország* [Seething Hungary], 63.

36 The recollections of Bartha can be read in: György Haas, *A szabadság tábornoka. Bartha Albert* [The general of freedom. Bartha Albert], (Budapest, Kairosz, 2002).

37 On the military policy of the revolutions of 1918–1919: Peter Pastor (ed.), *Revolution and Interventions in Hungary and its Neighbor States, 1918–1919*, (Highland Lakes, N. J., Atlantic Studies on Society in Change), 1988, 11–104.

38 Peter Pastor, *Hungary between Wilson and Lenin. The Hungarian Revolution of 1918–1919 and the Big Three*, (Boulder, East European Quarterly, 1976).

39 On the Central European revolutions and political changes: Tibor Hajdu, *Közép-Európa forradalma, 1917–1921* [The revolution of Central Europe, 1917–1921], (Budapest, Gondolat), 1989.

40 Magyarország népéhez! [To the Hungarian people!] *Népszava*, (October 8, 1918), 2.

41 The People's Act No. XVIII

42 Zsigmond Móricz, *A földtörvény kis kátéja. Az 1919: XVIII. néptörvény magyarázata és utasítása a földmíves nép földhöz juttatásáról* [Small catechism of the land reform. An explanation and statement to the XVIII. People Act of 1919 about 'The land to the peasants'], (Budapest, Néplap), 1919, 7., 12.

43 Béla Kun, *Accomplished!* [Elvégeztetett!] In: Béla Kun: *A Magyar Tanácsköztársaságról. Válogatott beszédek és írások* [About the Hungarian Soviet Republic. Collected speeches and essays], (Budapest, Kossuth), 1958, 127., 129–131.

44 György Borsányi, *Kun Béla. Politikai életrajz* [Béla Kun. A political biography], (Budapest, Kossuth Könyvkiadó), 1979. resp. György Borsányi, *The Life of a Communist Revolutionary: Béla*

Kun, (Boulder, Colo., Columbia University Press), 1993. Another significant work is the book of Rudolf Tőkés, published in the USA, on the Hungarian Soviet Republic, focusing on Béla Kun: Rudolf L. Tőkés, *Béla Kun and the Hungarian Soviet Republic. The Origins and Role of the Communist Party of Hungary in the Revolutions of 1918–1919*, (New York-Washington, Frederick A. Praeger, 1967).

45 György Nánássy: *Miért léptem ki a magyarországi kommunista-pártból? A magyar kommunista-vezérek üzelmei* [Why did I leave the Hungarian communist party? Dealings of Hungarian communist leaders], (Budapest, 1919).

46 On the life of Münnich cf Ferenc Münnich: *Viharos út* [Stormy Road], (Budapest, Kossuth Könyvkiadó, 1986).

47 András Simor, *Így élt Korvin Ottó* [The Life of Ottó Korvin], (Budapest, Móra Könyvkiadó, 1977), 71–108.

48 The newest publication of the novel: Ervin Sinkó, *Optimisták. Történelmi regény 1918–1919-ből* [Optimists. A historical novel from 1918–1919], (Budapest, Noran Libro, 2010). Sinkó was among the most peculiar members of the Hungarian Soviet Republic. He went as far as sending young army officer participants of the counterrevolution of Budapest in June 24, 1919, to a Dostoevsky seminar. Students of the Ludovika Academy had to read *The Brothers Karamazov* as a punishment. The recollections of Sinkó: Ervin Sinkó, *Szemben a bíróval* [Facing the Judge], (Budapest, Magvető, 1983).

49 József Lengyel, *Visegrádi utca* [Visegrád Street] (Budapest, Szépirodalmi, 1962).

50 L. Sebastian Haffner, *Az elárult forradalom. Németország, 1918–19* [The betrayed Revolution. Germany, 1918–19], (Budapest, Európa, 2007).

51 "A kommunisták vezéreit letartóztatták és a tolonczházba vitték—Kun Bélát félholtra verték a rendőrök" [Leaders of communists were arrested and brought to holding centers—Béla Kun was almost beaten to death by police], *Az Est*, (February 22, 1919), 3.

52 Tibor Hajdu, *Who was Mihály Károlyi?*, 120–121.

53 Dezső Szilágyi, "Harcban a proletárhatalomért" [In fight for the proletariat power]. In: Ernőné Lányi ed., *Nagy idők tanúi emlékeznek* [Witnesses of great times remember], 62.

54 Béla Kun, "Mi a Tanácsköztársaság?" [What is the Soviet Republic?] In: Béla Kun: *A Magyar Tanácsköztársaságról* [About the Hungarian Soviet Republic], 115.

55 Gábor Egry ed., *Kérdések és válaszok 1918–1919-ről* [Questions and answers about 1918–1919] (Budapest, Napvilág, 2018), 45–47.

56 Péter Csunderlik, *A "vörös farsangtól" a "vörös tatárjárásig"* [From the 'red carnival' to the 'red invasion'], 175–182.

57 'To the evolution and spread of the world conspiracy theories of Judeobolsheviks' l. Paul Hanebrink, *A Specter Haunting Europe. The Idea of Judeo-Bolshevism in Twentieth Century Europe*, (Cambridge, Harvard University Press), 2018.

CHAPTER 2

Councils and Revolution: The 1918 German Example

Marie-Josée Lavallée

Introduction

"Long live the German Republic!" shouted the Vice President of the German Social Democratic Party (SPD), Philipp Scheidemann, to thousands of workers massed in front of the Reichstag building in Berlin on November 9, 1918. The German Emperor Wilhelm II had just abdicated and World War I was just about to end. While Schiedemann's proclamation may have sounded rather bold to his colleague, Friedrich Ebert, the newly appointed German chancellor, Karl Liebknecht would raise the stakes even higher on the same day. Standing before the Imperial Palace and another big crowd of workers, the leader of the Independent Social Democratic Party of Germany (USPD) and the Spartacus League, Liebknecht would hail not just any but a "Socialist German Republic":

> We must strain our muscles now to construct the workers' and soldiers' government in order to create a new proletarian state, a state of peace, joy and freedom for our German brothers and our brothers throughout the whole world. We stretch our hands to them, and call on them to carry to completion the world revolution.[1]

Though it was a momentous event, the German Revolution of November 9, 1918, like the one in Hungary on March 21, 1919, is also described at times as one of those "forgotten revolutions"[2] that shook the European continent at the end of World War I, only to fade into oblivion. Centenaries provide us with an opportunity to fill the holes of oblivion. That Germany may have become a Communist country with a government based on Councils resembling the Russian or Hungarian Soviets may sound strange today. But if we remind ourselves that the workers' movement and most revolutionaries of the time, claimed to be the direct followers of Karl Marx, the connection with Germany becomes a matter of course. Since the Second International also rested upon

German foundations, the country had a "hegemonic position" in the international socialist movement at the end of the 19th century.[3] According to Marx and Engels, Germany would be the epicenter of the proletarian world revolution.[4] A high level of industrialization was considered by all Marxist revolutionaries at this time as a prerequisite for launching a successful Socialist revolution. Russia's level of industrial development was far behind that of Germany, it was not expected to be the pioneer.

Though Lenin would not respect this mechanical determinism, he subscribed to Marx's economic view of history. He actively stoked the flames of the revolutionary embers in Germany in order to strengthen and protect the Bolsheviks' own experiment in Russia. Like everyone else, he too was convinced that by virtue of its level of industrial development, the socialist revolution in Germany was just around the corner, and once it flared up, it would be the natural adjunct to his Bolshevik enterprise. The idea that Russia could go it alone was the furthest thing from Lenin's mind.

Let's pause for a moment: The 1917 October Revolution in Russia was a game-changer for Marxists everywhere. It provided them with conclusive evidence that revolutionary change is not necessarily a function of industrial indicators or statistics. Russia showed the world that the socialist revolution is a human enterprise. Paradoxically, no one learned this important lesson faster than the ruling political establishments of Europe. They began tracking not only with anxiety but with even greater determination, any and all developments in Europe that were similar to the revolutionary and pre-revolutionary conditions prevailing in Russia by 1917.

Strikes, protests for bread, work, and peace were raging for months in Germany prior to the end of the war. Mutinies were commonplace. The expected collapse of the imperial order put the building of a new regime on the political agenda and it was an open question which way Germany would go in November 1918. Would it become a parliamentary democracy or a dictatorship of the proletariat? Would it be a Democratic Republic or a Republic of Councils? Conditions in Germany were seen by many as identical to those that prevailed in Russia at the time of the February Revolution, in 1917, when the Tsar abdicated under popular pressure, and was replaced by a provisional government. By November of 1918, it was perfectly clear to most everyone that Germany possessed virtually all of the attributes that could tip her over "to the other side". But there was yet another similarity with Russia that should be noted.

Organs of popular government, Councils, or Soviets, appeared in Russia in the midst of the 1905 Revolution,[5] and re-surfaced again in February 1917. Though they did not exist in Germany before 1914, Councils, or *Räte*, were also spreading fast and furious throughout Germany's industrial heartland and in the Navy as the war dragged on and especially after 1917. Like their relatives, the Soviets in Russia, the *Räte* were viewed from the outset as a profound threat to the bourgeois order.

In Russia, at the dawn of its October 1917 Revolution, and in Germany, in November and December 1918, many among the protagonists wanted to create a republic based on the Councils i.e. the *Räte*. As Ernst Däumig, one of the actors of the German Revolution put it in 1920, the Councils were to become the engines of socialist production and of the self-managed communities they epitomized. The Council System would "establish the dictatorship of the proletariat" by "seizing political power... taking control of the production process and the state apparatus".[6] The proponents of this system expected that Germany's workers would reach out to each other across the land, organize themselves into a nation-wide, non-hierarchical network of Councils as an alternative to a parliamentary system based on political parties.[7]

As we know by now, both the Russian and the German attempts to build such a republic failed, as did the one in Hungary in 1919. In the Russian case, the Bolshevik party would monopolize power in the new Communist state, thus making the Soviets virtually powerless. On hindsight, Lenin's slogan—*All Power to the Soviets*—was a false sign, a lure that led the Russian proletariat into a blind alley. In Germany, the experience with Councils was rather different. Here, even the pretence was quickly extinguished by those Social Democratic Party leaders, Friedrich Ebert and Gustav Noske in particular, who seized the reigns of the revolution after it had triumphed over the ancien regime and quickly suppressed all revolutionary manifestations after December 1918.

There are two fundamental principles that must be clearly established and understood at the outset of any discourse about the role played by Councils in Germany. First: Councils were but one and by no means the most significant of the protagonists of the November 1918 German Revolution. Their activities, their impact on the events that were unfolding during this period were affected, and in many respects limited, not only by situational factors unique to Germany but by the necessity of having to share the stage of history with a number of other powerful actors.

Second: Contrary to what some apologists of the Councils claim, workers and soldiers in Germany were *not* acting as if they were parts of a single body. While the demands of the various participants in the German Revolution may have overlapped, and the motives which dragged them into revolutionary action may have been similar, the everyday life experiences of hundreds of thousands, nay, millions of German Council members, their understanding of, and predisposition to the class struggle, and their perception of the objectives of mass action, were often not only distinct but divergent.

The workers, sailors, and soldiers who organized themselves into Councils in

Germany did not do so according to a pre-existing, or centrally designed template. They were driven by their own experiences and circumstances. No one waved a magic wand over them. The German Councils rose spontaneously and in response to an un-scripted, un-choreographed movement by the German left and the activist milieus that came into play during the war. On November 9, 1918, and in the following days, uncertainty, improvisation, and discord about what has to be done were the rules rather than the exceptions in Berlin and throughout Germany.

The contrasting declarations of Philipp Scheidemann and Karl Liebknecht on November 9, 1918, already shows that progress towards establishing and sustaining a Republic of Councils in Germany—a *Räterepublik*—would not come easy. This chapter will examine a missed *rendezvous* with history. By focusing on the emergence of the Councils immediately prior to the November 1918 Revolution, it will help us to see more clearly the causes of the Councils' disempowerment by the end of 1918 to early 1919. The dice were already cast before the short-lived Bavarian Soviet Republic came into being in April 1919.[8] (We shall briefly return to this desperate attempt and the "March Action" of 1921 at the end of this chapter.)

The German Left and Activist Movements before 1918

During the last decades of the 19th century, the Social-Democratic Party of Germany (SPD) was *the* vanguard of the European and German left. It was recognized by most as the backbone of the Second International, which was founded in 1889. For decades, the SPD was the champion of the common people in Germany. It had no rival in that domain, and it consciously refused to join any of the governments of the day until 1890, when some of its leaders began to flirt with the idea of taking the parliamentary road to Socialism. This new strategy of pursuing the class struggle within the walls of the Reichstag and "waiting for the right moment" to act did not please everyone, especially not those in the radical wing of the SPD.[9]

The working class was the SPD's electoral base, but by the turn of the 20th century, the Party began to gain some votes from the ranks of the middle class as well.[10] While the Party had long been marginalized in the midst of right, centre-right, and conservative parties, the SPD suddenly became the dominant party in Parliament after the January 1912 elections. In the already belligerent atmosphere, fuelled by the arms race, which started in Europe in 1912, and by the increasing public support for the Kaiser's imperialist designs, the SPD at first opposed the idea of going to war. This was only natural given the ideological commitment of the Party and the Second International's own public condemnation of the war in 1912.

The resolute and principled stance of the SPD did not last very long. Pressured from all sides to stop its antiwar manifestations during the July crisis of 1914, the Party would vote for the credits needed by the government to mobilize the population for war.[11] Through a skilful propaganda drive, the government managed to convince most everyone that the war was to be a defensive one and that sending a whole generation to the *abattoirs* was in the national interest. The SPD was not alone in substituting patriotism for its internationalist commitments, many other socialist parties throughout Europe executed a similar *volta face* and under similar circumstances.[12] As Germany's own annexationist ambitions became apparent during the Reichstag sessions of 1915,[13] the real intent of this war, which the radical wing of the SPD never doubted or ceased to condemn, could no longer be ignored. Except for the latter, the leadership of the SPD, from July 1914, would unconditionally embrace the parliamentary game,[14] in order to preserve its new posture as a "respectable and patriotic party".

The next major challenge to the SPD's integrity came in 1916, when the Party would once again vividly contradict its earlier pacifist stance. 1916 was a difficult year for all of the nations at war in Europe. Peace movements began to gather greater momentum throughout the continent. Germany was no exception. The country was rapidly exhausting its reserves without any gain or advance in sight. The year 1917 did not start off showing any signs of improvement. In light of these growing difficulties, and the increasingly frequent expressions of anti-war sentiments, the SPD leadership began to waver. It put forth a rather half-hearted peace resolution on July 19, 1917, which carried no weight. Its cynicism was revealed just one day after it was passed. On July 20th the SPD would vote once again for a new round of war credits.[15] These contradictory signals should include those made by the Party during the spring of 1917, when it expelled some members for their participation in the anti-war movements, which consisted of strikes and protests often motivated by food and basic product shortages like coal.[16]

It is from the ranks of the excommunicated and dissident left of centre wing of the SPD that a new political party, the Independent Social Democratic Party of Germany (USPD) would be created in April 1917. This new socialist party came onto the political playing field just before the so-called "Bread Strikes" that were started by the rising anti-war movement in Germany. By founding a new party "in the interest of the working class", the USPD affirmed its opposition to the government, to the government's war policy, and to the SPD, which had endorsed those policies.[17]

Paradoxically, since it was the product of various opposition factions, the USPD would quickly reveal even more heterogeneity, or internal divisiveness, than the SPD. (To be fair, the USPD leadership was fully aware of its inability to present a consistent, coherent policy alternative.)[18] Its affiliates were the Spartacus Group, founded in January 1916,[19] which counted among its leaders Rosa Luxemburg and Karl Liebknecht, and the Revolutionary Shop Stewards (RSS). The RSS was an extra-parliamentary group, organized by shop stewards from the iron and metal-working industries who left the official Trade Union Movement dissatisfied with the low level of militancy shown by the latter.

Trade Unions were at the forefront of the workers' movement in Germany, but as elsewhere in Europe bureaucratization had set in by the turn of the century in Germany as well. Many of the unions became instruments for the domestication, rather than the radicalization, of the working class.[20] Most of the union bureaucracy came from the SPD in Germany and would therefore follow that party's moderate line rather than support the rank and file or their radical dissidents. The Revolutionary Shop Stewards arose in reaction to the central union bureaucracy's moderate political stance.

Though they were not seen as particularly close to each other, the RSS, the Spartacists, and the left-wing of the USDP would become the mainspring of virtually every major radical step taken by the German working classes by the beginning of 1917. And yet, it was the inability to agree on a common political strategy, ideology, and action plan that was the most characteristic feature of this loose alliance of radical political actors. As the parliamentarian wings would adopt increasingly moderate positions in response to the rising revolutionary tensions in the land, the extra-parliamentary factions would go in exactly the opposite direction. This disharmony reached its crescendo inside the Reichstag during those fateful November hours in 1918. By this time, the most significant bone of contention between them all was the role they would be willing to give to the Councils in the newly emerging Republican political arena. Let us now look at what this bone of contention, the Councils, stood for, and who spoke on their behalf.

The Councils in Germany before the November 1918 Revolution

Historians agree: Unlike in Russia, Councils as such did not exist in Germany prior to WWI. The majority of them came into being during the 1917 strikes and primarily in response to the impact of the war.[21] Scholars also agree, however, that the formation of Councils in Germany was accelerated by the demonstration effect of the 1917 Russian Revolution.[22] Let us examine more closely the rise of the German Council movement before looking at their demise.

Prior to WWI, fighting men in Europe did not come back from the various battlefields to turn on their rulers back home. In previous wars, they would follow their commanders to the battlefields, and the ones that came back alive would go back to their fields or factories, and resume their former lives. The war which started in 1914 changed all that. In this "Great Patriotic War", millions of peasants and workers were thrown into battle and perished quickly in the deadly cross-fires produced by the latest military technologies. The carnage, the wanton, senseless destruction of human lives that followed one hundred years of peace in

Europe, traumatized millions like never before and none more so than those who participated up front in this uncontrolled, mindless bloodletting.

While the war provided the context, it was the *volta face* and subsequent rupture of the SPD that diversified and flooded the political stage in Germany during WWI. In addition to the traditional party-political actors, hundreds of thousands of dissatisfied workers, peasants, soldiers and sailors would now climb onto the stage of history in order to give voice to their outrage, to register their just demands, and to take matters into their own hands. But while this flooding of the political arena was a Europe-wide phenomenon, it had a unique German current. It is this current that holds the key to understanding the direction taken by the German Council movement during WWI.

As the destructive and stalemated war carried on and central authorities in Germany became less and less effective in dealing with local circumstances, thousands of ordinary citizens, most of them industrial workers and sailors, would spontaneously reach out to each other to create small, local organizations—the Councils or *Räte*—for the protection and management of their common interests. While this process of local self-preservation was a direct consequence of the war, it was driven by the unique motivations, demands, and objectives of its members. As we have stated earlier, there was no central model, no all-encompassing schema indicating how to set up these Councils or program their agendas. The German Councils did not have a general staff or an overarching game-plan. They often behaved in a disjointed, unsynchronized manner, but this should not be taken to mean that they did not have a unique national character. *Au contraire*, Councils in Germany closely reflected the unique socio-economic characteristics of the German working classes. The German proletariat was in many respects different from its Russian, Hungarian, British, or other relatives on the continent. To understand the uniqueness of the German Council movement requires, in short, an understanding of the German proletariat's unique characteristics.

To begin with, the German working class before the war had a rather vague, and most certainly very different idea of the meaning of socialism than the neighbouring proletariat. To the German working class, socialism was a striving for justice. To German workers, a socialist was someone who struggled to eliminate the various forms of injustices felt in everyday life—at work, in society, and with regard to state power. Most observers agree that before and during the war Germany's workers did not conceive of socialism as the collective ownership of the means of production or the proletariat's control of production.[23] The strikers and street-protesters in Germany reacted to abuse and to the degradation of their working and living conditions as a consequence of the war.[24] Unlike elsewhere, the German proletariat was not driven by an omnipotent desire to go to war against the bourgeoisie because their bourgeoisie left them better off than their fellows in other parts of Europe.[25] While the German working class articulated political demands, it looked to achieve those through parliamentary democracy, not through the establishment of a proletarian dictatorship, the elimination of the private ownership of the means of production, or via the establishment of a socialist republic. They intended to improve the system, not to overthrow it.

Insurgent workers and sailors at the outset of the German Council movement did not contemplate the possibility that their committees could be bodies endowed with legislative, executive, and judicial powers.[26] This window of opportunity for the Councils in Germany would only open up during the fall of 1918, when all of a sudden they found themselves in the middle of a revolutionary fire that began to consume everything around them. Were they able to live up to this historic opportunity? The only way one can understand the answer to that question is by looking at how the Council movement came into being in Germany, what was, so to speak, its early childhood experience.

The first visible signs of efforts at autonomous, grassroots self-organization among Germany's workers and military personnel arises during the Bread Strikes of April 1917. This strike was motivated by a food shortage that followed that of the previous winter, and the adoption of the Auxiliary Service Law in December 1916. This new law compelled all workers to serve the armament industry, eliminated employees' right to choose their place of work or to quit their jobs, and cancelled all social and economic provisions granted by employers and the state before the war.[27] The government got the assent of the trade unions for this measure and the SPD did not lift a finger in defence of the workers.

The abandonment of the workers by their own Social Democratic/Trade Union leaders pushed the Revolutionary Shop Stewards (RSS) on the stage once again. This organization, which was already very active in the 1916 workers' protests, grew out of the munitions and metal-working industries and constituted an entirely new type of grassroots initiative, because it was not under the control of either the Trade Union or the SPD bureaucracy. The group's leader, Richard Müller, who organized the April 1917 strike, was arrested even before it broke out. His more compliant deputy, Adolf Cohen, would quickly cave to outside pressures for moderation. He tried to reign in the movement, dampen the fury of the protesters but their discontent was already too strong to be contained. In the absence of their trusted leader, the Shop Stewards followed their own impulses in 1917. They elected a small executive body to represent them and to gather and formulate their own demands without waiting for direction from the SPD or the Trade Unions. Eight factory delegates along with a representative of the unions' leadership and the metalworkers' leaders would form a commission to negotiate their demands with the authorities. They reiterated the pacifist demands first voiced in 1916, requested better food supplies and asked for the revocation of the

Auxiliary Service Law. They demanded an end to the state of siege and censorship. They also pressed for universal suffrage and the secret ballot.

Doubts have been expressed as to whether one could classify this first self-elected body in Berlin in 1917 as a Council. The existence of workers' councils in Leipzig by this time, however, is acknowledged. Their demands were very similar to those of their fellows in Berlin. During these events of April 1917, Luxemburg's and Liebknecht's Spartacists would also add their voices and organisational skills to support these spontaneous strike movements. The USDP, at the time, also advocated the pursuit of the strike. What became of these early radical initiatives? The 1917 unrests would eventually succumb to the military's call for order.[28]

There is significant consensus among historians that the January 28, 1918 General Strike, rather than the events of 1917, constitutes the start of the Council movement in Germany. Admittedly, the January 1918 events provide more persuasive, more conclusive evidence of the German proletariat's ability to engage in spontaneous, grassroots organizational activities than a year earlier. Be that as it may, the events that began in January 1918 also vividly exposed the growing divisiveness of the German left, the increasing opposition of the two socialist parliamentary parties to grassroots initiatives, the German proletariat's own wavering self-confidence in its own strength, and in its entitlement to taking matters into its own hands. Let's briefly review the dynamics of these countervailing forces since they hold the clue to the demise of the German Council movement and to the puzzling divergence of the revolution in Germany from the one in Russia, Hungary, or Austria.

Let's begin with the demands of the January 1918 protesters. They closely resemble those of the previous year. Central to them were once again demands for food and for the end of the state of siege. But there was a significant new demand this time: an end to the war and an end to annexationist schemes vis-á-vis the newly formed Workers' State to the East. (The Bolsheviks took Russia out of the war in 1917, and the peace negotiations between Germany and Russia began at Brest-Litovsk at the end of November 1917. Imperial Germany intended to impose harsh conditions on the new Communist country. The Bolsheviks launched a massive leaflet campaign to arouse the sympathies of the German proletariat. In fact, Russia's leaflet campaign—addressed to German soldiers and workers—intended to trigger revolutionary fever in their ranks and they proved to be highly effective.[29])

Apart from their support of the Russian Bolsheviks, the German strikers in January 1918 had come up with some additional items that did not serve on their earlier menus. They called for the restoration of the freedom of the press and universal suffrage that included women. They also pushed for a thorough democratization of the state apparatus.[30] There were, however, no demands for self-government, self-management, and the socialization of the economy, all features usually associated with Council movements elsewhere, most significantly in Russia.

It is acknowledged that the January Strike in Germany was orchestrated by the Revolutionary Shop Stewards in the armaments industries. It was also enthusiastically endorsed and supported by the Spartacists. The 400,000 workers who precipitated this strike by-passed the Trade Union and Party bureaucracies. They chose 400 representatives and set up a small Action Committee to lead this strike. As an afterthought (or as sign of their weak self-confidence), the delegates also invited the SPD and the USPD to send some representatives to the Action Committee deliberations, even though the leaders of these parties did not support the strike action. The Action Committees' gallant gesture opened the door to its own demise. Within days, the Action Committee would be declared illegal by the government. While the workers wanted to keep up the strike pressure, all the invited parliamentarians, including those from the USPD, would argue against it. The two parties' representatives would pressure the workers to break with their Action Committee, and put their fate in the hands of the General Committee of Trade Unions, and give up their autonomous fight. As this transfer of authority would have amounted to alienating the rank and file from its representatives, the Revolutionary Shop Stewards and their Action Committee refused to go along with this demand. But their barricades were already breached as a consequence of their own actions. Rather than having someone else speak for them, and in order to save face, they called off the strike themselves on February 3rd. This would prove to be the dress rehearsal for the grand retreat of November 1918.[31]

While the 1918 January strike was brutally crushed and may be seen as a pathetic failure for the German Council movement, it may also be seen as a critical step forward. Despite the obvious setback, these events also energized hundreds of thousands. They showed that the working classes are able to organize themselves from the ground up into a powerful social and political force. The strikers' ability to paralyse the armaments industry, even if for a short while, provided them with a heightened sense of empowerment. Their rising power and the fear they instilled in the Social Democratic political leadership of Germany is clearly acknowledged by Friedrich Ebert, the leader of the SPD, for whom the efforts by local workers' councils to take matters into their own hands was a recipe for a national disaster:

> The radical leadership had got the upper hand in the munition factories in Berlin. Supporters of our party, whom the radicals had terrorised into stopping work came to the Executive to ask it to send members into the strike leadership... I entered the strike leadership with the firmly-determined

intention of bringing the strike to an end as soon as possible, and in this way saving the country from disaster.[32]

This infiltration by the SPD of the initiatives from below would not remain an isolated case. From that point on, the Shop Stewards and the Spartacists would be forced to pursue their activities underground as waves of arrests would decimate their ranks right up until the autumn of 1918.[33] While the USPD was more radical in its approach than the SPD, its parliamentary representatives would also do their best to discredit anyone who would advocate the "dictatorship of the proletariat" and argue for a Republic of Councils.[34]

After the January strikes, and the ensuing repressions, two of the most active forces behind the establishment of politically driven workers' councils—the Revolutionary Shop Stewards and the Spartacists—temporarily lost connection with each other. They would only reconnect in the autumn of 1918, after Karl Liebknecht and Richard Müller were released from prison. This is when the Revolutionary Shop Stewards would begin to prepare for the revolutionary insurrection. By September, they were distributing leaflets and began to acquire weapons. They benefited from material support from the Russian Bolsheviks, with whom they had some contact.[35] They also organized a series of secret meetings throughout the fall, which welcomed some left-wing members of the USPD. The attendees would soon call themselves the Executive Committee of Workers' and Soldiers' Councils, or simply, the Workers' Council. This first general council anticipated the one they would organize during the November Revolution.[36]

By the fall of 1918, Rosa Luxemburg's and Liebknecht's Spartacists would take the lead in advocating for the formation of councils of workers and soldiers as political levers for the transition to Socialism. The Spartacists proclaimed their "solidarity with the Russian Soviet Republic". In their October 7 conference, they called for the expropriation of banks, mines, and factories, the abolition of the monarchy and of the German states (*Länder*). They announced that the task of implementing these revolutionary changes must be put into the hands of the Councils.[37] The Russian parallel was a recurring feature of their platform. Lenin reacted to the Spartacus' program on October 18, directly addressing himself to them:

Dear Comrades,
We have had news today that the Spartacus group, together with the
Bremen Left Radicals, has taken the most energetic steps to promote the
setting of Workers' and Soldiers' Councils throughout Germany.... The
propaganda work of the German Spartacus Group, which has carried on
systematic revolutionary propaganda in most difficult conditions, has really

saved the honour of German socialism and the German proletariat. Now the decisive hour is at hand: the rapidly maturing German revolution calls on the Spartacus Group to play the most important role. [38]

As events would shortly demonstrate, however, these hopes had very little foundation in reality. There was an obvious discrepancy between the Spartacists' confident call to form councils as organs of self-management and self-government, and the incertitude of the people who actually constituted the councils in Germany. Contrary to Lenin's conviction, the Spartacists would not be the main actors of this revolution. Their leaders would be murdered within a few months with the connivance of Germany's leading Socialist politicians.

Before turning to the climactic events of November-December 1918, a short pause is needed here in order to say a few words about the Council movement within the German armed forces.

Councils in the Armed Forces of Germany

Soldiers' Councils played important roles in Russia, in Hungary and elsewhere. What role, if any, did they play in the German Revolution? While Russia released German war prisoners into Germany at the end of 1917, these former prisoners did not figure largely in the German revolution like they did in Hungary.[39] Talking about *"Soldiers' Councils"* in the case of Germany is in fact somewhat misleading since they were organized almost exclusively by members of the German Navy. From the end of 1917, discipline broke down in the field army, the number of mutinies and desertions grew rapidly. Protests within the field army reached a high point when the High Command ordered the renewal of fighting after Germany was already defeated.[40] The fact is, most soldiers' councils were created rather late in the day, and most of them were infiltrated and manipulated by the High Command to deflate them.[41] This is why it was the sailors—who were, for the most part, kept out of action during the war—who became the most militant members of the German resistance within the German armed forces prior to November 1918.

The heightened revolutionary spirit of the German sailors may be explained by two other factors. First: Many of the sailors were, in fact, skilled workers with close ties to colleagues among the radicalized metalworking professions. Secondly: With the exception of the submarine core, the German navy experienced long periods of idleness throughout the war.[42] German sailors spent most of their time in the ports, among restless segments of the population rather than on the high seas. This force of circumstances enabled them to fraternize with their radicalized fellow workers. They had easier access to newspapers, leaflets, and revolutionary literature.[43] Many of them knew of and were inspired by the uprisings and protests within the shipyards themselves. For instance, the workers of the naval base in Kiel went on strike in March 1917, to protest against new cuts in flour rations after the harsh winter of 1916–1917.[44] Sailors would join the workers in Kiel, chanting "Long live Liebknecht!" And they would do so again during those fateful days in November 1918.[45] But we have to emphasise: the demands of the sailors, like those expressed by most of the German proletariat, were specific to their working environment. They did not spill over into demands for large-scale, revolutionary political change.

The sailors' mutinies of October and November 1918 occurred in a context full of possibilities, as the imperial regime was dying and steps toward a socialist transition were on the drawing board. Did the sailors who were at the forefront of this renewed militancy pursue a strategic political agenda in pursuit of socialism? The answer is no. As earlier, they were motivated, first and foremost, by resistance to power abuses and by the news that their officers were contemplating a last ditch effort to save face by throwing them into a senseless and suicidal action against the British Navy. In October-November 1918, Germany's sailors would organize themselves into sailors' councils. Within days, their movement would spread to a number of German cities triggering massive popular protests. By November 9, tens of cities had "turned red".[46]

Even if the sailors' councils have lit the revolutionary fire throughout Germany, with the exception of Berlin, these councils would not mutate into an enduring revolutionary political force. The "Fourteen Points" formulated by the Kiel's soldiers' council on the day it was officially created, on November 4, 1918, are representative of the aims and plans of the sailors.[47] Most of them were contextual and remind us of the demands voiced during episodes of unrest in 1917.[48] They asked for the release of arrested sailors and political prisoners, pleaded against reprisals, demanded more humane treatment from their officers, and asked for complete personal freedom when they were off duty. Even when they proclaimed that "political power has been placed in the hand of the soldiers", they did not go further than to ask for complete freedom of speech and an end to media censorship. Moreover, they expected the government of the day to implement their demands. They did not envision direct participation in the government or call for its replacement.[49] The presence of Gustav Noske from the SPD at this critical confrontation also must be noted. On November 5, Noske was elected chairman of the Sailors' Council. Two days later, and with the assent of the sailors, he would be appointed governor of Kiel.[50] The case of the Sailors' Councils vividly illustrates the problems which afflicted the German Council Movement from the onset and contributed to their early demise. Arnold Brecht, provides a succinct assessment:

When the Kiel soldiers thus suddenly held in their hands the power over the warships in the harbor and over the town, they did not know what to do next. Aimless and leaderless, they walked the streets. Then, Gustav Noske, Social Democratic expert on naval affairs, whom his party sent to Kiel on November 4 at the request of the (imperial) government, succeeded with great courage and skill in gaining control of the situation. The admiralty and the sailors willingly accepted him as governor of Kiel. Kiel was pacified.[51]

To be fair, there were some notable exceptions to the above. On November 7, 1918, the day Noske became governor, some dissenting soldiers and workers of Kiel formed a common council and established a provisional provincial government in Schleswig-Holstein. "Political power lies in our hands", they declared. They announced that their goal "is a free, socially-minded people's republic". The "new order" would be established "in cooperation with the existing authorities". They added that "an old democratic dream of freedom and unity, for which many of the best of you fought and suffered, will now become reality on a new and higher level".[52]

Whether the workers' and soldiers' council of Kiel intended to build a socialist republic in the full sense of the word is, however, open to discussion, as everyone at this time, even the most conservative minded elements, used the language of socialism to rally support and to demonstrate their affinity for the working classes in order to promote their own political agendas. No one did this more effectively than Noske and Ebert, the two "Socialist" leaders who probably commissioned the murder of two of the most active supporters of the German Council movement—Rosa Luxemburg and Karl Liebknecht.

To conclude: Germany's experience with Councils prior to the November 9, 1918 revolution was very different from that of Russia or even Hungary. While agitators and strikers in 1917 and 1918 did not hesitate to invoke revolutionary events in Russia to inflame the revolutionary fervour of Germany's workers and sailors, the emergence of Councils in Germany occurred under different cultural, and socio-economic circumstances. In Russia, councils were provided with an opportunity to fill a political void in February 1917. In Germany, such an option was not even on the drawing board. The Soviets had a pre-war history in Russia. They reappeared as soon as the Tsar fell, and were expected to be organs of self-government and self-management in the strongest sense, from the outset.[53] This was not so in the case of Germany. In Germany, the Councils were discouraged from aspiring to a leadership role in the transition to socialism by the parliamentary wing of the SPD/USPD. They were restricted to articulating more limited and immediate aims. The first noticeable shift in this posture only came in the fall of 1918, but this shift was far too late and did not possess sufficient force or conviction. While the Councils in Germany after the January 1918 events increased in numbers, they would not take on an overt political stance until virtually all of the cards were stacked against them.

The End-Game

It is often forgotten that a "republicanisation" process was already underway in Germany weeks before the November 11, 1918 armistice. This was a precondition required by the Entente to start peace negotiations. It is this "logic" that drives the Emperor's appointment of Prince Maximilian of Baden as his new, "liberal" chancellor on October 3, 1918. It was the Prince's task to lead Germany's transition into a new, post-war political realignment and save its political establishment from total annihilation. The appointment for the first time, of social-democrats to the German cabinet, was also a key element of this new political strategy. It is important to point out: a bourgeois-democratic republic was not the only alternative in this game plan. A renewed constitutional monarchy was an equally plausible option. The one option all of the mainstream players rejected outright was a Socialist Republic of Councils. They saw that option as a descent into chaos and disorder.

When news of the Emperor's abdication reached Berlin on November 9, as the huge strike planned for weeks by the RSS and the Spartacists was taking place, Prince Maximilian appointed Friedrich Ebert, the Chairman of the SPD as his successor in the position of Chancellor. He did so with the clear intention of using him and his party to save the last remnants of the monarchy. In hindsight, this was not at all a farfetched idea—Ebert would have been happy if Germany remained a constitutional monarchy.[54] This may explain why he was so furious with his socialist colleague, Philipp Scheidemann, who jumped the gun without consulting with him by proclaiming the end of the Monarchy and setting Germany on a Republican path.[55] Ebert was even less inclined to call this Republic a "socialist" one as Karl Liebknecht did that afternoon. But Liebknecht was guilty of a bigger crime in the eyes of Friedrich Ebert and the German political establishment. He and his colleagues were already circulating leaflets in which they called for the establishment of a Republic of Councils.[56] For the leader of the SPD and the majority of the USPD's parliamentary deputies this was the last straw. They went on the offensive by using the only weapon they thought might save them: the language of the Councils and Socialism.

Two camps faced each other, locked in a pitched battle on November 9. On the one side were the proponents of a Socialist Republic of Councils led by Karl Liebknecht, the Spartacists and the Revolutionary Shop Stewards. Their game-plan for proclaiming a Republic of Councils was in Liebknecht's pocket by the afternoon of November 9.[57] Soldiers' councils were meeting in the Reichstag, discussing the course of the revolution in a highly charged and turbulent atmosphere. Emil Barth and Richard Müller, from the Revolutionary Shop Stewards, took the lead in this debate in the assembly. Müller proposed the election of workers' and soldiers' councils in Berlin and to hold the first meeting of their representatives the following day. This was clearly an issue of power and governance.[58] As Ernst Däumig, a Revolutionary Shop Steward and USPD member would declare a few days later, the crucial question for their side was crystal clear: "Did we fight for a bourgeois-democracy or a socialist republic?... Power must be in the hands of those who fought for it". It must be vested "in the system of workers' and soldiers' councils".[59]

The second camp, composed exclusively of parliamentarians, decided to go into battle wearing a mask. They knew that their goal—a bourgeois-democratic republic—can only be attained if they disguise themselves, if they execute an elaborate affinity-fraud, by pretending to favour the Councils and grassroots organizing. In spite of their uneasy relations, the SPD and USPD leaders agreed to form a provisional "workers' government" based on a coalition of six members, three from each party. They called this "workers' government" *The Council of Peoples' Representatives*. The choice of the word "council" by the SPD-USDP strategists was purposeful—they used it to take the wind out of the sails of their adversaries.

In a proclamation issued three days later, this bi-partisan, provisional government would go even further in its misleading rhetorical offensive: "The government which has emerged from the revolution, the political leadership of which is purely socialist, has set itself the task of putting into effect a socialist programme".[60] While these "socialist" parliamentarians, and Friedrich Ebert in particular, were die-hard opponents of a socialist revolution from below, they were realistic enough to know that they could not stop it. As Richard Müller of the Revolutionary Shop Stewards would later observe, they jumped on the bandwagon in order to stop it. They generated political capital for themselves by appearing to show an affinity for the workers' and soldiers' demands.[61] As Liebknecht would also point out, the parliamentarians "ran to catch up because they feared that the mighty movement of the people would surge past them".[62] This duplicitous strategy did not fool everyone, as illustrated by the nickname— Radish—given to Ebert by his opponents (meaning, he was "red on the outside, white on the inside").[63]

Once they saw through the SPD-USPD affinity-fraud, Richard Müller and Karl Liebknecht decided not to support the provisional government headed by The Council of People's Representatives (CPR). They pushed through another resolution entrusting the Workers' and Soldiers' Councils with all executive, legislative, and judicial power. This new arrangement would have subordinated the CPR and the SPD-USPD parliamentary coalition forces to the Councils. To settle the matter, a meeting by 3,000 delegates of all the Councils would be held the following day at Circus Busch, where the six representatives of the coalition committee would also be elected.[64]

Space does not allow us to go at length into the elaborate manoeuvring that enabled the SPD-USPD forces to gain control of the momentous debate of November 10, 1918. Even though the future of the German Republic would only be officially settled in December, the fate of the Republic of Council option and of the German Council Movement was sealed on November 10, 1918. It is essential to underscore that while Councils were grassroots organizations, and were supposedly independent of Germany's political parties, they were, in fact, thoroughly infiltrated by activists of the SPD-USPD from the outset. This infiltration would prove fatal during those few hours when they had a real chance to seize power. The majority of the "Council" delegates to the momentous November 10th assembly were SPD-USPD activists.[65] They voted against the Spartacists' and Revolutionary Shop Stewards' alternative.[66] The latter's intense agitation in the following weeks against the holding of a Constituent Assembly, which would confirm Germany's transformation into a bourgeois parliamentary republic, and their struggles against the violence and acts of sabotage organized against them by Ebert and his accomplices would all be in vain.

After the November 10 meeting at Circus Busch, the Army threw its support behind the Council of the Peoples' Representatives against the forces advocating a Republic of Councils. Chancellor Ebert and General Groener decided to create a mutual assistance pact. Ebert pledged that in return for military support:

> ...the government would act to fight Bolshevism and the power of the councils and that it would support an early election for a National Assembly that would lay the basis for a representative parliamentary democracy.[67]

The "Executive Committee of the Greater Berlin Workers' and Soldiers' Councils" created on November 10 was supposed to share power with the CPR until December, but it was never allowed to do so. There was nothing like a "dual power" in Germany, even for a while, as in Russia after the February Revolution.[68] In Russia, the Soviets were a serious competing power from the start. In Germany, the Councils never had a chance. Rosa Luxemburg herself acknowledged this fact in a dramatic manner:

> On November 9, the first cry of the revolution, as instinctive as the cry of a newborn child, was for Workers' and Soldiers' Councils. This was our common rallying cry, and it is through the councils alone that we can hope

to realize Socialism. But it is characteristic of the contradictory aspects of our revolution… that at the very time when this great, stirring, and instinctive cry was being uttered, the revolution was so inadequate, so feeble, so devoid of initiative, so lacking in clearness as to its own aims, that on November 10 our revolutionists allowed nearly half the instruments of power they had sized on November 9 to slip from their grasp.…

The primary illusion of the workers and soldiers who made the revolution was their belief in the possibility of unity under the banner of what passes by the name of Socialism. What could be more characteristic of the internal weakness of the revolution of November 9 than the fact that at the very outset the leadership passed in no small part into the hands of persons— Ebert, Scheidemann, and [Hugo] Haase—who, a few hours before the revolution broke out, had regarded it as their chief duty to issue warnings against revolution, to make the revolution impossible.[69]

The stinging defeat of the Councils in Germany in November-December 1918 would not end quietly. It was followed by demonstrations and episodes of social unrest, which would reach a high point with the so-called "Bloody Christmas" of 1918 (an armed confrontation between sailors and soldiers on the morning of December 24, which become a bloodbath when workers would also be dragged in the *mêlée*). These and other events would cause a great stir in the ranks of the left, but would not fundamentally alter the outcome of the German revolution. The tragic events of December solidified the power of the SPD and led to a new split within the ranks of the left, as more radical elements of the USPD and the Spartacists created a new revolutionary party, the German Communist Party (KPD), eager to pursue the "socialist class struggle".[70]

In the "Founding Manifesto" of the KPD, Luxemburg declared that the distinctive character of the revolutions of the present and the future is the formation of workers' and soldiers' councils. In her view, extending the system of workers' councils "in all directions", was the key to halting the gathering counterrevolution in Germany:

We must make the masses realize that the Workers' and Soldiers' Council has to be the central feature of the machinery of the state, that it must concentrate all power within itself and that it must utilize all powers for the one great purpose of bringing about the socialist revolution. Those workers who are already organized to form workers' and soldiers' councils are still very far from having adopted such an outlook, and only isolated proletarian minorities are as yet clear as to the tasks that devolve upon them. The masses must learn how to use power—by using power.[71]

Unfortunately, the German revolution did not live up to Rosa Luxemburg's high hopes. In spite of the admirable and resolute struggles before and after November 9, 1918, the historical opportunity Luxemburg talked about, had passed.[72] She and her comrade, Karl Liebknecht, were murdered on January 15, 1919, after the so-called "Spartacist Uprising", by the far-right paramilitary *Freikorps*, which cooperated with the SPD led government in this and subsequent acts of aggression against the German working class. The *Freikorps* and the German army would implement a "White terror" throughout the country between 1919 and 1923, brutally crushing waves of revolts, popular protests, and strikes.

Armed struggles between the right and the left would become common in Germany[73] and would be decisive in crushing the ephemeral Republic of Councils founded in Bavaria on April 7, 1919. The Bavarian Republic was founded on November 7, 1918, but the SPD's resolute opposition to the participation of councils in the central government delayed the implementation of a councilsystem in Bavaria. The "Bavarian Soviet Republic" proclaimed the "dictatorship of the proletariat" after "the example of the Russian and Hungarian nations".[74] It was set up in a highly chaotic atmosphere after right-wing forces murdered Kurt Eisner, who headed the Bavarian government since November and was an advocate of the councils but had to abide until then by the SPD's will. The Bavarian Soviet Republic was plagued from the outset by the strength of the right-wing in Bavaria and Germany and by the polarization of the forces on the left. The Bavarian Republic of Councils had two governments during its three weeks of existence. Both succumbed to assaults launched by the SPD-led central government. The KPD's Red Guards would be defeated on May 1 by a massive attack of *Freikorps* and German troops sent to Bavaria by Noske. A thousand people died in the fighting. The Communist leaders were arrested, many were executed. Bavaria quickly became a bastion of right-wing political radicalism.[75] By this time, Hitler's party was already in existence and actively engaged in planting the seeds of the Third Reich.[76]

The right and the left would fight another harsh battle in March 1920. Their shared hatred for the SPD led-government reached a climax after the negotiation of the Versailles Peace Treaty. There would be a serious putsch attempt from the right by Wolfgang Kapp, supported by the *Freikorps* and army troops to overthrow the central government. The March Action of 1921, by comparison with Kapp's putsch, was child's play. This was triggered by isolated conflicts between mine workers and their employers in the industrial region of Prussian Saxony. It had a very limited impact on the rest of the country. The KPD[77] tried to turn these protests into a general revolutionary upheaval in pursuit of the strategy dictated by the Comintern after its Second World Congress of 1920, but it was bound to fail. (Both Béla Kun and Mátyás Rákosi would play a limited role in the so-called

March Action in Germany as Comintern agents, only to be chastised later by Lenin as putschists who failed to deliver.)

The councils born in the midst of the November 1918 Revolution in Germany would survive for a few more years, but the government would make sure to emasculate them. Their enshrinement in the Weimar Constitution, drafted in January 1919, was "not a gift, but a Trojan horse" as Ernst Däuming would later observe. "Making councils elements of a capitalist constitution means to strangulate, or at least paralyze any serious implementation of the council idea".[78] For a time, councils would remain useful tools of self-legitimization, until the last remnants of the socialist atmosphere of the November Revolution have vanished, and following the Bavarian example, overtly conservative and fascistic forces came to monopolize Germany's political arena.

Conclusions

The revolutionary leaders of Germany—people like Rosa Luxemburg, Karl Liebknecht, Ernst Däumig or Richard Müller—conceived of the Councils as the only effective counterweight to German Capitalism, the power of the German imperial elite and the bourgeoisie. But the Councils in Germany failed to match these expectations because the main actors of the German revolution, the workers, the sailors, the soldiers, in most cases, did not share this view. Of course, the intrigues of the political and military establishment share a great deal of the responsibility for this as well.

Beyond false consciousness and fraudulent political intrigues of the Socialist parties in Germany, one has to also acknowledge the structural factors that hindered the realization of Luxemburg's dreams for Germany. It is undeniable: the working class, broadly speaking, was better off in Germany than in any other European country at the time. Since the German working class had more than their chains to lose, they were not ready to risk everything. Between 1916 and 1918, workers rose up because of the pressures generated by longer work days, degrading working conditions, and food supply shortages. The specific hardships suffered by sailors and soldiers have to be added to the list. War has been exhausting for those on the home front no less than for those who fought or were on the vessels. Once the fever of the first days of November fell, the insurgents were clearly more concerned with food supplies, and a quick return to a stable and normal state of affairs, than with fomenting the world revolution and prolonging thereby their own suffering. The ruling SPD-USPD coalition and the Trade Union leadership fully understood this sentiment and structured their communications strategies and policy initiatives accordingly. The Council of the People's Representatives was eager to pass legislation satisfying the most pressing public demands in the very first days after the storm of November 9. It thus bargained for social peace, and its policy measures offered concrete proof of its capacity to facilitate the return to normalcy.

International pressures, whose importance is often overlooked, were also a strong impediment to the development of conciliar power in Germany. The Entente required that Germany become a republic before it would start peace negotiations with her. The victorious powers were also getting ready to decide what price they would make Germany pay for the casualties, the destruction she brought upon them all during the previous years. Clearly, it was in Germany's national interest to stabilize its domestic socio-political climate as fast as possible. Bolshevism was the worst nightmare of the Entente, and it was actively engaged in trying to crush the Communists in Russia at this time. Trying to replicate the Russian experience would have been suicidal in this context. The Entente let the Germans know privately and publicly that they would only negotiate with a bourgeois republic that embraced rather than rejected Capitalism.

As we have shown throughout this chapter, the Councils in Germany did not even consider themselves serious contenders for overarching political power until the eleventh hour. Even some of their strongest advocates have admitted as much.[79] Unfortunately, by the time they came to possessing such aspirations all the cards were stacked against them. The Social Democratic political establishment and the German Trade Union leadership were as opposed to this idea as the national and international bourgeoisie. They could not rise above their role as colourful, but tragically ineffective actors in a drama during which Germany shed its imperial, monarchical skin, took on that of a bourgeois republic, only to exchange that for a more ferocious, Fascist one. While the project of a council republic in Germany failed, its ghost has haunted German social and political theory for a long time afterwards. To this day, this German tragedy provides us with rich material for thinking about political alternatives to those systems that urge us to place our future into the unseen hands of unregulated market forces.

NOTES

1   Broué Pierre, *The German Revolution 1917-1923* (Chicago, IL: Haymarket Books, 2005), 209-210.

2   See Gaard Kets and James Muldoon, *The German Revolution and Political Theory* (Cham, Switzerland: Palgrave MacMillan, 2019), 1-2.

3   David Priestland, *The Red Flag: a History of Communism* (New York, NY: Grove Press, 2009), 52.

4   Gaard Kets, and James Muldoon, "The "Forgotten" German Revolution: A Conceptual Map", in Kets and Muldoon, *op.cit.*, 2-3.

5   Marc Ferro, *Des Soviets Au Communisme Bureaucratique*, 2nd ed. (Paris, France: Gallimard, 1980), 33-40.

6   Ernst Däumig, "The Council Idea and its Realization" (written in 1920), in Gabriel Kuhn, ed., *All Power to the Councils! A Documentary History of the German Revolution of 1918–1919* (Oakland, CA: PM Press, 2012), 51.

7   Paul Mazzocchi, "Insurgent Democracy and the German Councils", in Kets and Muldoon, *op. cit.*, 277-297.

8   As this chapter focuses on the November Revolution in Berlin, the preceding context will concentrate on the developments connected to these events. Specific cases like Bavaria will be left aside.

9   Priestland, *The Red Flag*, op.cit., 52-58. After the expiration of the Anti-Socialist Law, which made the party illegal in the Reichstag from 1878 to 1890, the SPD advocated this strategy to be more visible and strengthen its popular support (see Jonathan Sperber, "The Social Democratic Electorate in Imperial Germany" in David E. Barclay and Eric D. Weitz eds., *Between Reform and Revolution: German Socialism and Communism from 1840 to 1990* (New York, NY: Berghahn Books, 2005), 167-168.

10   Sperber, "The Social Democratic Electorate," 182, 186–187.

11   Heinrich Winkler, *Histoire de l'Allemagne XIXe-XXe siècle. Le long chemin vers l'Occident*, transl. Odile Demange (Paris: Fayard, 2005), 284–286.

12   Priestland, *The Red Flag*, 59-60.

13   "Opposition within the SPD (June 19, 1915)", in *GHDI, German History in Documents and Images*. Collection of primary source materials. http://ghdi.ghidc.org/sub_document.cfm?document_id= 963. Consulted on July 27, 2019.

14   James A. McAdams, *Vanguard of the Revolution. The Global Idea of the Communist Party*, (Princeton—Oxford, NJ: Princeton University Press, 2017), 106–107, 110–111. Rosa Luxemburg, *The Crisis in the German Social Democracy* (New York, NY: H. Fertig, 1969). is important in this respect.

15   Winkler, *Histoire de l'Allemagne*, 296–299.

16   "The Independent Social Democratic Party of Germany: Guiding Principles (April 1917)", *GHDI*, http://ghdi.ghi-dc.org/sub_document.cfm?document_id=969. Consulted on July 27, 2019.

17   "The Independent Social Democratic Party".

18   "The Independent Social Democratic Party".

19   The foundations of the Spartacus Group were laid a year earlier, in the midst of the internal battle within the SPD. Luxemburg and Liebknecht among others organized a faction called "International Group" which opposed itself to the party's support of the war (McAdams, *Vanguard of the Revolution*, 111).

20   Ralf Hoffrogge, *Working-Class Politics in the German Revolution: Richard Müller, the Revolutionary Shop Stewards and the Origins of the Councils Movement*, Keady, Joseph J., transl., (Leiden: Brill, 2015), 39.

21   The importance of the pre-November 1918 has been pointed out in recent research, for instance Hoffrogge, *Working-Class Politics*, Chapters 4-5 (especially p.35–71); Mazzocchi, "Insurgent Democracy and the German Councils", 286–287.

22   On the influence of these events on skilled workers, see Broué, *The German Revolution*, op.cit., 90-93, 95-96, 100–102; on workers in naval yards and sailors, see Michael Epkenhans, "'Red Sailors' and the Demise of the German Empire", in Christopher Bell and Bruce Elleman, eds., *Naval Mutinies of the Twentieth Century. An International Perspective* (London: Routledge, 2003), 80-105.

23   Eric D. Weitz, *Creating German Communism, 1890-1990. From Popular Protest to Socialist State* (Princeton: Princeton University Press, 1997), 51.

24   This is true of the workers and sailors, but also of soldiers. See Scott Stephenson, *The Final Battle. Soldiers of the Western Front and the German Revolution of 1918* (Cambridge:, Cambridge University Press, 2009), 53-55..

25   See Hoffrogge, *Working-Class Politics*, 63; Weitz, *Creating German Communism*, 22-35. (On prewar conditions).

26   These are general characteristics of the councils; see Mazzocchi, "Insurgent Democracy and the German Councils," 292.

27   On these prewar conditions, see Eric D. Weitz, *Creating German Communism*, op.cit., 22-35; on the changes during the war, 64-74.

28   Hoffrogge, *Working-Class Politics*, 39-43; Broué, *The German Revolution*, 92-96.

29   Broué, *The German Revolution*, 101–102. A journal, *Die Fackel* (*The Torch*), was also distributed on the front.

30 Hoffrogge, *Working-Class Politics*, 46-50.

31 Hoffrogge, *Working-Class Politics*, 49-57; Broué, *The German Revolution*, 103–108.

32 Quoted in Broué, *The German Revolution*, 108.

33 Hoffrogge, *Working-Class Politics*, 61.

34 Broué, *The German Revolution*, 131.

35 On the hypothesis of financial support and arm supply; see Hoffrogge, *Working-Class Politics*, 64-65. As early as October 1918, Lenin expressed his wish to see the Russian workers support their German fellows, especially by providing extra food supplies and soldiers; see Lenin's letter to Y.M Sverdlov and Lev Trotsky (October 1st, 1918) and his address of October 3 meeting of the leading bodies of the state. (See: John Riddell, ed., *The German Revolution and the Debate on Soviet Power. Documents: 1918-1919. Preparing the Founding Congress*, New York: Pathfinder. 1986, 48-52.)

36 Hoffrogge, *Working-Class Politics*, 61-62.

37 Broué, *The German Revolution*, 131–132.

38 Lenin, *Complete Works*, 35, 369, quoted in Riddell, John, ed., *The German Revolution and the Debate on Soviet Power. Documents: 1918–1919. Preparing the Founding Congress*, New York, Pathfinder, (1986), 55-56. Lenin also sent a congratulatory telegram to Karl Liebknecht after he was released from prison, on October 21, and the Soviet ambassador Joffe held a spectacular reception for him (Broué, *The German Revolution*, 132).

39 German soldiers on the Western front have not had the opportunities to "fraternize" with the Russians as their fellow in the East. The latter were called "Bolsheviki", a name evoking the influences they absorbed in this experience (Scott Stephenson, *The Final Battle. Soldiers of the Western Front and the German Revolution of 1918* (Cambridge, Cambridge University Press, 2009) 31, 43.

40 See Stephenson, *The Final Battle*, 17–18, 27, 45-50, 60-66.

41 See Stephenson, *The Final Battle*, 117–119, 129–134.

42 On the German navy's situation during the war; see Epkenhans, "Red Sailors", 80, 86-87.

43 Broué, *The German Revolution*, 97-98. Suggests that these ties have been decisive, but recent studies and source material nuance this picture.

44 Epkenhans, "Red Sailors," 90.

45 See for instance "The Wilhelmshaven Revolt. A Chapter in the History of the Revolutionary Movement in the German Navy, 1918–1919," in Gabriel Kuhn, ed. and transl., *All Power to the Councils! A Documentary History of the German Revolution of 1918-1919* (Oakland: PM Press, 2012), 6,9.

46 On these events, see Epkenhans, "Red Sailors," 86-87, 94–101.

47 "The Kiel Sailors' Revolt: Fourteen Points Raised by the Soldiers' Council (November 4, 1918)," *GHDI*, http://ghdi.ghi-dc.org/sub_document.cfm?document_id=3939. Consulted on July 31, 2019.

48 See Epkenhans, "Red Sailors," 90-91. Broué, *The German Revolution*, 98, 100.

49 "The Kiel Sailors' Revolt." A proclamation of the Munich Soldiers' Council of November 12 also reflects this focus on practical and contextual demands (quoted in Stephenson, *The Final Battle*, 123).

50 Epkenhans, "Red Sailors," 99.

51 As all retrospective accounts, Arnold Brecht's testimony may be considered with caution, but subsequent developments would confirm most of his observations. "Arnold Brecht on the November Revolution (Retrospective Account, 1966)," *GHDI*, http://ghdi.ghi-dc.org/sub_document.cfm?document_id=3821. Consulted on July 31, 2019. The text of the Fourteen Points rather indicates that Noske arrived late in the evening on November 3 ("The Kiel Sailors' Revolt").

52 "Appeal to the People of Schleswig-Holstein (November 7, 1918)", *GHDI*, Acessed on July 31, 2019. http://ghdi.ghi-dc.org/sub_document.cfm?document_id=3938.

53 In Russia, the « resurrection » of the Petrograd Soviet in 1917 responded to political needs from the onset. It gathered workers', soldiers', and citizens' representatives, along with members from each socialist party and other statesmen (testimony of Mstislvaski, from the left wing of the social revolutionaries, quoted in Marc Ferro, *Des soviets au communisme bureaucratique* (Paris: Gallimard, 2nd ed. 2017), 41-48.)

54 "Arnold Brecht on the November Revolution".

55 See Scheidemann's testimony, quoted in Hoffrogge, *Working-Class Politics*, 69, note 25.

56 Broué, *The German Revolution*, 145.

57 See Richard Müller," Democracy or Dictatorship," *All Power to the Councils!*, (1925), 70.

58 Hoffrogge, *Working-Class Politics*, 72-73.

59 "Ernst Däumig Advocates the Council System and Argues Against Summoning a Constituent Assembly, 16 November 1918", in Ben Fowkes, *The German Left and the Weimar Republic. A Selection of Documents*, (Chicago, IL: Haymarket Books, 2014), 48.

60 Fowkes, "Proclamation of the Council of People's Representatives," *The German Left* (November 12, 1918), 17.

61 Müller, "Democracy or Dictatorship," 59.

62 Liebknecht, Karl, "Was will der Spartakusbund", *in Gesammelte Reden*, 649-662, reproduced in Riddell, *The German Revolution and the Debate on Soviet Power*, 195.

63 Stephenson, *The Final Battle*, 114, note 16.

64 Hoffrogge, *Working-Class Politics*, 73.

65 Broué, *The German Revolution*, 158.

66 See Hoffrogge, *Working-Class Politics*, 76-80, 83, Broué, *The German Revolution*, 153–154.

67 Scott Stephenson, *The Final Battle*, (2009), 119–120. The details of this alliance were only revealed during the "stab-in-the-back" trial (told by Arnold Brecht; see note above); see a similar declaration from Groener's *Lebenserinnerungen*, quoted in Broué, *The German Revolution*, 169.

68 See Stephen A. Smith, "The Revolutions of 1917–1918," *The Cambridge History of Russia. Volume 3: the Twentieth Century*, Ronald Suny ed., Cambridge—New York, Cambridge University Press, (2008), 115–116.

69 Rosa Luxemburg, "Founding Manifesto of the Communist Party of Germany (KPD,) 1918," in Kaes, Anton, Jay, Martin, and Dimendberg, Edward, eds., *The Weimar Republic Sourcebook* (Berkeley—Los Angeles—London: University of California Press), 43-44. Ernst Däumig had a similar reading of the events ("The Council Idea and its Realization," *All Power to the Councils!* (1920), 53-54.

70 "Resolution on Founding the Communist Party of Germany," 216.

71 Rosa Luxemburg, "Founding Manifesto of the Communist Party of Germany (KPD,) 1918," in Anton Kaes, Martin Jay, and Edward Dimendberg, eds., *The Weimar Republic Sourcebook* (Berkeley – Los Angeles – London: University of California Press.1994), 43-44. Ernst Daumig had a similar reading of the events (See: "The Council Idea and its Realization" in Kuhn, *All Power to the Councils!* Op.cit., 53-54.

72 Hoffrogge, *Working-Class Politics*, 80, 87.

73 Eric D. Weitz, "German Communism", in Silvio Pons, and Stephen A Smith, eds *The Cambridge History of Communism. Volume 1: World Revolution and Socialism in One Country 1917-1941* (Cambridge: Cambridge University Press, 2017), 580-581. After Germany was defeated the High Command still wanted to continue the carnage.

74 See Fowkes, "Proclamation of the Bavarian Council of Republic, 7 April 1919," *The German Left*, 62-63.

75 Gavriel D. Rosenfeld, « Monuments and the Politics of Memory: Commemorating Kurt Eisner and the Bavarian Revolutions of 1918–1919 in Postwar Munich », *Central European History*, 30, 2, p.225–227; *All Power to the Councils!* 169.

76 The first political program of his party was drafted in 1920 (reproduced and translated in French in Richard Overy, *Chroniques du IIIe Reich* (Bruxelles: Ixelles, 2012), 22–25.

77 In December 1920, the KPD and the left faction of the USPD merged into the VKPD, the United Communist Party of Germany, simply called KPD from July 1921.

78 Däumig, "The Council Idea and its Realization", 55.

79 Vrousalis recently suggested that most dissenting elements, especially in the USPD, would have considered the councils and the parliamentary system as complementary, albeit in different ways. This idea is condensed in the concept of "council Erfurtianism" (Vrousalis, Nicholas, 2019). « Revolutionary Principles and Strategy in the November Revolution: The Case of the USPD », in *The German Revolution and Political Theory*, 114).

CHAPTER 3

Workers' Councils and the 1919 Hungarian Commune

Lajos Csoma

Introduction

Between 1917 and 1923, a wave of revolutions swept through Europe and many parts of the world. The primary aim of these revolutions was to put an end to the reign of those who engineered the four year-long massacre, known as World War I. Many of these revolutions were also committed to transforming their societies into ones that were based on communal values rather than on personal greed, private profit, exploitation, and imperial expansionism. These revolutions formed a chain of events that were closely connected to one another, from Argentina to Mexico, from Iran to Egypt, from Finland to Italy. The starting point of this global phenomenon was the 1917 Russian Revolution. Its end in 1923 was marked by the Bulgarian uprisings, the fall of the Labour Governments in Saxony and Thuringia, and the defeat of the Hamburg Uprising. To repeat: This global chain of events was ignited by the outbreak of WW1 and its catastrophic consequences everywhere.

The primary demand of these revolutions, which was in fact rallying cry as well, was "peace". In Russia, the revolutionary events in November 1917 swept away the Provisional Government that emerged after the downfall of the Tsar. The Provisional Government owes its downfall to its explicit desire to continue Russia's participation in the war. This was the pattern everywhere. The first revolutionary step in all of the countries that belonged to the Central Powers was a declaration to end the war. It was the rebellion of the German sailors that ended Germany's pursuit of the war, after which the imperial system collapsed in a matter of days. It was only after this collapse that the question of "what next" comes onto the German policy-making agenda. The German scenario was repeated elsewhere, including Hungary. It was defeat on the battlefront, and the enormous price ordinary citizens had to pay for the senseless carnage, that swept away the great Central and Eastern European empires.

In general, when the central political power, the State, is shaken, it produces civil unrest and rebelliousness, especially in cases where the state was seen to be oppressive and unjust. This is why the fall of the imperial, tsarist dynasty was followed by newer and newer revolutionary waves of unrest that spread to the furthest parts of Russia. Within a matter of weeks, "thousands of spontaneously organized councils ('soviets') popped up throughout that country" [1] and news of the Russian Revolution spread around the world like a wildfire. The organized labour movements had been waiting for this signal everywhere for decades. When it came, it affected in various ways not only the working classes but many of those who were, one way or another, politically active. The revolutionary fervor was especially strong in Central and Eastern Europe. As Hobsbawm writes: "The revolutions swept away all systems from Vladivostok to the Rhine". [2]

Most people greeted these events within the affected countries with a sense of hopefulness. After the hopelessness of the war, all strata of society expected something positive from these revolutionary changes sweeping through this part of the world. This was certainly the case in Hungary, a country that was Austria's partner in the Austro-Hungarian Monarchy.

It cannot be emphasized enough: The level of socio-economic development across this enormous revolutionary landscape separating Vladivostok from the Rhine was not at all uniform and showed a great deal of diversity. The capitalist mode of production (wage labour, market economy) and its technology (large-scale industrial production) was dominant in the western part of Europe and was rapidly spreading eastward. The level of development in the central and eastern parts of Europe was, however, highly fragmented and uneven. Unlike the western part of the continent, there were huge developmental gaps here between the cities and the countryside. There were isolated, island-like hubs of industrial development that were surrounded by vast seas of agricultural backwardness, nowhere more so than in Russia. Hungary was no exception to this pattern, which constituted a veritable "clash of civilizations": rapidly and mindlessly industrializing urban centers encircled by hostile feudal and semi-feudal forces, rightfully fearful of the disruptive transformations coming their way but weakened by their own internal contradictions.

Expectations of what was to follow after the collapse of the old order, were not uniform. The political, economic, and intellectual elites in most parts of Central and Eastern Europe expected national independence and possibly, some territorial expansion as well. The largest population strata in these countries, the peasantry, expected access to land via the break-up of the large, privately held estates, so it could finally begin to earn a decent livelihood from farming. While the share of the working classes was quite low as a percentage of the overall populations everywhere, it was in most cases well organized to articulate its interests in the urban hubs, via its trade unions and Social Democratic party organizations. The working classes welcomed and spearheaded the changes everywhere. At the peak of the revolutionary era, a part of the Central and East European working class tried to take direct control over the management of the factories that employed them: They created councils—or 'soviets'—throughout the region in order to achieve this objective.

As for the general public and ordinary citizens: Their overriding objective was peace. They simply wanted an end to the bloodshed and to be able to go back to work and provide for their families. The general public, especially in those countries that were defeated in war by the Entente, did not know what to expect from these revolutions, but it was more or less united in its belief that the old order had fallen because it was unsustainable. For ordinary citizens, it was unclear what was to come on the heels of the collapse. It was not at all preposterous for many to think that the world revolution may spread westward and succeed everywhere. Only a few had any concrete idea about the meaning of the word "Socialism", and what life would be like under such a system, but there was a general optimism about this new possibility as well: surely it had to be better than the preceding order. As Thomas Mann concluded in the spring of 1919: "Communism as I understand it, contains much that is good and humane. Its goal is ultimately to dismantle the state (which will always be dedicated to power and oppression), humanize the world, cleanse its body of the poisons that are infecting it. At bottom, who would be against that?" [3]

A General Overview of the Council Movements in Central and Eastern Europe

These movements, which emerged spontaneously from the bottom up at the beginning of the revolutionary era, should not be seen as the products of an ideological blueprint devoid of local or national characteristic. The various councils of workers, soldiers, peasants, and the national councils, which became the actual leaders of the revolutionary processes in many parts of this region, acted on the basis of their members' political orientations, activities and commonly shared experiences or values. They reflected local characteristics, class conditions as well as external circumstances. In some parts, the councils held de facto power for weeks, even months. In a number of cases, National Councils were the seeds of the new international order, by championing the objectives of national sovereignty for their nation states. This is particularly true in the case of Czechoslovakia, Poland, and the South Slavic states.

As we have stated above, there was a great thirst for land by the peasants in most parts of Central and Eastern Europe. The rural peasant councils in most cases coordinated the distribution of land to the landless peasants, and with varying degree of radicalism. In areas of great rural poverty, village council members would chase away the landowners and the priests, then divide their properties among the villagers. In areas populated by ethnic minorities, the actions of the peasant councils were often embraced by the ethnic councils, especially in the case of those expropriated landowners who were of a different ethnicity from the local population.

Military councils also played an important role in the early days of the revolutions while the enlisted men were still together. Most of the soldiers of the Central Powers rushed straight home from the battlefront in disarray, often carrying their rifles with them. Virtually all of the post-war governments—East or West—wanted to stop the revolutionary processes under their jurisdictions and were keenly aware of their need to possess military capabilities to do so. This is why all of them wanted to convince the soldiers' councils, who were controlling the individual units, to side with the government—and if they were unable to do so, to at least neutralize these military councils.

In Central and Eastern Europe, councils organized by the proletariat—workers' councils—became the single-most significant elements of the overall council movement. There are several explanations for this. In contrast to the rural population, it was the working class that had the highest proportion of organized activists, and with political experience to boot. The workers' councils were not simply organs driven by animosity towards the reigning political elites. All of them were driven by the desire to find a remedy for the disastrous supply-shortages and chaos that came in the wake of the war everywhere. They wanted to reboot production that came to a halt everywhere, to improve their own circumstances, to achieve better working conditions, fair compensation for the work of their members, etc. In many places, the workers who formed these councils, also realized that their goal of re-booting stalled production processes in a fair and sustainable manner can best be achieved if they take control into their own hands over the factories that employed them. As we have stated above, approaches varied from place to place and according to local circumstances.

The industrial proletariat at this time, especially in Eastern Europe, was concentrated in and around the capitals, the seats of political power, and in a few big cities. It was natural for them to think about organizing nationwide, or municipal councils as well in order to achieve the proletariat's overall objectives within the local, regional, and national political arenas. By 1919, the terms 'Soviet Republic' or 'Republic of Councils' had an utterly clear-cut and precise meaning for most in the East European workers' movements: State power was to be vested in bodies created by the workers' councils for the purpose of representing and acting on the interests of the exploited classes.

The events that took place in Hungary in 1919 should be considered in light of the above and as a part of the worldwide revolutionary process that began to gather force at the beginning of the 20th century. Rather than seeing it as a unique historical event, the Hungarian example should simply be looked at as a monumental phenomenon. The following segments of this chapter will highlight some of its remarkable dimensions.

The Workers' Councils of Hungary

From the 16th century onward, Hungary was a partitioned and much abused Central European colony of the Hapsburg and the Ottoman Empires. After the Ottomans retreated in the 17th century, the Hapsburgs monopolized the colonialist hegemony. There were a number of attempts on the part of the local Hungarian nobility to free itself from the Austrian yoke, but all of these attempts ended in defeat. The first popular, broadly based revolution against the Hapsburgs and patterned largely on the French Revolution came in 1848. It too was ruthlessly repressed by two of the Great Powers that kept order in Europe: Austria and Russia. Twenty years after the repression of the 1848 Hungarians' fight for independence and democratic rights, the Hapsburgs decided to offer a deal to the Hungarian nobility, by inviting them into their tent. In 1867, and in return for their support of the aristocratic order and Austrian hegemony, the Hapsburgs gave the Hungarian aristocracy and nobility a fifty–fifty partnership in their empire. In short, from 1867 until 1918, the Austrian-Hungarian aristocratic families ran a "joint venture" known as the Austro-Hungarian Empire which was one of the superpowers under The Congress of Vienna.

The enthusiasm that accompanied the outbreak of the war in Germany and Austria was widely shared by Hungarians as well. This early and patriotic enthusiasm quickly turned to bitterness in Hungary as millions began to experience the impact of the carnage on their own daily lives, and as news of the hundreds of thousands of fallen and wounded loved ones reached home from the battlefields.

By 1915–1916, food riots began to surface. On June 28, 1916, a mining strike broke out in Petroşani and between July 3 and 5 of that year, the workers of the ammunition factory of Manfréd Weiss went on strike in Budapest. In 1916, the government decided to introduce a safety valve in order to defuse the rising pressure against its authority from bellow. It set up a number of "complaint committees" to re-channel public resentment from the streets, into various bureaucratic chambers. In the summer of 1917, striking mine workers were given the right to unionize and to manage their affairs. A strike by the rail-way manufacturing workers between May 29 and June 3, gave them a 40–50% wage rise. These stopgap measures and the continuation of the war were unable to stem the rising tide of resistance.

On November 25, 1917, about 100,000 workers gathered in Budapest to express their hostility to the war, to raise their voice against the political establishment, and to express their solidarity with the Russian Revolution. One of the speakers at this public demonstration was Dezső Bokányi, a high-ranking member of the Hungarian Social Democratic Party (HSDP). He openly raised the possibility of setting up workers' councils, in order to serve as levers for change. His idea was quickly shot down by the top leadership of the HSDP. The idea, however, was fully embraced by more radical members among the shop stewards, and in the rank and file of the Trade Union Movement. From this point on, the organization of workers' councils quickly moved to the top of the agenda at factory assembly meetings. [4]

In Budapest, a group of young Socialist engineers teamed up with a group of shop stewards and set up an Inter-factory Organizing Committee[5], which quickly developed into an anti-war revolutionary group. (The catalytic agent for this was a small revolutionary cell headed by two 20-year-old students, members of the Galilei Circle, Ilona Duczynska, and Tivadar Sugár. They played a critical role, along with the anarcho-syndicalist Ervin Szabó, and his followers among the shop-stewards in organizing the giant demonstration at the end of November 1917 along Andrássy Street. Duczynska, the future wife of the political economist Karl Polanyi had just returned from Zurich, where she was studying engineering. She brought with her the latest declaration of the Zimmerwald Movement, calling on the workers of Germany, Austria, and Hungary to rise. Szabó put her in touch with a radical group of shop stewards from the large munitions factories in and around Budapest, and this encounter set the ball rolling in Hungary in the early fall of 1917).

By January 13, 1918, the HSDP had convened six large People's Assemblies in Budapest to deal with the economic crisis caused by the war, the increasing labour unrest, and the revolutionary events unfolding in Russia. On this day, the police arrested Duczynska, and members of her small revolutionary cell and padlocked the headquarters of the Galilei Circle. The Hungarian Social Democrats wanted their assemblies to focus on voting rights, whereas the Inter-Factory Committee (IFC) put the establishment of a Budapest-based and a national workers' council at the top of its list of priorities. Just a few days before the start of these meetings, Zsigmond Kunfi, a prominent member of the HSDP, made a last-ditch effort to talk members of the IFC out of their plans of organizing the movement into Councils that may eventually exercise control even over the HSDP. He was unsuccessful in his attempt. At these general assemblies a resolution was passed calling for the establishment of workers' councils, which would serve as the voice of the proletariat and have the right to monitor even the Social Democratic Party. [6] At a meeting of roughly 30 workers' representatives from different factories, a preparatory committee was set up, and around 20–25 workers' councils were founded in the following days, throughout the capital. From this point onward, the organization of councils in Hungary began to spread like a wildfire.

On January 14, 1918, a general strike broke out in Wiener-Neustadt on the outskirts of the Austrian capital. By January 17, many workers in Vienna joined the strike, and they were followed by workers in various parts of Germany. The first strikes in Budapest erupted on January 18 and expanded into a nation-wide general strike by the following day. With the exception of the electrical and waterworks, all factories shut down. Public transport, with the exception of the railways, also came to a halt. Neither restaurants nor shops would open—only bakeries were exempted by the organizers. About half a million people participated in this general strike in Hungary. Workers' assemblies were summoned everywhere, and they expressed a fairly consistent list of demands: Peace, the right to organize workers' councils, universal suffrage, and the release of those arrested on January 13. Demonstrations were held all over the country and local workers' councils as well as municipal councils were set up in cities such as Szeged and Nagykanizsa. [7]

Following the government's pledge to begin negotiations with the newly established government of Soviet Russia, and the introduction of legislation that would guarantee universal suffrage, the HSDP quickly called off the strike on January 21, 1918, and the trade unions quickly put in some new restrictions, aimed at preventing future labour unrests not of their own making. Trade journals were forced to disclose the names of the workers who went against the interests of the trade unions. [8] In response, the Revolutionary Socialists—the group that took over the baton from the imprisoned Duczynska and her comrades - came out with a leaflet: "Hungarian workers! Your first task is to implement the right of self-determination of the working class! Appoint ten members from each factory to a workers' board and subordinate the current party management (emphasis added) to the workers' councils made up by members of these workers' boards". [9] Károly Tóth's comments, at a hastily called congress of the HSDP, that aimed to address internal divisiveness within the party, reflected the views of many at the time: "Many of our members are angry with the Party leadership, because it repressed and disbanded the strike movement despite the will of the masses". [10]

On May 1, 1918, tens of thousands demonstrated in the streets of Budapest and throughout Hungary. This was followed by a nation-wide strike in June. With time, more and more factories ceased production (and not only because of labour unrest but supply management issues as well), and the discontent spread from Budapest to the rural industrial centers, with more and more shutdowns as a consequence. Increasingly, the main demand of the workers everywhere was for the establishment of workers' councils under the control of the local militants.

At first, and in order to control these new, spontaneous initiatives, the HSDP's local organizations took the lead in organizing many of the new councils. On 28 June 1918, it was these HSDP organized councils that issued a call to end the strike, claiming that it was impossible to achieve the strikers' objectives. [11] Despite these interventions by the HSDP, the strikes continued in a number of places. In Győr, for example, the workers held on for twelve more days. On October 13, 1918, at the Social Democratic Party Congress, 32 delegates put forward a motion to start establishing workers' councils throughout the country. Meanwhile, the level of dissatisfaction with the central government was increasing at a rapid rate. Within weeks, on October 25, a group of parliamentary and non-parliamentary politicians, critical of the government's and parliament's war policies and their handling of the country's internal and external affairs, decided to establish an extra-parliamentary counter government, the Hungarian National Council (HNC), led by Count Mihály Károlyi. This "provisional government", that set up its headquarters in one of Budapest's best-known hotels—the Astoria—would include for the first time some prominent members from the HSDP, which up to then had never held a seat in the Hungarian Parliament. Parallel to these developments, sailors' councils were quickly organized within the Austro-Hungarian navy, and they took control of a number of the ships. The larger corps of the Budapest garrison also joined a newly created Soldiers' Council as the rebellion against the old order spread like a wildfire via the Councils. The Students' Council was founded on October 25, initially with 50 members, but its membership also rapidly escalated. By the last week of October 1918, the country was on the verge of open rebellion, and the Councils were right in the thick of the action. In the 'Egyesült Izzó' ('United Incandescent Lamp') factory, 3,000 workers attended a general meeting in support of the newly formed National Council led by Károlyi. They demanded that it should be supported by the Soldiers' as well as the Workers' Councils that were being formed at this time.

The Soldiers' Council, in partnership with the shop stewards of the largest factories around Budapest, actually set the date of the uprising for November 4, 1918, but the revolution would not wait that long: on the evening of October 30, the Hungarian National Council declared itself in command of the country and the army refused the orders of the high command to stand in their way on October 31st. The same day factories in Budapest voted to elect their delegates to the Budapest Workers' Council which held its first meeting on the November 2.

It is important to underline that the election of delegates to the Budapest Workers' Council on October 31 was organized and coordinated, in most cases, by the trade union functionaries. As a result, the first wave of factory committees that would constitute the membership of the Budapest Workers' Council excluded many of the more radical revolutionary elements of the proletariat in Budapest. The Budapest Workers' Council voted to join the provisional government, the

Hungarian National Council, and delegated the Social Democrat Dezső Bokányi as its representative. How did the Hungarian Social Democratic Party, the Hungarian labour movement's political party, react to these rapid developments?

It is a documented fact, that the leadership of the Hungarian Social Democratic Party felt itself threatened by the grass-roots radicalism of the emerging council movement in Hungary. In order to prevent its own marginalization by this revolution from below, it attempted to take over the leadership of this groundswell revolutionary movement and use it as an instrument for its self-preservation. Accordingly, the HSDP leadership drafted and published the Operational Regulations for the Budapest Workers' Council on November 5. [12] The Party did not consult with anyone in drafting these guidelines, least of all with local factory representatives. The guidelines unilaterally stipulated that 126 of the 365 members of the Budapest Workers' Council were to be delegated by the HSDP leadership and 239 by the trade union leadership, which also consisted of party members. The new HSDP guidelines also stipulated that a meeting of the Budapest Workers' Council could only be convened by the HSDP leadership and only those could stand as delegates who had been HSDP or Union members for at least one year. The Operational Regulations left nothing to the imagination about who would exercise power over the Budapest Workers' Council and the newly emerging council movement in Hungary: "The leadership of the HSDP and the Executive Committee of the party caucus will serve as the central representatives of the workers' councils".

Many of the councils at the time would have nothing to do with this unilateral effort of the HSDP to impose central Party control over them. The relationship between the workers' councils and the HSDP continuously deteriorated between November 1918 and March 21, 1919. Factory and local, municipal councils, which were directly elected by the workers themselves were more closely aligned with the desires of their members than those of the HSDP bureaucracy. In the following weeks and months, these local councils would exercise increasingly greater say in matters that affected people at local levels. When needed, they opposed the central administration, and managed to get their way. They established complaint offices, took on profiteering merchants, seized their merchandise, and distributed them among the poor and needy, and replaced corrupt officials wherever they were identified.

The factory councils were actively engaged in improving the existential circumstances of the working class and did not hesitate to be heard at local, regional and national administrative levels. They worked as genuine representatives of their members and refused to take their marching orders from any political party even ones that claimed to have their interests at heart. As the well-known Hungarian historian, Tibor Hajdu concluded: "Following the October 1918 revolution, and right up to March 1919, a new power structure emerged and existed, side by side with the central administration, and it was better aligned with the desires of the people: the workers', soldiers' and national councils that operated in the factories, among the troops, within the villages and cities did so often in opposition to the official power structures. There was a dual power system operating in Hungary between the 1918 and the 1919 revolutions". [13]

Workers' and Soldiers' Councils Under the 1918 Peoples' Republic

The Soldiers' Council, which played an important role in the victory of the Chrysanthemum Revolution and brought Károlyi to power on October 31, 1918, disbanded itself within hours of achieving victory. It was immediately replaced by a new council, the Budapest Soldiers' Council. The HSDP took a leading role in the formation of this new council and appointed one of its high-ranking members, József Pogány as its leader. (The soldiers elected Tivadar Sugár, the 21-year-old partner of Ilona Duczynska, as this new soldiers' council's second in command in recognition of his role in the revolution. He and Duczynska were only released from jail by the revolutionary solders a few days earlier.) At the time of its creation the Budapest Soldiers' Council counted more than a thousand members. [14]

Returning soldiers from the battlefield also formed their own soldiers' councils in many of the towns and villages in order to restore order in the countryside. They would clash on more than one occasion with representatives of the local national guard, a holdover from the previous era, that was under the authority of the central government. Instead of disarming and disbanding the new and spontaneously created soldiers' councils, the Károlyi government would force them to hold monthly elections and to include some government appointed military personnel among their commanders. [15]

Decrees regulating the freedom of the councils would be passed in quick order. On November 5, the Károlyi government issued a decree which stated that decisions of the National Council enjoy precedence over the decisions taken by local councils throughout the country and in all cases. In spite of this, and at the urging of the central National Council, local national councils would be created as agencies of the central authorities. Oftentimes they too would begin to act independently of the capital and would unilaterally take over the functions of the former administrative bureaucracy, often by physically chasing away the former public servants. [16] These *local* national councils would organize armed militias to maintain law and order and call for the confiscation of property possessed by their former exploiters, such as traders and landowners.

In the industrial districts, towns and cities, even where the old territorial administration remained in place, another form of spontaneous organization, the workers' councils, would emerge to reestablish order. "Within weeks, after the Chrysanthemum Revolution of 1918, village councils had de facto power in the vast majority of cases, and they actively exercised that power. Their main objective was to maintain law and order, remedy shortages in public supply and services, establish their independence from the central bureaucracy that had subjugated them in the past, and prepare the way for a reform that was uppermost on everyone's mind—the distribution of land to the peasantry and agrarian reform to end the semi-feudal conditions that reigned in the countryside". [17]

The response from the center to these grass-roots initiatives was predictable: It increased the size of the gendarmerie in the rural regions of the country in November. Even the Social Democratic Party's daily newspaper, *Népszava*, joined the chorus. It began to publish alarming horror-stories about the rising "anarchy of the masses". in the countryside. [18] The post-October 1918 efforts of the "Peoples' Republic" to repress the activities of the village councils in the countryside resulted in the death of hundreds of peasants and left many thousands wounded. In some places, events moved at a much faster pace. The Semsey estate in the town of Balmazújváros, for example, was taken into public ownership, as part of a new "communist republic". [19] In Sátoraljaújhely, the local council proclaimed a proletarian dictatorship on November 16, 1918. In the Zsil Vallley (now inside Romania) the coal miners took power into their hands and refused to recognize any superior authority. In the first days of November 1918, bloody battles were fought in the mining villages of Bihar and Szatmár.

The relationship between the centrally inspired and initiated local national councils and the workers' councils during the Károlyi regime was complex. In general, and over time, the workers' councils gained the upper hand in more and more places. This was certainly true in the south of Hungary, in Szolnok County for example, the workers had more confidence in the workers' councils than the local national councils and preferred to turn to them with their problems. [20] In the city of Jászberény, for example, there was a general food shortage because of widespread hoarding. This is how the local workers' council reacted: "What is to be done about this? The industrial and the farmers' councils should take this matter into their hands because they are the real representatives of the poor and the dispossessed. They have the power to confiscate the hidden stockpiles". [21] In other cases, members of the workers' councils crashed (collectively attended) meetings of the local national councils, using this approach to exert pressure on them.

The rising power of the workers' and soldiers' councils was a continuous feature of the Károlyi era. They replaced the centrally controlled municipal administration in several places such as the cities of Sátoraljaújhely, Debrecen, Nagyvárad and the village of Dunapataj, occasionally with violence. "The endeavor to implement proletarian dictatorship spontaneously and locally has become more and more widespread". [22] On March 10, 1919, a three-member directorate took over control in the town of Kaposvár, led by Sándor Latinka. They then occupied the county hall, accompanied by a large crowd of people supporting them. The minister István Nagyatádi Szabó had no choice but to recognize this spontaneous change in local authority which was quickly followed by the seizure of large estates in this county. [23] On March 14, a five-member directorate got formed in Tolna County and on March 19th, the Workers' Council of Miskolc city took control of Borsod County. [24] From March 1–17, Government Commissioners and Lord-Lieutenants, or *főispán*, were dismissed in 13 counties and cities. District workers' councils were formed in several places across Pest County. In these places, the orders of the chief magistrates of the county's districts, or *főszolgabíró*, could become effective only with the countersignature of the local workers' councils. [25] On March 2nd, 1919, just two weeks before the establishment of the Republic of Councils, the Congress of Workers' Councils of the Great Plain of Hungary was held in Szeged. Participants at this gathering urged for a more deliberate and rapid progress towards socialization. Here and during a people's assembly held in the town of Csépa, the delegates condemned the local national council and finally, a workers' council was set up to oversee the work of the local national council. [26]

The power struggles between the workers' councils and the local national councils, were a constant and rapidly escalating features of the Károlyi regime. On November 26, the Minister of Interior issued a decree that requested the local, grassroots councils to resist from assuming public authority. [27] In order to eliminate the grassroots councils, an act was adopted on January 27, 1919, about the establishment of the so-called "people's councils". These people's councils—which cannot really be considered real councils—consisted of officials and delegates appointed by the Government Commissioner and they only possessed a minimal degree of authority. On February 11, 1919, a government decree[28] was issued, to prevent any further extension of the councils' power in Hungary. It established that "Governing Boards" rather than Workers' Councils should exercise management controls in the factories. Unlike the Workers' Councils, the Governing Boards were not autonomous bodies as the state and the trade unions had full control over them. A counter-revolutionary author would describe this change later in the following manner: "The decree clearly showed that Ernő Garami, a top member of the Hungarian Social Democratic Party, and the Minister of Commerce at the time, knew fully well, that the workers should not be entrusted with the management of the factories". [29]

This new initiative of the Károlyi regime to reign in the power of the workers' councils also failed. In most cases, the workers' councils changed their names to 'boards' and continued to operate just as before. [30] The workers either placed their own representatives in the companies' governing boards (as was the case with Ganz's Electricity Co.), or they established independent organizations that overruled and regulated the capitalist company management (for example, at the Weiss Manfréd Works in Csepel, the ship and wagon factories of the Ganz and elsewhere). [31]

According to Hajdu, the rising power of the workers' councils in Hungary prior to March 21, 1919 did not follow a straight line. The councils did not have a decisive say in many of the counties in the north-western parts of the country, with the exception of Győr. Progress was more rapid in the counties of Hajdu, Bihar, Zemplén, Bereg, Csanád, Nógrád, Szabolcs, Szolnok or in bigger towns like Nagykanizsa. The Councils also played a decisive role in Borsod, Somogy and Tolna Counties, as well as in the cities of Szeged, Kiskunfélegyháza, Aszód, Pécel, Szob and in the village of Nagyszénás. Within the capital, the Budapest Workers' Council became the most significant and determined political force by the beginning of 1919.

By mid-March, however, this uneven path, these tributaries of the Hungarian council movement had merged into a mighty river that was ready to overflow its banks. Sándor Juhász Nagy, the Minister of Justice of the Berinkey Government described the political situation in the following manner: "By March 1919, all differences between the Social Democratic and Bolshevik crowds have faded. The proletariat demanded the same things everywhere in Hungary". [32]

None of the above should be taken as evidence for unanimity of opinion or uniformity of operations by the workers' councils throughout Hungary before or after the March 21 declaration of the Dictatorship of the Proletariat. In the Workers' Council of Budapest, for example there was open warfare between Communist and Social Democratic members that often ended in fisticuffs. Indeed, this, the largest workers' council in the country, passed a resolution on January 28,1919 to expel anyone who is a member of either the Hungarian Communist Party or the Trade Union bureaucracy. In spite of this decision, the Budapest Workers' Council remained a steadfastly socialist undertaking as seen by its approval on March 7 of the economic proposals of Jenő Varga. The Budapest Workers' Council mirrored the behavior of most of the workers councils in the country in retaining its independence, sovereignty. The workers' councils during the Károlyi era took their marching orders from the local membership, rather than from the political parties that wanted to harness them for their own purposes. On March 21, the Budapest Workers' Council welcomed and unanimously approved the merger of the two left-wing parties and voted to disband itself.

The Workers' Councils and the Hungarian Bolsheviks

While there were Communist in Hungary prior to 1918, they did not have a political party of their own until November 24, 1918. Until that day, the Hungarian labour movement had only one political party representing its interests and that was the HSDP. (The party of the Hungarian Communists was founded in a Budapest apartment belonging to József and Jolán Kelen, who had rented it earlier to Ilona Duczynska after she came back to Hungary from Zurich to establish her small, revolutionary cell.)

The top leaders of this new, revolutionary party—Béla Kun, Ernő Pór, Ferenc Münich, Tibor Szamuely—spent the war years as prisoners of war in Russia. They did not possess deep roots within the Hungarian labour movement and became staunch supporters of the Bolshevik path to Socialism during their stay in Russia. The second-tier leadership and most of the rank and file of the new Communist party came from the ranks of the HSDP's left wing, and honed their combative skills within the trade union movement or as militant shop stewards in the factories around Budapest. There were some independent intellectuals as well, like György Lukács, who also joined the Party shortly after November 24.

Throughout the revolutionary period, and even in exile after the fall of the Commune, the Hungarian Communists were often at loggerheads with one another on both ideological and practical policy issues. (One of the biggest and earliest disagreements among them was about what to call their party—the Party of Hungarian Communists, or the Hungarian Communist Party. After some very heated debates, the second option was narrowly defeated in 1918. (In order to use a uniform standard of reference throughout this book, the editor has chosen to distinguish the two left-wing political parties of Hungary from each other prior to their March 1919 merger, by referring to them as the HSDP and the HCP).

The primary concern of the remaining parts of this chapter is to help us to understand the approach of the HCP to the Council Movement in Hungary, especially to the workers' councils that began to play a decisive role during the Peoples' Republic, and which clearly wanted to entrench, legitimize and institutionalize their role as authentic and direct representatives of the working class during the Dictatorship of the Proletariat as well.

What was the Bolsheviks'position towards the Councils? The HCP's position on this question was unambiguous when it established itself in November 1918. It openly proclaimed that capitalism can only be overthrown through the collective actions of the working class that organizes itself into councils. For the Hungarian Bolsheviks, councils were essential, indispensable tools of the revolution. The HCP actively fought for broadening the mandates of the councils during the Károlyi era and championed the formation of factory level workers' councils that would exercise supreme authority over the privately-owned enterprises. The

Party's rapid membership growth after November 1918 is largely due to this open-door policy vis-á-vis the councils. By the beginning of 1919, HCP membership rose to 30–40 thousand. [33]

To repeat: the HCP did not set itself up to serve as an agent but an enemy of the Chrysanthemum Revolution. It looked upon the Károlyi regime as an enterprise of the bourgeoisie and considered, that its mission was to overthrow it. This was not merely a tactical but a strategic objective for the party of the Hungarian Communists. The first issue of *The Internationale*—the theoretical journal of Hungarian Communist intellectuals is explicit about the "economic and technical necessities of the communist world revolution". [34]

Gyula Hevesi, who was to play a leading role in the direction of the Commune's economic policies was also categorical: "Captalism is bankrupt and must be replaced. Production must be taken out of the hands of those who can only produce for the sake of profit". According to Hevesi the working class wants to live better, and to work less. This can only be achieved by increasing productivity, i.e., by "the cooperative *efficiency* of communal work". This prerequisite—greater productivity and efficiency—can only be achieved under communistic production processes. (It should be stated here that Hevesi was an engineer and no doubt this coloured his understanding of the essence of Communism. For him, Communism was about enhancing the efficiency of industrial production, rather than eliminating efficient industrial production as the core value of human societies.)

For Hevesi and the new Bolshevik leaders in Hungary, the construction of the road to the future must be put into the hands of the councils organized by the proletariat. "The form of the Proletarian Dictatorship is The Republic of Councils, from which the bourgeoisie is completely excluded. The proletarian state power relies on the mass organizations of the workers—such as the trade unions, the party organizations, factory workers' councils and other, similar organizations—that engage millions of workers—to achieve its goals". [35]

The leaders of the Hungarian Communists did not see themselves as politicians who should bring semi-feudal Hungary into the bourgeois era, before they embark on constructing the Socialist base for a Communist society. They wanted to skip a phase in the Marxist historical blueprint. Accordingly, they designed a two-step strategy for skipping a historical phase separating Socialism from Feudalism. Step one involved the revolutionary transfer of power into the hands of grass roots councils, and furnishing them with executive, legislative and judicial supremacy in the fight against the bourgeoisie. Once the bourgeoisie was defeated, came the second step of their grand strategy. They stipulated that the councils should be transformed into transmission belts or adjuncts of the Bolsheviks as they lay out the path leading towards Socialism and the ultimate, Communist society. The Hungarian Bolsheviks wanted nothing to do with parliamentary democracy. "It is not parliamentary majority that we should strive for. For it is useless for us in a bourgeois democracy anyways. Instead, we must aim for the rule of the workers', the soldiers' and the peasants' councils, and to achieve that we must establish the dictatorship of the revolutionary proletariat". [36]

What Happened After the Seizure of Power?

The first pronouncement of the Dictatorship of the Proletariat via the Revolutionary Governing Council (RGC) after the bourgeois democratic order collapsed in Hungary on March 21, 1919, was unambiguous and was fully congruent with the HCP's 2 step strategy: "The new political party has given executive power to the Revolutionary Governing Council to establish and empower workers', peasants', and soldiers' councils nationwide. From now on legislative, executive, and judicial powers are to be exercised by the dictatorship of the workers', peasants' and soldiers' councils". [37]

Reality was, however, far more complex and contradictory, and immediately separated theory from practice. Within days it became clear, that the activities of the workers' councils most everywhere were not in harmony with the economic and industrial policies of the HCP and the Revolutionary Governing Council, with its HQ in Budapest. From the first day on, the policy goals and interests of the centralized state were often contravened by the territorially deployed local councils. The conflict between the center and the periphery was a constant feature of the 133-day long Hungarian Republic of Councils.

In order to cope with this reality, and to execute its own agenda, the RGC began to actively regulate the behavior of the local councils within a matter of days. It began by establishing a hierarchical and centralized power structure. [38] A new RGC decree not only prescribed, but prioritized the tasks of the local councils, and stated that their activities are subject to overrule by a higher council level. The one thing strictly forbidden to them was the distribution of the properties and lands of the large agricultural estates, including those of the Church that happened to be located on their territories.

Apart from telling them what they can or cannot do, and in what order, this new central decree also ordered all the councils to register themselves with the Commissariat of the Interior and include the names of their members in their registration forms. The decree established a rigid, top-down hierarchy—National, County, District, City, Village—and stipulated that "The superior councils and their executive committees shall have the right to change ex officio any decision of the subordinate councils". [39]

Decree No. XCVI of the Governing Council also introduced a measure that further limited the exercise of self-government. "The counties and the cities are to be headed by Commissars appointed by the Revolutionary Governing Council.

These centrally appointed Commissars will provide guidance for and control over the local councils and their executive committees". [40] (It should be noted: While this was a centrist design, most of the new Commissars appointed by the Revolutionary Governing Council were former local council members. Moreover, none of these new, centrally appointed Commissars would alter a decision taken by a county level council during the existence of the Hungarian Republic of Councils.) How did all this work out in practice?

The first strategic step of the Bolsheviks that we outlined in our previous section vis-á-vis the councils was relatively easy to achieve. The second step would become its greatest stumbling block. It would find it simply impossible to exercise its will and gain full control over the genie it let out of the bottle. (And that genie would come back to haunt it with a vengeance, in 1956.) No matter the restrictions, local councils were able to exercise considerable independence throughout the lifetime of the Hungarian Republic of Councils.

At the beginning of April, and largely in realization of its own failure to have its will prevail, the RGC issued a confidential instruction to the local councils: "Under exceptional circumstances—if it is not possible to re-establish production under their jurisdiction in the countryside, and in order to restore the confidence of the landless peasants, the local council may engage in land re-distribution". Under this secret measure, a family would now be able to receive up to five Hungarian acres (hold) of arable land and one Hungarian acre of meadow (a hold is 1.0665 acre). The landless peasants could also be given one Hungarian acre of land to build a house on and have a small garden plot next to it. This initiative came about not because, but in spite of the central will of the Dictatorship of the Proletariat. Some of the councils did not even wait for this decree and distributed land arbitrarily. [41]

All things considered, quality of life of a substantial number of landless peasants significantly improved as a consequence of the above "secret" measure. The local councils played a major role in the enhancement of public supply and the alleviation of the housing shortages. These rural local councils were not fearful to innovate in the face of the most unusual of challenges. In the village of Kápolna, for example, the local parish priest paid a visit to the council to complain that his livelihood was at risk because only a few of his parishioners had paid the church taxes. After giving it some thought, the local council decided to provide unemployment benefits to the priest. [42] Though the central Governing Council wanted to control the councils, the latter refused to remain passive.

In line with the first step of the Bolsheviks' two step strategy outlined earlier, revolutionary workers' and soldiers' councils were set up in almost all districts of the capital. Once they established themselves, they did not sit back to await their marching papers. They provided themselves in all cases with full autonomy. "In its proclamation of March 22, the council of the first district of Budapest announced that the council had the exclusive right to provide leadership for revolutionary order and the dictatorship of the proletarians in that district. As proven by their actions, these were more than just empty words". [43]

Many of the district councils began to issue decrees even before they were formally constituted and recognized by the central authorities. They also tended to be more radical in the measures they took, and this brought them into frequent conflicts with the trade unions. As Samu Jászai, a trade union leader, summarized in the *Népszava* newspaper: "A lot of people are getting together to create councils in order to dictate to the leadership". [44] Albert Király also reported on the rising political competition between the workers' councils and the trade union bureaucracy. The conflict between the revolutionary district councils and the social democratic commissars for Budapest ended in the resignation of the commissars on April 1. [45]

To cite a similar case: the council of the first district of Budapest organized an armed protest to demand the resignation of József Pogány, one of the two Commissars of Defense. Pogány and the Second Defense Commissar, Böhm were even assaulted at the demonstration. At the Revolutionary Governing Council's meeting of April 3, Zsigmond Kunfi, another high-ranking Commissar cut right to the chase. "Who is in charge here", he asked his fellow Commissars? He stated that there are only two ways to answer this question: either abolish the councils outright or hand them all power, because the current arrangement is unsustainable.

At another early meeting of the RGC on April 6, Commissar Bokányi went even further. He told his colleagues that the pursuit of equality by the councils is at the expense of the Revolutionary Governing Council. "If we don't take action against them, they will step on our necks within a matter of weeks"[46] (Bokanyi exaggerated the severity of the problem, the confrontations were nowhere near as serious as he suggested, but his comments clearly reflected the negative feelings of the Commissars on the Revolutionary Governing Council about the local, self-governing councils).

It was in response to these early but very pronounced challenge to its two-step council strategy, that the RGC decided to call for immediate council elections on April 7. The April 11 issue of the Communist Party daily, *Vörös Újság,* (Red News), did not mince its words about the division of labour between the workers' councils and the newly formed, but yet to be named political Party created from the merger of the HSDP and the HCP. The daily reiterated that the workers' councils possess legislative and executive powers in order to prevent the emergence of a new central bureaucracy. But it also underlined, that they function as critical components in a centralized chain of command. The district workers' councils were designated as the top decision makers in local matters, the National Congress of Councils was the highest legislative authority on matters of national concern. The supreme executive power was in the hands of the Revolutionary Governing Council. This national chain of command had to be respected on the ground. The Party's position was expressed in a colourful manner: the workers' councils were "the sprouts of the new social order, that will blossom into a communist society organically", the gardener-botanist in charge of the new seedlings was the Party high brass. [47]

This consolidation was clearly an open retreat from the original, grassroots driven design of the path to socialism. From here on in, local councils and directorates were reprimanded if they put local interests ahead of the central will. "The local workers' councils and directorates should rise above their local interests: They should follow only the interests of the proletarian community as a whole" i.e., as expressed and ordered by the Party dominated RGC. [48] The establishment of this new, subordinate-superior relationships was easier said, than done. As one of the most respected authorities on this subject concluded: "The power struggles between the government and local councils became one of the fundamental problems for the construction of a new socialist state". [49] Let us briefly illustrate these power struggles with some concrete examples.

On April 26, the RGC delegated the delivery of social services to the central workers' council in Budapest, the city workers' councils in the cities and the rest of the country under the county councils.]. This centralization of responsibilities set off a series of confrontations in Budapest between the local district councils and the central authorities. Their key complaint was, that the Governing Council has greatly limited the autonomy and maneuverability of the local councils, and by doing so, it is no longer "a true proletarian dictatorship".

On April 14, in a move similar to the above, the Commissariat of Defense abolished the soldiers' councils by a unilateral executive decree and replaced them with party-political appointees in all of the military units.

The National Congress of Councils, which was to be the Republic's supreme legislative body, was only called into session on June 14. Until then, the Revolutionary Governing Council ruled by executive decree and consulted with no one, other than the Workers' and Soldiers' Council of Budapest, which had around 500 members who were elected by and from the ranks of the Budapest district councils. Candidate selection was in the hands of the ruling political Party, rather than the local citizens. The first assembly of the Budapest Workers' and Soldiers' Council was on April 11, and notwithstanding Party control over its membership, the relationship between the Budapest Workers' and Soldiers' Council and the Revolutionary Governing Council was fraught with conflict from its first day of operation. As stated above, the Republic of Councils' supreme legislative body—the National Congress of Councils—was only called into session on June 14. Members of the NCC were elected by the county and city councils, one member per 50,000 residents. The majority of delegates were HSDP party members, since candidate selection was handled by local Party organizations, and the Communists had virtually no organizational base outside of Budapest. The first days of this large, unwieldy legislative body were exhausted by a myriad of local issues and controversies. On June 23, the NCC approved the Republic's new constitution (a document prepared without any public consultation by the ruling political party). After delegating power to a smaller, 150-member Central Executive Committee, the NCC adjourned and never met again during the remaining days of the Republic. In practice, there was not a functioning or independent legislative or judiciary branch of the Hungarian Dictatorship of the Proletariat—governance by central executive decree was its modus operandi from its first to its last day.

While a bitter struggle for power between central and local authorities was a constant feature of every one of the 133 days, these confrontations should not be simplified or portrayed as conflicts between city dwellers and the rural populace. The RGC's impulsive efforts to control the local councils in the countryside were understandable: it felt that the predominance of local interests would pose a great threat to the capital's food supply. Hungary was blockaded by the Entente, occupied by troops of neighboring countries. Over two million citizens were crowded into the capital, and they had to be fed. To repeat, the impulse to retain control over the councils in the countryside is understandable. But it should also be established that the rural councils, virtually everywhere were fully committed to maintaining solidarity with their brothers and sisters in the cities, who were dependent on them for their sources of food. There were only very rare examples of the alleged selfishness of country folk vis-á-vis their countrymen in the cities. The Bolsheviks' fears were not proven in practice. *Au contraire*, there were numerous examples that support the opposite—i.e., rural councils taking the interests of the big cities into consideration and in an unselfish manner. A good illustration of this solidarity between city and country folk is a resolution taken by the workers' council of Kaposvár, a rural town in the Western part of Hungary: "The Workers' Council of Kaposvár calls upon all workers' councils in Transdanubia to make all efforts in order to transport food to the proletariat of Budapest". There were many other similar resolutions taken by local councils during the lifetime of the Republic of Councils that underlines this spirit of solidarity between the urban and the rural populations. [50]

We should also pause here, to underline the increasing public attention paid by workers' councils, and without central compulsion, to the advancement of women, and gender equality within their own deliberative bodies. For the first time in the country's history, women became important participants in the process of deciding who was to get what, when and how within Hungary. Women played important roles in many of the newly established councils and often without central prodding. A directive by the Szolnok County Council in the south of Hungary is a good illustration of this new trend. "The Republic of Councils has liberated women from the oppression of the capitalist state system. Proletarian women are provided rights and are treated as the equal of men. We call upon the workers', soldiers' and farmers' councils and on all the comrades, who are working to uphold the interests of the Hungarian Republic of Councils, to give their full support to the women's movement, and assist the movement in every way possible, and with full understanding". [51]

The unselfish initiatives of the rural councils had other positive benefits for the central authorities. For example, at the end of April, when the Eastern part of Hungary was literally turned into a battlefield by invading troops from Rumania, "the district directorate of Tiszafüred diligently drafted soldiers, collected horses, requisitioned wagons and fodder day and night, without waiting for orders from above". [52]

The challenge of harmonizing central and local interests was most difficult in the pursuit of strategic national economic objectives. The RGC's Decree No. IX, issued on March 26, 1919, was driven by this all-encompassing challenge or imperative. It proclaimed that: "The task of the workers' councils is to maintain proletarian work discipline, protect the properties of the working people, and supervise production within the factories". [53] The decree, however, introduced a measure that immediately restricted the autonomy of the workers' councils, because it created an entirely new level in the chain of economic command—the Production Commissars—who were centrally appointed by the RGC, reported to the RGC and were given supreme executive authority. According to the new regulations, the Production Commissars took over the right from the workers' councils for establishing pay scales within the production units. The workers' councils retained the right to formally approve the new pay scales. If they disagreed, the center would have the final word. Subsequent RGC decrees, such as the ones of April 17 and 20, further limited the workers' councils' autonomy. The RGC introduced yet another participant into the process of governing the production and distribution of goods and services, who was not accountable to the local workers' councils—the centrally appointed trade union representative.

We should also insert into this catalogue of centralizing trends the arrival on the scene of the world's first socialist trade union of engineers, the National Association of Applied Engineers (AMOSZ). They burst onto the scene with the support of the RGC, by addressing not the proletariat, but "The Technicians of the World" and proclaimed that the socialist way of production in Hungary heralds the arrival of a "...new world of true knowledge and aptitude". [54]

The AMOSZ declaration was the opening scene of a new play, in which, the technical expert replaces the worker as the hero of socialism. The engineers who created the AMOSZ had the full backing of the Hungarian Bolsheviks. They were unhappy about being shunted aside during the first days of the revolution by the plebs, the amateurs, the non-technicians who were unhappy about their earlier conduct. The technical, engineering experts were unhappy with the loss of many of their former privileges—such as those related to annual leave—along with their administrative and technical prerogatives. The AMOSZ was a clear reflection of the intensification of conflicts between manual and intellectual labourers and the growing tendency of the new Republic to limit the autonomous activism of the locally organized proletariat. Jenő Varga, the People's Commissar for the Economy was unambiguous about which side was represented by the central government. "Factory level workers' councils have misunderstood their roles and have exceeded their powers. They arbitrarily and recklessly removed some engineers from their positions in the factories. I say arbitrarily, because they did not have the right to do so and recklessly because often, shortly after these expulsions, the officers were called back to the factory and some even got elected to be the chairman of the workers' council itself". [55] Varga emphasized that the relationship between the blue-collar and the white-collar workers should not be aggravated. Gyula Hevesi another economic Commissar was even more emphatic in his criticism of the workers' councils: "They should not exercise an obstructive or delaying influence on the implementation of the technical measures ordered by the professionals in charge". [56]

The evidence is irrefutable: For left-wing technical intellectuals, for most of the new Party leadership, especially the Bolsheviks, and for a large segment of public opinion, it was not a blue-collar, agrarian-proletarian but a technocratic, engineering-based communism, that will replace the bankrupt capitalist order. The next general assembly of AMOSZ was emphatic about where the chips will fall under the dictatorship of the proletariat: "The communist state is based on more and better production. This can only be organized and managed by professionals. These professionals should be given all the powers they need for the efficient and productive organization of the factories and their technical management". [57]

At the May 17 meeting of the Revolutionary Governing Council yet another agreement was reached about the necessity of limiting the powers of the workers' councils over the production and distribution of goods and services on the path to socialism. At this meeting Béla Kun made it clear to his colleagues on the RGC that the supervisory powers given to the the workers' councils at the start of the revolution was a limited term appointment, brought on by the force of necessity.

According to Kun, the councils' supervisory roles can now be gradually restricted with the active assistance of the trade unions. They have fulfilled their temporary and historical assignments in overthrowing the bourgeoisie. [58]

In his article published on May 28, Gyula Hevesi followed a similar logic. He argued that the early wage increases were a product of necessity and had to be incurred even if they led to deficits. In the future, however, this problem has to be solved by planned and rational management. On the issue of labour discipline, he claimed that in far too many cases, "the workers did not fulfill their proletarian obligation with as much conscientiousness as it was expected of them by all trustworthy fellow proletarians and those on the battlefronts". He argued that the resolution of these problems should be delegated to the newly appointed Production Commissars, to the trade unions and to more socially conscious workers. Hevesi did not once mention the workers' councils as a part of the solution. [59]

The official view quickly shifted thereafter: Workers' control would be reframed as a hindrance on the path to Socialism. Once the forces of production are expropriated the center requires responsible leadership. Supervision of the production and distribution of goods and services by the workers was dismissed as a harmful phenomenon that strengthens the factory's "particularism", creates a new bureaucracy, and weakens work discipline.

The trade union leadership became as critical of the workers' councils as the party leadership. They saw the rising power of the workers' councils as a threat to their powers and prerogatives. They complained that "In the factories and the districts, the workers' councils often made wage-related decisions without consulting with us".[60] In a frontal assault on the sovereignty of the councils, they proclaimed: "It is necessary to bring the workers' councils under the trade union's chain of command". [61]

The gang-up by the central Party leadership and the trade unions on the workers' councils would only intensify from May 1919 onwards. On June 11, the People's Economic Council (an agency of the Revolutionary Governing Council) expropriated for itself the right to organize elections to the factory level councils and provided the Trade Unions with the right to oversee the entire process. From here on in, the factory councils could not make any decisions without trade union supervision. [62] Following the People's Economic Council's decree of July 10, the factory councils were pushed even further back: all they could do by then was to look into the books of the production units. Management controls were to be exercised without any supervision by the workers' councils. This became the exclusive prerogative of the Production Commissars, and the Chief Technical Manager. [63] According to the orders of the Commissariat for Labour and Social Welfare, issued on June 17, workers in the healthcare institutions, were similarly stripped of their rights to form workers' directorates (factory workers' councils or supervisory councils). [64]

In the increasingly turbulent cross currents that we have described above, it is not at all surprising, that many of the pre-revolutionary managers were also able to find a niche for themselves after March 21. As a former chief executive officer indicated: "Socialization in the mining sector meant that a Department for Coal Mining was set up by the government to supervise and manage the country's coal production and distribution. The members of this department were men from the companies themselves and they managed to protect the interests of their former companies—as well as they could". [65] The former executive officer of another factory pointed out that the head of the supervisory workers' council had always met the needs of the company management and kept the communist elements away from the factory.[66]

It is not the task of this chapter to provide an analysis of the economic policies of the Republic of Councils. A few salient features should, however, be noted regarding the scale of nationalization. In the iron and metal industries 144 factories were nationalized within the first month of the Republic of Councils— employing 36,386 workers. To this should be added the premises of 22 mining companies with 26,750 employees.[67] Production commissioner were appointed to 400 factories by April 23 and their numbers increased to 1073 factories by May 5. By May 31, 3,585 nationalized companies in Budapest alone had separate, state supervised bank accounts. [68] Summaries from the counter-revolutionary era put the number of companies that were nationalized at 4,159. [69] (Several small factories could belong to each company.)

Financial management was a largely neglected area within these socialized enterprises. The goal was to create large distribution centers in various sectors of the economy and to eliminate free trade and retail trade as quickly as possible. Compensation for work in the majority of cases was provided in kind. Socialized companies generally ruled out barter trade and the use of money.

The industrial centers became the commanding heights of the economy during the Hungarian Republic of Councils. The People's Economic Council—which was to supervise the economy, was ultimately unable to fulfill its mandate. The inherited circumstances—blockade, invasion, financial collapse—would have defeated the efforts of those with the best of intentions. The inappropriateness of the RGC's centralized and single-minded economic strategy was evident even to its own architects by the middle of June 1919. On June 14, Jenő Varga proposed that the Materials' Distribution Council should rank the distribution of raw materials and fuel according to the following order of priorities: military necessities, transportation, food supply, heating, lighting, and supply of other factories. [70] The Hungarian Republic of Councils was everything but a planned economy. Improvisation, crisis management, rather than rational planning was the order of the day. Decree No. LXIX ordered the establishment of local and district industrial production councils, [71] and Decree No. 45 called for the establishment of district level economic people's councils, to help meet the challenge of coordination. Neither of these decrees were implemented. In fact, on July 17, Decree No. CXXX. abolished the operation of the district industrial production councils. The economic relationship between the center at Budapest and the countryside remained an unsolved problem during the entire term of the Republic of Councils.

Conclusions

It has become conventional wisdom throughout the former Soviet Empire to argue that workers' councils are a hindrance on the path to Socialism after the bourgeoisie is cast aside, because they impede central planning and coordination, limit the speed of industrialization, restrict the rate of economic growth and the maximization of productivity and efficiency. This was the view of the German Social Democratic Party, and it became the orthodoxy already under Lenin as well. Rather than the engines of Socialism, workers' councils were reframed as burdens on the path to Socialism. It was for her support of the German workers' councils that got Rosa Luxemburg shot in January 1919 on the orders of the German Social Democratic leaders. It was her insistence upon this vehicle, that got her into hot water with Lenin, then later Stalin. It was Ilona Duczynska's sympathies with Rosa Luxemburg's ideas that got her expelled from the Hungarian Communist Party in exile in Austria in 1922 as well. Wherever they resurfaced in the Soviet Empire—in Hungary, during October 1956, for example— they were immediately bulldozed into the ground, their leaders were either executed or jailed.

One of the clearest expressions of the conventional Bolshevik wisdom on workers' councils in Hungary is in the writings of the economic historian, György Péteri, who considers workers' councils as unnecessary hindrances to efficient industrial management. With a short pause in October 1956, this was the view of all the Hungarian Communist parties between 1919 and 1990. Another Hungarian socialist historian Tibor Hajdu recalled his own arguments with Péteri's views during the post-1956 era in Hungary, with the following words:

> I told Péteri, that he may be right about one thing: The delegation of power
> to the workers' councils over production may not produce optimal
> economic efficiency. But he must also recognize: There is no socialism in a
> place where the workers' councils do not exist and where they are not
> allowed to have an influence on the production and distribution of goods
> and services. What kind of socialism is that?[72]

The Hungarian revolutions of 1918–1919 raised several problems that were hard to solve by the newly formed Hungarian Socialist Party that replaced the People's Republic of Mihály Károlyi on March 21, 1919. Let us not be mistaken: This newly created Party was a revolutionary party, based on its ideology, but it was badly fragmented over the application of its revolutionary ideology. Its fragmentation and divisiveness were not restricted to questions of ideology but even to such mundane questions as what to call itself.

One of the biggest challenges for this badly divided party was how to interpret the concept of workers' self-management and how to put into practice the dictatorship of the proletariat over the production and distribution of goods and services. What this chapter showed was, that neither the Social Democrats nor the Bolsheviks could walk the talk of revolutionary change. It was the social democratic party that had to face up to this reality first during the Károlyi regime. While the Hungarian Bolsheviks warmly embraced the idea of giving all power to the Councils during the Károlyi era, they dropped the idea like a hot potato when they got into power.

The authority aspired to by the councils did not meet with the approval of either the Hungarian Social Democrats' or the Bolsheviks' concept of the proletarian dictatorship. Due to the short timescale—133 days—the multiplicity of the challenges facing the revolutionary leadership, its internal divisiveness and inexperience in governance, no real solutions or answers could be given to this grand historical question at the time. The inability to resolve this question persists however, to this day, and remains perhaps the greatest theoretical as well as practical challenge for socialists everywhere.

NOTES

1   E.J. Hobsbawm, *A szélsőségek kora*. [The Age of Extremes] (Budapest: Pannonia, 1998), 62.
2   Hobsbawm, E.J. *Ibid.* 68.
3   Letter to Josef Ponten, Munich, March 29, 1919 in, *The Letters of Thomas Mann: 1899-1955*, trans. Richard and Clara Winston, (New York, NY: Vintage Books, 1975), 86.
4   Tibor Hajdu, *Munkástanácsok Magyarországon 1918-1919-ben*. [Workers' Councils in Hungary:1918-1919.] (Budapest: Kossuth, 1958), 12.
5   Gyula Hevesi, *Egy mérnök a forradalomban*. [An Engineer During the Revolution] (Budapest: Európa, 1959), 95.
6   Gyula Hevesi, *Internationale* 1, no. 3-4 (February 22, 1919).
7   "Dokumentumok a magyar párttörténet tanulmányozásához" [Documents for the Study of Hungarian Party History], Vol II., 1917 November–1919 August. (Budapest, *Szikra*. 1954), 18.
8   Gyula Hevesi, *op.cit.* 134.
9   Documents… *op.cit.* 20.
10 Gyula Hevesi, *op.cit.* 138.
11 *Népszava*. June 28, 1918.
12 *Népszava*. November 5, 1918.
13 Tibor Hajdu, *A magyarországi Tanácsköztársaság*. [The Hungarian Republic of Councils] (Budapest: Kossuth, 1969), 14.

14 *Népszava.* November 3,1918.

15 *Népszava.* December 4, 1918.

16 According to the estimation of Oszkár Jászi, about one third of the public administration leadership fled. Jászi, Oszkár. *Magyar kálvária, magyar feltámadás.* [Hungarian Calvary, Hungarian Rersurretion]. (Budapest: Pallas, 1989), 66.

17 Tibor Hajdu, Munkástanácsok. op.cit. 1958. 61.

18 *Népszava.* November 3,1918.

19 *Debreceni Újság.* (Debrecen News) November 12, 1918. also. Dokumentumok... op.cit. 53.

20 *Szolnok megye 1918/19-ben.* (Szolnok County in 1918/19) Szolnok, Damjanich Museum. 1961. 20.

21 *Jászberényi Újság.* (Jászberény News) December 22, 1918. (Quoted in Szolnok megye 1918/19. ibid. 20.

22 *Szolnok Megye,* Op.cit. 29.

23 *Magyarországi Rendeletek Tára.* (Hungarian Government Decrees) (Budapest: 1918), 2423.

24 Gyula Hevesi, op.cit. 217.

25 Sándor Kávássy, *Somogy vármegye Direktóriuma 1919-ben.* (The Directory of Somogy County) (Szeged: Teacher Training College, 1964).

26 Hajdu, *Munkástanácsok... op.cit.,* 135.

27 János Kende, *Forradalomról forradalomra.* (From Revolution to Revolution) (Budapest: Gondolat, 1979), 120.

28 *Budapesti közlöny.* 1071/1919. M.E. sz. rendelet Az üzemi választmányokról. (Decree No. M.E. 1071/1919) Budapest City Registry, (February 11, 1919).

29 Sándor Matlekovits, "A Tanácsköztársaság közgazdasági politikája." (The Republic of Council's Economic Policy) in Gusztáv Gratz ed. *A bolsevizmus Magyarországon* (Bolshevism in Hungary) (Budapest: Franklin,1921), 343.

30 Tibor Hajdu, *Munkástanácsok 1958.* op.cit., 105.

31 György Péteri, *A Tanácsköztársaság ipari irányítási rendszere.* (Industrial Management Under the Republic of Councils) (Budapest: Közgazdaságz, 1979), 43.

32 Sándor Juhász-Nagy, *A magyar októberi forradalom története.* (The History of the Hungarian October Revolution) (Budapest: Cserépfalvi, 1945), 475.

33 János Kende, *Forradalomról... op.cit.* 83

34 Hevesi's article appeared in the first issue of *Internationale* in the middle of December 1918 but was dated January 1919.

35 *Vörös Újság.* "Red News," 1, no.1 (December 7, 1918).

36 *Vörös Újság* no. 15. January 23, 1919.

37 *Mindenkihez!* (To Everyone!) (March 21, 1919).

38 2221. *K.E.T./1919. XXVII. számú rendelet. A vidéki munkás-, katona- és paraszttanácsok és direktóriumok hatásköre.* (Decree XXVII on the responsibilities of the rural workers', soldiers' and peasant councils) *Vörös Újság.* April 1, 1919.

39 Tibor Hajdu, *Munkástanácsok..* op.cit. 221.

40 Tibor Hajdu, *Munkástanácsok..,* ibid. 229.

41 Tibor Hajdu, *Munkástanácsok..,* ibid. 240.

42 Tibor Hajdu, *Munkástanácsok..,* ibid. 242.

43 János Kende *Forradalomról... op.cit.* 155.

44 János Kende op.cit. 156.

45 János Kende *Ibid.* 156.

46 Lajos Varga, A szocializálás illúziói és buktatói a proletárdiktatúra első, békés-békétlen hónapjában (The Illusion and Hurdles of Nationalization During the Peaceful and Unpeaceful Months of the Republic of Councils). *Múltunk,* 2015/4. 43.

47 *Vörös Újság.* 2, no. 54, (April 11, 1919).

48 *Vörös Újság.* 2, no. 62, (April 20, 1919).

49 Tibor Hajdu, *Munkástanácsok..* op.cit. 228.

50 *Népszava* June 3, 1919.

51 *A megyei direktórium rendelete. 1919. június 28.* (The June 28, 1919 Decree of the Szolnok County Directorium) in *Szolnok megye..*, *op.cit.* 37.

52 From a manuscript by Lajos Kolacskovszky quoted in Tibor Hajdu *Munkástanácsok..*, op.cit. 195.

53 *Vörös Újság.* March 27, 1919.

54 Gyula Hevesi. op.cit. 249.

55 *Vörös Újság.* May 23, 1919.

56 *Szociális Termelés* (Socialist Production) June 4, 1919.

57 AMOSZ. Vol I, No. 64. June 15, 1919.

58 *A magyar munkásmozgalom történetének válogatott dokumentumai.* 6/a kötet. (Selected Documents from the History of the Hungarian Workers Movement. Volume 6/a) Budapest, Kossuth.1959. 504.

59 *Szociális Termelés.* May 28, 1919.

60 Samu Jászai. *A szakszervezetek föladatai a kommunista társadalomban.* (The Role of the Trade Unions in Communist Society) *Szakszervezeti Értesítő.* (Trade Union News) Vol XVI. No.7. May 31, 1919.

61 *Szakszervezeti Értesítő.* Vol XVI. No 6. May 24, 1919.

62 *Szociális Termelés.* June 18, 1919.

63 György Péteri. *op.cit,.* 236.

64 *A magyar Tanácsköztársaság szociálpolitikája.* (The Social Policy of the Hungarian Republic of Councils) Budapest, Gondolat. 1959. 86.

65 The comments of Ferenc Chorin Jr at the Board Meeting of the Salgótarján Coal Mine Co on August 22, 1919, are quoted by György Péteri, *op.cit* 254.

66 See György Péteri. *op.cit.* 258 on the Rimamurány-Salgótarjáni Iron Ore Co.

67 Sándor Matlekovits. "A Tanácsköztársaság közgazdasági politikája" (Economic Policy of the Republic of Councils) *Közgazdasági Szemle.* Vol. 62. 1920. 52.

68 György Péteri, *op.cit* 220.

69 *Népszava.* April 23, 1919.

70 György Péteri, *op.cit.* 187.

71 *Népszava.* April 23, 1919.

72 Lajos Csoma, "1918-1919 forradalma és a történelmi emlékezet. Hajdu Tibor történésszel beszélget Csoma Lajos." (The 1918-1919 Revolutions and Historical Memory: Lajos Csoma in Conversation with Tibor Hajdú) *Eszmélet*, no. 121, (Spring. 2019. 32).

CHAPTER 4

Exploring The Public Policy Universe of the 1919 Republic of Councils

András B. Göllner

A New Compass for a New Journey

Before embarking on this new journey into the public policy universe of the 1919 Hungarian Republic of Councils (HROC), it's imperative to say a few words about the compass that will guide us on our way. Its first, and perhaps most notable feature, is that it is a *moral* rather than *amoral* compass. Its value preferences are drawn from a small stream of consciousness that began with the Greek philosopher, Aristotle, and grew into a roaring mainstream over the centuries as others joined the flow of ideas from different parts of the planet, to express the universal rights and freedoms to which each and every human being on earth is equally and inalienably entitled.[1]

The central idea that unites the streams of consciousness flowing into this roaring river or *mainstream,* and shaped our compass as well, is the one which recognizes that we're "in this wash" together: this idea rejects selfishness as a virtue,[2] it embraces solidarity,[3] and acknowledges that we are our sisters and brothers' keepers. We are confident that this moral mainstream will continue to gather strength, it will outlive this book, and will go on to inspire others to create even more advanced compasses in the future than the one we're about to unveil here.

The 3 communal values that our compass is most sensitive or attuned to as it scans the signals emanating from its designated public policy universe is *justice, constitutionally guaranteed equal rights for all* in deciding who gets what, when and how in pursuit of *ecologically sustainable, communal well-being.* Our compass recognizes that attendance to these values cannot be left to chance or unregulated market forces: their achievement demands moral leadership and a climate that protects, nurtures and maximizes the *capabilities*[4] of all citizens to engage in fearless and informed *public reasoning* about the path that will lead them towards ecologically sustainable communal well-being.[5]

It's important to underline that the value preferences of our compass are not drawn from a pie in the sky but from the salt of the earth. These value preferences are endorsed by the covenants of today's two major international organizations, the United Nations and the European Union. (The explanation of why so many members of these organizations cannot swim within their mainstream belongs elsewhere.) The value preferences of our compass are not tangential but central to the concerns of the oppressed, abused, misled working men and women of the world. They are values that were broadly embraced by millions of ordinary Hungarians in 1848, as well as in 1919 and have, therefore, a legitimate place in our policy evaluation toolkit.

In order to distinguish it from compasses that were used on previous expeditions,[6] we need to reveal not only our compass's value preferences, but its settings vis-á-vis four other inspiring areas of human ingenuity: politics, the State, government, and public policy. The *idea* of politics that encases our compass is as universal as its value preferences. It pre-dates categorizations that have divided the world of politics into left and right-wing hemispheres. It should not cause any irritation to the hands of those who like to look upon themselves as conservatives, liberals, socialists or even anarchists. The designers of our compass trace the roots of politics back, once again, to those ideas of Aristotle that are as valid today as they were when they were first formulated three hundred years before the birth of Christ.[7] It would be an American political scientist, Harold Lasswell (1902–1978), who would reduce Aristotle's lengthy tome into a universally acceptable working definition of politics as a struggle over who gets what, when, and how in a community.[8] The political sensors of our compass reflect this Lasswelian or neo-Aristotelian approach.

The approach of our compass towards the State will require a bit longer elaboration than its approach to politics, but it must be undertaken because we cannot enter the public policy universe of the 1919 Hungarian state unless we identify its dimensions. In Aristotle's time the locus of organized political activity, the *polis,* was the city.[9] City politics did not die out with the Greeks—it merely expanded into larger and larger territorial enclaves over time, reflective of population growth and *Homo Sapiens'* unmatched ability within the animal kingdom to organize themselves into larger and larger communities in order to go after what their leaders wanted them to.[10] Today, most of the world's human population is subdivided into 206 distinct *states*, of which 193 are full, though not necessarily equal or fully sovereign members of the United Nations.[11] The Hungarian state is one of the member of this exclusive group.

There is surprising unanimity of opinion between the political Right and the Left about a universally valid "means test" for qualifying an organization as a State. It was developed by the German Sociologist, Max Weber (1864–1920), who argued that what distinguishes a State from any other political organization is its claim to "a monopoly on the legitimate use of physical force within its territory".[12]

Though it's universally embraced, Weber's means test did not put an end to arguments between the Left and the Right, liberals and conservatives, about the *origins* and nature of the State.[13]

West Europeans like to think of the State as an organizational form they invented after the Treaty of Westphalia in 1648, and as something they gave as a present to the rest of the world through their colonial exploits afterwards. With a few exceptions, most Hungarians (not to mention the people of Africa and of other non-European parts of the world) have a different take on this matter. Hungarians, for example, had been taught for centuries that their state came into the world over 1,000 years ago for the purpose of fulfilling God's will on a part of the planet they came to occupy after they left their former hunting grounds in Asia at the end of the 7th century AD.

Our compass does not question the ability of the Magyars to craft a state for themselves 600 years before that skill set was mastered by their European neighbours to the West. It has, in fact, detected states in many non-European parts of the world nine thousand years *prior* to the birth of the Hungarian state. The reason why *our* compass can reach back further in time and space than the Westphalian one is this: it possesses a *universally valid teleological sensor* in addition to the universally valid *means test* that was discovered by the aforementioned Max Weber.[14]

Our compass traces the origin of the State back to the start of the Agricultural Revolution, to a time and space when our ancestors began to abandon life "on the road" (the life of the hunter, gatherer), and to establish permanent settlements for themselves—initially in Northern and Central Africa. It's not the falsely pious, self-serving language of the Machiavellian princes of the West but *the logic of settlement*, the desire to give the settlement an *afterlife*, to end the limbo of uncertainty, to provide enduring safety and a livelihood to the founders' off-springs that gives birth to the state as an *institution*. The idea to acquire statehood comes to the leaders of the Magyars not before, but after they had been taught a lesson in warfare by a Bavarian Prince and decided to *settle down* in the Carpathian Basin rather than carry on looting and raping their neighbors to the West.[15] (Looking at the practices of Viktor Orbán, the leader of the Hungarian government during the past decade suggests, that old habits die hard within Hungary's political elite, especially when the statues of the ancestors who terrorized the West 1,200 years ago are prominently displayed on Budapest's Heroes Square.)

The architects of the State are driven to this day everywhere on the planet, first and foremost, rightly or wrongly and regardless of their final blueprints, not by the desire to monopolize force but by the desire to secure *sustainability* for their systems.[16] István, the first King of the Hungarians didn't want his lifework to go to waste.[17] Louis XIV of France (1637–1715), at the prime of his power, proclaimed "*L'État c'est moi*" and reminded the citizens of France of his *systemic* or institutionalized sustainability on his deathbed as follows, "*Je m'en vais, mais l'État demeurera toujours*". The British echo this idea to this day: *The King is dead, long live the King!*[18] The American federal state endures to this day because of the attentiveness of its architects to providing it with a formula of sustainability. It's the quest for systemic sustainability that drives the narrative of *The Communist Manifesto*, *The Wealth of Nations*, as well as Viktor Orbán's *System of National Co-operation* (NER). Communal sustainability is not a 21st-century idea. It has been embedded into *Homo sapiens'* DNA since the start of the Agricultural Revolution. The princes of Europe did not invent it—they merely paid lip service to it after they were taught how to do so by Machiavelli. The beginning or end of every state is like the beginning or end of a dream, or of a nightmare.[19] Our compass recognizes, in short, that states are *political symbols* purposefully implanted in the minds of members of a community by their leaders—the architects of the State— in order to fill them with not only a *feeling* of common identity, but first and foremost, a *feeling* of *communal sustainability via subservience to the established political order.*[20]

In addition to registering the value preferences, the persuasive or coercive ability, and the *telos* of a State, modern policy compasses should also be able to register the key that enables a State to secure recognition for itself from its neighbours and those that matter in their time and space outside of their territories.[21] There are many paths towards acquiring and maintaining critical third party recognition.[22] Modern compasses should not ignore but address this fourth dimension of statecraft especially in the case of the 1919 Hungarian Republic of Councils.

The distinction between States and governments can be dealt with much more rapidly now. Our policy compass looks at governments as *agents* that manage the affairs of the State. It is the State's prerogative to decide what powers and organizing principles it applies to the management of its affairs on the territory under its jurisdiction. Most states organize their governments along *functional* (vertical) and *territorial* (horizontal) lines. Functional organizational models of governance come in two varieties: One bases itself on the *separation of powers* principle (also known as the Presidential Model) the other follows what is commonly known as the *fusion of power* principle (also known as the Parliamentary Model). In the first case, a State's government is divided into separate branches—the executive, legislative, and judiciary—that may or may not check and balance each other.[23] The latter fuses these branches, puts them into one or two houses of Parliament and in the case of democratic states, uses a variety of instruments to prevent this fusion of power from becoming abusive or autocratic.[24]

As far as territorial (or horizontal) organizational models of governance are concerned, states tend to choose between one of three types of arrangements, in order to manage their affairs in a sustainable manner. These are commonly known as the *Federal, Confederal* and *Unitary* models.[25] The important thing to keep in mind in all of the above cases is that it is the State and not the government of the day that decides whether the affairs of the State will be managed in a Presidential or Parliamentary, a Federal or a Unitary fashion. Compasses that are insensitive to the above distinctions cannot serve as reliable guides to the public policy universe of politically organized communities such as states.

Having identified the moral values of our compass, its approach towards politics, the State, and governments, we have only one more setting to elaborate upon: the one towards public policy. Our compass looks at public policy as that which governments consciously, deliberately set out to do or *not* to do during the course of managing the affairs of their states.[26] Though many people outside of governments can and do participate in the manufacturing of public policies even in an autocracy, our compass will only recognize a policy as "public" when it has governmental authority behind it.

Deliberate intent is an important element to highlight in the above definition. Public policies have side effects, and those that are unintended should not be granted public policy status. (The ban of alcoholic beverages by the State may, for example, increase the sale and consumption of other narcotics. Such an outcome may be intentional or unintentional. It is the job of the policy analyst to distinguish between deliberate intent, and the unintended side-effects of governmental actions or inactions.) Our compass does *not* classify the unintended side effects of governmental actions or inactions as public policy but draws attention to them when needed.

Ever since Aristotle, political theorists had been hard at work trying to construct a grand theory, a "one-size fits all" formula along the lines of Einstein's Theory of Relativity, that would reveal the "laws" of the public policy universe in an empirically verifiable and predictable manner. While such a tool is still but a dream, "Big Data" analytics enables us today to design compasses that provide simultaneous, 360-degree scanning of a State's public-policy universe along many of the co-ordinates of our currently fashionable grand theories, be they *structural* (e.g. Marxism, World Systems Theory, Institutionalism), or *dynamic* (e.g. Pluralism, Game Theory, Public Choice Theory). Rather than locking onto a single signal—pattern, such as the one favored by Marxists,[27] or Pluralists[28], our compass follows a holistic approach.[29]

Our "holistic" compass is "state-of-the-art" in the sense that it recognizes that the public-policy universe of the "world system" (to use Wallersteinian language for a change[30]) consists of distinct "Galaxies", "Constellations", "Solar Systems" and "Planets". In the policy sciences, we refer to these collectively as "policy subsystems". Policy subsystems come in many shapes and forms and under different labels such as *iron triangles, issue networks, policy paradigms, advocacy coalitions, policy regimes* and the like.[31] As one of the innovators of the public-policy template used in the design of our compass notes: "By the end of the 1980s it was clear from the work of scholars in many different countries that a variety of different subsystems existed (in the policy universe) depending on the structural interrelationships among their component parts".[32]

An important feature of our compass' public-policy sensors is that which enables them to approach the public policy-making process as:

> A series of discreet but related sub-processes that together form an entire policy-cycle. The stages in that cycle correspond to the *five* (5) stages found in other instances of applied problem solving whereby problems are recognized, possible solutions are proposed, a solution is chosen, the selected choice is put into effect, and finally, the outcomes are monitored and evaluated.[33]

These five stages of the public-policy cycle are now commonly known by scholars all around the world as "agenda setting, policy formulation, decision-making, policy implementation and policy evaluation."[34]

To sum up: Our compass approaches the public policies of the Hungarian Republic of Councils along each of their developmental stages and focuses on 3 targets: the identifiable *actors, ideas* and *institutions* that play a decisive role in each stage of the policy cycle. The designers of our compass's public-policy sensors provide a lucid statement of the rationale for this kind of targeting:

> ... Actors, Ideas and Institutions form the common ground where all policy theorizing converges, from different directions and with distinctive points of view. It is in adopting and adapting these conceptual particularities that the potential for greater insight into policy making and policy outcomes can be realized.[35]

With these technical matters out of our way, and the sight-lines of our compass fully revealed, we are now ready to enter into the public policy universe of the 1919 Hungarian Republic of Councils. Though this chapter, as indeed all of the chapters of this book, is driven by the desire to reveal aspects of the 1919 Hungarian Republic of Councils that have been distorted and forgotten by historians, it has to be a selective rather than exhaustive survey. A single chapter, such as this one, cannot possibly capture the entire policy universe of the 1919 Hungarian Republic of Councils in all of its aforementioned dimensions. Such a venture, while much needed, has to be left to a much larger vehicle, manned by a crew that can utilize the navigational system that we outlined on the preceding pages. What follows is not a final but an opening statement, an important test run with a new, state-of-the-art compass that will provide us not only with some important discoveries about fundamental aspects of the Commune's policy universe (its core, the constituent parts of its public-policy engine, its judicial policies, its approach to law enforcement, the exercise of physical force over its territory, its alleged reliance on terror) but open the way for others where no one has gone before.

The Core of the Commune's Policy Universe: The Proletarian State and its Governing Machinery

The opening paragraphs of the temporary constitution of the new Hungarian state leave nothing to the imagination:

> The goal of the Hungarian Republic of Councils is to abolish the capitalist production and social order and build in its place a socialist production and social system. The way to achieve this goal is by ensuring that workers exercise control over their exploiters. The dictatorship of the Hungarian proletariat will be exercised by the National Congress of Councils together with the local workers', soldiers' and peasants' councils. The people who work in workers', soldiers' and peasants' councils will make the laws, will execute them, and exercise judicial control over those who break them.[36]

It is clear from the above, that the Founding Fathers of the Hungarian Republic of Councils wanted to design and operate a state that would meet all of the systemic pre-requisites of statehood that we outlined earlier: communal sustainability, constitutionally guaranteed justice, and equal rights to its long-exploited underclass, the monopoly of physical force on its territory, and, last but not least, the achievement of recognition from those neighbours that mattered. Its design, in other words, was harmonious with the universal template presented in the previous section.

The HROC's constitutionally prescribed vertical power plant followed the fusion of power principle: executive, legislative and judicial power was to be housed in the National Congress of Councils (NCC), whose members were to be chosen by a network of local councils of workers', soldiers' and peasants' deputies. The horizontal power plant of the HROC was a hybrid machine: structurally it was a federal system, but operationally it followed the principles of democratic-centralism. The right to appoint and remove deputies cascaded upwards, from the lower village councils right up to the National Congress, but the decisions taken by deputies of a higher-level council were binding on the levels directly below them. The Greater Budapest Workers' and Soldiers' Council could overrule the decisions of the district councils in the capital. A county council could overrule a district council that could, in turn, overrule a village council and so on. Members of the base, the local councils, from whom power extended upwards to the National Congress, were to be chosen freely and according to the principles of universality. A lower-level council could recall its representatives higher up if it did not like how it was being governed.

Until the National Congress of Councils met in the middle of June, to finalize the country's constitution and take full control of the ship of state, a newly created and limited-term executive body, the Revolutionary Governing Council (RGC) was to run the affairs of the new state by decree but in close consultation with the country's largest local council, the 500 member Workers' and Soldiers' Council of Greater Budapest and its 80-member Executive Committee. The RGC was in effect the executive arm of the Proletarian State during the first three months of the HROC's 4-month long existence but it did not have free reign. After the NCC passed the country's new constitution on June 23, 1919, the RGC dropped the "Revolutionary" prefix from its name and became known simply as the Governing Council. Whereas prior to June 23 its main rival was the Executive Committee of the Workers' and Soldiers' Council of Greater Budapest, from this point on, it had yet another supervisory body imposed upon it on which the Communists were in a small minority—the newly-elected 150-member Executive Committee of the National Congress of Councils: the RGC fell under even greater public scrutiny near the end of its mandate than at its beginning.

While the architects of the new Hungarian state possessed hardly any governing experience, they were fully cognizant of the template that we outlined in the first part of this chapter. Initially, they managed to enthral millions with their design not only within the lower but the middle and upper-middle classes as well. With the active and enthusiastic assistance of the local councils throughout the country—councils that pre-dated the Dictatorship of the Proletariat and were organized spontaneously by Hungary's working men and women after the end of WWI—the HROC managed to organize the first free elections in Hungary's thousand-year history. Anyone over 18 within the non-propertied classes could cast a vote.[37] Think of it: millions of formerly disenfranchised working men and women were able to vote for the first time in their lives. The People's Republic of Mihály Károlyi was unable to master this challenge during its five months in office. The Republic of Councils did it in just over two weeks. Those who to this day still do not recognize the transformation from the 1st to the 2nd Hungarian Republic as a revolutionary event cannot be categorized in any other way than as ill-informed, or blind.

Who were the key *actors*, what were the *ideas*, what was the *institutional setting* that combined to push this particular design of the State, this type of governing machinery through the various stages of the public policy cycle in Hungary? The narrative of the past century identifies the key architects of the first Hungarian proletarian state as "Lenin's boys", sent to Budapest from Moscow at the end of 1918 in order to organize a Bolshevik coup and to beat the false consciousness out of the ill-informed minds of the Hungarian public at large through a Soviet-designed reign of "Red Terror". This narrative that identifies Béla Kun and his Soviet trained colleagues—working hand in glove with the Kremlin—guided by Lenin's blueprints and working within a cohesive and well-structured institutional setting, which provided them with preferential treatment inside the walls of the new Hungarian state, is pure fiction. This conventional narrative[38] is as false as the one given to Lenin by Béla Kun, after the Soviet leader called him in Budapest because he could not believe what he had just heard in the news in Moscow on March the 22nd, 1919.[39]

Let us begin setting the record straight regarding the Founding Fathers of the Dictatorship of the Proletariat in Hungary by casting our eyes backwards onto the evidence presented by Peter Csunderlik and Lajos Csoma in earlier chapters of this book. The HSDP was the undisputed vanguard of the Hungarian labour movement going back to the second half of the 19th century. While there were many revolutionary cross-currents at play in Hungary outside of the HSDP's control (e.g. the agrarian socialists, the Anarchists—the religious, the syndicalists, and others—the socialist revolutionaries, various factions of the Galileists, the shop stewards, the inter-factory committee, the socialist engineers, Lajos Kassák's followers, and last but not least, Béla Kun's Bolsheviks), the HSDP had by far the largest, best organized, political machine within the country in March 1919. The HSDP controlled virtually all of the Trade Unions, and one of the most influential women's organization at the time. By 1919 it had more than 1.5 million card-carrying and unionized members. The Hungarian Communist Party had a fraction of this political capital. It was just shy of its 4-month birthday, its top leadership was badly divided, and the entire front line of its Central Committee was in jail until the afternoon of March 21, the day when the Republic of Councils was proclaimed.

The majority of the Founding Fathers of the 1919 Hungarian Republic of Councils came *not* from Lenin's drawing room but from the centre and left-wing of the Hungarian Social Democratic Party's leadership, who learned their socialism not on Lenin's but on August Bebel's, Rosa Luxemburg's, and Anton Pannekoek's knees.[40] The HSDP executive managed to convince the Communists to give up their powerful, independent administrative machine on March 20, 1919, and to fold it into the Social Democrat's much larger operation. From that point on, "Lenin's Boys" in Hungary were in a minority position within their own tent.[41] Of the powerful 11-member Party Secretariat, that ran the operations of the newly fused party, only 2 were former Communist Party members. The situation went downhill from there. Of the 327 delegates to the new Party's first Congress in June 1919, held just prior to the first meeting of the National Congress of Councils, less than a quarter were members of the disbanded Communist Party. During the first round of voting at this first Party Congress, the delegates refused to elect a single former Communist to the Party's newly constituted Executive Committee. Kun had to threaten withdrawal from the party alliance before the delegates grudgingly agreed to give 4 of the 13 seats on the Party's Executive Committee to Kun's followers. As the American-Hungarian Political Scientist Rudolf Tökés points out, "...the Communist drive for control of the united party was doomed from the beginning".[42]

The situation within the State apparatus was equally distant from Lenin's formula. The hand of the HSDP majority shows clearly when we look at who was put in charge of the performance after the curtain was raised on the new state on March 22, 1919. The Head of State (the President) and the head of the State's governing machinery (the Prime Minister) became Sándor Garbai, a high-ranking member of the HSDP. The temporary executive branch of the new government— the aforementioned Revolutionary Governing Council—was organized into 13 Commissariats (or ministries). Only one of these ministries, the critically important Foreign Relations Commissariat, was put in the hands of a Bolshevik Commissar, Béla Kun. 11 were headed by a high ranking member of the HSDP executive, and one, the Agricultural Commissariat, was headed by a *troika* of whom only one, Jenő Hamburger, was a former member of the HCP.[43] The actual drafting of the constitution was put into the hands of the Commissar for Justice, Dr. Zoltán Rónai, an academic (a political scientist, no less), a centrist member of the HSDP, who never set foot in Russia, had not read a word by Lenin and was opposed to the fusion of the two left-wing parties as late as March 21.[44] Members of the Communist Party were in an even greater disadvantage within the organs of the powerful Workers', Soldiers' and Peasants' Councils. They only had a handful of representatives on the 80-member Executive Committee of the Workers' and Soldiers' Councils of Greater Budapest, and possessed virtually no representatives on the regional and local councils outside of the capital. On the constitutionally designated commanding levers of the NCC's 150-member Executive Committee, Béla Kun's Communists only had 20% of the votes. The Hungarian Republic of Councils was as close to a Communist Party dictatorship as America to a Donald Trump Presidency after January 6, 2021.

The *ideas* that moved the policy-cycle through its first three stages as far as the State and its governing machinery were concerned, were once again not those that one would associate with Lenin, the principal architect of the Soviet state. The ideas behind the design of the 1919 Hungarian proletarian state were drawn from a German, rather than a Russian well, even in the case of those Bolsheviks who did play a significant role in the design of the proletarian state (e.g. Béla Kun and his chief theoreticians, László Rudas or György Lukács). As Peter Kenez rightly observes:

> It would be anachronistic to think of the Hungarian Communist Party at that time as a Bolshevik organization... The Hungarian Communists' conception of the Party was more Luxemburgian than Leninist... Béla Kun had little understanding of Leninist ideology and the theoreticians had not yet freed themselves from their Western European Socialist background... György Lukács, on the Party's right and László Rudas, a leader of the Communist left wing both agreed with Luxemburg's idea of spontaneity... [45] The Communists and the left-wing Social Democrats drew from the same ideological source.[46]

And that source was neither Russian nor Leninist.[47]

It was György Lukács's Commissariat of Public Education in March 1919 that ordered and paid for the translation and publication of Rosa Luxemburg's *Mass Strike*.[48] Lukács wrote a glowing introduction to the work, making it explicitly clear where he and his Commissariat stood at the time.[49]

In a similar and noteworthy essay, written during the agenda and policy formation stage of the newly emerging Hungarian state, and written before he read and translated Lenin's *State and Revolution* into Hungarian, Rudas was still echoing Luxemburg's and Pannekoek's core ideas which explains why workers' councils were entrusted with executive, legislative, and judicial suzerainty in the new Hungarian constitution on March 21, 1919: "Parties play only a secondary role in revolutions for on these occasions it is precisely the least organized elements of the working classes which acquire crucial importance".[50] The genuine Leninists within the HCP at the outset, such as Tibor Szamuely, were as surprised and disappointed with the design of the Proletarian State and its governing machinery on the morning after March 21, 1919, as Lenin himself.[51]

To sum up: While everyone on the Left in Hungary was buoyed by the Russian revolution, they were far more familiar with the ideas of Georges Sorel, Rosa Luxemburg and Anton Pannekoek at the moment of their creative engagement than with those of Lenin. This is why their design of the State and of its governing machinery is so unlike the one installed by the Bolsheviks in Moscow. Comparing the two systems is like comparing apples and oranges.

As far as the *institutional* frame of the agenda setting, policy formulation, and decision-making phases of the policy-cycle vis-á-vis the architecture of the proletarian state and its governing machinery is concerned, the facts here are also at odds with the conventional narrative. While there were some negotiations by some of the founding fathers of the Hungarian proletarian state inside Béla Kun's prison cell prior to March 21, 1919, the institutional setting for the final design of the Hungarian proletarian state was much wider and reached all the way into the institutional headquarters of universal capitalism which was temporarily located in Versailles and under greater influence by the French government of the day than it would be under normal circumstances.[52]

Hungary's Communists and Social Democrats didn't unite their troops in Budapest at the drop of Mihály Károlyi's liberal hat on March 20 in order to "finally fulfill their long repressed and morbid desire to destroy Hungary's Christian-National identity"[53] but to defend the 1,000-year-old Hungarian state against the forces of those external institutions that wanted to make it unsustainable. The founding fathers from the two political parties on Hungary's left began to look for a common path to the future outside of their parties' institutional setting and behind their own members' backs, weeks before March 21. They wanted to see if they could "bury the hatchet" and work together to help working men and women to the centre stage of Hungary's political arena after the destruction wrought upon them by the Imperial order and by WWI. The external force, the external *institution* that pushed the hitherto hostile political parties into each other's arms in Hungary on the afternoon of March 21, 1919, and launched the Hungarian proletarian state, was the so-called "Council of Ten" of the Paris Peace Conference.[54] Its nuclear decision, taken behind Hungary's back [55] on February 26, 1919[56] was only made fully known to Hungary's leaders on March 20, 1919.[57]

The Entente's ultimatum did not allow for protracted negotiations within Hungary's political arena. Kun's institutional setting was the prison cell where he was being held—a place from where he had no access to Lenin. The HSDP's institutions were fully functional but they were locked into the same 30-hour time capsule as everyone else. Their leaders were right in concluding that they could only come out of that time capsule alive if they secured the support of the Workers' and Soldiers' Council of Budapest, and that of the second-largest political party, the Communists. Sándor Garbai, one of the HSDP's top negotiators, the one who would become the Head of the Proletarian State, rushed over to a meeting of the Budapest Workers' Council and advised them of the joint plan of the two left-wing parties to give all power to the Councils. The Budapest Workers' Council gave unanimous consent to the shot-gun marriage plan without any debate. And why wouldn't they? They were given an offer they could not refuse.

To conclude: The West has only itself to blame for the temporary collapse of one of its bastions in the East. It provided the "shotgun" for this sudden marriage between the Hungarian Social Democrats and the Bolsheviks that would manifest itself in the form of a new, anti-capitalist, proletarian state. The observations of the liberal historian and legal scholar, Oszkár Jászi, provide to this day the clearest and most accurate assessment of the critical role played by external institutions in this first, and decisive policy initiative of the Hungarian state:

> If the Entente had wished it, legality and democracy in Hungary might have been preserved… But all this was of no interest to the diplomatists of the Entente.. They were interested only in two things: that the Hungarian Treaty of peace should be signed *sans phrase* and that the country should be kept a close preserve of foreign capitalists and profiteers.[58]

The Hungarian Left refused to buckle under this gun. "Horthy and his associates agreed to both conditions with the generosity of true Magyar gentlemen".[59]

According to our compass, the limited endurance of this hastily constructed revolutionary state and its governing machinery was due to problems that would emerge during the 4th phase of the policy cycle—the implementation of its core elements. The erratic, often contradictory roll-out of the proletarian state and its governing machinery (which Lajos Csoma illustrated with great clarity in the previous chapter), reflected not only the divisiveness, the numerous fault-lines within the newly fused political party but the strength of the spontaneously organised workers', soldiers' and peasants' councils. The latter refused to roll over and die, refused to be used simply as "delivery boys", as window dressings in a Hungarian "Potemkin village" scene. The challenge of having to confront perhaps the biggest existential challenge in its entire 1000-year history with an untried revolutionary state and a governing machinery, whose parts were not in tune with each other was bad enough: the united opposition to this experiment by the great powers of the day, the military invasion by three of the neighbouring countries, the unwillingness of the two country's that could help—the USSR and Austria— to do so, sealed the fate of Hungary's working men and women. They were brutally swept off the centre stage of Hungary's political arena by a series of counter-revolutions that will be highlighted in the closing chapter of this book.

The Proletarian State's Approach to Justice, Law Enforcement and Coercion

As we have stated at the beginning of this chapter, a *"monopoly on the legitimate use of physical force"* is universally recognized as one of the essential prerequisites of statehood and one that applies equally to democratic and autocratic states. Our aim in this section is to examine the approach of the Hungarian Republic of Councils to the demands for law and order, the use of physical force, especially the use of "terror" as an instrument of public policy.

Is terror an objective necessity for the movement of working men and women to the center stage of history? Is it an indelible part of the Marxist revolutionary formula? We have studied these hotly contested questions for decades, but cannot concern ourselves at length with them in this chapter.[60] Our task here is strictly limited to identifying the political *actors*, *ideas* and *institutions* that propelled the Hungarian Republic of Councils' coercive policies through the five stages of the public policy cycle between March 21 and August 1, 1919, and to examining what role if any, state sanctioned terror played in these processes. Though our focus is narrow, our conceptualization of "state sanctioned terror" is universal. It was designed to transcend ideological boundaries in order to enable socialists, capitalists, liberals, conservatives, the Left, the Right, to feel equally comfortable navigating with it.

In our political lexicon, "state-sanctioned terror" is a uniquely targeted and extreme form of coercion that seeks to create profound fear (terror) in the minds of community members (civilians and non-civilians alike) about the dire consequences of being caught thinking, planning or implementing acts that challenge the authority of the State's governing machinery. This type of coercion—ideologically driven intimidation—involves the legal and indiscriminate use or threat of violence up to and including deadly force by state actors against any suspected *political* opponents and rivals who are identified as "enemies of the State" or "enemies of the people". To achieve its desired effect, the State actors who use this coercive instrument must be able to demonstrate to one and all, that they are invincible, and in possession of uncontestable and legitimate monopoly over the use of such force on the entire territory of the State.[61]

As a preamble to the *alleged* use of terror by the proletarian state in Hungary, it has to be established that while terror is *not* a prerequisite of statehood, the use of this form of coercion is as old as the State itself. It is a policy instrument that respects no ideological boundaries and comes in many colours and shades including white, red, black and brown. Those states that sanctioned its use throughout human history, had generally done so because they considered it, rightly or wrongly, a *legitimate* "system-maintenance device", indispensable for their state's survival.[62] Those governments that applied it, or apply it today, generally do so because they believe they cannot manage the affairs of their state without it, or survive in office unless they use it. Terror, in other words, is not an objective but a subjective necessity: it's a "mind game" that "manufactures consent"[63] by making us believe that dissent is immoral because it threatens the sustainability of the community, and the State has a *moral obligation* to deter potential dissenters by not only flexing or "showing off" its awesome muscles in public,[64] but by using it as well, and in a violent and merciless manner, against anyone caught in the alleged act of thinking, planning or engaging in political dissent.[65]

The conservative historical narrative of the past century inside and outside of Hungary argues that "Red Terror" was the all-encompassing, all consuming feature of the 1919 Hungarian Republic of Councils' pursuit of that essential, Weberian maxim we have spoken of earlier.[66] According to this school of thought, the use of terror as a public policy instrument by the Hungarian Republic of Councils was unavoidable and was the result of a double-bind. First: since the architects of the Hungarian proletarian state were all "Lenin's boys", they had no choice but to copy faithfully their master's teachings and practices on terror in Hungary. Second: the illegitimate, unpopular "coup" by Béla Kun and his Soviet trained Bolsheviks could only sustain itself by terror in Hungary. The senseless, unpopular, anti-Christian, anti-Hungarian agenda of the Leninist and Jewish led Revolutionary Governing Council, they tell us, could only be advanced by terror in Hungary.[67]

The liberal-conservative academic mainstream's take in Hungary today on the use of terror by the 1919 proletarian state differs only marginally from its older conservative relative.[68] It reduces the number of the 1919 Red Terror's victims by a couple of hundred (from 560 to just over 360).[69] It corrects an important false impression, by pointing out, that the vast majority of the perpetrators of the terror on the ground were Christians rather than Jews.[70] It presents its movement through time and space as a wave rather than a straight line.[71] It acknowledges that part of the responsibility for the alleged application of terror by the proletarian state in Hungary in 1919 rests with the brutalization of many of the country's citizens in the killing-fields of WWI.[72] Last but not least it follows the latest American fad, popularly known as *whataboutism*. (The liberal "new wave" in Hungary today does not think its "kosher" to talk about the Red Terror without talking about the White Terror, in the same breath.)[73]

We shall argue, and provide verifiable evidence for our argument, that the still dominant liberal conservative narratives which claim that terror was baked into the "formula" of the *Hungarian* transition to socialism in 1919 (i.e., that it was ideologically predetermined), and was a deliberately chosen policy instrument of the Hungarian proletarian state, is an empirically unsustainable fairy-tale.[74]

The quest for the *legitimate monopoly of physical force* by the proletarian state began on the first working day of the 1919 Republic of Councils and was rightfully one of its chief public-policy preoccupations throughout its lifetime. The Revolutionary Governing Council mandated three Commissariats with explicit responsibilities in this, perhaps most important quadrant of the Commune's policy-universe: the Commissariat for Justice, the Commissariat of the Interior and the Commissariat of Defense. They put Social Democrats, rather than Communists (Zoltán Rónai, Jenő Landler, and József Pogány respectively[75]), at the head of each of these Commissariats.[76] Not one of these men had read a single line from Lenin, or been to Russia before or during the lifetime of the Republic of Councils. While all of them applauded the Russian revolution, along with tens of millions throughout the world at that time, the one thing they shared in common with each other and with the majority of an albeit badly divided Revolutionary Governing Council was the desire *not* to model "their shops" on the one in Moscow, and not to rely on terror as the cornerstone of the Hungarian proletarian state's justice and law enforcement policies.[77]

To ensure that the objective outlined above would be upheld, the independence of all the Commissariats was tightly curtailed by the Founding Fathers of the 1919 Hungarian Republic of Councils. The Commissars had to account for their actions to the RGC, to the Soldiers, and Workers' Council of Greater Budapest and ultimately to the National Congress of Councils once that body was duly constituted and operational as the executive, legislative and judicial engine of the proletarian state.[78]

The old rules, along with the old court system were the first to go, as the proletarian state's acting executive (the RGC) geared up its policy-making engine on March 22, 1919. As we have stated earlier, the two Commissars who were entrusted with leading the team that was to revamp the Republic's judicial system, were neither Bolsheviks nor "party hacks". The Social Democrat Rónai not only bristled at the idea of going to bed with the Bolsheviks, but was given a deputy, István Lékai, who wasn't even a member of *any* political party.[79] Both of these Commissars were legal scholars with doctorates, who surrounded themselves with some of the best and most progressive legal minds available at the time who were both willing and able to participate in the execution of the Herculean task that lay ahead.

The halls and offices of the Commissariat of Justice in Budapest were not crawling with hotheaded Bolsheviks out for blood in 1919. This Commissariat was perhaps the "safest haven", the one government agency without any of "Lenin's Boys" among its staff.[80] Equating the judicial system they concocted in great haste with the one in Moscow at the time is just one of the oft repeated fairy-tales about the Hungarian Republic of Councils that refuses to die.[81]

The newly unfolding Hungarian justice system was driven by the same desire for sustainability as its feudal and semi-feudal predecessors were: one gave primacy to individual, the other to collective rights; one favoured the propertied classes, the other favored the hitherto 'disposable' commoners. The earlier ones evolved over a long period of time, the one in 1919 did not have such a luxury.

Hungary's lawmakers of 1919 reversed the long-standing order with the stroke of a pen. They abolished all discriminatory measures against commoners, put working men and women at the front of the line, the nobility and the fortune hunters at the back so they would never ever be able to force millions of commoners into bondage, or be able to march them off to their death in pursuit of the fortune hunters' insatiable appetite for wealth, privilege and conquest. Not surprisingly, on March 22, 1919, any attempt to remove working men and women from the front of the line, from the center stage of Hungary's political arena, or to overturn the Dictatorship of the Proletariat, became a crime.

Given the shortage of space, we cannot enter into a detailed analysis of the Republic of Councils' judicial policies. All we can do with the aid of our compass is to draw attention to some of the newly emerging evidence that was kept hidden from public view until relatively recently. Three young female Hungarian scholars in particular deserve honorable mention for their pioneering work and their courage to speak publicly about their findings at a time when it is, once again, dangerous to do so.[82] According to Zsófia Nagy, the policy makers within the Commissariat of Justice "wanted to create a new criminal code and assigned an important role to a special institution called the Department of Experimental Criminology (the DEC), that was especially sensitive to social and psychological factors in the assessment of criminal behavior".[83] Henrietta Trádler directs our view to the "interdisciplinary teamwork that integrated legal, psychological and historical knowledge into the DEC's guidelines",[84] while Viola Lászlófi has shown that "The DEC provided judges and lawyers with psychoanalytic training. For the first time in Hungarian history, psychoanalysis was used as a criminological tool in the judicial process".[85] The commentator on these recent findings, the aforementioned András Patrik Erdős, concluded his assessment with the following words: "The proletarian dictatorship did not want to create a new type of man with its new methods of justice, but to change society so that everyone would have a place in it".[86]

Parallel with the work of the aforementioned is that of another historian, Sándor Nagy, who studied the entire collection of court documents held in the Budapest Municipal Archives from that era. Here are his findings, publicly shared for the first time in English in this book:

> The primary task of the Revolutionary Tribunals was to protect the proletarian dictatorship. In short order, however, they began to administer justice not only in political cases, but in all areas of public law.[87] They assumed many of the functions of the old (royal) justice system. This transformation of the Revolutionary Tribunals was formally authorized by the RGC's Decree No. XCIV on May 17, 1919 [88]... The largest jurisdiction,

the Budapest Revolutionary Court, was established on March 26, 1919 under Ferenc Rákos.[89] During its 4 months of operation, the Budapest Court heard 2,233 cases (which constituted about a quarter of all the court cases in the entire country during the life of the Republic). 60% of the cases brought before the Budapest Court were thrown out without a formal hearing. Only 20% of the accused were found to be guilty (446 in all). Only one-fifth of all those convicted fell into the "political" category (i.e. 89 cases). The Budapest Court handed down a total of 21 death sentences, of which only four were carried out.[90]

Let us turn our attention to the behavior of the two other Commissariats—the Commissariats of the Interior and Defense—and see what role if any they played in the alleged "reign of terror" during the 1919 Republic of Councils.

The Revolutionary Governing Council put the Commissariat of the Interior in charge of the activity we tend to lump under the heading of "domestic law enforcement". Without going into the details, law enforcement in Hungary after WWI was in the same chaotic state as it was throughout the territories of those three empires that collapsed at the end of WWI—the Hapsburg, the Ottoman and the Romanoff. Millions of mostly illiterate fighting men were "back home" from the battlefields, dejected and utterly brutalized by the senseless bloodletting they had to participate in during the preceding months. Many had lost not only their homes, but their homelands, their jobs as well as their belief in the established order that put them through this hell. Starvation, poverty and disease was rampant everywhere on the territories of the vanquished. The wounded, the sick, the homeless, the unemployed, the hungry, the justifiably enraged and uncivil underclass ebbed and flowed in the streets of the former capitals like garbage after a heavy downpour. Public authority had broken down everywhere, blue- and white-collar crime was rampant and reached levels never before seen. The Károlyi government in Hungary was as unsuccessful in handling the rampaging lawlessness as her neighbours everywhere. Its challenge was heightened by Hungary's status as a defeated power, a pariah barred from Versailles. The country was a shadow of itself, its territory dismembered, a blockade imposed upon its truncated body by the victorious imperial powers. The Károlyi government's challenge was also heightened by the invasion and systematic plunder of Hungary's remains by three of her neighbors (the so-called "Little Entente" made up of Czech, Yugoslav and Romanian troops) and last but not least, by its own inexperience in statecraft, especially in navigating what was a rudderless and rapidly sinking ship of state.

In the hope it may be more successful in gaining the upper hand over this desperate situation, the Revolutionary Governing Council of the Commune decided to fold into one newly created law enforcement agency—aptly called *the Red Guards*[91]—all the former members of the more than a dozen law enforcement agencies that operated as separate entities under the Károlyi regime,[92] and put a 26 year old young man in charge of this police force, the aforementioned Ferenc Rákos, who received his doctorate in law in 1916, was not a prisoner of war in Russia and knew about as much about the ways of the Russian Cheka, or Lenin's theories on terror in 1919, as the proverbial man on the moon.[93]

There is no space here to engage in a lengthy analysis of this new, rag tag proletarian law enforcement agency other than to acknowledge that throughout its four months of existence, the Commissariat of the Interior and the Red Guard high command itself were never looked upon in any other way, and rightfully so, than as a liability by the Soviet-trained, terrorist-minded minority within the Communist wing of the newly formed Socialist-Communist party alliance. The best that this bloodthirsty minority got out of the newly fused Party executive and the RGC was the replacement of the first Social Democratic Commissioner of Defense, József Pogány, at the beginning of April and the creation of a Political Investigation Unit under the *Red Guards'* national command that was to keep a close eye on any and all counterrevolutionary activities throughout the country. Even these concessions to the "terrorist fringe" of the Communist minority was bitter to swallow. Pogány's replacement, Vilmos Bőhm, promptly disarmed József Cserny's self-appointed terror gang and promised to apply martial law against anyone who attempts to utilize terror as a tool for the construction of socialism.[94] The RGC did not put two Soviet trained graduates of the Cheka in charge of the new political unit of the Red Guards but two men, Otto Korvin and Imre Sallai, who were both strangers to Leninism and the ways of the Cheka, and were not known as advocates of terror on the path to socialism.[95]

While there were some horrific cases of abuse committed by some units of the Red Guards,[96] not to mention those under the command of Tibor Szamuely within the Commissariat of Defense, which we shall turn to momentarily, not even the Horthy regime's scribes look upon the Red Guard itself as *the* "command center" of the terror as such.[97] The view of the Soviet comrades was similar. Virtually the entire top leadership of the Hungarian Red Guard that escaped to Russia was executed or sent to the Gulag in the 1930s.[98]

Let us finally turn to the Commissariat of Defense, the third institutional pillar of the 1919 Hungarian Republic of Councils' coercive policies. Initially, the founding fathers of the proletarian state did not envisage that the Commissariat of War (or Defense) would play any other coercive role than as a defender of the State from its external enemies. The newly merged Communist-Socialist Party executive dominated by the Social Democrats, didn't appoint a Soviet trained, Leninist member of the Hungarian Communist Party to the head of this

Commissariat, but one who they considered at the time to be one of their own moderate members, the aforementioned József Pogány. The latter was well known for his earlier run-ins with the Soviet-trained minority faction of the Hungarian Communist Party that wanted to see blood flowing in the streets of Budapest, as the sign of progress towards socialism in Hungary.[99]

For the Cheka trained terrorist who formed a tight knit minority within the Hungarian Communist Party, the choice of József Pogány as Minister of Defense of the Hungarian proletarian state was indigestible so they organized a virtual insurrection against him outside his office on the afternoon of April 3, 1919. During a heated cabinet shuffle on the evening of April 3, 1919, Pogány was removed after serving for less than three weeks as head of the proletarian state's military, and was given a new post in the government.[100] This "victory" by the "terrorists" within the RGC was a pyrrhic one: Instead of succeeding Pogány, the RGC also removed his chief rival, Tibor Szamuely, from the top of the Defense ministry. As we had pointed out earlier, the new defense chief, Vilmos Bőhm, was the strongest advocate of Pogány within the RGC and a man who was even more of an outspoken opponent of terror as an instrument of the proletarian state than his predecessor.

It was the renewed advances of the armies of the Little Entente on the territory of Hungary near the end of April and especially the Romanian Army from the East that enabled the "terrorist" wing of the Communist Party to regroup. They engineered an end-run around the RGC, the Commissariat of Defense, Bőhm's military commander for Budapest, the Social Democrat József Haubrich and the increasingly exasperated opposition from the Workers' and Soldiers' Council of Greater Budapest. On April 21, 1919, Szamuely managed to convince his colleagues on the RGC, and Bőhm himself, that under the heightened external threats to the proletarian state, and the widely documented activities of both the Entente and the Little Entente in trying to sow dissent behind the military lines in order to overthrow the increasingly fragile proletarian state, the Ministry of Defense should play a leading role in maintaining "law and order" in the homeland and not leave this task entirely in the unreliable hands of the Commissariat of the Interior, and its unreliable Red Guards. Accordingly, Szamuely was appointed to head up a unit of the Red Army (the so called Committee for Security Behind the Lines), with the right to use martial law powers along with deadly military force against anyone it suspected of dissent. Szamuely was provided the services of a number of those "Lenin-Boys" from Cserny's gang, along with others under the Red Army's control in order to get the job done in an orderly manner. Szamuely was provided with his own steel-reinforced bullet-proof military train, and began to travel the width and length of the rapidly shrinking country, imposing swift and merciless punishment upon anyone, rightly or wrongly accused of opposition to the government. Time flies when you have little of it. By the time the RGC had realized in May what was taking place under its umbrella and called for the release of the hostages taken by Szamuely and Cserny, by the time Korvin admitted to the RGC that he cannot control Cseny's men, and Bőhm faced up to Szamuely in the Army, by the time the supreme executive, legislative, judicial head of the Republic of Council (the NCC) had a chance to meet for the first time in June, and call for a halt to this madness, the terror claimed over three hundred lives and left a permanent stain on the heroic attempts of Hungary's working men and women to move from the periphery, to the center of their country's political arena.

Conclusion

On the 100th anniversary of the 1919 Hungarian Republic of Councils, this is how László Kövér, the President of the Hungarian Parliament and second in command of the current Hungarian autocracy, ended his reflections on the subject that was the focus of our attention: "There are still some who feel nostalgic about those killers, those foreign trained terrorists who ruled our country in 1919 during the so-called Republic of Councils and kept millions of Hungarians fearing for their lives".[101].

Our backward glance onto Hungary's long-forgotten revolution came to a different conclusion than Mr. Kövér, not just because of our use of a better, more sophisticated compass than the one at his disposal, but because of our acknowledgement that the lives of working men and women matter. Rather than glorify terror, this chapter attempted to recapture the long-forgotten and regularly sullied dignity of those millions of working men and women in Hungary who struggled mightily, at a pivotal time in world history, to demonstrate that terror is *not* their weapon of choice on the path towards justice, equal rights under the law and ecologically sustainable communal well being.

Our investigation acknowledges that there were people in high places in Hungary and in the Soviet Union in 1919 who referred to themselves as Marxists[102] and who considered terror as a legitimate coercive tool along the path to socialism.[103] We concede that terror was a publicly declared, *intentional* policy tool of the Russian Revolution and Lenin advocated its use to his comrades in Hungary as well in 1919 and on more than one occasion.[104] What we question is not the Russian Bolsheviks' or some of their Hungarian disciples' affinity for or acceptance of terror as a legitimate public policy tool on the path towards socialism, but the projection of this preference or value into the public policy universe of the 1919 Hungarian Republic of Councils. The projection of Lenin's "mind" onto the Luxemburgian "body politic" of the Hungarian Republic of Councils[105] is not just a poetic sleight of hand but a historical slander against the heroic attempt of millions of working men and women in Hungary to move in a dignified manner, under the harshest of circumstances, from the periphery to the center of their political arena.

Of the many takes that we looked at during our exploration of the above questions, perhaps the most instructive yet most ignored is the one taken by Oszkár Jászi a century ago. A life-long opponent of the Republic of Councils and of Béla Kun's Communists, Jászi acknowledges the "bad boys" within the Commune but refuses to smear the entire enterprise of Hungary's working men and women with the bestial actions of a small minority. He portrays the Hungarian Communist Party leadership—the minority partner of the Social Democrats—as a chair with three legs each of a different length. According to him, the smallest, or shortest leg on this unstable communist stool was indeed tainted "by the *idée homicide*":

> This group was composed of the intellectually unhinged... The central obsession of these people was the idea of massacre as a simple and rapid panacea. If the bourgeoisie were exterminated in a night there would be an end once and for all of the danger of counterrevolution... Fortunately, the more sober elements of the dictatorship were able to hold this group in check.[106]

Until now, one of the great untold stories of the 1919 Hungarian Republic of Councils was the combined opposition of the *leading actors*—the newly amalgamated Socialist Party executive, the three Commissariats for law and order, the Revolutionary Governing Council itself, and last but not least, the Budapest and National Congress of Councils—to the use of terror as an instrument of public policy.[107] With the use of a new compass, this story has now been not only told, but can be empirically verified for the first time.

What our compass had led us to see is that the leading actors of the Hungarian Proletarian State, the leadership of Hungary's much maligned labour movement, much to Lenin's and some of his Hungarian "boys'" chagrin, did not follow Vladimir's *ideas* but stuck with those of Rosa Luxemburg, Pannekoek, Bebel, and "Council Socialism" to the bitter end.[108] The Soviet-trained minority most definitely wanted but was never able to secure the majority of their colleagues' support for the use of terror as the propellant of working men and women to the center stage of Hungarian history.[109] Rather than its weapons of choice, the Cheka trained "Lenin-boys" of Szamuely and Cserny were constant thorns in the side of the 1919 proletarian state.

There is no disagreement between historians on the left and the right: the overnight transition from the People's Republic to the Hungarian Republic of Councils was non-violent (if we discount the March 20 ultimatum and the threat of violence by the Western Imperialist Powers which resulted in the collapse of the Károlyi regime).[110] As Péter Csunderlik had shown in his opening chapter to this book, the movement of working men and women to the center of Hungary's political arena was "blowing in the wind" well before the end of WWI and was gathering force throughout the Károlyi era. By March 21, 1919, it was embraced not only by millions of oppressed men and women in Hungary's cities, towns and villages but by significant segments of the Hungarian bourgeoisie, and nowhere more so than in the capital. The break with capitalism was considered by most as a risk worth taking, one that was not only a legitimate but a timely undertaking and this is why it was achieved peacefully. The dictatorship of the proletariat came to Budapest on little cats' feet like the fog in Carl Sandburg's unforgettable 1916 poem and left more or less the same way as it came. Béla Kun and his colleagues hopped on a chartered train for Vienna on August 1. It wasn't the Hungarian masses, or the restless bourgeoisie that chased them out of town but the troops of the Romanian monarchy, who were armed, financed and put up to the task by the imperialist great powers.

The words of József Berzsák, a simple labourer and a leading member of a rural workers' council in the county of Szolnok offer perhaps the best summary of how the 1919 attempt by Hungary's working men and women to move to the center stage of their political arena ended after the fog had lifted in Budapest. They also explain how the 1919 Republic of Councils became a forgotten revolution:

> We would not have acted any differently even if we could have seen into the future, and saw the terrible shadows of the fate that awaited us. What became of us, after the fog had lifted? Who doesn't know? Crushing defeat and imprisonment, loss of livelihood, hatred, ridicule and unending scorn, the executioners' ropes and bullets, the bottom of a freshly dug pit awaited countless numbers of our good companions. Those of us who survived have been left behind by time. We are getting older, there are fewer and fewer of us left as time passes by, but we always think back to our honest endeavor, our good-willed, noble constructive intent with a pure heart and proud self-awareness. The past is closed, the present lives, we look to the future with hope.[111]

NOTES

1   The 1948 Universal Declaration of Human Rights, which all members of the United Nations have endorsed, is perhaps the clearest expression of the mainstream, the "gold standard" today for people to aspire to in every corner of the world.

2   Those whose compass sees virtue in selfishness will not find much to cheer about on the journey we're about to embark upon. If they would rather stay within their own bubble, they should go directly from here to Ayn Rand. *The Virtue of Selfishness.* New York: Penguin. 1964 and then visit with George Reisman. *Capitalism: A complete understanding of the nature and value of human economic life.* Jameson Books. 1996. The compass used by the last two authors is about as far from ours as that proverbial Hungarian village of Makó, from Jerusalem.

3   "Solidarity" is a prominent current in the mainstream. It lifted up, carried aloft the great Pericles
     in ancient Greece, the youth of Budapest in March 1848, the Communards of Paris in 1871. It was
     astutely singled out by that Russian Prince, Peter Kropotkin late in the 19th century and left an
     indelible imprint on the minds of tens of millions by the start of the 20th century, including those
     "upper crust" Hungarians who would join the struggle for workers' rights before and during the
     1919 Republic of Councils (e.g., Ervin Szabó, Ervin Batthány and "that gentry girl", Ilona
     Duczynska). For a recent English language edition of Kropotkin's focus on this current see: Peter
     Kropotkin. *Mutual Aid: A Factor of Evolution.* For a good discussion of the impact of this current
     on the minds of Hungary's early 20th century revolutionaries see: András Bozóki and Miklós
     Sükösd. *Anarchism in Hungary: Theory, History, Legacies* (originally published in Hungarian in
     1994 as *Az anarchizmus elmélete és magyarországi története*). Translated from the Hungarian by
     Alan Renwick. New York. Columbia UP. 2005). The current of solidarity would vividly re-surface
     as *Solidarnos* under the banner of Gdansk's ship-workers in Poland during the 1970s and is the
     main force that unites blacks and whites in the BLM movement today.

4   The word is consciously borrowed from the vocabulary of the Nobel Laureate Indian economist,
     Amartya Sen; see: Amartya Sen, *The Idea of Justice* (London: Penguin Books, 2010).

5   There are notable differences between the justice theories of John Rawls (John Rawls, *A Theory of
     Justice* (Cambridge, MA: Belknap Press, 1971), and those of Amartya Sen, but the fulcrum for both
     is *public reason* based on the type of discourse ethics that Habermas proposes, among others.

6   This comment is not intended to belittle the efforts of those pioneers who have gone before us. It
     merely seeks to draw attention to the fact that the compass we are using on this journey is of a
     very recent vintage—the culmination of decades of rigorous work by some of the finest public
     policy scholars from around the world—and was simply unavailable on previous expeditions.

7   For a recent exposé of Aristotle's political ideas in English see: Carnes Lord, *Aristotle's Politics* 2nd
     ed. (Chicago, IL: University of Chicago Press, 2013).

8   See: Harold D. Lasswell. *Politics: Who Gets What, When and How?* (New York, NY: Whittlesey
     House, 1936).

9   This is why those in the English speaking world still refer to those who pursue political activities
     in their countries as citizens. The French call them *citoyens*. The word in Hungarian is also
     reflective of this attachment to the original Greek term, the *polis*. In Hungarian, the politically
     minded citizen is a cultivator, a caretaker of the *polis* and is known as a *polgár*.

10   The secret of this unparalleled organizational ability is discussed at length by the Israeli historian
     Yuval Noah Harari, *Sapiens: A Brief History of Humankind* (New York, NY: Signal Editions, 2016).

11   The term United States was already taken when the UN came into being after WWII. United
     Nations is obviously a misnomer, not because its members are everything but united but because
     of the organisation's pretension to represent all the nations of the world. Canada, for example, is a
     State consisting of over 600 Indigenous nations speaking over 50 different languages. If you added
     up all the first or Indigenous nations of Europe, Asia, Africa, the Americas, the Middle East, we'd
     be well over 10,000 in number.

12   First published in German in July 1919, Weber's thesis was only translated into English after
     WWII. (See: Max Weber, *Politics as a Vocation* (New York, NY: Fortress Press, 1965). After
     probably the most exhaustive analysis of European states between 990 and 1990, Charles Tilly also
     concluded that the State has always been, and will always be a *"coercion-wielding organisation"*. See
     his *Coercion, Capital, and European States* (New York, NY: Wiley and Blackwell, 1993). Marxists
     and Anarchists will of course agree. For the latter, even the workers' state is anathema because of
     its monopolization of coercion. (This is why the political mentor of Ilona Duczynska, the
     Hungarian anarcho-syndicalist, Ervin Szabó (1877–1918)—a cousin of Karl Polanyi—looked more
     favorably upon Kropotkin than upon Lenin.

13   For reviews of competing state theories, the following will be more than enough: Martin Carnoy.
     The State and Political Theory (Princeton, NJ: Princeton University Press, 1984); Ronald Cohen
     and Elman R. Service eds, *Origins of the State* (Philadelphia, PA: Institute for the Study of Human
     Issues, 1978); David Held *et al*, eds, *States and Societies* (Oxford: Basil Blackwell, 1985). And last
     but not least, Andrew Vincent. *Theories of the State* (Oxford: Basil Blackwell, 1987).

14   Ours is not the only compass that looks at the State through a teleological sensor. The various
     social contract theorists (Hobbes, Rousseau, and Locke) all had one. The Marxist, anarchist

compasses both have their teleological view-finders along with such outliars (sic) as the one used by the white-supremacist Christian-Nationalists in Viktor Orbán's orbit in Hungary today. The problem with all the aforementioned models is that their teleological sensors are not compatible with each other, they do not accept each other's readings: Our teleological sensor is universal, theirs' isn't. As we shall demonstrate, even Mr. Orbán can travel comfortably with ours if he wants to gather an empirically verifiable sample from the public policy universe of the Hungarian Republic of Councils.

15   István, the founder of the Hungarian state in 1000 AD reached for the same preservative as the one that helped to sustain the Holy Roman Empire since 312 AD. He was done with the home remedies suggested by his nemesis, Koppány. In the preamble to his *First Book of Laws*, István declared that he would govern his realm "by the will of God". See: János M. Bak, György Bónis, James Ross Sweeney (Eds, and translators*). "The Laws of King Stephen I (1000–1038)" in The Laws of the Medieval Kingdom of Hungary, 1000–1301.* 2nd ed. (Charles Schlacks, Jr. Publishers: 1999), 1. It is from the preamble of István's fundamental law that József Szájer, the recently disgraced author of Hungary's 2011 constitution got the idea of putting God into the preamble of the text he concocted on his laptop while commuting between Budapest and Brussels during the last months of 2010 as a representative of his party—the Fidesz—in the EU Parliament. (Mr. Szájer, the father of the Orbán Constitution was busted in a police raid on a Brussels apartment at the end of 2020. He was caught climbing down a drainpipe trying to escape the raid on an all-male sex party that was in violation of Belgium's regulations on crowd size during a high point of the Covid 19 pandemic. By the grace of God—aka *diplomatic immunity*—he was not charged for endangering the lives of his fellow European citizens.) For additional information on István the King see footnote No. 17 underneath.

16   Aristotle also recognizes that all states have a purpose, or a *telos*. He argued that the best among them will pursue *the greatest good*, which he considered to be *autarkeia*. Autarkeia has been interpreted in various ways throughout the ages. Most often it's looked upon as a hybrid of self-sufficiency and independence. The word would acquire an utterly false and anti-Aristotelian meaning in the hands of the Bolsheviks in the USSR after 1928, and most markedly after Stalin's 1948 rejection of the original, Aristotelian thesis as expressed, for example, by Karl Polanyi in his celebrated 1945 essay on regional cooperative planning. (Stalin punctuated his sentence with the 1949 Moscow murder of the Bulgarian Communist, Georgi Dimitrov, who happened to be, after Tito, the leading political advocate of regional developmental planning in East Europe at the time. Polanyi was secretly tipped off by an associate of his from his student days, Mátyás Rákosi who happened to be Stalin's leading Hungarian disciple by 1948 and told never to set foot in Hungary again. His wife Ilona happened to be in Hungary that year also quickly packed her bags. Neither returned to Hungary until well after Stalin's and Rákosi's passing. To conclude: Aristotle's concept of *autarkeia* has nothing in common with Stalin's because it can only be achieved by those states that encourage their citizens to engage in public reasoning—fearless and informed speech—and pursue the greatest good in a continuously learning environment that maximizes justice and equal rights under the law. (See: Wolfgang Weissleder, "Aristotle's Concept of Political Structure and the State." in Cohen and Service, op. cit., 187–203).

17   It is challenging but not impossible to summarize in a footnote the almost 1000 year-long official church and state-sanctioned fairy-tale that sustains the Hungarian state from its inception to this day. According to this officially endorsed story, the founder of the Hungarian state, King István, brokered a divine contract on his deathbed in 1038 between the mother of Jesus—the Holy Virgin—and his coronation crown. (The coronation crown was given to István 38 years earlier as a joint Christmas present by the head of the Roman Catholic Church, Pope Sylvester II (946–1003AD) and Otto III (980–1002AD), the Bavarian head of the Holy Roman Empire, because István married a close relative of Otto, was willing to get his people to pray to Jesus, and to bring his flock into Otto's tent rather than burn it down every now and then, like in the old days.) By virtue of brokering this 1038 "deal" between the Holy Virgin and his Holy Crown, István secured the sustainability of the Hungarian state. Mary, the mother of God, agreed to serve as the country's *eternal regina* or queen. Who could ask for more? She agreed to grant *divine personhood* to István's crown. Ever since 1038, whoever puts that crown on their head has a stairway to heaven, and a ticket to ride in Hungary. The bottom line is this: István's crown symbolizes the State of Hungary to this day. No one is wearing the crown today but it sits in the Hungarian

Parliament and keeps its eyes on the lawmakers while Mary, sitting next to Jesus, does so from the heavens above. For a more detailed exegeses I recommend a version penned by one of my PhD advisors and intellectual mentors at the London School of Economics, Professor László Péter (1929–2008), who I look back upon with fondness and respect. See: László Péter. "The Holy Crown of Hungary, Visible and Invisible." *The Slavonic and East European Review*, 81, no. 3. (2003), 421–510.

18   This is why Prince Harry's decision to step out of line and move to LA is so disturbing to the British royals and their followers. That fracture poses a mortal threat to the sustainability of the British state's original design.

19   The holy man, Black Elk, one of the Lakota survivors of the massacre at Wounded Knee in 1890 provides a fitting confirmation of this statement: *"I did not know then how much was ended. When I look back now from this high hill of my old age, I can still see the butchered women and children lying heaped and scattered all along the crooked gulch as plain as when I saw them with eyes still young. And I can see that something else died there in the bloody mud, and was buried in the blizzard. A people's dream died there* (emphasis ABG). *It was a beautiful dream".* The account is from John G. Neihard. *Black Elk Speaks.* (New York, NY: Suny Press, 2008), 281.

20   There is no room in this book for a discussion of the indispensable role played by "narrators" (priests, witch-doctors, spin-doctors, historians, ideologues, opinion leaders, teachers, the media, etc.), the "communications technologies" (hot, cool, print, electronic, digital), and the emotionally charged "narratives" themselves (fairy tales, religions, mythologies, ideologies) and the "rituals" that are relied upon by the architects of every state to impregnate *the minds* of a critical segment of their community with the *feeling* that their state will provide the community with an enduring "after-life". The embrace of the priesthood and creed of Christianity by Emperor Constantine in 312 AD is a testament to the importance of these variables. *"Constantine's conversion to and support of Christianity… served an entirely conservative end, the preservation and continuation of the Empire".* Hans A. Pohlsander, *The Emperor Constantin* (New York, NY: Routledge, 2004), 78–79.

21   The people of Israel for example have existed for thousands of years in the Middle East and had an ancient Kingdom, a State of their own making, thousands of years ago which would fall victim to a series of invading Empires, prior to and after the birth of Christ. It would take the Israelis almost two thousand years after the birth of Christ, to re-acquire statehood. (The official birth date of the modern state of Israel is May 14, 1948). The ability of the Israeli state to sustain itself since 1948 is due to more than the desire and ingenuity of the newest Israeli state-crafters. Ultimately it is the willingness of a critical mass of outsiders to recognize and support the State of the Israeli settlers combined with the inability of those who oppose it to destroy it that holds the key to its sustainability since its newest reincarnation. The sole possession of a thermonuclear bomb is also, of course, an immensely persuasive instrument in the hands of the Jewish state. The acquisition of such a tool by one of Israel's unfriendly neighbours, say, Iran, would greatly complicate the equation. This partly explains why those Western powers who have agreed to guarantee the sustainability of the Israeli state, are so reluctant to allow Iran to acquire such a weapon.

22   The Kurds used to have a State before the Ottoman Empire took it away from them. Their dream turned into a nightmare following the collapse of the Turkish Empire in 1918 when three European Imperial leaders—Lloyd George. Woodrow Wilson and Georges Clemenceau refused to recognize their claim and redrew the map of the Middle East to suit their own imperialist ambitions, by leaving the Kurds without a homeland. (Actually, the lines were drawn already by the beginning of 1916 well before the guns fell silent, by that secret agreement between France and Britain that is known as "The Sykes-Picot Agreement". See: Edward Peter Fitzgerald. "France's Middle Eastern ambitions, the Sykes-Picot negotiations, and the oil fields of Mosul, 1915–1918," *Journal of Modern History* 66, no. 4 (1994), 697–725, and James Barr. *A Line in the Sand: Britain, France and the Struggle That Shaped the Middle East* (New York, NY Simon & Schuster, 2012). The latest episode of the Kurd's 100 year-long nightmare came in 2019 as a consequence of the collusion between Donald Trump, Vladimir Putin, Recep Tayyip Erdogan, Bashar al Assad and their local minions. For a revealing exposé of the Kurd's struggle to provide themselves with an ecologically sustainable habitat based on the principles of justice and equal rights see: Thomas Jeffrey Miley and Frederico Venturini eds., *Your Freedom and Mine* (Montréal, QC: Black Rose Books, 2018).

23   In a democratic state, the various branches check and balance each other, in an autocratic state, they do not.

24   For a discussion of some of the challenges posed to the democratic state by the fusion of power principle see: "The Rule of Law and the Sovereignty of Parliament" in Tom Bingham. *The Rule of Law* (London: Penguin Books, 2010), 160–171. For a brief discussion of the problems associated with this arrangement in Hungary after 2010 see András B. Göllner. "Portrait of an Abusive Relationship: Parliamentary Sovereignty vs The Rule of Law in Hungary" *The Journal of Parliamentary and Political Law* 12. no. 1, (April, 2018), 67-75.

25   For a detailed elaboration upon the various organizational arrangements discussed above I suggest: L. Morlino, D. Berg-Schlosser, and B. Badie, B., *Political Science: A Global Perspective* (New York, NY: Sage Publications, 2017).

26   This is the stripped-down definition or conceptualization of Thomas R. Dye, *Understanding Public Policy* (Englewood Cliffs, NJ: Prentice Hall, 1972). and it is broadly accepted everywhere on the planet by now because of its *initial* ideological neutrality. (It's when Dye begins to discuss *why* or *how* governments choose to do or not to do something that he runs into ideological turbulence.)

27   Those who are interested in strictly a neo-Marxist as opposed to the classical Marxist, or Leninist manual should begin to practice their entry into the public policy universe of the 1919 Hungarian Republic of Councils with Antonio Gramsci and Nicos Poulantzas. See: Antonio Gramsci, *Prison Notebooks* 1-3 (New York, NY: Columbia University Press, 2011). and Nicos Poulantzas, *State, Power, Socialism* (New York, NY: New Left Books, 1978). along with J. Martin ed., *The Poulantzas Reader: Marxism, Law and the State* (London: Verso, 2008).

28   Those who prefer the pluralist manual could find happiness with Thomas R Dye. Op.cit.

29   To be precise: Our compass is not insensitive to the signals picked up by the compasses of Marxists, pluralist, game theorists or by any of the other compasses that are listed in the public policy catalogues, it simply refuses to be guided exclusively by any one of them. In a somewhat superficial way, Amitai Etzioni's "Mixed Scanning" approach to decision-making may be analogous to our approach to the public policy universe. See: Amitai Etzioni. "Mixed Scanning: A Third Approach to Decision-Making," *Public Administration Review* 27, no. 5. (1967), 385-392. For a good, though not exhaustive listing of the various analytical approaches to public policy see, Lydia Miljan, *Public Policy in Canada* (Oxford: Oxford University Press, 2012).

30   See: Immanuel Wallerstein, *The Modern World-System* (New York, NY: Academic Press, 1974). And *World Systems Analysis* (Durham, NC: Duke University Press, 2004).

31   For a good review of this latest, holistic approach see M. Howlett, M. Ramesh and A. Perl. *Studying Public Policy: Policy Cycles and Policy Subsystems* 3rd ed. (London: Oxford University Press, 2009), 81-89.

32   *Ibid.*, 8

33   *Ibid.*, 199

34   *Ibid.*, 199

35   *Ibid.*, 48

36   See: A Tanácsköztársaság ideiglenes alkotmánya. A Forradalmi Kormányzótanács XVI. sz. rendelete. (The Temporary Constitution of the Hungarian Republic of Councils. Decree No XVI of the Revolutionary Governing Council). Budapest, April 2, 1919. The final version of the Republic of Councils' constitution was passed by the National Congress of Councils on June 23, 1919. See: A Magyarországi Szocialista Szövetséges Tanácsköztársaság alkotmánya (The Constitution of the Hungarian Socialist Republic of Councils) Budapest. T*anácsköztársaság*. no. 78. (June 28, 1919). As in all cases, and unless otherwise indicated, all translations from the original Hungarian text are by the author.

37   The voting age was set at 18 for men and women. The country's fortune hunters, members of the nobility and the aristocracy, members of the bourgeoisie who engaged in commerce and profited from the labour of others, along with members of the clergy, the mentally challenged and the criminally incarcerated could not vote. The participation rate in this first election was low, due almost entirely to the shortness of time for campaigning and the raising of public awareness about the issues, platforms and personalities involved. How to survive in the midst of a post-war tsunami that flattened the country was uppermost on the minds of everyone in Hungary in

March-April 1919. The participation rate in the capital was just over 30% of the eligible voters and barely reached 20% in the countryside.

38   Even one of the more recent and balanced account of this era by a young Hungarian historian Gergely Bödők is coloured by this conventional historical view: "The Hungarian Republic of Councils that was proclaimed on March 21, 1919 (its name was translated from the Russian Soviet Republic), set up a Russian Bolshevik-type state system and government machinery". See: Gergely Bödők. *Vörös- és fehér terror Magyarországon* (1919–1921) [Red and White Terror in Hungary: 1919–1921]. PhD Dissertation submitted to the Department of History, Doctoral School of the Eszterházy Károly University. Eger. 2018. 114. As we shall show, nothing could be further from the truth than the above claim.

39   As we have stated in our Preface, "the big lie" about the identity of the 1919 Hungarian Republic of Councils, which refuses to die to this day began with Béla Kun in that telegraph sent to an agitated Lenin, who could not believe his "boy" would hand over the Hungarian Bolshevik Party to the Social Democrats, and provide Hungary's workers' councils, rather than the Bolsheviks the leading role on the path to socialism. Kun claimed that "Since there are no real workers' and peasants' councils in Hungary and he's holding the Social Democrats in the palms of his hands" he can do as he pleases. ("Radio Message from Comrade Bela Kun" Moscow *Pravda*. (March 28, 1919). Kun's "big lie" was as false as Donald Trump's about scoring a "tremendous victory" in the 2020 US Presidential elections which the vast majority in the Republican Party, and close to 100 million Americans accept as the truth today

40   For a discussion of the merger and the founding documents of the new state, which were published at the start of the Republic and cannot be dismissed as after the fact rationalizations see: Jakab Weltner (ed). *Az Egység Okmányai*. (The Documents of the Union). Budapest. Commissariat for Public Education. 1919. For the actual text of the agreement see: *ibid*, pp. 5-6. There is nothing in the final agreement or in any of the founding documents that proclaims or suggests that the Hungarian Bolsheviks must play a vanguard role in either the new party, the RGC or in the duly constituted bodies of the workers', soldiers' and peasant' deputies during the transition to Socialism. The entire edifice of the "big lie" rests on that deceptive telegram to Lenin by Béla Kun at the start of the revolution in which he professes to be in charge, because in Hungary, "there are no Workers' Councils" and the Social Democrats are at his beck and call.

41   László Rudas, a leading left-wing theoretician in Kun's Party would claim decades later that he met Lenin in Moscow at the end of March 1919 where the Soviet leader told him outright that: "I regard this unification (between the HCP and the HSDP) as dangerous. It would have been much wiser to form a bloc in which both parties retained their independence. In this case, the Communists would be able to increase their strength day by day and if the Social Democrats neglected their revolutionary duties, the Communists could split off from them". *Szabad Nép*. January 21, 1949.

42   Rudolf Tőkés. *Béla Kun and the Hungarian Soviet Republic. The Origins and the Role of the Hungarian Communist Party in the Revolutions of 1918–1919* (New York, NY: Frederick A. Praeger, 1967), 167.

43   This was the initial line-up. The RGC would undergo two major shuffles after March 21st due in large measure to the Bolsheviks' unhappiness with their allotted role. Though they sought it, they never managed to come anywhere near to parity, let alone the leading role insisted upon by Lenin.

44   Rónai's deputy commissar in the Justice Commissariat, Dr. István Lékai was also a highly regarded legal-scholar, and a non-party member (!) of the RGC,. Both were hated by "Lenin's Boys", but no one could touch them. The Workers' and Soldiers' Deputies of Budapest stood staunchly behind them during the 133 days of the Commune. The power and authority of these "homegrown" constitutional experts was increased rather than diminished by the National Congress of Councils at the end of June 1919.

45   On the meaning of this core concept in the works of two prominent Western Marxists—Rosa Luxemburg and Anton Pannekoek—who, together, had a powerful grip on the minds of the architects of the 1919 Hungarian state; see: Ottokar Luban, "Rosa Luxemburg's Concept of Spontaneity and Creativity in Proletarian Mass Movements: Theory and Practice." *International Critical Thought* 9. no. 4, (2019). And Paulina Tambakaki, "Why spontaneity matters: Rosa Luxemburg and democracies of grief". *Philosophy and Social Criticism* 47, no. 1, (2021). Also: John P. Gerber, *Anton Pannekoek and the Socialism of Workers' Self Emancipation, 1873–1960*. (New York, NY: Springer, 1990). Pannekoek, for whom the idea of a party led path to workers'

emancipation was anathema, was named as an honorary member of the Hungarian Republic of Councils by none other than Bela Kun, before Lenin would straighten him out and tell him that Pannekoek was possessed by "an infantile disorder."

46   Peter Kenez, "Coalition Politics in the Hungarian Soviet Republic" in Andrew C. János and William B. Slottman eds., *Revolution in Perspective: Essays on the Hungarian Soviet Republic of 1919* (Berkeley, CA: University of California Press, 1971), 70-71.

47   The Hungarian Bolshevik leadership's realignment with Leninist theory would begin haltingly after the start of the Republic, pick up speed in Vienna after they fled to the Austrian capital in August 1919 (resulting in a bitter split within the Party) and reaches its zenith after the adoption of Lenin's "21 points" by the 2nd Congress of the Commintern in August 2020.

48   Rosa Luxemburg, *Tömegsztrájk* (Mass Strike) (Budapest: Public Education Commissariat, 1919).

49   This should not be taken to mean that Lukács was anti-Leninist at the time. He simply didn't know much about Lenin's theory of the State, or of any of Lenin's revolutionary ideas for that matter. The following are his words, upon looking back from 1967: "We knew hardly anything of Lenin's theory of revolution and of the vital advances he had made in that area of Marxism... of those who had taken part in the Russian Revolution some (like Szamuely) had little talent for theory... It was not until my emigration to Vienna (after the collapse of the HROC, ABG) that I was able to make a thorough study of Lenin's theory... Intellectually we were unprepared and I was perhaps less prepared than anyone—to come to grips with the tasks that confronted us." From the Preface of Georg Lukács, *History and Class Consciousness* (London: Merlin Press, 1967). Lukács was educated in Germany and by his own admission, drew his inspiration from such non-Bolshevik sources as Hegel, Weber, Sorel, Bebel, Luxemburg and Pannekoek. For additional confirmation and insights; see: Georg Lukács, "Bolshevism as a Moral Problem", trans. Judith Marcus Tarr, *Social Research* 44, no. 3, (Autumn 1977), 416–24 and "Tactics and Ethics," Georg Lukács, *Political Writings*, ed. Rodney Livingstone, trans. Michael McColgan (New York, NY: Harper and Row, 1974), 3–11. Also: Zoltán Tarr, "A Note on Weber and Lukács." *Socialism, Revolution, and Ethics* (September 1989). And John E. Seery "Marxism and Artwork: Weber and Lukács in Heidelberg, 1912–1914" *The Berkeley Journal of Sociology* 27 [Special Feminist Issue,] (1982), 129–165. For Lukács's transition from his Luxemburgian posture to his Leninist and quasi Stalinist stance then back to the position of his youth, see: Michael Löwy. "Lukács and Stalinism." *New Left Review* (May-June 1975), 25-41

50   László Rudas. "Lényeg és Forma" [Essence and Form,] *Internationale.* (May 1919). This reference is from Peter Kenez. Op.cit cf 15. P. 71. Duczynska, the liaison person in Moscow between the German Communist Party delegation and the Commintern high brass at its 2nd Congress in 1920, fully agreed with this Luxemburgian, Pannekoekian position as well and would remain true to it all her life. She would be expelled from the Hungarian CP in exile in 1922 at the urging of, among others, the by then anti-Luxemburgian, anti-Pannekoekian György Lukács and László Rudas. By 1936 Rudas was a Stalinist, and remained so until his passing in 1950. He endorsed Kun's execution in Moscow in 1938. He did not object to the assault on the 1919 veterans after he returned from Moscow with the Red Army in 1945. He led the assault against the ideas of Bibó and Lukács after 1948. He shed no tears for Dimitov in 1949, and applauded the arrest and execution of László Rajk in 1949. When I asked Ilona Duczynska one late evening in 1977 what she thought of Rudas, she just let out a big sigh.

51   Szamuely, went to Berlin in December 1918 and left Berlin for Budapest on January 3, 1919, just before the start of the Spartacus uprising, disgusted not only with the direction taken by the leadership of the German Social Democrats, but also with Rosa Luxemburg and her criticism of the Leninist path. Szamuely, a prominent Moscow trained member of the Hungarian Bolshevik Party played literally no role in the design of the new Hungarian proletarian state, and resented being kept at arm's length at its conception by Kun even though he was the Chairman of the Party's second tier Central Committee. While he was rewarded with a deputy commissar title at the outset, he remained perhaps the most passionate critic of the original design. He even flew to Moscow in May to brief Lenin personally on how the Soviet leader's design was being bastardized in Budapest. More on this in the following section.

52   For the full story see: Margaret MacMillan. *Op.cit.*

53   This is the rough and short summary of the official line which prevailed in Hungary between 1920–1945, and which is once again the official line in Hungary today, under Viktor Orbán's rule.

54   Initially, the Council of Ten was the supreme decision-making body of the Paris Peace Conference, It consisted of the leaders of the 5 victorious imperial powers and their foreign ministers. It would eventually shrink in size and become a closed shop of 3—Wilson, Clemenceau and George.

55   Hungary was barred from the peace negotiations in Versailles and was not privy to the deliberations of the Council of Ten.

56   In a nutshell: this closely held decision by the Entente was in clear contravention of the armistice terms that Hungary signed in good faith in Belgrade on November 13, 1918. February 26th 1919 is the day when the Entente decided to turn its back on Woodrow Wilson's concept of national self-determination in favor of its own imperial ambitions by ceding, among others the entire Eastern part of the Hungarian State and the more than three million ethnic Hungarians who had lived there for centuries to Romania, in return for the Romanian Monarchy's support of France's military and imperialistic ambitions in the Balkans and points beyond. The first and hazy news of this decision was leaked to the Hungarian President on March 15, 1919 by a visiting American military attaché from Romania, Lieutenant Colonel Halsey E. Yates. The official ultimatum was hand delivered to Hungary's President Mihály Károlyi on March 20th 1919 by the Entente's local representative Lieutenant colonel Ferdinand Vix, who is, to this day the villain in a story he had literally nothing more to do with other than as a messenger boy.

57   The ultimatum was non-negotiable. The Hungarian President and his Prime Minister, Dénes Berinkey were given 30 hours to convey their favourable response after which, the country would be in breach, and subject to military reprisal. Berinkey refused to comply and handed in his government's resignation to the Hungarian President on the spot. The President then turned to the leader of the country's largest political party, the HSDP, and asked him to form a government, rally the troops and stand up to the military blackmail that threatened to turn Hungary's dream into the kind of nightmare the Lakota chief, Black Elk was talking about in reference to the massacre at Wounded Knee. For details of this ultimatum and its role in the creation of the proletarian state. See: Mária Ormos. "A Vix jegyzék" (The Vix Memorandum) in *Padovától Trianonig: 1918.1920* (From Padua to Trianon) 3rd ed., (Budapest: Kossuth, 2020), 164–190. See also two excellent analyses by Peter Pastor, "The Vix Mission in Hungary, 1918–1919: A Re-examination," *Slavic Review* XXIX, no. 3, (1970). And the one in which he relied upon recently released archival material by the French government which was not available to anyone until 1970. "Franco-Rumanian Intervention in Russia and the Vix Ultimatum: Background to Hungary's Loss of Transylvania". *Canadian American Review of Hungarian Studies* (1974), 12–28.

58   Oscar Jászi. *Revolution and Counterrevolution in Hungary.* op.cit, 152–155.

59   *Ibid,*

60   Our short answer to both questions above is an emphatic *No.*

61   The ice-pick planted in the skull of Stalin's political rival Leon Trotsky in Mexico in 1940, on the orders of his nemesis in Moscow, or the live surgical dismemberment of the Saudi dissident journalist Jamal Khashoggi in Istanbul, Turkey, in 2018, on the orders of Saudi dictator Mohammed bin Salman are only two examples of how terror can be extended outside of the boundaries of the State itself by its most dedicated practitioners.

62   This is why an entire line of Roman rulers fed the Christian dissidents to the lions in front of a live audience. Its champion during the French Revolution, Maximilien Robespierre, looked upon terror as an exceptional form of justice. "Terror", said the leader of the Committee on Public Safety in his oft quoted speech of February 5, 1794, "is nothing more than speedy, severe and inflexible justice; it is thus an emanation of virtue; it is less a principle in itself, than a consequence of the general principle of democracy, applied to the most pressing needs of the fatherland (*patrie*)". Paul Halsall. "Maximilien Robespiere: On the Principles Of Political Morality." *Modern History Sourcebook* (New York, NY: Fordham University, 1997). This is the logic that compelled the Hungarian "Red Terrorist" Tibor Szamuely to force family members and entire villages to watch the public beatings and executions of their loved ones.

63   The phrase is respectfully borrowed from Noam Chomsky and the title of the book he co-edited with Edward S. Herman. *Manifacturing Consent: The Political Economy of the Mass Media.* Op.cit.

64   Witness the "Lenin-Boys"unilateral occupation of the majestic Batthany palace in the middle of the busiest thoroughfare in downtown Budapest on March 22nd, 1919, the cannons, and machine guns pointed at the passerbys from its windows, the clothing of Cserny and his terrorist gang

(long black leather coats, fine leather gloves, long red scarves slung over their shoulders, aviator goggles on top of their Derby-caps, hand-grenades , pistols and carabines draped around their bodies like ripe fruit, ready to burst) and a huge sign in freshly painted large letters above the entrance to their "man-cave" proudly proclaiming their function and identity: "The Lenin-Boys: The Terror Team of the Revolutionary Governing Council". If these "proud boys" had not committed over 200 murders and kept thousands more freaked out of their minds in Budapest and in the surrounding countryside with their antics, this could have been straight out of a Hollywood movie set. For a close look at the genesis of America's 21st century *Proud Boys*; see: Adam Leith Gollner, "Original Sins," *Vanity Fair* (July-August, 2021).

65 Russia today under Vladimir Putin, China under Xi jinping, North Korea under Kim Jung-un, Saudi Arabia under Mohammed bin Salman or Belarus under Alexander Lukashenko are just five and by no means isolated or exhaustive examples of states, that utilize this tool within their coercive policy mix today irrespective of their state's signatures on the United Nation's Universal Declaration of Human Rights, that forbids the use of such tools by its member states. While former US President Donald Trump did *not* use terror to sustain himself in office during 2016–2020, he constantly played with it in public, and is continuing to do so after his electoral loss in November 2020. He began his "mind game" by targeting his chief political rival, Hillary Clinton, by promising to "lock her up" after he is elected and by branding journalist critical of his administration as "enemies of the people", and followed up by surrounding himself with lackeys, who were clearly willing to execute his orders. Trump professed his admiration throughout his presidency for many of the practiotioners of state sanctioned terror and for authoritarian rulers in general, including Viktor Orbán of Hungary and Chairman Xi in China. As recently as January 6, 2021 he professed his "love" to those of his enraged supporters, who terrorized the men and women guarding the people's representatives in the US Capitol building, and stampeded through the building in order to summarily hang his own Vice President and the elected Speaker of the House from the nearest lamp-post because they dared to uphold the US Constitution and the rule of law. With such a man as the undisputed leader today of not only the Republican Party, and the US billionaire class but a significant majority of America's white-skinned, god-fearing blue-collar workers, the use of terror as a public policy-tool in American politcs is just a short hop, step and a jump away from that country's public-policy universe. If terror could become an everyday occurance during the first half of the 20th century in what we commonly recognize as the heartland of "Western Civilization"—Germany and Italy—is it inconceivable that it may also re-emerge (a hundred years after the massacre in Tulsa, Oklahoma) in the global headquarters of Universal Capitalism during the Roaring Twenties of the 21st century? The concentrated assault on Americans' ability to distinguish fact from fiction, illusion from reality, via the asymmetric flows of public information through that country's profit driven mass and social media outlets does not inspire confidence.

66 The first conservative accounts of the 1919 "Red Terror" in Hungary surfaced as soon as admiral Nicholas Horthy marched into Budapest in November 1919 and took control of the country's public information flows. They are still in vogue 100 years later. Albert Váry, *A vörös uralom áldozatai Magyarországon* (The Victims of the Reds in Hungary) 3rd Hungarian ed. (Budapest: Szegedi nyomda, 1993), and Gusztáv Gratz. *A Bolsevizmus Magyarországon* (Bolshevism in Hungary) new ed., (Budapest: Méry Ratio, 2016), Zoltán Somogy. *A rémuralom napjaiból—Túszok és egyéb történetek* (The Days of the Reign of Terror: Hostages and other Events) (Budapest: Pátria Irodalmi Vállalat és Nyomdai Részvénytársaság, 1922), along with Cecile Tormay's *Bujdosó Könyv* (An Outlaw's Diary.) (Budapest: Pallas, 1920), and Váry's own sequel, *A forradalmak kora. Magyarország története 1918–1920* (The Age of Revolution: Hungary's History, 1918–1920) (Budapest: Magyar Szemle Társaság, 1935), constitute the conservative *canon* on the 1919 proletarian state, especially on its choice of terror as its favorite system-maintenance device. These "classics" serve as the basis for such recently "refried" versions as the one by Veritas Institute "historian" (sic), László Anka. "A Vörösterror Magyarországon" (The Red Terror in Hungary). Budapest, *Magyar Hirlap* (August 1, 2019); Gergely Bödők. "Kegyelmes urak a Gyűjtőfogházban: A vörös terror fővárosi túszai". *Múltunk*, no. 4 (2014); Ádám Gellért. "Temessétek élve a holttestek közé". *Index.hu*. August 13, 2019, or the book length manuscript by B. Tamás Müller. *Vörösterror az Országházban, 1919* (Red Terror in Parliament,1919). Budapest. Office of the Hungarian Parliament. 2016. They serve tangentially as the ammunition for the repositioning of Ilona

Duczynska as a "terrorist" by one of her former literary collabourators and "friends" (sic) Kenneth McRobbie. (See Kenneth McRobbie. "Ilona Duczynska Meets Ervin Szabó: The Making of a Revolutionary Personality—From Theory to Terrorism" *Hungarian Studies Review* no 1–2, (2006).

67   As we stated in our introduction to this book: the first line of defense of capitalism is to declare that its chief rival, socialism, kills. This is the thesis advanced by the highly popular *Black Book on Communism, op.cit*, as well. It dedicates a section to the 1919 Hungarian Commune, in order to drive home the alleged "universality" of the fatal attraction between terror and the movement of working men and women to the center stage of history. In Hungary after 1919 and under the leadership of Admiral Nicholas Horthy, the socialist is no longer just a killer, but a Jewish killer, driven by the desire to hit a home run by exterminating capitalism along with Hungary's "Christian National Identity".

68   This is the view of the most recent and "authoritative" historical accounts to emerge from the largely state-funded liberal-conservative "think-tank", the Clio Institute of Budapest, and from its two principal investigators, Gergely Bödők and Ádám Gellért. The CI's thesis was actually first aired by Gergely Bödők in his 2018 doctoral dissertation See: Gergely Bödők. *Vörös és Fehér Terror Magyarországon: 1919–1921* (Red and White Terror in Hungary: 1919–1921. PhD Dissertation. Eszterházy Károly University. Department of History. 2018. http://disszertacio.uni-eger.hu/54/4/Bodok_disszertacio.pdf. (Bödők's thesis supervisor was Ignác Romsics, the current doyen of modern liberal Hungarian historiography.) During a series of public conferences on the 100th anniversary of the Commune, organized by the Clio Institute, Bödők and Gellért argued that terror was a purposefully chosen public-policy plank of the Republic of Councils. In their view, this policy choice was driven, albeit not exclusively, and with fewer victims than hitherto listed, by the "terrorist DNA" in the ideological genes of the Council Republic's "Communist leadership". These young historians reaffirm the canon: the political leaders of the HROC had no choice: they were Lenin's boys, they had to follow Lenin's "ideological blueprint", besides, they did not have legitimacy, they came to power through a coup, objective necessity doubled-down upon them, they could only proceed via terror. Bödők's and Gellért's arguments can be listened to in full on the following URL: <https://www.youtube.com/watch?v=MuJPW4LmzcQ>. To read a third person summary of their theses; see: Zoltán Szőts. "Mennyiben következett Bolshevik ideológiából a Vörös Terror" (To What Extent was the Red Terror the result of Bolshevik Ideology) Budapest, *ujkor.hu* (Nov 7, 2019). <<https://ujkor.hu/content/mennyiben-kovetkezett-vorosterror-bolsevik-ideologiabol.

69   There are problems even with the Clio Institute's reduced numbers. The two co-directors can't even agree with each other on the number killed by the "Red Terror" (Gelért's victims total 425, Bödők's is 367). Gellért's numbers include, for example those Bolsheviks who entered Hungary during early July 1919 with the tacit approval of Lenin, to overthrow Garbai and Kun and introduce a "real" Leninist system.

70   This of course does not alter the central pillar of the profoundly anti-Semitic conservative narrative according to which, the "adoption of terror" by the 1919 "proletarian state" was the idea of its Leninist, ethnically Jewish, therefore, anti-Christian, anti-Hungarian high-command. The predominantly Christian make-up of the terror-gangs, we're told, is merely the exception that proves the rule.

71   Gellért argues that there were no "terrorist kills" by the Commune until April 19. His numbers begin to climb during the last week of April (49 killed according to his extrapolation from Váry's body-count). He records two big jumps in May and June (108 and 232 respectively) followed by a sharp curtailment in July (36 victims). He could not offer a full explanation in 2019 for this fluctuating, wave-like profile in the number of the Commune's victims. We'll offer one at the close of our section.

72   This is particularly well argued by Bödők in his 2018 dissertation. Op.cit.

73   Bödők served as one of the academic commentators at the launch of the Orbán regime's most-recent "history book" on the "Red Terror" (the one penned by B. Tamás Müller, op.cit and published by the Office of the Hungarian Parliament, under László Kövér's Presidency). Bödők's only criticism of Müller's outlandish hatchet job was that it neglected to talk about the terror committed by the Whites after the collapse of the Commune. For a review of the launch and Bödők's comments see: Maróti Zsolt Viktor *ujkor.hu* Budapest, (March 22, 2016), <https://ujkor.hu/content/legyozni-az-uri-magyarorszagot-vorosterror-az-orszaghazban>.

74   To repeat ourselves for the sake of those who may have missed our earlier disclaimer and still entertain the idea of reframing our position as one driven by nostalgia for the acts of terror committed during the 1919 Republic of Councils: Our analysis does not excuse the inhuman actions committed during the 133 days of the Commune by some of its "bad boys" (the term is consciously borrowed from the title of the most recent book on the 1919 Republic of Councils. See: Pál Hatos, *Rosszfiúk világforradalma: Az 1919-es Magyarországi Tanácsköztársaság története* [The World Revolution of the Bad Boys: The History of the 1919 Hungarian Republic of Councils], (Budapest: Jaffa Kiadó, 2021). We do not minimize the suffering of the innocent victims (the ones who were murdered, held hostage or were simply afraid for their lives through no fault of their own). We have not come here to praise terror, but to bury those parts of it that do not belong in the public policy universe of the 1919 proletarian state.

75   All three were thorns in the side of the Bolshevik minority that favored the use of terror as a public policy tool. Rónai smartly avoided fleeing with the "heavy hitters" to Russia after the collapse of the Republic. He took his own life in Belgium in 1940 rather than submit to either the Nazis or their new Bolshevik allies who jointly raped Poland in an orgy of violence in 1939. Landler also avoided Russia and died in Cannes early in 1928, so the Russian Bolsheviks executed his younger brother Ernő instead, then buried Jenő's remains next to the Kremlin's wall to pretend that they actually cared. Pogány was the least cautious of the four. He sought refuge in the Soviet Union and was executed there in 1938 along with many of his former Social Democratic and Communist comrades.

76   Pogány was replaced by Bőhm at the beginning of April, but his replacement was also a lifetime Social Democrat, and perhaps the loudest critic of terror within the entire RGC. Böhm was already in Vienna before the collapse of the Commune as Hungary's Ambassador to Austria and lead negotiator with the Entente's representatives in the Austrian capital. After the fall of the Commune, this ex-leader of the Hungarian Iron Workers, and the formidable Commander in Chief of the Commune's Red Army stayed clear of the territories controlled by the Hungarians, Germans or Soviets till the end of WWII. He died of natural causes in Sweden in 1949 but not before Hungary's post-WWII Stalinist leader and his 1919 nemesis, Mátyás Rákosi stripped him of his Hungarian citizenship on the 3rd of June, 1949.

77   As we have stated earlier, the ideological roots of the 1919 Hungarian Republic of Councils were not in the East but in the West, not in Lenin's but in Luxemburg's garden. As we have quoted Lukács himself, not only the Social Democrats, but most of the Communists in the RGC were more familiar at this time with the ideas of Luxemburg than those of Lenin.

78   We must at all times remember: this proletarian state did not aspire to Parliamentary but to Council Socialism. This is why it studiously avoided using the country's majestic Parliament building as the seat of its own executive, legislative and judicial powers. Much to Lenin's chagrin, the new Social Democratic-Communist alliance did not provide itself the leading role on the path to socialism. It gave away this possession to the Councils themselves. As Lajos Csoma had shown in the previous chapter of this book, the working men and women of these councils insisted on exercising their hard won rights against the party bureaucracy and against all those who attempted to push them around by force rather than reason. This book celebrates rather than minimizes *their* spirit, heroism and sacrifices.

79   Lékai's nomination was warmly seconded and supported by none other than Béla Kun.

80   Many of them were former students or colleagues of Rusztem Vámbéry (1872–1948), the father of 20th century Hungarian criminology. Others, such as the pioneering psychoanalyst Lilly Hajdú, the medical doctor József Madzsar or Rónai himself were prominent members of the progressive Galilei Circle, and of the Association of Social Scientists who gravitated around such figures as Ágost Pulszky, Sándor Ferenczi, Gyula Pikler, Oszkár Jászi, the aforementioned Vámbéry or Karl Polányi, and published their works in such well known, progressive journals of that era as *Nyugat* (West), or *Huszadik Század* (Twentieth Century). Lilly Hajdu would be subjected to continuous harrassment after 1919 not so much for the role she played during the Republic of Councils but for being a Jew and an outspoken woman devoted to the methods of Freud. (See: Anna Borgos. "Elhárító mechanizmusok: Pszichoanalízis és politika találkozásai Hajdu Lilly életútjának tükrében" (Denial Mechanisms: The Encounters of Psychoanalysis and Politics on the Life-Path of Lilly Hajdú) *Thalassa* 20, no. 1, (2009), 21-46.) Hajdú managed to elude Horthy's police during the roundup and deportation of Hungary's Jews that began in 1941 and really took off in 1944. Her

husband was caught, deported and died in the Terezin death camp operated by Hungary's wartime ally, Germany. Hajdú's son, Miklós Gimes was executed in Hungary along with Imre Nagy in 1958 on the orders of Hungary's Communist Party boss, János Kádár (she heard the news of her son's death sentence and execution on the radio). Her daughter, Judit Gimes, managed to escape to Switzerland after the Soviet repression of the 1956 revolution. Lilly Hajdu took her own life in Budapest on May 27, 1960 after she was repeatedly denied an exit visa by the Kádár regime, to visit her daughter and grandchildren in Switzerland. Madzsar, one of Ilona Duczynska's mentors prior to 1919, was executed in the Soviet Union in 1938. As we have stated earlier, Rónai killed himself in Belgium in 1940, rather than wait to be killed by the Nazis or the Bolsheviks.

81 The unreliability of the politically biased "studies" during the Horthy era are paralleled by those of the Stalinist and post-Stalinist one-party years in Hungary. See, for example András Szabó. "A Magyar Tanácsköztársaság büntetőjogának fő kérdései" (Key Aspects of the Republic of Councils' Criminal Code) in Pál Halász (ed). Tanulmányok a Magyar Tanácsköztársaság államáról és jogáról [Studies on the State and Legal System of the Republic of Councils] (Budapest: 1955), 115–166. The last comprehensive analysis of the Republic of Council's judicial system was completed more than half a century ago, during the Kádár era in 1961. It is a somewhat rosy-eyed look back from the blind alley of Gulyás Communism by Béla Sarlós. A Tanácsköztársaság forradalmi törvényszékei [The Courts of the Republic of Councils]. (Budapest, 1961). It is only very recently that some younger historians, such as Patrik András Erdős and others have begun to devote some attention to this long-neglected policy area, albeit with a historical rather than a public-policy compass.

82 The young historians presented their findings at a scientific conference jointly organized by the aforementioned Clio Institute and the Budapest Municipal Archives on May 31st, 2019 (the latter also deserve credit for their opennes). For a summary of the historians' findings; see: Zoltán Szőts, "A Tanácsköztársaság alternatív büntető politikája" [The Alternative Punitive Policies of the Republic of Councils] Újkor.hu, (June 14, 2019).

83 Ibid,.

84 Ibid,.

85 Ibid,.

86 Ibid,. For his own earlier study of the DEC see, András Patrik Erdős. "A Tanácsköztársaság alternatív büntetőpolitikája: A Budapesti Forradalmi Törvényszék Kísérleti Kriminológiai Osztályának működése [The Alternative Punitive Policies of the Republic of Councils: The Budapest Revolutionary Court's Department of Experimental Criminology] Clio Műhelytanulmányok no. 3, (2018).

87 Civil Law (divorce, births, deaths, inheritance, etc) were handled by the old court system, but under a new set of rules that respected gender equality, the rights of ethnic minorities, children and eliminated preferential treatment for the country's fortune hunters.

88 The go ahead in urgent cases was already granted on April 8, 1919.

89 Rákos was a Galileist, with a law degree. Like so many others, he also sought refuge in the Soviet Union after the collapse of the HROC. He was sent to the Gulag by Stalin's henchmen in 1938. Like József Lengyel, he also managed to survive the harsh conditions in the forced labour camps and after he completed his sentence he was able to return to Hungary in 1947.

90 Sándor Nagy, A Budapesti Forradalmi Törvényszék Iratai [Documents of the Budapest Revolutionary Courts] Budapest Fővárosi Levéltár. Hungaricana.hu, (2019). It's important to underline: the above cases do not include ones handled by the millitary and martial law tribunals, especially those headed by Tibor Szamuely or József Cserny that fell under the supervision of the Commissariat of Defense, and the Red Army's military commander of Budapest, Haubrich József (who was also executed in Moscow in 1938). We shall deal with these cases shortly.

91 The Red Guards were organized into 12 territorial districts—11 in the countryside , 1 in the capital itself. Three of the 4 men who headed the largest Red Guard division in the capital at different times (Ernő Landler, Ernő Seidler, and Ferenc Jancsik) sought refuge in the Soviet Union after the collapse of the Commune and were executed in Moscow in 1938-39. Of the national directors, the only one to escape persecution in Moscow was Mátyáa Rákosi, and he only held the post during the last week of the Commune when it was at the edge of the precipice and he was already packing his bags. One of Hungary's current crop of young, conservative historians, Tamás M. Tarján, is as far off the target as his predecessors by arguing that the Commune's police force was

based on a "Leninist blue-print", and that it was headed by a Cheka trained terrorist, József Cserny. Cserny never even came close to heading one of the 12 divisions of the Red Guards, let alone its national command. For Tarján's ill-informed theses, which were subsequently reproduced by virtually all of the pro-governemnt media throughout Hungary on the centenial of the 1919 Commune; see: Tamás M. Tarján, "Puccskisérlet a Ludovikán" *Rubicon*, June, 2019, <http://www.rubicon.hu/magyar/oldalak/1919_junius_24_puccskiserlet_a_ludovikan/>.

92 For an overview of the Károlyi regime's law enforcement agencies see Tamás Révész. "Nemzetőrök, polgárőrök, népőrök: A Károlyi kormány karhatalmi szervei" [National Guards, Public Guards, Peoples Guards: The Law Enforcement Organs of the Károlyi Government,] Budapest, *Rubicon*, no. 3, (2015).

93 Rákos would of course become very familiar with the ways of Soviet security forces *after* the collapse of the 1919 Commune. He only evaded execution in the Soviet Union by a whisker but was the NKVD's prisoner in the Gulag for a decade, after his capture and torture on trumped up charges in the 1930s. That experience, however, did not stop him, as it stopped Ilona Duczynska's best friend, József Lengyel, from shamelessly serving both the Rákosi and the Kádár regimes after his release and return to Hungary in the late 1940s. Rákos's first act after his return to Hungary from the Gulag was to translate into Hungarian Yuri German's stomach-turning ode to the terrorist who started the bloody affinity-fraud in Russia in 1918—Felix Dzerzhinsky. See: Jurij German, *Történetek Drzezsinszkij életéből* (Stories from Dzerzhinsky's Life) (Budapest: Új Magyar Könyvkiadó, 1949). This is what the jacket cover, composed by Rákos, had to say about the architect of the Bolsheviks' terror-machine. "We shall finally learn, from Yuri German's book, who was this man (Dzerzhinsky), who was endowed with extraordinary talent, in whom honor, self-discipline, and willpower were coupled with the most self-sacrificing love. Only historical ages produce such proudly and lovingly recalled heroes as him who remain part of our folklore and epics for centuries afterwards. Anyone who reads this book will learn how to love their fellow human beings and make the greatest sacrifices for their community".

94 Their ability to regroup elsewhere, their protracted but diminishing successes in committing murderous acts throughout the territory of Hungary until the end of the Commune are addressed by Péter Konok, *op.cit*, (2010).

95 A Galileist, an associate of Ilona Duczynska, older brother of Commissar Jozsef Kelen, (the latter was one of the many Commune leaders to be executed in the 1930s in the Soviet Union), Korvin was a highly intelligent, T.S. Eliot like figure of the Hungarian revolutionary movement at the end of WWI (he just turned 24 when the war ended).. He was not a Russian trained Bolshevik but an aspiring young poet, highly thought of by none other than Mihály Babits. Korvin had a permanent physical disability that kept him at home and away from the battlefront. Well to do, but sensitive to the suffering of the oppressed, he was a Socialist Revolutionary at night, a well paid bank executive during the day. He became the underground leader of the Hungarian Socialist Revolutionaries *after* the January 1918 arrest of the then 21 year old Ilona Duczynska and her group. As we had pointed out earlier, the Hungarian SR's political role models were Bebel, Kropotkin, Pannekoek, and most notably Luxemburg. Korvin and Sallai did not become Luxemburgians because they opposed Lenin. They were Luxemburgians because they, like Lukács at the time, were not familiar with Lenin's thoughts. Korvin joined the Communist Party in November 1918. Three months later, in February 1919, he was interned, along with Kun and the top HCP leaders by the Károlyi government. Apparently he was the one who typed up the final text of the merger between Kun and the Social Democrats in Kun's prison cell on the night of March 20. Kun, not to mention Garbai and the top leaders of the Social Democrats, trusted him much more with internal security than Tibor Szamuely who was the Cheka's point man in the Hungarian Communist Party and who loudly disapproved of the merger between the two parties and was openly out for blood.

96 Most notably, by Jozsef Cserny and a group of his self-appointed "Lenin-boys" during the month of May and June, when they ran circles around their RGC appointed "state controllers"—Korvin and Sallai. After Korvin managed to oust them from his shop at the beginning of June, they relocated themselves to the 2nd precinct in the capital under an openly accommodating precinct commander, Ferenc Bandl. Here, and with the assistance of a disgruntled acting national Red Guard commander, Ede Chlepko (who wanted to use Cserny's thugs to embarrass Bela Kun and the RGC for passing him over for the top job as National Director of the Red Guards) Cserny's

men were able to continue their atrocities, albeit on a much smaller scale, until they were finally disbanded following their last murderous acts in July. (On the details of the latter, please see Péter Dónáth's thoroughgoing discussion, *op.cit.*)

97 The fate of Dezső Bíró, one of the men who headed the largest of the Red Guards' 12 regional units (i.e. the one in the capital), offers some proof of this. Bíró did *not* follow his colleagues to the Soviet Union but stayed in Vienna after fleeing Budapest with Béla Kun on August 1, 1919. He was allowed back to Hungary by the Horthy regime during the early 1920s and was never charged with any abuses of power. Bíró became the Deputy-head of the Hungarian Football Federation and died of natural causes in his bed and in his home in 1932.

98 By July the leading perpetrators of the terrorist acts of May and June such as Szamuely and Cserny were the targets of increasingly severe censure and reprimand by the RGC, the Red Army commander of Budapest, the Workers' and Soldiers' Concil for Budapest along with the newly constituted Executive Committee of the National Congress of Councils. By late July it was not the aforementioned "terrorists" but the combined pressure of the Imperialist blockade, the economic chaos and hunger throughout the land, the growing frustration of Hungary's 4 million peasants with the blatantly and proudly anti-Leninist agrarian policies of the RGC, and the aggressive penetration of the Romanian Army into Hungary, along with news of widespread rapings and lootings by its soldiers that kept Hungary's citizens in fear.

99 Pogány was a university graduate, an intellectual rather than a physical labourer, an aspiring playwright and literary theorist with a number of publications under his belt by the end of WWI. He rose quickly to the top of the HSDP leadership, was a Social Democratic member of the Károlyi government and approved of the arrest of Kun and the top Communists in February 1919. He submitted a proposal to the newly merged party executive for the reorganization of the Ministry of Defense and the Army that was strikingly different from one submitted by the Moscow trained Chekist, Szamuely. Even Béla Kun voted for Pogány's approach and for his appointment as head of the military on the night of March 21, 1919.

100 Pogány became one of the three Commissars for Foreign Affairs after this shuffle (Béla Kun and Péter Ágoston were the other two). Pogány was put in charge of the Commissariat's International Propaganda Unit—he became for all intents and purposes Ilona Duczynska's boss in this Ministry. After the collapse of the Commune, Pogány spent some years in the USA as a high-ranking member of the American Communist Party and used the name John Pepper rather than his Hungarian one. Eventually he too sought refuge in the USSR, where he was executed on the orders of Stalin. For a relatively recent, and not altogether sympathetic biography that utilizes some recently released archival materials; see Thomas Sakmyster: *A Communist Odyssey: The Life of József Pogány/John Pepper* (New York, NY: Central European University Press, 2012). My brief discussions with Ilona Duczynska decades ago about her ex-boss inside the Ministry of Foreign Affairs in 1919 did not leave me with the impression that she was a fan. Within a few weeks of her appointment, she began looking for a way out and left her high-power position in Budapest by the end of May for an anonymous and low ranking post as a stringer for a left-wing newspaper in Zurich. See: András B. Göllner, *Ilona: Portrait of a Rebel* (Forthcoming, 2022).

101 Kövér was quoted on June 6, 2019 by the same pro-government daily, *Magyar Hírlap* that distributes not only the government run Veritas Institute's historical fallacies, but all of the Orbán government's mind-bending narratives to a defenseless and ill-informed Hungarian public. Kövér, his boss Orbán, and the spin-doctors that work on behalf of the EU funded Orbán regime have regurgitated this line thousands of times during the last decade so by now it has become as veritable a "Hungaricum" as Paprika or that incomparable firewater, Pálinka. This chapter neither dismisses the terrorist acts that occurred during the Republic of Councils nor waxes nostalgically about them. It simply puts them into a place in the public policy universe of the Commune where they belong.

102 While Marx certainly looked upon the movement of history as a struggle between opposing social forces, he did not argue anywhere that the success of the transformation from one historical stage to another is predicated upon the use of terror by the agents of change. For Marx, the movement of working men and women to the center of their country's political arena does not require that they become terrorists, or rally behind those who choose to follow this path to power.

103 The loudest Hungarian advocate and practitioner was, of course Szamuely but he was by no means the only representative of this counterproductive, inhuman approach in Hungary during the 133 days of the Commune.

104 The use of terror on the path to socialism was accepted as a legitimate public policy alternative by Lenin as early as 1908, much to Rosa Luxemburg's chagrin (See Ottokar Luban. "Rosa Luxemburg's critique of Lenin's ultra-centralistic party concept and of the Bolshevik revolution". In *Critique* 40, no. 3, (2012), 357–365. And Bertram D. Wolfe, "Rosa Luxemburg and V. I. Lenin: The opposite poles of revolutionary socialism." In *The Antioch Review*, no. 21, (1961), 209–226. Lenin restated his earlier position in *The State and Revolution*, as well as in his celebrated polemics with Karl Kautsky that began in the fall of 1918. See: Karl Kautsky. *The Dictatorship of the Proletariat* (Ann Arbor, MI: University of Michigan Press, 1964), xv-xvii. (First published in 1918); V. I. Lenin. "The Proletarian Revolution and the Renegade Kautsky" in *Collected Works. Volume 28, July 1918-March 1919.* Moscow: Progress Publishers, 1965 (first published in response to Kautsky in 1918); Kautsky's rejoinder is in *Terrorism and Communism: A Contribution to the Natural History of Revolution* (London: National Labour Press, 1921). (It was written in 1919 and was first published in 1920.

105 My sincere apologies to Suzanne and to Leonard Cohen for this poetic license.

106 See: Oscar Jászi, *Revolution and Counterrevolution in Hungary.* op.cit., 119–120.

107 A cursory glance at the sudden and sharp decline in the number of victims of "terror" after the June meeting of the National Congress of Councils stands as a testimony to the resistance of Hungary's working men and women to the attempted hijacking of their revolution.

108 They would try to resurrect their broken dream in 1945, then try one last time in 1956.

109 As we have stated earlier while László Rudas, to the left of Lukács in 1919 would change his colour earlier (shortly after he read and translated Lenin's *The State and Revolution* into Hungarian, and met Lenin in Moscow in May, 1919), the Bolsheviks' center and the recalcitrant right wing, including Lukács, only shredded their Luxemburgian roots after they fled to Vienna and were read "the Riot Act" by the 2nd Congress of the Commintern in the summer of 1920. The Hungarian Social Democratic majority on the RGC stayed firmly opposed to the use of state sponsored terror. Ilona Duczynska stayed true to her principles. Like her early mentor, Angelica Balabanoff, like Emma Goldman, she also left Moscow early and was expelled from the Hungarian Communist Party in exile by 1922 for her "Luxemburgian" deviation. She bravely gave it another try with the Austrian Communist Party in 1934, only to be expelled for a second time, in 1936, this time on the direct orders of Moscow.

110 It's this absence of blood on the streets of Budapest on March 21, 1919 that enables everyone on the Right to dismiss the movement of Hungary's working men and women to the center of their political arena in 1919 as a coup d'état and blinds even many on the Left from seeing this as a genuine social revolution.

111 Originally quoted in *Szolnok megye 1918/19-ben* (Szolnok County in 1918/19) Szolnok. 1961. p.5. This author had taken it from the 2020 Doctoral Dissertation of Lajos Csoma, op.cit. Footnote no. 576.

CHAPTER 5

Working Women and the 1919 Commune

Part I: Introducing Magda Aranyossi

Susan Zimmermann

THE FIRST PART of this chapter on women and the 1919 Republic of Councils is a brief introduction to English-speaking audiences of a remarkable member of the Hungarian and international women's and workers' movements, Magda Aranyossi. The second part of the chapter immediately afterwards contains the first English translation (by András Göllner) of large segments of Aranyossi's 1954 study on "The impact of the Russian Revolution and the 1919 Republic of Councils on the working women's movement in Hungary, 1917–1919", published originally in *Századok*, which was then and possibly even today the most prestigious periodical of the historians' profession in Hungary.

Less than a year older than Ilona Duczynska, Magda Aranyossi was a prolific writer and lived an eventful life. Like so many of her generation, she was both an eyewitness to and participant in the 1919 Hungarian Republic of Councils. During the interwar years, she was active in the international women's movement. During World War II, she participated in the Hungarian underground movement against Fascism. After 1945, she became a founding member of the Democratic Alliance of Hungarian Women (Magyar Nők Demokratikus Szövetsége) and became founding editor of the Alliance's journal *Asszonyok* (Women). From 1949 to her death in 1977 she was a researcher at the Institute of the Hungarian Labour Movement (Magyar Munkásmozgalmi Intézet), later Institute of Party History (Párttörténeti Intézet) in Budapest.[1]

When in the middle of the 1990s I did research on the history of the pre-1918 Hungarian women's movement, I soon discovered a number of female historians who had written, during the period of state-socialism—books, pamphlets and articles—about the history of women in Hungary in the period before 1945. Magda Aranyossi was one of them, and she was, quite like some of her peers, a more or less "self-made" historian. Her involvement with writing and editing publications highlighting women's history, dating to the interwar period, would culminate in her 1963 monograph *Rebellious women: The history of the Hungarian woman workers' movement 1867–1919*.[2]

In the early 2010s, some 15 years after my first encounter with the writings of Aranyossi and other women of her generation and younger, I began to gather material for a new historiographical study on Hungarian women's history written between 1945 and 1989. Screening key journals of the historical profession and a number of library catalogues, I discovered Aranyossi's study on the Republic of Councils, parts of which are now published for the first time in English translation here. I also came upon a larger body of her writings as well as those written and edited by many others.[3] From the perspective of the ever-changing politics of history, I chose to characterize the positioning and fate of this diverse body of writing on women's history as follows:

> On the one hand, given the fact that women's emancipation as a political and cultural project formed one indispensable element of the overall state-socialist project for change, these writings, from the perspective of the official core of the Hungarian political system and the historians' profession, must have been perceived as something to be condoned, benevolently tolerated, or patronized, or as something that was both unavoidable and in substance irrelevant. … On the other hand, the writing on women's history, because it was and remained associated with the official women's organizations or trade unions, or the Institute of Party History, was perceived and visibly coloured as connected to social movements and activism that related to both a leftist pre-socialist past and to state socialism. Therefore, many who felt alienated from the Hungarian one-party system, or disliked some of its components, must have perceived these publications as belonging to the ideological mainstream of that system. … By associating the history of women's emancipation (and writing about it) with both the past and present of the Western world and state socialism as a system, the memory of writing women's history as a social critique, which as a social praxis had been vividly present under state socialism, was erased from the public consciousness after 1989.[4]

The historiographical study just quoted is no more than an exploratory one; due to restrictions in time and space I did not include several genres of publications that abound with additional information on women's history in Hungary, including source and reprint editions, Hungarian folk-life studies, popular women's magazines, and autobiographies. The publication of works belonging to the latter genre was highly cultivated in state-socialist Hungary, and Magda Aranyossi was one of those who recounted their life history in a series entitled

"Women in history". Her *Unorderly autobiography* was published shortly after her death in 1977.[5]

While to date there is no systematic historical scholarship discussing the life and work of Magda Aranyossi there is a wealth of material, including and beyond her own work, from which we can (or in some cases could in principle) learn surprisingly much about her life and personality.

First: there are archival holdings on Aranyossi kept in the archival division of the Institute of Political History (Politikatörténeti Intézet), the successor of the Institute of Party History in Budapest. Of importance here is an archival collection containing material on and written by Aranyossi and her husband Pál Aranyossi,[6] as well as a lengthy life history interview conducted in 1970 by Aranyossi's colleagues at the Institute of Party History; at the time Aranyossi had already begun to write her memoirs.[7] The life history interview forms part of a large collection of such interviews recorded by the Institute of Party History and kept today at the Institute. Neither the names of the interviewees nor the interviews themselves can be accessed by researchers. The Institute pursues this policy in order to protect the interviewees in the extremely hostile and aggressively anti-communist political environment that has developed in Hungary after the end of the state-socialist system in 1990.

At present neither the library nor the archival division of the Institute of Political History can be used for research purposes; hidden behind a myriad of legal stipulations implemented by the hostile Orbán system, the Institute was forced to temporarily close down the aforementioned services; it has been forced to leave its premises and is experiencing tremendous financial difficulties.[8] One cannot but hope, that the regime will not use its newly acquired power over key archival material pertaining to the period of state-socialism, to destroy, alter or abuse vital archival evidence about Hungary's 20th century history.

Second: the internationally well-known Hungarian writer Péter Nádas, who is the nephew of Magda Aranyossi, has recently come out with two important publications that give substantial information on the life and personality of his aunt. It's important to note here, that Aranyossi became Nádas's guardian after the death of his parents in 1955 and 1958 respectively (Nádas himself was born in 1942). The first of these books, Nádas's autobiography *Luminous details: Memory sheets from the life of a storyteller*, appeared in 2017.[9] In 2018 Nádas complemented his own memoirs with a copious volume entitled *My old, drowned world. With annotations by Péter Nádas* which makes available a new, commented edition of Aranyossi's *Unorderly autobiography*, and rich additional information compiled by Nádas and a team of associates. Both volumes—which in and of themselves are of great value for any future study on Magda Aranyossi and her circles—build on Nádas's extensive family archive, which, once available for historical research, will certainly constitute a vital resource for research on the history of women's activism in Hungary and beyond in the 20th century.[10]

We learn from Aranyossi's autobiography and the volume *My old, drowned world* containing its re-edition that Aranyossi was born as Ida Magdolna Neumayer in 1896 into a family belonging to the "well-to-do Jewish bourgeoisie". The family name was Hungarianized as Nádas in 1911. Magda was the third of eight children and the elder sister of Péter Nádas's father.[11] The volume *My old, drowned world* published in 2018 contains, on top of the re-edition of Aranyossi's 1978 *Unorderly autobiography*, those portions of the manuscript of this text that were not included in the published version, and a precious variety of additional information and original documents, including: extensive annotations related to a myriad of individuals, places and events mentioned in *Unorderly autobiography*, many of them authored by Péter Nádas and directly "correcting" and adding to Aranyossi's autobiographical account; a large number of letters from and to Aranyossi (from both Nádas's family archive and the archival division of the Institute of Political History), most of them dating from the period between 1943 and 1946 and exchanged between Aranyossi, her husband, and her son, one letter (by Péter Nádas to his aunt) from 1958, and a few more letters from the 1960s; Aranyossi's 20 pages study "A pince [The basement]", written in 1962,[12] on key circumstances of the underground work of the resistance group to which she belonged in Hungary in 1943/1944; and many photographs and facsimiles of personal and other documents, (including e.g. the certificate of the enrollment of Aranyossi in the liberal-progressive women's organization Feministák Egyesülete [Feminist Association] in 1918), accompanied by extensive quotes from Nádas's 2017 autobiography.

The published material on and by Aranyossi can be characterized as a rich source for historical research. In Nádas's *Luminous details* his aunt Magda Aranyossi features as "one of the central characters".[13] His two-volume autobiography refers to Aranyossi on countless occasions, and it is impossible indeed to briefly 'summarize' Nádas's perception and evaluation of her character, her journey through life, and her personal and political commitments. In one place he talks of her in the following manner: "My aunt Magda was one of the most intelligent beings whom I met in my protracted life. However, there was a little blemish in her temper. She did not always manage to harmonize her passions, intentions, sense of reality, and ideals;"[14] in another place he characterizes Aranyossi as:

> … much likely to be admired with her sense of reality, fortitude, and grand dame manner which did not brook discussion or contradiction … the older she became the more she was like this, a born lady, not a ladified woman

with her acquired manners, but a born lady, who was indeed a communist, but only en passant. Even if she herself thought it to be the other way around.[15]

Unorderly autobiography, Luminous details, and *My old, drowned world* together give insight into the transformation of Hungarian society in the 20th century, left-wing politics and women's activism and organizing in Europe and Hungary during Aranyossi's life time, Aranyossi's personality and biography, and, last but not least, the politics of history both during Aranyossi's life time and the decades after the end of one-party rule in 1990.

The politics of history are visible in the most eye-catching or concise manner in some of the quotes taken from Nádas's autobiography and attached to the family documents published in *My old, drowned world*, which repeatedly underline his evaluation of things. Yet the politics of history are boldly present in *Unorderly autobiography* and the lengthier narratives contained in *Luminous details* as well. Two anecdotes, related to Aranyossi's personality and biography may serve as examples here. In a captivating section of his memoirs, Nádas recounts a series of long discussions between himself and his aunt towards the end of the 1950s, when the nephew conversed with the aunt in her room during the latter's sleepless nights. *Luminous details* interweaves these encounters with a narrative that shares with the reader Nádas's own, somewhat complex yet unambiguously negative take on Aranyossi's political world view and commitment.[16] Nádas had just turned 14 when in the autumn of 1956 the Hungarian uprising/revolution—he discusses various names for those events and rejects all of them—took place. During the lengthy nighttime discussions with his aunt only a few years later Nádas was a self-described "frantic youngster, unfair and extreme". Aranyossi, says Nádas, was plagued at the time by both the barely suppressible inner strife with deformations plaguing her personal life and the inner contestations evolving around her life-long political commitment to communism. Nádas characterizes communists as "adnate with their party"; they couldn't "recognize that only they themselves were their party. They were not any longer a persona apart, yet then a party could not have a personality, whatever party that may be".[17] Communism he describes as a preposterous, failed, and murderous ideology and practice, even whilst historically it achieved a few important basic things. Why doesn't his aunt speak out? Why doesn't she turn away from her political commitment, if "she sees all of this so clearly", he asks his aunt during one of these late-night conversations:

After some hesitant silence she answered: Only my party may bury me.
I confess, her answer caught me unexpectedly, her arrogant foolishness hit me in the face and incensed me.

You don't say in earnest that you will be there at your own funeral?
You don't say in earnest that you shape your life from the perspective of
your funeral?
You don't say in earnest that your own funeral is more important than the
life of others?
Why don't you just shit on your own funeral from up here from your
second-floor balcony?
… With her I spoke deliberately in such rough manner, I used words she
herself would never in her life pronounce, I provoked her. On the other
hand, both of us had already been over all possible funerals, the exhumation
and re-burial of the humiliated and executed, we knew what such
necrophile rituals meant. To say (no more than) the least, the pink of
infamy, parody, burlesque, perfidy. It doesn't mean a fuck. …
Only my party may bury me, nobody else, this was her obstinate answer, and
that I was not to speak with her in such tone, or I was to be so kind as to
leave her room.[18]

The other anecdote comes from Aranyossi's 1978 *Unorderly autobiography*. In the
section "On illegal ways" Aranyossi describes the vicious, random violence against
Jews and other persecuted groups and individuals, and those who tried to help
them in 1944 and early 1945 in Budapest under Nazi occupation. Aranyossi and
her husband Pál Aranyossi, called "Pali", at the time had to spend their nights
changing flats and hideouts. One of their hideouts was the home of the Orodi
family. Here is how she looks back upon this time:

> … ever more people took refuge. The most diverse of people. A criminal
> police detective who didn't want to follow his commander and flee to the
> West. A silly old beau, driven by his fear of the carpet bombing, came
> here from his flat on the outskirts of Budapest. He tried to scare me by
> saying that the Russians will 'communalize' me. If only I could see them
> already—I said to Pali—I wouldn't even mind if I was communalized.[19]

All three volumes discussed here also can serve as sources for the study of the
broadly defined history of left-wing movements and women's activisms and
organizing in Europe and Hungary. I can mention only a few highlights, to be
found where Nádas and Aranyossi give more extensive narratives and detailed
descriptions. Aranyossi's *Unorderly autobiography* closes with the historical
moment when "the first two Soviet soldiers entered our shelter" in Budapest on
13 January 1945.[20]

Luminous details contains information on the time thereafter too. For instance,

Nádas recounts his impressions and insights about Aranyossi's friendship circles evolving from the women's networks in and around the Democratic Alliance of Hungarian Women (Magyar Nők Demokratikus Szövetsége, 1945–1956). As I alluded to this at the beginning of this introduction, Aranyossi was a founding member of the Alliance and the founding editor of its journal *Asszonyok*. Her activities were focused on these circles in the first years after the Second World War. Nádas paints a vivid picture of the character of these personal as well as institutionalized relationships, and the habits and some of the personalities involved. He gives information for instance on how the women built a network of child protection institutions all over the country and their encounters with Hungary's *de facto* head of state, the leader of the Hungarian Communist Party, Mátyás Rákosi, over this question. He talks of their encounter at a literacy campaign for women, and so on. Another narrative worth mentioning is Nádas's description of a meeting between Aranyossi and Countess Katinka Andrássy on the occasion of the latter's visit to Hungary in 1963.[21]

Aranyossi's *Unorderly autobiography*, while detailed and multi-layered on the emigration years and the life and work in the underground communist resistance movement in Hungary during World War II, does not have much to say about the Republic of Councils. While she opens up in great detail about that event in her 1954 study re-published here, she avoids talking about it in her autobiography. She of course is not alone in doing so.

A highlight of relevance for the history of communist and popular front international organizing of women in the 1930s is the section contained in *Unorderly autobiography* on her involvement with organizations, representatives and activities in Paris of key importance internationally at the time. Aranyossi describes the preliminaries of the World Congress of Women against War and Fascism held in the French capital in the summer of 1934, and the event itself. The Congress gave rise to the *Rassemblement mondial des femmes contre le guerre et le fascisme* and its *Comité mondial des femmes contre le guerre et le fascisme* (Women's World Rally Against War and Fascism, and Women's World Committee Against War and Fascism), an organization working closely with Moscow and aimed at being fully inclusive of women from all political camps engaging for peace and against fascism. In the Paris Secretariat of the Committee Aranyossi was responsible for the daily operation of its journal *Femmes (dans l'action mondiale)* in the years to come; *Unorderly autobiography* reveals that she was also a member of (what Aranyossi labels) the "international plenary" of the organization, under the pseudonym "Helène". Aranyossi paints a multi-facetted picture of the *modus operandi* and character of the leaders of the organization, including Gabrielle Duchêne and Bernadette Cattanéo, and discusses in detail the workings of the Secretariat and the organization.[22]

I hope that this brief introduction into Aranyossi's life and work and the sources available to study her generation of women activists in the context of the history of progressive social movements, and Eastern European state-socialism, can serve as an incentive for others to engage in such research. For now, Aranyossi's own words may serve as a non/final chord leading up to the closing sentence of *Unorderly autobiography* quoted above (on the Soviet soldiers entering her bomb shelter in Budapest in January 1945). Aranyossi says: "My approach from childhood on towards my surroundings has changed profoundly during the long journey I made through this gorgeous and gruesome 20th century. I have seen many horrors, and a lot of suffering and injustice, yet I invariably *believe in the human being*".[23]

NOTES

1   Ágnes Kenyeres, "Aranyossi Magda, Nádas," in *Magyar Életrajzi Lexikon: 1000-1990* (Budapest: Arcanum Adatbázis, 2000), <https://mek.oszk.hu/00300/00355/html/index.html>; Péter Kozák, "Aranyossi Magda", in *Névpont.hu* (2013), <http://www.nevpont.hu/view/428>.

2   Magda Aranyossi, *Lázadó asszonyok. A magyar nőmunkásmozgalom története 1867-1919* [*Rebellious women: The history of the Hungarian woman workers' movement 1867-1919]* (Budapest: Kossuth Könyvkiadó, 1963).

3   Aranyossi's publications involve a variety of genres, exemplified by the following titles: a series of articles in 1950 entitled "A turjánon beérett a rozs" (The rye has matured in the Turján lands) which gave a "sociographic account of the agrarian misery" of the 1930s; *Clara Zetkin*. (Budapest: Hazafias Népfront, 1956); Magda Aranyossi and Tibor Erényi, "Aus der Geschichte der Arbeiterinnenbewegung in Ungarn. Die Periode der Jahrhundertwende [On the history of the women workers' movement in Hungary. The period of the turn of the century]", in *Internationale Tagung der Historiker der Arbeiterbewegung. XIV. Linzer Konferenz 1978. Linz, 12. bis 16. September 1978. Die Frau in der Arbeiterbewegung 1900-1939. Geschichte der Arbeiterbewegung. Bearbeitet von Gerhard Botz unter Mitarbeit von Hans Schafranek [International Conference of Labour Historians. 14th Linz Conference 1978. Woman in the labour movement 1900-1939. Adapted by Gerhard Botz with the assistance of Hans Schafranek]*, Bd. 13/1, ITH-Tagungsberichte (Wien: Europaverlag, 1980), 343-72 (published posthumously). Aranyossi also published biographies, including an extensive book on Leó Frankel [1952; German translation 1957]. The information on and summary description of "The rye" incl. the quote above is taken from Magda Aranyossi, *Az én régi, elsüllyedt világom. Nádas Péter széljegyzeteivel [My old, drowned world. With annotatons by Péter Nádas]* (Budapest: Jelenkor Kiadó, 2018), 499.

4   Susan Zimmermann, "In and Out of the Cage: Women's and Gender History Written in Hungary in the State-Socialist Period", *Aspasia* 8, Nr. 1 (2014), 142-43, <https://doi.org/10.3167/asp.2014.080107>.

5   Magda Aranyossi, *Rendszertelen önéletrajz [Unorderly autobiography]* (Budapest: Kossuth Könyvkiadó, 1978). In the following, when referring to and quoting from *Unorderly autobiography* I use the reprint edition (which does not give this original title) contained in Aranyossi, *My old, drowned world*, 5-292.

6   Politikatörténeti Intézet Levéltára [*Archive of the Institute of Political History*] Section VI: Személyi gyűjtemények, visszaemlékezések [Personal collections, recollections], Call no. 857.f.: Aranyossi Pál és Aranyossi Pálné [Pál Aranyossi and Mrs. Pál Aranyossi], o. J.

7   The information on the 1970 interview stems from a short biographical account on Aranyossi contained in Aranyossi, *My old, drowned world*, 499. The interview was conducted in eight sessions between 2 July and 31 August, 1970.

8   "Politikatörténeti Intézet," [*Institute of Political History*], http://polhist.hu/english/archives-and-library/.

9   Péter Nádas, *Világló részletek. Emléklapok egy elbeszélő életéből* [Luminous details. Memory sheets from the life of a storyteller], *2 volumes* (Budapest: Jelenkor Kiadó, 2017).

10   The family archive will be made available in the future in a public archive (Information received from Péter Nádas, email 16 June 2020).

11   Aranyossi, *My old, drowned world*, 5, 473, 495, 499, and the detailed pedigree contained in the volume. The quote is from Aranyossi's 1978 memoirs.

12   ... says Aranyossi in her *Unorderly autobiography*, Aranyossi, 269.

13   The phrase is used in the short description given on the cover of Aranyossi, *My old, drowned world*.

14   Nádas, *Luminous details*, vol. 2, 26.

15   Quoted from *Luminous details* in Aranyossi, *My old, drowned world*, 495.

16   The section opens at p. 80 of Nádas, *Luminous details*.

17   Nádas, *Luminous details*, vol. 2: 100 (I would like to add here that my translations of Nádas's literary text certainly do not live up in all instances to the standards of professional literary translation.)

18   Nádas, *Luminous details*, vol. 2: 103.

19   Aranyossi, *My old, drowned world*, quote on p. 271.

20   Aranyossi, *My old, drowned world*, 292.

21   Nádas, *Luminous details*, 2: esp. 106–111, 128–129, 243–251, 257–262, 276–277, 410-422, 443-449.

22   Aranyossi, *My old, drowned world*, 190–201 (spelling of "Helène" as given in this reprint edition).

23   Aranyossi, *My old, drowned world*, 292 (emphasis in the original).

Part II: The Impact of the 1917 Russian Revolution and the 1919 Republic of Councils on the Working Women's Movement in Hungary: 1917–1919*

Magda Aranyossi

On November 7, 1917, the Russian working class, under the leadership of V.I. Lenin and the Bolsheviks, seized power and launched the dictatorship of the proletariat in that country. The news of this revolution was greeted with considerable enthusiasm and hope by many in Hungary. The soldiers facing death and mutilation on the bloody battlefronts away from their loved ones, the exhausted and long exploited workers and peasants back home knew what they had to do. They knew that they had to put an end to the rule of those who led them into this senseless war. They knew almost instinctively that they must overthrow the system that kept them, and their families enslaved and in misery for generations. Soon, the entire country was rocked by strikes and protests, demanding an end to the wanton butchery, and calling for a socialist revolution. Working class and peasant women played a major role and often in the front lines of this revolutionary movement that finally swept the old political elite out of power in Hungary on March 21, 1919. This study is an hommage to their heroic struggle.

The main roots of the proletarian women's movement extend back into the early days of the Hungarian Social Democratic Party (HSDP). Our own examination will begin with the establishment of the Party's National Organizing Committee for Women (NOW) in 1903. As soon as the NOW began to exercise its voice, however, it found itself increasingly at odds with the party leadership that was entirely in the hands of men. At the 1910 party congress, some members from the women's wing of the Party did raise objections to the leadership's sabotage of the fight for women's suffrage, but their voices were quickly silenced. From 1912 on, the leadership of the women in the HSDP fully supported the Party executive and fell in line with the men in what constituted for all practical purposes a betrayal of the struggle for gender equality in Hungary. The NOW proclaimed that the role of women in Hungary was to support their men on the

* This text forms part of a longer study by Magda Aranyossi, published in Hungary after the death of Stalin. It appeared in the Hungarian journal, *Századok*. (Budapest. 1954. Vol 88. No 1). This abridged adaptation was translated into English by András B. Göllner, the editor of this book, who wishes to thank Professor Susan Zimmermann for bringing it to his attention as a worthy tribute to the heroic struggle of working women in Hungary during the Hungarian Republic of Councils.

battlefront by doing as they are told, and by increasing their efforts in the factories and in the fields. It agitated in support of the war effort, saying that, those who stayed behind must do their part to hasten victory on the battlefront.[1] The NOW suspended the class-struggle and argued that the war had in fact eroded class differences in the country.[2] As the military situation rapidly deteriorated and the consequences of this war became increasingly clear for all to see, these exhortations quickly lost their persuasiveness among working-class women. The suffering brought on by the war, the entry of ever larger numbers of women into the labour force, and their first-hand experience of workplace exploitation and abuse, quickly radicalized many. Working women began to look for ways to organize, to resist their exploiters, and to help in putting an end to the pursuit of a senseless war.

From 1915 onwards, and in ever increasing numbers, Hungarian working women actively joined the fight against the war, and the push for improved working conditions and full voting rights. The strike at the Wolfner Factory in the spring of 1915, the demonstrations at the Csepel market in June, against the poor quality and high prices of food, similar initiatives in Soroksár and Erzsébetfalva were spearheaded by working women.[3] The demonstrations at the women's division of the Worvarts Workers Training Center in Pozsony (now Bratislava) in January 1916 were a continuation of this struggle.[4] Hundreds of women joined the local agricultural labour union in Almáskéri, to replace their menfolk who had been sent to the battlefront.[5] They initiated a solidarity strike with the workers of the Manfred Weiss Factory on July 3–6. As a sign of their militancy, they succeeded in electing female shop stewards at this factory for the first time in Hungary.[6] Following the March 1916 Women's Day, this militancy and engagement by working women in the struggle for greater justice expanded by leaps and bounds in the large factories around Budapest (especially the Ganz Electro, the Airplane and the Armaments Factories) and in many of the small and medium sized manufacturing shops, and enterprises that were operating in the outer districts of the capital.

Not to be outdone, the NOW began to plan the release of pamphlets and publicity materials to reflect this trend. According to a secret 1916 report by one of the high-ranking members of the HSDP leadership, "These materials were not designed to promote anti-war agitation. Their only aim was to recruit more and more women to join the associations of working women".[7] It was, however, plain to see that a growing number of Hungarian women were publicly opposed to a war that dragged their husbands and sons off to die under horrible circumstance and which locked them, along with their children, back home into the hellholes of factories, where they were brutalized, stripped of any rights, and forced to put in 12–16 hour shifts at slave labour rates in order to feed the war machine.[8]

By 1917, virtually every factory in Hungary had a prison on its grounds to punish disobedient workers and those who objected to the inhuman working conditions. Meanwhile, the number of kindergartens were totally inadequate—in the entire country there were only two publicly funded day-care centers for the small children of working women. It's this and other examples of gross neglect that fired the anger of hundreds of thousands of Hungarian working women—the mothers who lost their sons, the young war widows, and the sisters who lost their brothers. This is what compelled the exploited women in the factories and on the large privately-owned agricultural estates to join the labour movement, and to become increasingly conscious of the need to put an end to the political system that sanctioned this madness. The radicalization of Hungary's working women was greatly aided by those secret but well-known underground organizations, such as the Revolutionary Socialists, The Interfactory Committee, the Galilei Circle.

In the first mass demonstration against the war on November 25, 1917, tens of thousands of working women were out in the streets of Budapest, demanding peace and social justice.[9] This was followed on January 18, 1918, by a country-wide general strike that lasted for days and in which, large numbers of working women participated throughout the country.[10] In Szeged, a large agricultural city in southern Hungary, every one of the factories that employed primarily women, were on strike—including the tobacco and rope making factories that employed over a thousand people each.[11] In the big demonstration for the universal franchise in Budapest on April 22, 1918 many of the papers commented on the unusually large numbers of women among the demonstrators. "The large number of working women from the factories was especially striking, and they appeared to be particularly angry with Prime Minister István Tisza, as they sang protest songs against the war-time minister".[12] This report also mentioned the large number of domestic women employees among the demonstrators—maids, nannies, and servants—along with many from the tobacco factories, and singled out the 2000 working women who joined the march from the canning factory just on the outskirts of Budapest.

Throughout the year the number of industrial unrests increased as did the brutality of state repression against the protesters. In all these events, local working women played an active and often heroic role. They often were severely punished for their bravery. The repression of the workers in the Rope Factory of Szeged is a good illustration of the heroism shown by working women in Hungary during the struggle for social justice and an end to war. During the 1918 strike at this factory in Szeged, the police and local militia arrested 19 male and 129 female employees and took them all down to the local military barracks and applied great physical pressure on them to return to work. The 19 men broke and went back to work under military escort. The 129 women would not break and were all imprisoned in the local county jail under harsh punitive conditions.[13]

Another example of the spirited and heroic fight of Hungarian working women for justice is provided by the local municipal clerk at the town of Lajosmizse. He spoke of a veritable revolution outside the county hall on July 19, 1918 set off by a group of women, most of whom had 5–6 children at home and their spouses out on the battlefront.

> The women laid siege to the County Hall and if we had not received military protection, we could not have left our place of work …it was only a matter of hours. Without the help of the military the demonstration would have ended in bloodshed.[14]

Working women took the lead in organizing many of the hunger strikes that became common during the middle of 1918. Another police report from Nyitrabánya spoke of an assault on the coal mine company's offices by a group of enraged women on July 22. Apparently, the women turned on the local militia who used live ammunition and their bayonets against them. The women then marched to the local military headquarters and began to attack the troops there, throwing sticks of dynamite and bullet cartridges at the men, who had to defend themselves against the assault. Two hundred soldiers were needed to put an end to the protest organized by the women.[15] These and similar actions illustrate well the combative nature of Hungarian working woman throughout the war.

Data on the entry of women into the organized labour movement is another indicator of this growing radicalization. Whereas in 1916, 8,314 women were registered as members of a Trade Union, by 1917 the figure is 48,818—a 487% increase in one year alone.

As news of the Russian Revolution spread in Hungary, the National Organizing Committee of Woman decided to alter its tactics: it began to glorify the revolution but continued to support the Trade Union leadership's duplicitous strategy and shed very little light on the Russian Bolsheviks' achievements in promoting gender equality. Instead of highlighting the beneficial consequences for women of revolutionary change, the NOW advocated "a measured and careful learning process" for Hungarian women, arguing that rigorous education and discipline is the first prerequisite of effective political action.[16] Instead of offering encouragement to the militants, the NOW came out in support of the HSDP and the Trade Union leadership's stand to call off the general strike of June 1918, arguing that "We're not strong enough, not sufficiently organized to take on the well-organized forces that have been lined up against us".[17]

The fact is that while the NOW verbally embraced and applauded the Russian

Revolution, it was fully subservient to the Social Democratic Party leadership that supported the 'peace policy' of the Austro-Hungarian Monarchy, and which showed not even the slightest desire to overthrow the Hungarian bourgeoisie. The NOW's main demand was to broaden the franchise for women, but, it did not advocate revolution to achieve that objective. The desire of Hungary's working women for peace and revolutionary change revealed itself not because but despite the HSDP leadership's or the NOW's agitation. A good example of the voices from below is given by a working woman from the small town of Balmazujváros:

> Our wise old men are still wedded to the old ways. But we are no longer willing to stand for this. Mothers and working women of Hungary! Let us unite, and topple this rotten, self serving, oppressive disorder and give birth to a more beautiful and better order.[18]

One could never find a passage similar to the one above on the pages of the Social Democratic Party's press. It is only from secret police reports, for example, that we get any evidence of the vital role played by the country's working women in hiding the more than 100,000 war-time deserters who abandoned the killing fields because they could not take the insane butchery and suffering any longer. Many of the deserters were young boys in their late teens and early twenties and had to be hidden for they faced court-martial and most likely death after their arrest. It was only when the Austro-Hungarian Monarchy was virtually at the edge of the abyss, on October 15, 1918, that the NOW would finally issue a call to Hungarian woman to rise up and join the fight for democracy. But even at this late date, they followed the HSDP leadership's call for a peaceful rather than a revolutionary change. When the revolution finally broke out on the 31st of October 1918, the leadership of the NOW was fully behind the HSDP leadership: "We have confidence in this new, provisional government, the National Council, because leaders of our Party are part of it. Our comrades are part of the government and this is the guarantee that our aims will prevail".[19] The NOW's newest fliers called on Hungary's girls and working women to "Participate in the establishment of calm and order so you can all enjoy, as early as possible the fruits, the blessings of peaceful work".[20]

Members of the women's movement who accepted these words of assurances were quickly disappointed. The new liberal-democratic government, with the support of the HSDP, would embark on a set of policies that swept many of their claims under the carpet. The National Council offered a refuge, an olive branch to the bankers, the great landowners, the factory owners, the exploiters, and created a new army cleansed of any Bolshevik elements. It attempted to emasculate and bring under its direct control the newly created revolutionary soldiers' and workers' councils that were the heart and soul of the 1918 Revolution that toppled the ancien regime.

How did the NOW react to these changes? It followed blindly the HSDP leadership as before, even though that leadership sold out Hungarian women in its very first post-revolutionary act. The new franchise gave all men over 21 the right to vote. It restricted this right in the case of women. Women would have to wait until they turned 24 and showed clear-cut proof of their ability to read and write, before they could cast a ballot. This new electoral law, in effect, eliminated the rights of millions of working women to participate in their country's political life, especially in the countryside where illiteracy was rampant due to the systematic efforts of the Hungarian Catholic Church and previous governments to make a virtue out of keeping women out of the classrooms, working in the fields with their small children from sunrise to sunset, or pregnant, ignorant, and barefoot in the kitchen.

The liberal-social democratic government also rejected the principle of equal pay for equal work in its employment and social policy and left working women once again in second-class status at a time of great hardship. In a country where women became the heads of many households, because more than a million men were left dead, mutilated, or diseased during the war, the government would set the unemployment pay for women at a rate one-third below the one for men. These discriminatory measures, and the new government's clearly preferential policies towards the privileged classes quickly raised new tensions between the government and millions of ordinary citizens.

It's under these circumstances that a new political party, the Party of the Hungarian Communists (HCP) comes on the scene at the end of November 1918 and heralds not only a split but a life and death battle between two political wings of the Hungarian labour movement: the Hungarian Communists, who wanted to establish the dictatorship of the proletariat, and the Social Democrats, who were basically an adjunct of the Hungarian bourgeoisie. The latter were not prepared to embark on a radical revolutionary path. They wanted to consolidate the liberal democratic order in the country based on capitalism and a free market economy. They had no intention of overthrowing the Hungarian bourgeoisie.

The bitter political emnity between the two parties was quickly reproduced within their respective women's organizations. The HCP co-opted several radical working class and intellectual women who would be bitterly attacked by the HSDP's women's organization, the NOW, as "Well poisoners".[21]

The battle against the Communist Party's women's network and leaders was quickly joined by newly created and even more conservative women's organizations in Hungary. Catholic and Protestant women's organizations led by the writer Cecil Tormay[22] and Countess Zichy created the National Association of Hungarian Women (NAHW) which in barely disguised form, was an anti-Semitic and a chauvinistic organization that used the language of Christianity, patriotism and family values to try to build a bastion in the hearts of Hungarian women against the "globally expanding poison" of Communism.[23] These efforts by the Social Democrats and more right-wing elements in Hungary could not stop the radicalization of Hungary's working women, their demands for justice and gender equality, and for radical change. They gravitated by the thousands towards the Communist Party that promised to deliver what so many had demanded.

Despite this groundswell of support by working women for the HCP, the leadership of the working-class women's movement in Hungary would remain in the hands of the Social Democrats throughout the coming months. The NOW managed to keep its ties with many of the newly created women's organizations in the capital and the regional centres of Hungary and used these connections with maximum efficiency. It advocated peaceful reforms and held up the revolutionary changes proposed by the HCP as a recipe for disaster, and a return to bloodshed and suffering.[24] One should not try to hide the fact, that the HCP was not able to fully harness the forces that were lining up behind it. It could not fully capture the hearts and minds of Hungary's working women with its own messages and actions. This was a failure by the party that would prove to be an increasingly serious handicap for the Republic of Councils.

The Working Women's Movement During the Republic of Councils

In one of its very first decrees, the Hungarian Republic of Councils provided Hungarian women with something that they never had before—full and equal rights to participate in local and national elections. On April 2nd, 1919, the Revolutionary Governing Council passed a decree that all working men and women over the age of 18 would be able to vote in local and national elections under the dictatorship of the proletariat. The first council elections were scheduled for April 7. The government granted women not only full voting rights but devoted a great deal of effort in various communications campaigns, to encourage women to exercise their voting rights.

Unfortunately, the Republic of Councils did not provide similar guarantees to uphold the principle of equal pay for work of equal value. While it provided lip-service to the principle, it never enshrined it in a decree or in the new constitution. This was a serious omission. The Revolutionary Governing Council's decrees on wages gave a wide lassitude to workers' and local councils in setting wage levels, but in the absence of any legal and constitutional guarantees, women's wages were often set at levels that were well below the one set for men. The socialist daily that targeted working women, *Nőmunkás*, openly spoke of the abuses, but put the onus on the women to fight against these abuses at their place of work, rather than on the Revolutionary Governing Council.[25]

Before the Commune, most of Hungary's working women were unskilled labourers. The ancien regimes devoted no attention to the education or training of women workers. The less a woman knew, the more easily she could be exploited. This area saw a dramatic change after March 21, 1919. The Revolutionary Governing Council passed a whole series of decrees that were designed to enhance the competitiveness of women in the workplace. Attendance in school up to grade 8 became compulsory for both girls and boys. The gates of high schools, vocational colleges and universities were thrown open to the daughters of the working classes and the children of agricultural labourers regardless of gender. The discrimination against women in technical education was greatly curtailed. A series of decrees were passed to liberate women from the debilitating burdens of housework and childcare. Publicly funded nurseries, day cares, school lunch programs, vacation programs for inner city children were introduced to assist working mothers.

In addition to these important initiatives, women were provided with a whole series of long overdue rights, in property and family law, and much effort was devoted to education and counselling to restrict engrained and discriminative practices and prejudices. On the territory of greater Budapest, every Thursday, "women's assemblies" were held to educate women about civic issues and on how to strengthen and defend their acquired rights and the aims of the Republic.[26]

Special mention should be made of the measures taken to protect working mothers and their infants, because they were taken during a period of great external hardship—Hungary was under blockade by the great powers, invaded by its neighbors, suffering from the aftereffects of a lost war and bleeding from a thousand wounds. The enormous challenge in this domain is dramatically laid out in a report from this period:

> On March 21, 1919 there were at least 30,000 babies in Budapest who were wrapped in newspaper instead of proper sanitary diapers. 100,000 were gravely ill, suffering from tuberculosis and other childhood diseases, many of them were starving and underfed. 180,000 children of the working class lived 7 or 12 to a room, in rat infested, unheated premises without running water or proper toilet facilities. 38.000 proletarian women were pregnant and looking forward with desperation to bringing another child into the world under these hell-like conditions... A series of new regulations were passed by the Revolutionary Governing Council during the first months of the revolution to radically alter these deplorable conditions. ... several large

convents were turned into children's hospitals, hundreds of mansions housing the rich were turned into daycare centers and nurseries, tens of thousands of children were housed in bright, airy homes, the supply of milk to working families was centralized. The law required that pregnancy should be reported to the municipal authorities and they had to provide appropriate, publicly funded training and education to expectant and nursing mothers and publicly guaranteed hospital facilities when they were due to deliver. Newspaper diapers became a thing of the past. A whole set of decrees were passed providing women with help in the case of unwanted pregnancies, and protection against abuse in the family or in the workplace. Strenuous efforts were undertaken to create safe public playgrounds for thousands of children in the inner cities and to provide school children in the cities with publicly funded vacation time in the countryside, in the fresh air and in healthy surroundings.[27]

With the merger of the HSDP and the HCP on March 21, 1919, the NOW found itself in an unusual position. It was not disbanded by the joint party leadership but was asked to serve from here on in as the organizing committee for women for the new, united party. From its former position as the HSDP's frontline critic of the HCP's policies on women's issues, it had to now embrace the Communist Party's more radical approach. This *volte face* obviously did not come about smoothly or with sufficient resolve. Though substantial personnel changes were undertaken in the top leadership of the NOW, this important organization was unable to fully adjust to its new mandate. It neglected to engage in vigorous organizational work at a time when it was most needed. It chose to devote most of its energies to the publication of idealistic propaganda materials about the virtues of a future communist society, rather than organize working women in the defense and construction of socialism. This failure greatly limited the efficacy of the Commune to maximize its full capital of human resources in defense of the Republic which was fighting a life and death struggle on so many fronts— embargo by the Imperial powers, invasion by three of the country's neighbors, not to mention the activities of the counterrevolutionary forces within the country. Instead of leading the struggle, the Party's strategic committee for women was swept along by the events that were unfolding, events in which, nevertheless, hundreds of thousands of working women played an important, albeit spontaneous, often neglected but heroic role.

An example of this spontaneous grassroots initiative by the working women of Hungary was the creation of the Red Amazon Brigades in Budapest in support of the newly formed Red Army. Its goal was to provide rapid, vocational training for women in various skills and to make their 'graduates' available throughout the country as a vital, skilled labour resource in place of the men who left their workplaces in order to join the Red Army to defend the homeland against the invaders. This is how Zsuzsa Nagy, one of the members of the Brigade spoke at the launch of this initiative:

> After all that we suffered, we working women demand an active, and equal role in the defense of the Republic. We intend to place our brigades into appropriate positions according to their members' skills throughout the country where they are needed.

Another militant, Berta Mentzer, put forth a resolution that defined the conditions under which female members of the Red Army would gain full membership in the Women's Brigade.[28] Perhaps the most passionate and heartfelt words belonged to Sári Mánuel, who stood up at the critical May 2nd meeting of the Greater Budapest Workers' and Soldiers' Council, where many were calling for an end to the dictatorship of the proletariat and said:

> We held a few meetings among us women in Budapest before the situation became as dire as it is today. There was not a single one among us who would not give her life to provide a better future for her child. I feel that we, the mothers, the working women of this city are more aware of the seriousness of the crisis that faces us than our men. I tell you this in the name of my sisters, and all our women: If called upon, we shall defend Budapest to the end, and not only Budapest but the dictatorship of the proletariat as well. If our men are unwilling to do their share, they will have to face their wives when it's all over!"[29]

The crisis abated for a short while, the Red Army managed to score some early victories, and the number of women's organizations and committees in the country continued to expand by leaps and bounds, but by June, the tide once again turned against the Republic. As the NOW began to prepare for a series of critically important national Congresses (the HCP's Congress scheduled for June 12–13, the National Congress of Women between June 14–15, and the Republic's legislature, the National Congress of Councils, between June 14 and 23), the revolutionary leadership's shortcomings of the past months would begin to become increasingly apparent.

The first voices raised about the failure to implement the Republic's promises to working women came during the Party Congress. "In many cases the voices of working women are being stifled and ignored by the Party's local authorities" was a frequent complaint.[30] At the Women's Congress, 62 rural and 52 Budapest women's organizations were represented by delegates. Most of these organizations represented a variety of local women's groups (e.g., the women's organization from the city of Győr represented 53 local women's groups that were active in that city). While the Women's Congress expressed its full solidarity with the revolution, it did not shirk from listing the dictatorship's shortcomings and broken promises to Hungary's working women. It asked, that the government walk its talk on the principle of equal pay for work of equal value.[31] The women demanded that children under 14 should not be allowed to work not only in the cities but in the countryside as well. It demanded that the age for compulsory education be raised from 8 to 14 and should be applied uniformly regardless of gender. The Congress called for an end to segregation of girls and boys into separate schools, demanded a host of overdue policies for the protection of pregnant women, maternity leave, appropriate educational and healthcare measures for expectant working mothers, and a host of measures to close the widespread gender gap that continued to persist under the dictatorship of the proletariat. The aim of all these declarations was the same. "To bring about gender equality in the country, to ensure that working men and women, girls and boys, are treated with equal respect, are provided with uniform rights and protection under the law".[32]

The delegates to the Congress put forward a detailed proposal for the nationwide reorganization of the NOW but the old reflexes kicked in once again. The leadership of the NOW failed to recognize the legitimacy of interest representation for women outside of the Party's direct, top-down control. Leadership in the women's movement was tied to Party membership, and strict subservience to the decisions of the central Party leadership became the top priority for everyone in the newly reconstituted NOW. The right to organize mass movements outside of party control was eliminated. This step was particularly harmful at a time when the newly formed Socialist Party—just renamed as the *Party of Hungarian Socialist and Communist Workers* (PHSCW)—was badly divided, unable to speak clearly, or provide a coherent, commonly agreed to Marxist-Leninist path toward socialism.

The Hungarian Republic of Council's Legislature—the National Congress of Councils—was called into session for the first time, three months after the start of the revolution, and started its deliberations on the same day as the Women's Congress. The National Congress of Councils also heard from the women of Hungary, especially after the Women's Congress was over. But the fact is, all three of the Congresses in Hungary during the middle of June 1919 carried the scars of generations of neglect towards women in Hungary. All three gave ample evidence of the distrust and disrespect of women's voices by Hungary's male dominated political elite. Virtually every one of the women who spoke at the National Congress of Councils spoke of the divergence between revolutionary theory and practice under the dictatorship of the proletariat, the difficulty of electing women to leadership positions within the councils and onto bodies that exercised national or local public authority. To illustrate their claim, the women pointed out to the legislators that of the more than two hundred delegates to the Party Congress that ended just days earlier, only 8 were women. They pointed out that there were hardly any women delegates in the Legislature itself, not even one woman from the countryside. They pointed out that the Budapest Council had an 80-member delegation in the Legislature, of which only two were women. It is these conditions that explain why so many of the declarations of the earlier Women's Congress included demands for full participatory rights for women in the leadership of the ruling Party and State administration.

Notwithstanding these glaring shortcomings, it is evident, that during the Republic of Councils, Hungary's working women set into motion a broadly based social movement that energized and raised the political awareness of hundreds of thousands of working women throughout the country to social justice and to the rights of women to participate fully in the decisions that affect who gets what, when and how in society. This was indeed a revolutionary break with the past, one that constituted a heroic manifestation of courage and social solidarity. The voices of Hungary's working women during the June 1919 Congresses were not raised in vain, and some slight progress became noticeable from early July onwards, and during the last weeks of the Republic, but these were too little and too late. With the collapse of the Republic in August 1919, any further progress was crushed. Had the leadership of the Republic of Councils been more resolute and committed to the working women of Hungary, had they devoted more attention to their voices, to harnessing their enthusiasm, and desire to participate in the Republic's decision-making processes, it would have improved not only its own chances of survival but would have made a lasting contribution to improving the status of women in Hungary, and to political progress based on full gender equality.

NOTES

1   In the HSDP's paper targeting working women, *Nőmunkás* [Woman Worker], (August 1, 1914).

2   *Nőmunkás*, (December 1, 1914).

3   *MMI Archives*, A.XV.1/1915/1, MMI is the abbreviation for the Institute of the Hungarian Labour Movement.

4   *Nőmunkás*, (January 1, 1916).

5   *Nőmunkás*, (April 15, 1916).

6   *MMI Archives*, A.XV.1/1915/1 and A.XV.1/1916/2.

7   *MMI Archives*, A.XV.1/1916/13.

8   *Decree No. 89,000* by the Ministry of Defense, issued on December 15, 1915, ordered that all enterprises or businesses that were supplying war materials must replace all their male employees who were called up to fight, with women.

9   Editor's note: Though Aranyossi knew her, she does not mention Duczynska by name . After 1948

and during the Rákosi era, Ilona Duczynska's name was taboo. In fact, she and her secret cell played a critical role within the "well known underground organizations" listed by Aranyossi. The sparkplug of the November 25th 1917 demo, was the small cell started by Ilona with the help of Ervin Szabo in September 1917. She and the key members of her cell were arrested by mid January 1918 for starting the avalanche that led to 1919. She and her three mates, including her lover, Tivadar Sugár were released from prison by a group of factory workers from Csepel on October 31, 1918 the start of the Chrysanthemum Revolution. Her name and the prominent role she played in sparking the 1918–1919 revolutions would only surface haltingly from 1957 onwards. By now she is once again the *béte-noire* of the Hungarian alt-right.

10 *Népszava* [*People's Voice*], (Budapest: January 22, 1918). (The official daily of the HSDP.)

11 *Délmagyarország* [*Southern Hungary*] (Szeged: January 23, 1918). (Large daily in southern Hungary).

12 *Az Ujság* [*The News*] (Budapest: April 23, 1918).

13 *MMI Szeged Municipal Archives and Chief County Magistrate's Office*, Document No. 1139.

14 *MMI. Arch. Chief Magistrate's Office for Pest County*, Document 3797/1918.

15 From the July 22, 1918 telegram of the district police (Csendőrség). H.L.H.M. 1918.63.4.a.18650.

16 *Nőmunkás*, January 15, 1918.

17 *Nőmunkás*, July 15, 1918.

18 *Nőmunkás*, May 1, 1918.

19 *Nőmunkás*, November 1, 1918

20 *MMI. Arch.* Röpiratgyűjtemény (Fliers). II. 11/1918/XI/1915/1.

21 Editors note: This was a commonly used term of dismissal in Hungary, especially in the countryside, where piped water systems did not exist, and people depended on their own private wells or the village water well for their daily supply of fresh water. Poisoning a neighbor's or a village's well was seen as the most cruel, gutless kind of act, more despicable than murder.

22 Aranyossi cites the 2nd edition (1921) of Cecile Tormay's *Bujdosó könyv* (Outcast Diary) which is highly popular among the anti-Semitic, Christian-Nationalist right in Hungary to this day.(For a recent edition Budapest. Magyar Ház, 2005)

23 See: Stolpa Józsefné, *Magyar Asszonyok Nemzeti Szövetsége Évkönyve* [The Yearbook of the National Association of Hungarian Women] (Budapest: 1945), 25.1.

24 *Nőmunkás*, January 15, 1919.

25 *Nőmunkás*, May 10, 1919.

26 Aranyossi cites the 1929 Special March edition of *Új Március*, [*New March*], a journal published in Vienna by exiled Hungarian Socialists.

27 Ibid.

28 *MMI. Arch.* A.II.11/134/415.1.

29 *MMI. Arch.* A.II.14/14.

30 *Nőmunkás*, June 21, 1919.

31 Ibid.

32 *Nőmunkás*, June 28, 1919.

CHAPTER 6

Vienna and Budapest After WWI: A Tale of Two Cities

Kari Polanyi Levitt

THROUGHOUT THE various parts of the Hapsburg Empire, the impact of the 1917 Russian Revolution was enormous. Unlike Budapest, Vienna did not experience a Soviet-style revolution led by communists. The Austrian Social Democratic Workers Party, founded by Viktor Adler, took a different course. The Austrian Social Democrats were a mass party and their membership included many revolutionary socialists. Like all European social democratic parties of the late 19th century, the intellectual source was Marx. However, Austrian Marxism differed from interpretations in Russia, Germany, and Hungary. Budapest and Vienna shared the status of sister cities, but while the Hungarian Commune lasted only 133 days, the Social Democrats of Red Vienna held power from 1918–1934.

Vienna, with a population of 2 million, was the capital of the Hapsburg Empire, with a population of approximately 50 million. When the Empire collapsed, Vienna became the capital of a small country of only 6 million people.[1] In all parts of the Habsburg Empire the war was unpopular. Young men were used as cannon fodder. Outrageous profits were made by companies producing war materials. Sacrifices were demanded of the middle-class population of Vienna to finance the endless war which brought inflation. Ordinary people sold their precious metals to the regime to melt down into money and jewellery. In a testament to the growing resentment towards the war, the son of Viktor Adler, Friedrich Adler, was lionized in Vienna after he assassinated the Minister-President of Cisleithania in 1916.

The Russian Revolution of 1917 was a spark that signalled the possibilities following the end of a horrible war. For a number of countries in Central Europe that experienced revolution, it was the end of monarchies. In Germany, it was the end of the Kaisers. New Republics were established in the states aspiring to nationhood, like the Czech Republic, which later joined with the Slovak Republic to make Czechoslovakia. Similarly, in the south, the joining of Croatia and Serbia to make what was known as Yugoslavia, although they had a king.

Social disintegration followed the war. Soldiers laid down their arms and returned to their towns. Pension hungry officials descended on Vienna from the five corners of the Empire to claim their backed wages and salaries. The systems in Vienna broke down. Systemic disintegration led to severe shortages of food, fuel, and other essential supplies. Soldiers returning from the front and urban workers established councils in an attempt to meet the needs of the population. The Social Democratic Party organized the collection of wartime arms to be stored in secret armouries known only to trusted party members.

Unlike Vienna, the communists seized power after the war in Hungary and Bavaria. In the interest of stabilization, British and French creditors supported the fragile currencies of the succession states which replaced the imperial Krone. A coalition of British and French military, economic, and political interest, known as the Entente, encouraged the Romanian army to invade Hungary and capture Budapest to restore government to the traditional Hungarian ruling classes.

The counter-revolution was led by Admiral Horthy, an Admiral without a fleet, since the Hungarian Port Fiume was returned to Italy by the Peace Treaty. The Italian port at Trieste became the most important European port on the Adriatic Sea. 'The White Terror' was aimed at a broad section of the population, which sympathized with the communist regime of the councils, giving rise to an emigration to Vienna, including Ilona Duczynska and Karl Polanyi who met and married in Vienna in the early 1920s, and where their only child was born in June 1923. Among the émigrées was Oszkár Jászi, who was Polanyi's mentor since earlier times, who created a publication servicing Hungarian refugees, called *Bécsi Magyar Újság*. Polanyi contributed several important articles before he was employed as a journalist by the *Der Oesterreichische Volkswirt*. Ilona found an elegant and spacious apartment at Vorgartenstraße 203, shared by her mother, Helene Békássy, and mother's companion, Erzsi, who cooked for the whole family.

Hungarian leaders during the Commune requested military assistance from Vienna, but this request remained unanswered. In her book, *Workers in Arms*, Ilona Duczynska criticized the Austrian Socialist leaders for their refusal to support the Hungarian commune with military aid.[2] Although several thousand Austrian workers did volunteer to go to defend Budapest, no significant shipment of arms took place. Subsequent research revealed that important military equipment was stored at the Vienna arsenal in joint trusteeship of Socialist and Conservative parties for the defence of the Republic. The prominent Austrian Socialist leader Julius Deutsch collaborated with representatives of the Conservative party to this effect, rather than use his position to assist his Hungarian brethren or to hide weapons for future defence of Austria. Otto Bauer, the most prominent leader of the Austrian Socialist Party, was a cautious man. Bauer was anti-communist. He feared that assistance to the Hungarian communists would not be well-received by the Entente who supplied Austria with essential food and energy during their occupation of the country. The overthrow of the Hungarian Commune lasted only a few days and its demise in August 1919 put to rest communist aspirations of securing a revolutionary socialist zone across Europe anchored in Budapest and Vienna and Bavaria and Berlin.

Meanwhile, in Vienna, the first national elections in the First Austrian Republic gave a majority to the Socialists from 1919–1920. After 1920, the federal government of Austria was led by majority coalitions of Conservatives. However, Vienna remained majority controlled by the Social Democratic Party from 1919–1933. While Vienna was a city it had the same provincial status as the other provinces of the Republic of Austria. The socialist city administration of Vienna used this status to organise effectively for the livelihood of the working class and to create what is known as Red Vienna, the city of my childhood. Red Vienna was renowned for its impressive affordable housing, education, and arts.

My parents both independently wrote that, in their later years, they believed the Socialist administration of Vienna was the greatest achievement of any society in Western Europe in the 20th century. My childhood played a role in this enchantment. I belonged to the *Österreichische Kinderfreunde*, Vienna's children organization run by the Social Democratic Party.

The social housing of Red Vienna remains an important historical model. The Karl Marx Hof—the longest residential building in the world, designed for 5,000 residents—is an iconic monument to the success of Red Vienna's municipal housing program. As a direct result of low rents and affordable living conditions, the working class were a privileged class. The financing of social housing was raised by progressive taxation on private apartment buildings. The housing that was built with money from this tax was inscribed with a variation of the declaration:

BUILT BY THE
COMMUNITY OF VIENNA
IN THE YEARS OF 1923–1934
BY MEANS OF THE HOUSING-CONSTRUCTION TAX.

The owners of these private buildings were, of course, not very pleased. None other than Friedrich Hayek published a pamphlet about how awful it was that the owners of private apartment buildings were being charged for housing those 'useless' people—the workers—and how they would let these buildings deteriorate because they could not manage to keep them up.

At that time in Vienna there was an intellectual atmosphere, an intellectual activity of not only a very high quality, but that was not dominated by the narrow and restrictive boundaries of academia. The University of Vienna was a very conservative institution, but the Socialist Party organized what one might call the People's University. My father lectured there on guild socialism along with many other eminent and well-known intellectuals.

Following the publication of Mises's book *Socialism*, in which he tried to prove that it was not possible to organize a socialist economic system because it would require not only markets for all factors of production, but particularly capital markets and a stock exchange, a famous controversy unfolded in the pages of the best-known German-language social science academic journal of the time, *Archiv für Sozialwissenschaft und Sozialpolitik*. My father was able to publish a reply to Mises in that same journal, although, he had no academic standing. He was not a university faculty, but he taught for the People's University. The intellectuals of the Socialist Party, generally known as Austro-Marxists (popularly referred to as the 'Two and a Half International') was somewhere between the more conservative Social Democrats to the West and the Third International of the Communists, with its headquarters in Moscow. Polanyi was associated with the Austro-Marxists, as Alexander Gerschenkron would have been. (Gerschenkron was a student at the University of Vienna and, on account of his political affiliations with Austro Marxism, when he got his degree, he worked as a manager in a bicycle factory for quite a while, but eventually, of course, became an important intellectual and professor at Harvard.)

An unforgettable part of my childhood in Red Vienna was May Day. May Day was not only a national holiday, or at least a holiday in Vienna, but I remember that on May Day my father would get the broom, take the brush off the bottom, and we would fix a big red flag onto it and hang it out of our window. Up and down the street red flags hung out of windows. I myself marched in May Day parades belonging to the children's section of the *Arbeiter Turnerbund* (Workers' Gymnastics Association) and we marched on the Ringstrasse, which is a broad boulevard that circles the central part of the city. I remember wearing a little black skirt, a white shirt, and a little red scarf. We would march there for hours—May Day marches were a major event. I remember asking, "who were the people in the front row?" I was told that they were the railway and streetcar workers. At that time, there were not many manufacturing industries in Austria. The working class was largely employed in transportation.

The workers of Vienna were well-respected not only in political and social life but also in the arts. The socialist hymn *Die Arbeiter von Wein* (The Workers of Vienna) paid tribute to them. The song is set to the tune of *Bandiera Rossa* and the words are:

Wir sind das Bauvolk der kommenden Welt.
Wir sind der Sämann, die Saat und das Feld.
Wir sind die Schnitter der kommenden Mahd.
Wir sind die Zukunft und wir sind die Tat.
So flieg, du flammende, du rote Fahne,
voran dem Wege, den wir zieh'n.
Wir sind der Zukunft getreue Kämpfer.
Wir sind die Arbeiter von Wien.
(We are the builders of the coming world.
We are the sower, the seed and the field.
We are the reapers of the coming harvest.
We are the future and we are the deed.
So fly, you blazing, you red flag,
Before the path we are laying.
We are the loyal fighters of the future.
We are the workers of Vienna.)

The fact that this song and the music that goes with it remain in my memory is remarkable. I don't remember any nursery songs from my childhood in German. One or two, but very few. But I remember this hymn.

There was no 1919 communist commune in Vienna because there was no space for it—there was no need for it. The revolutionaries in Vienna were inside the Social Democratic Party. It was not a typical social democratic party, the kinds that are better known for selling out the workers rather than championing their cause. Vienna was a different development. Vienna had a small, but relatively powerless Communist Party at the time. The role it might have played was occupied by the Social Democrats and Austro-Marxists, unlike Budapest.

It's a tale of two cities and the Austrian experience was as important, and perhaps even more important, than that of Budapest. Eventually, of course, and inevitably, you might say, socialism on a municipal scale cannot survive and did not survive. Red Vienna collapsed during the Civil War of 1934 when the reactionary forces brought out tanks and guns and destroyed what was left of the workers. This marked the beginning of Austrian fascism and the end of the legal Socialist Party of Austria.

NOTES

1   Before World War I, the Socialist Party in Austria had been supportive of the last Kaiser of the Hapsburg Empire, Kaiser Franz Josef. Other nationalist parties were opposed to the Kaiser, particularly the Czechs, Slovaks, the Croats, and the Serbs.

2   Ilona Duczynska, *Workers in Arms: The Austrian Schutzbund And The Civil War Of 1934* (New York: Monthly Review Press, 1978).

CHAPTER 7

The Exiled Voice of the 1919 Commune: The Hungarian Communist Press in Canada

Christopher Adam

ONE OF THE LONG-NEGLECTED features of the 1919 Hungarian Republic of Councils is the apparent loss of its voice, or more precisely, its migration abroad to distant parts of the planet, after it was silenced at home by the repressive right-wing dictatorship of Admiral Nicholas Horthy. In Hungary, the voice of the Councils would not be heard for close to 40 years, until suddenly, it rose briefly, from the ashes, during the short-lived anti-Bolshevik uprising of October-November 1956.[1] Canada was one of the places the voice of the 1919 Commune migrated to after it was banished from Hungary. Here, it could not be silenced, in spite of strenuous and coordinated efforts by Horthy's diplomatic representatives in Canada, and local backers of Horthy's Christian-Nationalist autocracy. This chapter will examine the efforts of Hungarian Communist migrants to Canada to keep the language, the vocabulary, the spirit of the 1919 Commune alive in a hostile environment, thousands of miles from home.

It is well documented that after the collapse of the Republic of Councils, and the Treaty of Trianon, which radically redrew Hungary's historic borders, close to 200,000 Hungarians fled their homeland and the "White Terror" that would be unleashed by Horthy's militias on those who stayed behind. A sizeable cohort of those who fled—close to 30,000—ended up in Canada. It would be an exaggeration to say that all the new Hungarian immigrants to Canada were enthralled supporters of the two, short lived post WWI Hungarian republics. The leaders of the Republic of Councils had done much on their own, to earn the wrath of not only the Hungarian nobility and middle classes but significant segments of the urban and rural working classes and those who formed the backbone of the Hungarian Council Movement. The origins of the Canadian-Hungarian community go back in time to a period well before the 1919 Commune. What cannot be denied, however, is that the Canadian-Hungarian community experienced its first and to this date, most intensive divisiveness and internal tensions as a direct consequence of the influx of new immigrants who spoke the language of the Councils, and were, rightly or wrongly, infected by the spirit of the 1918–1919 revolutions.

Divisions between communist and Christian-Nationalist community leaders and newspaper editors would reach unseen heights in Canada during the decades following the collapse of the 1919 Hungarian Republic of Councils. In a sense, the organized Canadian-Hungarian diaspora would divide into two solitudes, with the leadership of each promoting a mutually exclusive ideological narrative of the Hungarian nation, as well as events in the world. Christian-Nationalist conservative Hungarian-Canadians enjoyed the active political and financial support of the Horthy regime. The creation of an institutionally complete Hungarian communist diaspora in Canada, with a newspaper, social clubs and mutual benefit societies, relied mostly on a grassroots effort and on only limited support from communist parties in the US and Canada. Theirs was a voluntary community affair undertaken at significant risk and self-sacrifice.

The leaders of the Hungarian communist diaspora in Canada used the *Kanadai Magyar Munkás* (The Canadian-Hungarian Worker), a weekly newspaper, as a tool to build a collective consciousness and identity for Hungarian workers and agricultural labourers in Canada. Using strident revolutionary language strongly reminiscent of the days of the 1919 Commune, the publication sought to organize traditionally oppressed demographic groups within the Canadian-Hungarian diaspora against Christian-Nationalist forces seen as doing the bidding of the Horthy regime in Canada. The writers, editors and publishers of the *Munkás*, took it upon themselves to speak out against not only the economic injustices they encountered in their new homeland in Canada, but those that plagued their brothers and sisters left behind in Hungary. Their only weapon was a language, a vocabulary that they brought with them to the New World from their earlier struggles back home.

The Political Significance of the Press in the Canadian-Hungarian Diaspora

It was a common desire of leaders within ethnic and immigrant communities with roots in Europe to portray an image of national and ideological unity especially vis-á-vis the Anglophone majority in Canada. As such, public debate was often discouraged and dissent rejected by community leaders.[2] Ethnic newspapers, however, were not under such heavy pressures. Since they tend to reveal a more authentic, fragmented picture of diaspora realities, they serve as an invaluable resource for historians who are interested in exploring the language of political discourse within these communities. Additionally, as the status of secular community leadership increases within these communities over time, and the near monopoly of the clergy diminishes, editors of diaspora newspapers begin to play an increasingly critical role in diaspora power dynamics.[3]

In the case of the Canadian-Hungarian press during the interwar period, the existence of rival and dogmatic newspapers also reveals that leaders on opposing sides of the political divide spoke *past* each other, rather than debating or engaging the other side. Neither the *Munkás* nor its primary right-wing competitor within the community—the Horthy-sponsored *Kanadai Magyar Újság* (Canadian Hungarian News) and the right-wing *Kanadai Magyar Hírlap* (Canadian Hungarian Journal)—were open to divergent views. The *Munkás* focused on rallying its own supporters and promoting an alternative narrative of Hungarian identity and history. It was portrayed by its two opponents as both unpatriotic and dangerous to the very existence of the Hungarian nation. As in the case of Slavic émigré communities in Canada, where newspapers served as platforms to broadcast grievances about the politics of the home country and views on national history,[4] the *Munkás* worked on the margins of Hungarian identity in Canada to propose a vision of the Hungarian nation at odds with the government of Hungary and much of the organized diaspora.

North American sociologists like Susan Olzak have argued that the ethnic press of white diaspora communities in the US served to bolster group solidarity among co-nationalists at a time when they faced discrimination or hostility from the majority population.[5] In the case of the Hungarian press in Canada during the interwar period, and especially in relation to the *Munkás*, this assessment is only partially accurate. While the *Munkás* did serve to build solidarity among Hungarian workers in Canada and to make them more conscious of their oppression within the context of Canadian capitalism, there was no sense of a broader Hungarian solidarity, based on language or national affiliation, extending across the ideological divide. More than anything, the *Munkás* sought to win an ideological battle within the Canadian-Hungarian community. It fought against Hungarian adversaries, rather than struggle for rights as the voice of a minority within an English-speaking majority population.

The Arrival of Hungarian and Eastern European Labour to Canada in the Early Twentieth Century

Central and Eastern Europe was perceived by both the government of Prime Minister Wilfrid Laurier and politically influential industrial and business interests, as a source of cheap labour for Canada, especially within the agrarian sector. For instance, the Sugar Beet Growers Association of Canada struck an agreement with the Czech International Institute to settle farm labourers from Moravia around Lethbridge, Alberta.[6] In 1901, the Laurier government's Minister of the Interior, Clifford Sifton, was instructed to follow a largely "open door" policy, rather than quotas, when it came to the acceptance of agrarian workers from eastern Europe, and especially from the lands of the Austro-Hungarian Empire.[7] Labour interests in Canada, specifically the Trades and Labour Congress (TLC), were critical of this open doors policy, as the mass influx of agrarian and industrial workers from Eastern Europe was perceived as a strategy by businesses and industrialists to drive down wages for Canadian workers and cement poor working conditions.[8] Canadian labour leaders successfully petitioned the Laurier government to place restrictions on immigrants from East Central Europe, referring to these arrivals as being members of a racially "inferior class".[9] The Immigration Act of 1906 provided the Canadian federal government with the right to limit different "classes" of immigrants but in practice, this legislation did not stop the influx of Eastern Europeans.

By 1910, however, Canadian labour began to gradually see greater value in Eastern European immigrants, from the perspective of increased unionization in Canada. For instance, in 1913 Slovak and Ukrainian immigrants were central in establishing the first coal miners' union in western Canada, while the Toronto branch of the Amalgamated Clothing Workers of America was established, in no small measure, by the efforts of a Ukrainian worker and labour organizer.[10]

While Canada's labour movement seemed to move beyond its initial racist reaction to the presence of Eastern European workers, with the arrival of World War I, both the Canadian government and the English Canadian press focused much more on the race of the new arrivals, and concerns about their feared inability to assimilate, than before. The War Measures Act, which labeled more than 80,000 immigrants from the diverse lands of the Austro-Hungarian Empire as "enemy aliens" and led to the internment of 8,579 men, women and children in 24 Canadian internment camps was one example of the changing mood towards Eastern Europeans.[11] The other seismic event in how Eastern Europeans were perceived was the 1919 Winnipeg General Strike. The fear that Eastern Europeans were importing communist unrest to Canada meant that business interests were loath to continue advocating for an opens doors immigration policy when it came to continental Europeans. Winnipeg, being an important centre for both the Ukrainian and Hungarian community, and the site of the most significant example of Canadian labour unrest to date, also saw striking xenophobia directed against immigrants from Eastern Europe. John W. Dafoe, the editor-in-chief of the *Winnipeg Free Press*, went on a particularly raucous tirade, referring to the "fanatical allegiance of the Germans, Austrians, Huns and Russians" and adding that Canadian authorities ought to "clean the aliens out of this community and ship them back to their unhappy homes in Europe, which vomited them forth a decade ago".[12]

By the time the first Hungarian communist activists arrived in Canada in 1925 (they initially came via the US to help pave the way for a Hungarian left-wing diaspora north of the border), Eastern European immigrants, along with Finns, had already played a crucial role in establishing the Communist Party of Canada (CPC), earning immigrants a place at the heart of a fledgling Canadian radical left. The CPC, at this time officially operating as the Workers' Party of Canada, was co-founded by John Boychuk, a Ukrainian, and one-third of its Central Committee was comprised of Eastern Europeans and Finns.[13] In 1921, the Ukrainian Temple Labour Association was among the largest of radical left associations to spearhead the foundation of a national communist movement in Canada. Four years later, in 1925, one-fifth of CPC members were Eastern Europeans.[14]

The first Hungarian to have played a documented role in the pioneer days of Canada's labour movement was Mark Szalatnay, a revolutionary from the repressed 1848 Hungarian Revolution who arrived in Canada as a settler by way of the United Kingdom and the US, ultimately playing a central role in organizing a cigar workers' strike in Toronto 1872. Szalatnay, who was arrested and served a jail term for his role in organizing this labour unrest, displayed the type of revolutionary radicalism that characterized his Hungarian Canadian successors of the interwar period.

Hungarian communists also ended up on the RCMP's radar due to their involvement in the Communist Party of Canada and then in the 1930s, the Spanish Civil War. Hungarian Canadians, like other Eastern Europeans, were active among Canadian volunteers fighting in the Spanish Civil War as part of the Mackenzie-Papineau unit of the International Brigade. In many cases, the Communist Party of Canada coordinated the recruitment and transportation of these Eastern European volunteers and as such, the RCMP monitored these activities. For instance, the RCMP's secret Weekly Summary report from June 10, 1937, documented the many forums and meetings, some attracting between 500 and 1,000 participants, organized for, and by the Communist Party's volunteers in the Spanish Civil War. The Russian Workers' Club in Montréal, as well as the Ukrainian Labour Farmer Temple Band, were among the Eastern European émigré organizations actively present at these events. Hungarian Canadians affiliated with the communist diaspora made their presence felt too. The RCMP noted in 1937 that the Communist Party of Canada succeeded in recruiting four Hungarians from Lethbridge, Alberta, to fight in Spain. The men traveled on Hungarian passports and the Communist Party of Canada was responsible for coordinating their journey.[15]

The Left and the Growth of Hungarian Communities in Canada in the Interwar Years

The pioneers of the Hungarian communist community in Canada were activists of Hungarian origins from the US, affiliated with the Hungarian Workers' Mutual Aid and Self-Improvement Society of the American Communist Party. Prior to establishing a Hungarian-language communist paper in Canada, *Új Előre* (New Forward), an American publication edited by Lajos Kovess, an active participant in the 1919 Commune who fled Hungary after its collapse, was circulated and sold in Canada, with Hungarian Canadians proving successful in organizing subscription campaigns north of the border.[16] The success of these subscription campaigns after 1926, and the dedication of an entire page to news from Canada pointed to the viability of a new Hungarian-Canadian communist publication. The first leaders of the Canadian movement, however, were people from the US, like Kovess, sent to Canada, for having a proven revolutionary record from the days of the 1919 Commune.

In a clever move that caught conservative Hungarian Canadians off guard, especially the editors of the Horthy-sponsored *Kanadai Magyar Újság* and the right-wing *Kanadai Magyar Hírlap*, Kovess was initially able to obtain the support of the mainstream émigré community in supporting the Canadian efforts of the US based Mutual Aid and Self-Improvement Society by concealing its ties to communism. By 1927, however, the conservative Horthyite Hungarian Canadians realized that they had been misled into supporting a communist cause and the attempt to remove and marginalize all suspected communist elements from the community took hold.[17]

The establishment of the Hungarian communist diaspora in Canada in 1925 coincided with major changes to Canadian immigration laws in September of that year, and specifically the new Railway Agreement, which allowed for the arrival of 185,000 so-called "non-preferred" workers in a matter of only five years. "Non-preferred" immigrants referred specifically to East Central Europeans, notably ethnic Hungarians, along with Slovaks, Poles and Ukrainians.[18] This is the period during which the industrial centres of southern Ontario and Montréal also began attracting large numbers of Hungarians, thanks to the ability of businesses to apply for special immigration permits. The organized Hungarian communities of Montréal and southern Ontario, including most churches, date back to this period in the mid to late 1920s.

These were years of rapid expansion for the Hungarian community, with 27,600 Hungarians arriving in Canada during these years, and much of the growth shifting from the Prairies to Ontario and Québec.[19] By 1941, the Hungarian Canadian population stood at 54,598, with Montréal now home to 3,763 Hungarians, thus becoming the largest urban centre of Hungarian immigration in Canada.[20]

The *Munkás* and its right-wing rival, the *Kanadai Magyar Újság*, were both products of this era of growth in the Hungarian community. The *Újság*, established in 1929 in Winnipeg, counted on the support of the Horthy regime through the two recently opened Hungarian consulates—one in Winnipeg and the other in Montréal. Initially, the Horthy regime tried to stop the drain of labourers from Hungary to Canada. When it became clear that no effort could likely halt this out-migration, the regime decided to exert influence over the burgeoning Canadian diaspora community instead through their consulates and the *Újság*.[21] The *Újság* engaged in a balancing act of being a vociferous supporter of the British Empire and English Canada (all the while displaying xenophobic views of French Canadians), while also fomenting loyalty in the diaspora to the clericalism and irredentist conservatism of the Horthy regime in Hungary. By the early 1930s, the *Újság* was mailed to approximately 4,000 subscribers. As a constant reminder of its loyalty to Horthy era irredentism, the paper's masthead carried the well-known anti-Trianon slogan: "Truncated Hungary is not a country, pre-Trianon Hungary is heaven".

The disdain that communist activist and eventual *Munkás* editor István Szőke had for *Újság* editor Gusztáv Nemes could hardly have been deeper. This antipathy stemmed from the demise of the 1919 Commune and the "white terror" that followed it. Szőke accused Nemes of involvement in the white terror, as an officer of the Horthyite guard. Nemes, despite his paper's clear support of the Horthy regime throughout the interwar period and having been accused of fascism by the *Munkás*, claimed, curiously, that his publication was in fact above politics and beyond ideology, and was simply in support of the Hungarian nation. In an open letter addressed to "True Hungarians" Nemes explained that the *Újság* was a defender of "pure-spirited Hungarian and Canadian ethics and truth. It is not our responsibility to judge the governments of our homeland or those of other countries, nor must we deny our origins, or agitate against our own".[22] The implication was simple: while the *Munkás* represented radical, unpatriotic fringe politics, the Horthyite, reactionary *Újság* was beyond politics and ideology, and served as the voice of decent, patriotic Hungarians. For good measure Nemes added a direct reference to the *Munkás* and the communist diaspora: "We do not subscribe to the time-tested ways of the Communists. We do not terrorize, we do not threaten and we do not demand... we know that our red 'Hungarians' will see our honesty as a grand opportunity, but we are at peace, since our conscience is clear and our cause is just".[23]

The Polemics of the *Munkás*

The inaugural issue of the *Kanadai Magyar Munkás* appeared as a weekly on July 16, 1929, in Hamilton. It occupied modest office space in a building at 276 Britannia Avenue. The new paper made no effort to conceal its mission: It wore it proudly on its masthead. It declared itself at war with international fascism and the forces that could lead humanity into yet another world war. It proudly proclaimed its commitment to the emancipation of the working class. Most importantly, however, the paper declared that it aimed to develop among Hungarian

Canadian workers a collective political identity. The main editorial piece, using language that would define the rhetoric of the *Munkás* for decades to come, emphasized that the paper was established by "a few tattered, grey Proletarians, with the support of workers ready to sacrifice". In the headline article appearing in the paper's first issue, the *Munkás* had no reservations wading into the thick of a political battle within the mainstream Canadian-Hungarian community.

The Horthy regime, through its diplomats in Canada, funded two right-wing, pro-Horthy Hungarian-language newspapers (the aforementioned *Kanadai Magyar Újság*, based in Winnipeg and the *Kanadai Magyar Hirlap*, published in Toronto). The two right-wing Hungarian-Canadian publications competed, currying favour with the representatives of the Horthy regime in the hopes of increased funding and preferential treatment, while the *Munkás* rose from complete obscurity and as a grassroots effort with almost no funding to become a serious and competitive press organ within the Canadian-Hungarian community. Picnics and small-scale auctions, led by volunteers, were typical forms of grassroots fundraising to help the paper remain financially viable. In 1934, five years after the establishment of the paper, the *Munkás* reported on a group of volunteer women in Windsor who had organized a picnic and auctioned off a handmade pillow manufactured by a local comrade for $11, all for the benefit of the publication. In an article signed by a "Mrs. Simon", the women in Windsor were credited with having "toiled for our own weapon, through which we can spread justice and to reach every deceived worker. Through this they will find where they belong and come together to fight for the toppling of this rotten regime".[24]

Women played a key role in the *Munkás*' grassroots fundraising campaigns. During the 1930s, in most major Canadian centres, associations of communist women gathered on a regular basis to learn new skills together, discuss the state of the movement in Canada and to organize social events. One of the more active women's groups was based in Montréal, where women met every Tuesday evening at Prince Arthur Hall to practice sowing and various crafts, to read and learn, as well as to raise funds for the *Munkás*.[25]

Grassroots *Munkás* associations in the different Canadian cities were encouraged to compete with each other in raising funds for the paper and in attracting new subscriptions. On the front page of the January 7, 1937 issue, the *Munkás* published a list of statistics to inform readers which city's associations attracted the newest subscribers. The paper set a quota of attracting 600 new subscribers by the end of January. By January, 426 new subscriptions had been collected. Activists in Montréal and Winnipeg were the most successful in obtaining new subscribers and the *Munkás*' editors were quite happy to intensify the sense of competition between the two urban centres. "The fast pace at which

Winnipeg is advancing suggests that Montréal can only remain in the lead, or rather return to the top, if it mobilizes its fighters".[26]

The paper's political militancy and its drive to organize a radical workers' movement was already evident in the language of its first issue, especially in how the paper greeted its readers:

> Our fate back home in Hungary was one of abject poverty and suffering. The disgraceful rule of Horthy and Bethlen, the landowners, the factory owners, the gendarmes and the bailiff sucked our blood and what few assets we had to such an extent that we were barely left with a beggar's cane, with which we journeyed to other lands. We were filled with hope that it would be different in Canada. We arrived here and what did we find? Perhaps the gendarme and the bailiff are not hopelessly on our tracks, but the industrialist and the factory owner holds power within his hands just like in Hungary. We experience exploitation here too. There is nowhere further to journey. We must take a stand here and it is here that we must fight to ensure that our lives are not taken from us by the overlords... Our battle is also more difficult because the murderous Horthy regime has sent its gofers after us and our fellow workers...They want to dig their extended claws into our bodies and they want to plant the ghost of white terror in this soil. Our newspaper will be the sword with which we cut off the bloody thieving hands that try to reach for our pockets and our hearts. [27]

The *Munkás* used the language of the Councils to energise its base. In Carbon, Alberta, a local association of Hungarian communists appeared to get into a veritable frenzy, at least according to the dramatic language of the *Munkás* report in January 1945, due to an attack against the Hungarian Canadian left by a right-wing Hungarian publication. "The membership of the Hungarian group in Carbon responds with their clenched fist and collective work to Hungarian reactionaries".[28] The paper referenced Lenin, noting that even visceral attacks against Bolsheviks are useful in that they can be used by the attacked as a tool of propaganda. The report provides a snapshot of how a small community of Hungarian communists in rural Alberta formed a local network and found subscribers for the *Munkás* in order to fight back. Hungarian workers, mostly miners and their families, were invited to meet in the home a man referred to simply as "Colleague Kakuk", situated three miles from Carbon for a tea and light meal. The *Munkás* emphasized the grassroots and collaborative nature of the event, which raised $43.56, and the active involvement of many. The weekly's report provides a glimpse into the life of a long-forgotten Hungarian communist community in rural Alberta:

The following people donated to the tea: Colleague Mrs. Dénes a stuffed chicken, Colleague Mrs. Nagy a box of pears, shopkeeper J. Balla ten oranges, Colleague Mrs. Fecske chocolates, Colleague Fury cigarettes, Colleague Varga cigars. All of these items were raffled off, resulting in $7.50. Colleague Mrs. Kakuk donated a live goose, which was auctioned off and brought in $9.10...Rise up, Colleagues, rise to battle! Let us not watch passively as the Bourgeoisie attacks us![29]

The success of the communist community's tea in Carbon was juxtaposed on the same page of the *Munkás* with the reported failure of a tea organized by Windsor's Hungarian Lutheran minister, János Papp. The tea and his religious service was poorly attended. The *Munkás* suggested that the empty pews and the lack of interest in the tea could be connected to the minister's right-wing political views and his involvement in an anti-communist initiative.[30] Similarly in the case of Calvinist minister Béla Bucsin, the *Munkás* reported on poor attendance at his Calgary church and not with sarcasm and mockery: "Business isn't going well at all. He is unable to capture in his net the workers and so now he is trying to spread the thin gruel of the afterlife in Lethbridge and Taber".[31] Local communists in rural Alberta were set on stopping Bucsin from establishing local congregations. One local, a certain Mrs. Pesznyák of Taber, Alberta, caused a scene at Bucsin's first Sunday service. She allegedly knew Bucsin from Hungary. After the minister finished preaching, in which he also urged his congregation to steer clear of the Hungarian communists, she rose from the pews and accused Bucsin of oppressing workers and peasants back home in Hungary, and of owing her $50. The report, which turned into an op-ed by the end, urged workers not to "fall" for priests who, according to the writer, are nothing more than the veiled agitators of the ruling class. "Soon rather than later, the working class will make sure that it does away with its oppressors, in order to establish a homeland for workers".[32] It was not uncommon for the *Munkás* to insinuate that there were many more in the broader Hungarian community who were quietly sympathetic to the cause of the communist movement and that church or community leaders who actively propagated anti-communist views lost members of their flock.

What the *Munkás* had that was not present to anywhere the same degree among Canadian-Hungarians outside of the Hungarian communist diaspora was a sense of mission and self-sacrifice. Not only were members and supporters pressured to fulfill quotas in terms of how many new subscribers they signed up, but the paper even called on readers to go without food at times, in order to provide for their paper instead. In early 1931, less than two years after being established, the *Munkás* found itself in dire straits and had to publish biweekly, due to a lack of funds. A front page letter from March 1930 demands: "The *Munkás* must not be forgotten, even if we have to eat only once per day!" The letter writer, a certain P.P. from Taber, Alberta, was apparently a contrite Canadian-Hungarian communist who wrote to apologize to the editorial board for having failed to renew his subscription. He writes:

> I am sorry for not having lived up to my responsibilities and for having neglected my subscription. Unemployment has really set us back. Regardless, we must have the Munkás, we must not let go of our only weapon, we must not give up on a single issue, even if we are to eat only once per day…This battle will be the last, let us not give up hope, as victory will be ours. Do not sleep, proletariat![33]

P.P. signed off his letter with "Proletarian greetings" and the editors added their own thoughts as well at the end, encouraging readers to organize grassroots fundraising events to support the paper.

A critical component of the *Munkás'* polemics was its particular narrative of Hungarian national history and its opposition to the narratives promoted by the rest of the organized Hungarian diaspora in Canada. The divergent treatment of key turning points in Hungarian national history offers us a good illustration of this phenomenon. As in other years before or after, in 1938, the Hungaria Social Club, located on Montréal's Saint-Laurent Boulevard, (then the city's largely Eastern European 'Main Street'), Our Lady of Hungary Catholic Parish and the Hungarian United Church, cooperated in commemorating the 1848 Hungarian Revolution. As always representatives of the Horthy regime—notably diplomats from the Consulate in Montréal—participated actively in these commemorations. In 1938, the advisor to the consul, József Szentágotai gave the keynote address. János Bence provided a detailed report and op-ed of the Montréal event for the *Munkás*. Bence was furious that the consul spoke about the Hungarian revolutionary spirit, of loyal and disloyal Hungarians and of enemies, but failed to mention the 1919 Commune. In Bence's reading, the enemies of the Hungarian nation are the aristocratic classes, including Tsarist Russia in 1849, while the heroes of the nation are the Hungarian peasants and workers, and the communist leaders of the 1919 Commune.[34]

In stark contrast to Montréal's 1938 commemoration of the 1848 anti-Hapsburg rebellion, the one organized by the Ady Endre Association in Saskatoon, had a very different approach and message. Here the members of the local Hungarian democratic front organization, cooperated with the local communists. The keynote speaker here reached across the isles. In the process of remembering the heroes of the 1848 war of independence the keynote speaker spoke about the "pillaging of the Prussian-Nazi and fascist Italian assassins".[35] These divergent approaches to celebrating the anniversary of a landmark Hungarian event requires a brief elabouration.

In 1938, on the cusp of World War II, commemorating 1848 was of special significance for the Canadian-Hungarian communist diaspora. The *Munkás*, especially in its editorials, referenced the ideals of 1848 and its heritage in warnings about the imminent danger posed by Hitler and their Hungarian collaborators in the Horthy regime. In a passionate and even prophetic editorial, the *Munkás* noted:

> Many people, to this very day, did not believe what we have been saying for years, namely that Hungary and its people stand before the open mouth of the fascist dragon. The wild beast is waiting for the ideal moment to devour our homeland and our people...The situation is fatally severe in that even countries known to be democratic are silent in the face of this looming catastrophe...[36]

The Munkás editorial called on Hungarians in Canada and further afield to return to the ideals of 1848 radicals, like Lajos Kossuth or Sándor Petőfi, as well as Mihály Táncsics, and to recognize that "Hitler stands before the Hungarian gates, and his collaborators in Hungary are prepared to let him in".[37]

This, in fact, happened in March of 1944, when tens of thousands of German troops entered Hungary, and not a shot was fired against them. Soon afterwards, the Hungarian gendarmerie rounded up close to 500,000 Hungarian Jews, crammed them into cattle wagons and deported them to the death-camps of Auschwitz. The Hungarian armed forces fought alongside the Nazis till the last days of the war. 60,000 of them were captured by allied troops inside German territory at the end of the war. Several pro-Nazi Hungarian officers captured in Germany ended up in Canada. A number of them would become Hungarian community leaders in various Canadian cities, most prominently in Toronto and Montréal, by working with the RCMP as anti-Communist informers, and posing as Christian-Nationalist, anti-Communist patriots. A good illustration of this is Gyula Detre, who was the head of military security for Hungary's Arrow Cross Dictator, Ferenc Szálasi. Detre was captured in Germany alongside Szálasi. The latter was sent back to Hungary and executed. Detre emigrated to Montréal, and served as an RCMP informer, and lead the Montréal Hungarian community for the next 50 years praising the heroics of Admiral Horthy and leading the crusade against Communism among Canadian Hungarians.

On numerous occasions, the *Munkás* drew explicit parallels between 1848 and the 1919 Commune. In each instance, the core narrative was the alleged treason and treachery of the Hungarian upper classes against the average Hungarian peasant and worker, and indeed against the country as a whole. In one piece, the *Munkás* asserted: "While both [1848 and 1919] had their weaknesses and in fact their fatal flaws too, both were popular revolutions of the Hungarian people against the slaveholders and the traitors of the nation".[38] In this reading, the upper classes in Hungary, like in 1848, decided to ally themselves with foreign powers, so as to "turn against their own nation, rather than accept that their oppressive privileges had come to an end".[39] The author of the op-ed, listed simply as "Sz. I"., almost certainly editor István Szőke, credits both 1848 and 1919 for building a certain class consciousness and identity among the oppressed. He argued that both revolutions can serve as beacons, guiding Hungarians in the diaspora in their efforts to save their country from domestic and external oppressors.

While polemical editorial and op-ed pieces dominated the first issues of the *Munkás*, the paper also shared brief news items on strikes in Canada, workers rights issues in the US, as well as news snippets from the "old country" on poverty and oppression of fellow workers back home. The paper frequently reported on the dangerous working conditions that Hungarian immigrant workers faced in Canada, highlighting the not infrequent cases of workplace injuries and deaths. Appearing under the title "Another Victim", the *Munkás* remembered the passing of a recent immigrant worker, Mihály Sipos, who only arrived in Canada a year prior and lost his life on the job site. According to the paper, "the foreman, fearing for his own livelihood, mercilessly pushed those in his crew, neglecting all safety considerations".[40] Sipos' death was also used as a cautionary tale urging Hungarian Canadian workers to join the sick benefit society—the organization that not only provided benefits and assistance to workers in case of illness or death, but also served as a tool to unite and organize the Hungarian communist community in Canada. It was understood that in 1929 only a fraction of Hungarian workers in Canada, just 15% according to the estimates of the *Munkás*, even belonged to one of the Hungarian mutual benefit societies, with the vast majority not being within the immediate orbit of the nascent communist movement.

The *Munkás* made it clear that it represented the principles of uncompromising revolution. As such, in the paper's view, social democrats in Europe were little better than the lackeys of fascism—people and parties who, through their lack of zeal and tolerance, open the gates for fascist rule. In light of this, the *Munkás* had a dark view of so-called Red Vienna (Rotes Wien), even whilst many on the left saw in the Social Democratic-led Austrian capital between 1918 and 1934, as a model of how a city could be governed in a socially just and conscious manner. The *Munkás* believed, however, that "The Austrian Social Democratic Party, the pride and joy of the Second International, is in fact making a home and is serving as quarterback for the fascists in that country". The *Munkás* was especially disenchanted with the fact that Vienna's Social Democratic mayor instructed the police to stop radical left-wingers from engaging in a street battle with fascistic elements. Using fiery language, the *Munkás* informed its readers that the more moderate elements in Austria were, in fact, insidious adversaries of the workers' cause. It concluded that the average worker probably thinks to himself: "I will deal with the fascist-capitalist gang, but first I must free myself from my 'friends', especially from the Menshevik barnacles!"[41]

Ilona Duczynska, the woman who lit the fuse of the 1918–1919 revolutions in Hungary and who worked for a while in Bela Kun's Commissariat in the Hungarian Republic of Councils, until she had enough, left Hungary in June 1919. She lived in and admired Red Vienna throughout its reign. She fought in the Austrian civil war between 1934 and 1936 and eventually settled in Canada spending the last 30 years of her life in Pickering, Ontario and writing among others for the *Munkás*. While she was a great admirer of the progressive achievements of Vienna's socialist administration, she was equally critical of its failure to prepare itself militarily against the onslaught of fascism.[42]

The Battle for the Hungarian Canadian Working Class

The *Munkás* and the *Újság* battled for more than merely subscribers for their respective publications. The *Újság* was not ready to cede to its communist competitor the growing number of Hungarian workers in Canada, most of whom were not ideologically wed to Leninism or Marxism. As such, the Horthyite publication launched a column in its weekly entitled "The Workers' Paper" in which it attempted to speak to Hungarian labourers in Winnipeg and further afield in Canada, but also in the hope of suggesting that the radicalism of the labour movement was to be rejected. The *Munkás* responded to a column appearing in the *Újság* in September 1933, at the height of the Great Depression, in which the right-wing paper warned its readers not to be deceived by the "red agitators" who were organizing illegal strikes. (This article in the *Újság* specifically referred to the labour action in Winnipeg in August 1933 organized by Hungarian furriers.) It would appear, however, that the *Újság* and its workers' column was not well received, even by some Hungarian workers in Winnipeg who were not otherwise affiliated with the radicalism of the *Munkás* nor with the communist movement more generally but had supported the Hungarian furriers' strike. The *Munkás* reported that Hungarian workers in the Manitoban capital demanded that the community organizations cut ties with the *Újság* following its denunciation of the Hungarian furrier strike. The *Munkás* added: "These workers do not belong to revolutionary workers' movements, but rather they are workers who are still far from us. Naturally, however, the *Újság* and the Consulate General of the kingless Kingdom of Hungary do not hear that there is no fertile soil here for reactionary politics, even though recent events have clearly proved as much".[43]

The Hungarian furrier workers in Winnipeg invited the editor of the *Újság* to a public debate on the issue, or as the *Munkás* referred to it, a "people's assembly", but the Horthyite publication did not respond to the invitation.

In the same September 1933 issue of the *Munkás,* a letter to the editor appeared, signed simply by "M.L.", in which the reader encourages others who subscribe to "even sacrifice our last cents on the Munkás, because the weapons of the workers are not supported by the Bourgeoisie. We, the oppressed, must support this, as this is the only weapon in our hands, with which we can both access the incredible tool that is knowledge and then bring to its grave the rule of robber baron capitalism".[44] The memory of Winnipeg's strike in 1919 and recent action by Hungarian furriers in the city, boosted the confidence and also the rhetoric of the Munkás to declare: "The capitalists of Winnipeg see the great development of the workers' organization, with one strike after another and one battle after another... Young workers will also assist in the establishment of a Soviet Canada".[45]

In this battle with the *Újság*, one reader's letter published in the *Munkás* and signed by "A.V". sought to connect the Horthyite Winnipeg-based paper to the murder of 36 intellectuals, workers and peasants, some of them Hungarian Jews, killed during the White Terror against the 1919 Communards. (This was the infamous mass murder, in the forests of Orgovány, Hungary, where many of the victims were buried alive.) The letter writer asserts that the *Újság* "came to life in the forests of Orgovány" and goes on to chronicle the trauma of poverty-stricken mothers having to engage in prostitution in order to provide the basic essentials for their starving children in Horthy's Hungary. The letter writer adds: "Of course, the Horthyite insects aren't hammering on about this...The Horthyite dogs don't wail about the fact that Canadian beet workers live in filthy shanties and that they are unable to secure an existence even with their relentless labour".[46]

The *Munkás* also found it problematic, that in addition to doing the bidding of the Horthy regime in Canada, the *Újság* was actively trying to boost an idea increasingly common in Canadian circles: namely, that the future and wellbeing of workers rested in conciliatory, reform-minded workers' movements, as opposed to radical revolutionary ones. Following in the traditions of the 1919 Commune, the *Munkás* placed itself firmly in the latter camp.[47]

The Hungarian Canadian Campaign to Save Mátyás Rákosi

Mátyás Rákosi, who after 1948 would become Hungary's Stalinist leader (for additional details turn to Chapter 8), served as the Deputy People's Commissar for Trade in the 1919 Commune and later served in the leadership of the Red Guards as well. After the collapse of the 1919 Commune, Rákosi spent around four years in exile before returning to Hungary in 1924 and joining the

Communist underground. He was swiftly arrested and imprisoned and faced the possibility of execution for his role in the Commune. The Hungarian Canadian communist diaspora, with the *Munkás* at its helm, launched an extensive campaign in 1934 to have Rákosi's life spared. The Rákosi campaign also allowed the *Munkás* to make the case to Hungarian Canadian workers that the 1919 Commune is an integral part of their heritage and that it represented an alternative Hungary, in which workers finally had control of their own destiny.

> Hungarian workers! The Hungarian Republic of Councils was your power. The commissars of the Republic of Councils led your battles against the Hungarian Bourgeoisie. The Red Guard fought your battle against both Hungarian and international counterrevolution. The Hungarian Council of Republics was betrayed by social democracy and it was beaten by counterrevolution. But Comrade Mátyás Rákosi and the communists always remained loyal to the cause of the Commune, that is to your cause! [....] The leaders of your struggle, the Hungarian communists in exile, have not abandoned your battle.[48]

The campaign and call to arms, initiated internationally and in Canada, called for the creation of local worker committees with the goal of saving Rákosi's life and securing his release from prison. The *Munkás* organized protests and letter writing campaigns targeting Hungary's Consulates. In Montréal, for example in May 1934, the *Munkás* called on local workers to "flood" with letters and telegrams the Royal Hungarian Consulate, located in the Castle Building, at 1410 Stanley Street and pressure Hungarian Consul, Károly Winter, by demanding Rákosi's release.[49] The Munkás set ambitious goals for itself. It felt that it would be possible to not only rally the obviously "converted" within the Canadian-Hungarian community to this cause, but significant segments outside its orbit. It targeted even the Hungarian churches, non-Hungarian middle-classes, and liberal-conservative diaspora associations to advocate for Rákosi. "Let there not be a single Hungarian organization in Canada that does not register their protest, in which we demand the immediate and unconditional release of Mátyás Rákosi".[50] The *Munkás* warned that the Hungarian regime had sent its spies to the diaspora in Canada to spread false information about the likelihood that Hungary and the Soviet Union would strike an agreement leading to the release of Rákosi.

The *Munkás* also launched a petition in support of Rákosi and reportedly collected 11,000 signatures. When their efforts were strongly criticized by the *Újság* and right-wing Hungarian Canadians, some 400 supporters of the *Munkás* gathered outside of the rival paper's offices in Winnipeg to protest.[51] This and their successful fundraising drives suggest that within five years of the establishment of the paper and less than a decade after the Hungarian communists were sent from the US to Canada to organize a left-wing diaspora, the communist émigré community had significant mobilizing and organizational capacity.

Rákosi did, in fact, escape execution and he was released to the Soviet Union, after Budapest and Moscow struck a deal that in exchange, the Russians would return to Hungary flags that had been captured by Tsarist forces following the repression of the 1848 Revolution. In the years following World War II and even in the shadow of the 1956 Hungarian Revolution, which rejuvenated the long-suppressed workers' councils, and thoroughly transformed the shape, outlook and trajectory of the Hungarian Canadian diaspora, the *Munkás* remained steadfast. It supported to the end the dictator who would become infamous after WWII as Stalin's most faithful and most ruthless Central European disciple.

Conclusions

During the interwar period, the unjust and anti-democratic activities of the Horthy regime in the "old country", the memory of the oppression following the 1919 Commune and Horthy's embrace and alliance with Hitler and Mussolini provided more fuel and fodder to the causes pursued by the Hungarian communist diaspora in Canada. To the credit of this movement, while the broader Hungarian community was either supportive of the autocratic Horthy regime, even as Hungary allied itself with Nazi Germany, or was quiet on the subject, and while western powers failed to recognize the dangers posed by Adolf Hitler, the *Munkás* had sounded the alarms prophetically already in the early 1930s. It was an unrelenting opponent of fascism, and spoke with a thundering voice on behalf of the wretched of the earth.

The *Munkás'* failure, and that of the community built around it, was its cult-like behaviour, its inability to adapt, to change with the times. Its strident and militant polemics would continue to rouse the most zealous, but was alarming to those who were less ideologically committed and who were repelled by the excesses of the Bolsheviks and Stalinism. The *Munkás* echoed the fierce language of the 1919 Bolshevik leadership, it spoke a language that was not conducive to expanding the base, nor to securing the future of the movement in the diaspora beyond the interwar period. While the *Munkás* survived the 1956 Hungarian Revolution and refugee crisis, it became even more marginalized due to the continuation of its hardline position after de-Stalinization of the early 1960s.

In a desperate attempt to adjust, the paper changed its name to *Új Szó* (New Word) and managed to survive into the 1970's and early 1980's as a faint shadow of its former self. While it received support from Hungary's Kádár regime during the 1960s, its rigid ideological convictions and its connection to the 1919

Dictatorship of the Proletariat meant that it eventually fell out of favour even with the Kádár regime and its diplomats, who wanted to strike a more conciliatory, cooperative tone vis-á-vis the Western powers during the new era of detente. Peaceful co-existence was not in the vocabulary of the émigrés from the 1919 Hungarian Commune, who landed on Canada's shores. They did not experience Stalin's, Rákosi's or Kádár's brutal betrayal of the council movements in their homeland. They were stuck inside a rhetorical bubble, cut off from home, prisoners of a language that no one spoke or understood anymore. The interwar period was the "golden age" of a vibrant Hungarian communist émigré community in Canada—a unique, socially righteous, combative community, whose voice was captured and locked forever inside the preserved pages of its polemical weekly.

NOTES

1   Bill Lomax, *Hungarian Workers' Councils in 1956* (Boulder, CO: Social Science monographs, 1990).

2   Jack Jedwab, "Leadership, Governance and the Politics of Identity", *Canadian Ethnic Studies*, Vol. XXXIII, No. 3, 2001, 25–26.

3   *Ibid.*, 13–14.

4   J.M. Kirschbaum, "The Ideological Orientation of the Canadian Slavic Press", *Slavs in Canada* (Vol. 3) Inter-University Committee on Canadian Slavs, 1971, 297.

5   Susan Olzak, "Ethnic Conflict and the Rise and Fall of Ethnic Newspapers", *American Sociological Review*, Vol. 56. No. 4. Aug. 1991, 459.

6   Jan Raska, *Czech Refugees in Cold War Canada* (Winnipeg, Manitoba: University of Manitoba Press, 2018), 22.

7   Donald Creighton, *Canada's First Century: 1867–1967* (Toronto: Macmillan, 1970), 76.

8   James W. St. G. Walker, "Race", Rights and the Law in the Supreme Court of Canada—*Historical Case Studies*, (Waterloo: Wilfrid Laurier University Press, 1997) 251.

9   *Ibid.*, 252.

10   Charles Lipton, *The Trade Union Movement of Canada*, 1827–1959 (Toronto: NC Press, 1973), 125.

11   Bohdan Kordan, *Enemy Aliens: Prisoners of War: Internment in Canada During the Great War* (Montréal-Kingston: Queen's University Press, 2002), 36.

12   Barrington Walker, *The History of Immigration and Racism in Canada*, (Toronto: Canadian Scholars Press, 2008), 136.

13   John Kolasky, *Prophets and Proletarians—Documents on the History of the Rise and Decline of Ukrainian Communism in Canada* (Toronto: Canadian Institute of Ukrainian Studies, 1998), 113.

14   Anne Burger, *The Communist Party of Canada During the Great Depression—Organizing and Class Consciousness* (Simon Fraser University, 1980), 71.

15   RCMP Report on Revolutionary Organisations and Agitation in Canada, No. 859. Weekly Summary, June 10, 1937, 241.

16   For the most comprehensive history of the establishment of the Hungarian proletarian camp in Canada; see: Carmela Patrias, *Patriots and Proletarians: Politicizing Hungarian Immigrants in Interwar Canada* (Montréal: McGill-Queen's University Press, 2014).

17   *Ibid.*, 148.

18   Valerie Knowles, Strangers at our Gates—Canadian Immigration and Immigration Policy, 1540–2006, (Toronto: Dundurn, 2007), 142–143.

19   N. F. Dreisziger, *Struggle and Hope: the Hungarian-Canadian Experience* (Toronto: McClelland and Stewart in association with the Multiculturalism Directorate, Dept. of the Secretary of State and the Canadian Govt. Pub. Centre, Supply and Services Canada, 1982).

20 The community in Toronto was a distant second at this time, with 2,194. Pál Sántha, "Kanada Magyarsága," [Canada's Hungarians], (Winnipeg: Kanadai Magyar Újság, 1946), 20.

21 Carmela Patrias, *The Kanadai Magyar Újság and the Politics of the Hungarian Canadian Elite*, (Toronto: Multicultural History Society of Ontario, November 1978), 6.

22 Gusztáv Nemes, "Igaz Magyarokhoz!" [To True Hungarians], *Kanadai Magyar Újság* (November 4, 1941), 2.

23 *Ibid.*, 2.

24 "Windsori Női Csoport jelentése" (Report from the Women's Group in Windsor)() *Kanadai Magyar Munkás* (June 28, 1934), 8.

25 "Montréal csoportunk komoly munkába fogott" (Our Montréal group has begun serious work) , *Kanadai Magyar Munkás* (January 7, 1937), 3.

26 Winnipeg utólérte Montrealt", (Winnipeg Has Caught Up With Montréal), *Kanadai Magyar Munkás* (January 7, 1937), 1.

27 *Kanadai Magyar Munkás* (July 16, 1929), 1.

28 "Forradalmi Munkával Feleleünk a Kiáltó Szóra" (We Respond With Revolutionary Work to the Call)), *Kanadai Magyar Munkás*, (January 15, 1935), 5.

29 *Ibid.*, 5.

30 "Papp Jancsi tea estje 'befagyott' (Jancsi Papp's tea 'froze'), *Kanadai Magyar Munkás*, (January 15, 1935), 5.

31 "Bucsin csuhás a pergőtűzben" (Shaveling Bucsin in fire), *Kanadai Magyar Munkás*, (March 19, 1931), 3.

32 Ibid., 3.

33 "Ha egyszer eszünk naponta sem szabad elmaradni a Munkásnak " (The *Munkás* must not be forgotten, even if we eat only once per day!) " *Kanadai Magyar Munkás*, (March 19, 1931), 1.

34 "Amiről Szentágotati úr nem beszélt" (What Mr. Szentágotai Did Not Talk About), *Kanadai Magyar Munkás*, (March 24, 1938), 3.

35 "Méltó keretek között ünnepelte Saskatoon magyarsága március idusát" (Saskatoon's Hungarians Celebrated the Ides of March in a Worthy Manner), *Kanadai Magyar Munkás*, (March 24, 1938), 3.

36 "Oda haza és itt " (At Home and Here), *Kanadai Magyar Munkás*, (March 24, 1938), 4.

37 *Ibid.*, 4.

38 "Rokonok, 1848 és 1919" (Relatives, 1848 and 1919), *Kanadai Magyar Munkás*, (March 18, 1943), 4.

39 *Ibid*, 5.

40 *Ibid.*, 5.

41 "A Fassizmus (sic) hátvédjei" (The Quarter-Backs of the Fascists)), Kanadai Magyar Munkás, (July 16, 1929), 4.

42 See: András B. Göllner, *Ilona: Portrait of a Rebel* (Forthcoming 2022), and Ilona Duczynska. *Workers in Arms. The Austrian Schutzbund and the Civil War of 1934.* (New York, NY: Monthly Review Press, 1978).

43 "Itéljenek a winnipegi munkások" (Let the Workers of Winnipeg be the Judge) , *Kanadai Magyar Munkás*, (September 21, 1933), 5.

44 "Let Us Make Great the Workers' Press", (Építsök naggyá a munkássajtót), *Kanadai Magyar Munkás*, (September 21, 1933), 5.

45 "Nemzetközi Ifjúmunkásnap 'Pegen (International Youth Workers' Day in The Peg), Kanadai Magyar Munkás, (September 21, 1933), 5.

46 "Saját portánkon nézzük széjel" (sic) (Let's Look Around our Own Porch") *Kanadai Magyar Munkás*, (September 21, 1933), 5.

47 In and editorial piece covering a four month long strike of the United Mine Workers, the *Munkás* argued that radical demands and eschewing compromise is what leads to victory for the workers. *Munkás*, (September 21, 1933), 6.

48 " Mentsük meg Rákosi Mátyást", (Let Us Save Mátyás Rákosi), *Kanadai Magyar Munkás*, (June 28, 1934), 1, 7.

49 "Gömbösék titokban akarják kivégeztetni Rákosi Mátyást" (Gömbös and Co. Want to Execute Mátyás Rákosi in Secret), *Kanadai Magyar Munkás*, (May 17, 1934), 5.

50 "Állítsuk meg Horthy gyilkos véres kezét", (Let Us Stop Horthy's Murderous and Bloody Hand .), *Kanadai Magyar Munkás*, (January 15, 1935), 1.

51 *We Are Canadians—the National Group of the Hungarian-Canadians*, (Toronto: Hungarian Literature Association, 1954), 84.

CHAPTER 8

The Rhapsody of the Permanent Counterrevolution in Hungary

András B. Göllner

The events of Eastern Europe have the strange aftertaste of something that has already happened before, something unfolding retrospectively— an aftertaste which does not bode well for a meaningful future. Our only surprise is that we were not able to foresee them and our only regret that we do not know how to draw any consequences from them.

—Jean Baudrillard, *The Illusion of the End, 1992*

Ouverture

I cannot think of a better way of opening this last chapter—a chapter that will chronicle the *"secret attachment"*[1] of Hungary's rulers to their counter-revolutionary past—than with a passage written at the end of WWII by a man who, serious students of European intellectual history would agree is the most significant *political* thinker produced by Hungary during the 20th century.[2]

During the 100 years that began with the repression of our 1848 revolution and ended with Hungary's defeat in World War II in 1945, the people of Hungary lived under systems of governance that did not allow things to be called by their real names. This was a period in our history, when facts could not be illuminated for the public in terms of their simple cause and effect relationships. During this time the interpretation of reality followed a different set of procedures than those prescribed for us by the Enlightenment. Our leaders chose a path for us that had as little to do with the truth or with the facts as it's humanly possible. Public thinking was shaped by noblemen who were driven by whims, unfounded expectations, or divine inspiration. They wasted enormous resources trying to resolve artificial problems and

ignored the ones that would eventually drown us all.... All the distortions
that have manifested themselves during this period and in all walks of
Hungarian public life can in some way be traced back to the false, the
artificial foundations of our country's basic political and social
construction... After the 1867 compromise with the Hapsburgs, after the
counter-revolution that followed the collapse of the Republic of Councils
in 1919, you could not become a minister, a municipal notary, a bank
president, the head of a corporation, of a university or hold any kind of
supervisory position anywhere in the country unless you would publicly
embrace, pay homage to, and repeatedly exalt the lies on which the entire
edifice of public life rested in Hungary.... Gradually, this situation utterly
corrupted the moral and intellectual fiber of the leading strata of Hungarian
society. As for the general public's ability to attend to its civic responsibilities,
its ability to respond thoughtfully to issues of mutual public concern? After
the destruction of its own moral fiber, the political establishment's single,
overriding concern was to destroy the public's ability to distinguish illusion
from reality. Ours is a classic example of how the mechanisms of fear can
seduce and overwhelm the mechanisms of reason in politics.[3]

The role of the above passage in this closing chapter is that of a prism that focuses
the light from the past, the present and the future, in order to reveal why the 1919
Hungarian Republic of Councils became a forgotten revolution, and why it is
slandered to this day by the Right, and the Stalinists of the Left. Bibó was first
silenced by the Nazis in 1944, then by the Bolsheviks in 1948. His embrace of
workers' councils as a legitimate form of self-rule by Hungary's working men and
women almost got him executed in '56 were it not for the intervention of India's
Prime Minister, the late Jawaharlal Nehru (1889–1964).[4] His unmitigated embrace
of socialism earned him the scorn of Hungary's neo-liberals after the collapse of
the Berlin Wall.[5] Hungary's current 'illiberal' government is as fearful of and
desperate to distort his words as those that ruled before it. Tyrus Miller's
observations in connection with an even earlier essay of Bibó's than the one I've
chosen above [6] are right on the money: "The overall argument of Bibó's essay rests
on the importance of emotional attachments (and revulsions) in aligning the
various social elements of a society with its political structures".[7]

My purpose with this final chapter is to highlight this emotional attachment
in three, clearly discernible movements followed by a *finalé* and an epilogue that
will draw the appropriate consequences and suggests an approach towards
ending it.

The First Movement: 1919-1945

Béla Kun and his Commissars took the last train out of Budapest for Vienna on August 1, 1919, well before Admiral Horthy "liberated" Budapest—"that sinful city"—on November 16, 1919.[8] There wasn't a single shot fired in opposition to Horthy as he rode through the capital on the back of a white horse at the head of his newly formed National Army.[9] The desire of Hungary's workers and peasants to fight, to resist, had long been extinguished by the brutal impact of a lost war and the subsequent and relentless military attacks against the Commune by the neighboring countries. The Spanish Influenza, various other diseases, combined with the great powers' sanctions, the inability and or unwillingness of the Austrian and Russian political leaders to lend a helping hand, and the chaos produced by the Revolutionary Governing Council's own policies—as seen from earlier chapters—utterly drained the last drop of resistance from the exhausted and starving citizens of Budapest. When Horthy marched into the capital, the only shots heard were those fired by Horthy's armed "detachments" that began to round up and summarily execute those who participated in or sympathized with the Commune.

Horthy's men would massacre the skeletal Bolshevik crew that stayed behind in Budapest and instituted a roughly two year-long "White Terror" in order to punish the sinners and to deter Hungarian working men and women from taking matters into their own hands ever again.[10] Once the dust settled, Horthy's scribes began to rewrite the history books in order to ensure that not only the witnesses but future generations as well would forget about the 1919 Hungarian Republic of Councils and come to hold only distorted, and grotesque pictures in their minds of the time when Hungary's working men and women attempted to take charge of their own lives.[11]

For the next 25 years, until the defeat of Hungary's military forces at the end of WWII, only the Horthy regime's official version of the events of 1918–1919 would be allowed to be published or circulated in Hungary along with some remorseful and apologetic memoirs written by former Social Democratic colleagues of Kun.[12] The disastrous war losses, the excessively punitive terms of the Treaty of Trianon, the entire post-WWI debacle prior to Horthy's entry into Budapest would be blamed on "the Left". As Hungarian historian Tamás Krausz would observe decades later:

> The counter-revolutionary system of Horthy destroyed and criminalised the 1918–1919 revolutionary tradition of the workers' councils of the Hungarian working class... it declared in the name of the sanctity of private property that communal property—which was defined as the essence of socialism from Marx and Lenin till Zsigmond Kunfi, Justus and Lukács—was a sinful idea.[13]

The "Left" under Horthy's regime was not restricted to the Bolsheviks who bastardized and hijacked the ideals of Marxism after they abandoned their initial mentor, Rosa Luxemburg. The "Left" in Hungary is, to this day, a catchphrase consisting of a wide assortment of "sinners" and "degenerates" who happen to agree with the passage I quoted from Bibó at the start of this chapter. "The Left" includes all who are critical, for whatever reason, of Admiral Nicholas Horthy's destruction of Hungary's post-WWI democracy. In Horthy's counterrevolutionary Hungary, 'The Jew' was reframed as the "alien soul" of the Left with a singular, and overarching mission: the destruction of Hungary's "Christian-National *identity*".

Under Horthy's 25-year watch, Hungary's fragile, young post-WWI democracy would be cut off at the knees. Two thirds of the population would lose their right to vote. The secret ballot would be abolished outside of the capital. This is how a member of the Hungarian bourgeoisie—a former director of the Hungarian National Bank under the Horthy era described Horthy's realm:

> The interwar governments retained their power not so much by genuine popular support, but by exerting pressure to achieve safe majorities in the elections.... Far reaching reforms could be advocated... but the opposition... was never allowed to show its prowess in taking over government, and the government could seldom be compelled to yield or offer redress.[14]

The economic state of affairs was similar. While the late 1930's began to show signs of rapid industrial growth, the foundations of this economic 'virility' were brittle. Industry's raw materials supply was insecure (an obvious result of the country's dismemberment by the Treaty of Trianon): it was concentrated around Budapest and was surrounded by a sea of semi-feudal agricultural backwardness. By the late 1930s Hungary was the European Fascists' economic satellite. Her economic development was fueled first and foremost by Italy's and Germany's war preparations. Hungary's workers became the slaves of the military industrial complex that sustained European Fascism to the bitter end.[15]

Agriculture, the mainstay of the Hungarian national economy up to 1945, suffered from even more severe structural distortions, the most visible of which stemmed from the uneven distribution of landownership. Most of the country's arable land was owned by one percent of the land-owners. Beneath a thin veneer of wealth and privilege stood a large peasant class—numbering close to four million people, roughly half the population—who spent much of the year unemployed, in deep poverty, under-educated and overworked by the great landowners, the rural nobility, and by the Catholic Church, which ran most of the schools in the countryside, and owed much of the country's arable land.[16]

After the collapse of the 1938 Munich agreement,[17] the gang-rape of Poland by Germany and the Soviet Union in 1939, and the start of WWII, Mussolini's and Hitler's Hungarian pit bull would go on his own rampage by trying to *Make Hungary Great Again*. In 1941, Horthy sent his first Hungarian shipment of 21,000 "illegal" Jewish immigrants straight into the arms of the SS executioners who just happened to be waiting for them at the Hungarian-Ukrainian border town of Kamanets-Podolski. After the "illegal immigrants" lined up nicely to be processed, the Germans would machine gun all 23,000 of them—men, women and children—into a giant open pit dug in a forest clearing near the railway tracks.[18]

Horthy would follow Germany's lead by declaring war on the Soviet Union, and by sending her troops into Yugoslavia, Romania, Czechoslovakia, and the Ukraine. At the end of 1942, 200,000 poorly fed, ill equipped Hungarian soldiers were sent to the Soviet Union to "teach the sponsors of the 1919 Budapest Commune a lesson they'll never forget".[19] This entire army would perish within months on the Russian front near the river Don, in minus 30–40 Celsius weather and under the most brutal and inhuman of circumstances.

Back in Hungary, and under Horthy's reign, Hungary's 800,000 Jews would be herded into ghettoes and made to wear the yellow star to make them easy pickings for those who hated them as a consequence of the relentless state and church sponsored propaganda of the previous decades. Close to 500,000 were deported by Horthy's administration to Auschwitz and Birkenau in sealed freight cars and then gassed to death by the operators of the camps. When the trains could no longer run, thousands of others from the Budapest ghetto would be shot into the Danube or beaten to death in muddy ditches after they could no longer pull their aching, starving bodies as members of the Jewish auxiliary units alongside the enlisted men who were sent out by Horthy, then Szálasi, to hold the fort for Hitler and Mussolini during the closing months of the war.[20] Altogether, 600,000 of Hungary's Jews would perish as a consequence of this hatred.

Horthy's National Army defended the Third Reich against the Allies, right up to the gates of Berlin to the very last days of WWII. They fought not only the Russians, but the Canadians, the British, the Americans and anyone who attacked Fascism in the neighborhood. More than 60,000 Hungarian troops would surrender to the Americans, and the British in Austria and Germany at the end of the war. The enlisted men would return to their families in Hungary. Thousands of their commanding officers would not, especially the ones that swore allegiance to Ferenc Szálasi, Hungary's "Führer" during the last months of the war. They feared persecution back home especially after the Communist Party came to power in Hungary in 1948. By the early 1950s, thousands of these defenders of Fascism would end up in distant capitals of the "Free World". Like Eichmann, or

Dr. Mengele, many sought refuge in Argentina, others in Canada and the USA, where they reinvented themselves as fierce anti-Communist "freedom-fighters" and defenders of "Christianity", "the rule of law" and "Western values". They distinguished themselves in Roy Cohn's and Senator McCarthy's anti-Communist crusades during the early years of the Cold War in America. Hundreds snitched for the CIA, the FBI, or the Royal Canadian Mounted Police on people whose only crime was that they sympathised with the oppressed.[21] These officers created their own diaspora organization—the *Magyar Harcosok Bajtársi Közössége* (The Hungarian Community of Fallen Warriors)—to keep alive the counter-revolutionary spirit of the Horthy era outside of Hungary, to suppress the memory of 1919, and to spawn a host of other diaspora groups that participate to this day in the assault on those, who want to be free of the crooks who use Hungary's *"Christian-National Spirit"* as their instrument of abuse and personal gain.[22]

The Second Movement: 1945–1990

It is impossible to understand not only why Hungary's 1919 Republic of Councils became a forgotten revolution, but why it's so hard to prick the global neo-liberal bubble with a socialist needle, unless we confront what was done to working men and women by successive leaders of the USSR, of China and by their local Bolshevik surrogates in Hungary between 1945 and 1990.

April 4, 1945 is the day Hungary was liberated by the Allies from Fascist oppression. For better or for worse, this day heralded the beginning of a new era for everyone in Hungary. Obviously, we cannot attempt to retell the experiences of the various classes of people who lived through the 45 year long stretch of time that ended in the spring of 1990. Everyone has a story to tell. This section will focus only on the experiences of the working men and women of Hungary who rightfully thought their time had finally come after what they had to endure after their 1919 Republic of Councils was suppressed and forgotten.

In 1945, there was virtually unanimity of opinion, much like on March 21, 1919, that a fundamental and socially just transformation of Hungary's polity, economy, and society was at hand. It is this widespread belief in the need for a national and regional reconciliation in support of the common people of the region, an unshaken belief in the necessity of a cooperative, consciously planned pathway to an ecologically sustainable future based on justice and equality before the law for the oppressed that's echoed by Karl Polanyi in his celebrated 1945 essay.[23] That essay, the direction it pointed towards, was wholeheartedly supported by his wife, Ilona Duczynska, and is as relevant today as it was when it was originally penned in 1945.

The scale of Hungary's post WWII challenge

One cannot verbalize the traumatic state of a people that has been sent into the vortex of two world wars by its political elite in 25 years only to suffer such devastating defeats each time as Hungary did. The citizens of Budapest suffered the second longest military siege of any city in the world during WWII (Stalingrad suffered the longest).[24] Aerial shots of the city taken after the war ended provide a picture similar to the surface of the moon. Not only did this country of 9 million suffer more than a million dead during this second war (the number includes the 600,000 victims of the Holocaust), but she lost almost a million more who fled or were expelled from the scene of the crime over the first 3–4 years following the end of WWII (the expelled included 250,000 of Hungary's German speaking minority, the "Schwabs"). Hundreds of thousands were left permanently scarred and crippled by the war. The survivors faced hunger, economic uncertainty, disease and random arrests in the streets by the occupying Red Army and a one-way ticket to the Gulag and years of slave labour building "Socialism in one country".[25] To say that by 1945 the people of Hungary were suffering from an acute case of PTSD would be an understatement.

With the armistice agreement of 1945, the people of Hungary were compelled to pay a very heavy price for the foolishness of their former leaders. The USSR was given rights to war booty. The country was levied a very heavy reparations burden payable to the USSR, Czechoslovakia and Yugoslavia.[26] While most other states in East Central Europe (e.g., Poland, Czechoslovakia, Yugoslavia, and Romania) received substantial financial and material support from the UNRRA, Hungary received virtually nothing.

No one was more willing to participate in the task of rebuilding their war savaged country than Hungary's labouring classes. During the first couple of years of economic reconstruction that began on April 5, 1945, they displayed an almost superhuman effort, not unlike that which they exhibited at the end of WWI. Once again, many of them rose to the challenge by taking matters into their own hands via spontaneously organized local councils and committees throughout the country.[27] Often working on empty stomachs, frequently without pay or roof over their heads, they regularly worked 12–14 hour days, seven days a week, hoping that this time their sacrifices would not be in vain.

Historians tend to look at the first three years after the end of WWII in Hungary as a short-lived window of opportunity after the end of the Horthy era. Many years ago I concluded otherwise: this "window of opportunity" was in fact a construction site for a blind-alley.[28] These were years, during which this traumatized and crippled people were literally stripped naked of their remaining assets by the occupying Soviet Red Army. These were the years of the so-called "Dry Road" to socialism, the years for laying the economic foundations for the

Bolshevik rule that would begin in 1948 and remain in place for the next 42 years in Hungary.[29]

According to the Potsdam Agreement, the Berlin Foreign Ministers' Conference, and the Paris Peace Treaty that restored "order" in Europe after WWII all formerly German and Italian-owned assets and companies in Hungary became the property of the Soviet Union after the war. Berend and Ránki cite the Horthy regime's former Premier Pál Teleki, according to whom, *"The German Empire in 1939 had such an extensive and widespread network of economic interest in our country that through this she could check and indeed influence the whole of Hungarian economic life"*. [30] That share became much higher during the war. The assumption of Germany's and Italy's colonial mastery over Hungary was as easily achieved by the Soviet Union at the end of WWII as changing one's shoes, but it fundamentally altered the lives of Hungarians afterwards for generations.

After Hungary's workers cleaned up the rubble in Budapest and in the countryside, and after the Soviet Union's stranglehold on the Hungarian economy was firmly established, it was time to put Hungary's working men and women on the Stalinist assembly line. The Bolsheviks pulled the switch on Hungary's workers on March 12, 1948. Without prior consultation with anyone—not even Parliament, the Trade Unions or the Factory Committees—all firms employing more than 100 people were nationalized and were provided with new "working class managers". [31]

Hungary's newly appointed working-class managers did not have any advance notice of their promotion. They were not only pleasantly surprised but utterly unprepared for their new responsibilities. They were not selected on the basis of their ability to take care of the people's wealth but on the basis of their inability to resist the Bolsheviks' advances. Sleeping Beauty was rendered defenseless – *Prince Charming put his hand over her mouth and pointed a dagger at her heart*. Arguing that the inexperienced new managers needed "expert guidance to carry out their great patriotic duties" the Bolsheviks put all of them within a matter of days into an utterly subservient and supine position. They became the subjects of twenty new ministerial directorates whose orders could neither be questioned nor disobeyed from that point onward by anyone.[32]

The Bolshevik leadership, which hitherto maintained that the proletariat had been working like slaves under capitalism, suddenly began to proclaim that the workers should work even harder now: "We looked at the statistics comrades. It turns out that our workers are producing much less for our democracy than they did for Horthy. This is not progress, comrades. Increasing productivity; this is the decisive question for our democracy now. We must create order in this area".[33] And "order" they did.

Act no. 34 of 1947 had already eliminated the right to oppose centrally defined wage levels and the right to strike. The Workers Councils and Factory Committees created spontaneously by Hungary's workers in 1945 were disbanded. Trade unions were placed into that well-known "transmission belt" function which only the Stalinist-type command economy has been able to reserve for them. Their primary function became the application of pressure upon their members to obey the wishes of the Bolshevik bureaucracy. Opposition to any and all "plan directives" (sic) was outlawed. This was the antithesis of a discursive democracy. Some of the more extreme anti-labour measures prompted a hostile reaction from some members of the working classes, especially in cases when the workers overfilled the centrally-designed piece rate norms. Instead of receiving the extra payment stipulated in their contracts, they were informed that the norms had been erroneously set too low by the "comrades ", and they should simmer down. The most celebrated case of resistance against this theft involved a series of wild-cat strikes in the Csepel industrial center during October 1948.[34] The ring-leaders were arrested and shot. The construction of the blind-alley continued with even greater fervour and discipline. By the end of 1948, collectivization of agriculture was also in full swing.[35] and thus Hungary's workers and peasants found themselves once again on the bottom, gagged and bound, unable to resist "Prince Charming" who called himself Mátyás.While putting a precise dollar sign on the colonial exploitation of Hungary during its first "socialist" (sic) decade is well-nigh impossible, the evidence of a ten-year long rape of Hungary's working classes by their overlords at a time when they were at their most trusting and vulnerable position is, however, irrefutable.

October 23, 1956

It was the revolting assault on Hungary's working men and women, with the aid of the sacred word—socialism—that blew the lid off the Soviet Union's Hungarian 'power-plant' on October 23, 1956. This was not the bourgeoisie striking back at the dictatorship of the proletariat. It was the children of the industrial and agricultural labourers and their parents in the cities, towns and villages of Hungary who turned on their disgusting Stalinist abusers. As in 1919, they are the unsung heroes of Hungary's second social revolution of the 20th century and they are as forgotten and ignored today as those who made 1919 happen 100 years ago.

What made Hungary's rebellion against a nuclear superpower bully next door so remarkable was not so much the bravery or passion of its working class warriors but the spirit that moved them.[36] It was identical to the one that sent shivers down the spines of the Imperialist powers in Versailles in 1919, scared the daylight out of the Social Democrats of Germany and Austria and caused even Vladimir Ilyich Lenin sleepless nights in the Kremlin, until Béla Kun put his mind at rest by lying to him about it.[37] While the scribes of Nicholas Horthy, Rákosi and Kádár would do everything to erase or distort it, 1956 provides us with irrefutable evidence of its immortality.

Workers Councils sprang up miraculously and in an utterly spontaneous manner throughout Hungary at the end of October 1956 demanding the same rights for working men and women as their predecessors did 37 years earlier.[38] The Councils' demands, their right to play a leading role in the revolution of '56 was fully and publicly embraced by the revolutionary government of Imre Nagy at its last official cabinet meeting. The workers' councils of Hungary during the 1919 and 1956 revolutions had the same message for the Bolsheviks as they had for the advocates of Capitalist restoration: "Our factories and land belong to the people, and we will never surrender them".[39]

It needs to be retold, rather than forgotten, that 1956 was not a revolution against the ideals of socialism, but against those who chose to abuse the working classes under the label of socialism ! Hungary's social revolution in 1956 was not a movement to provide for the free movement of capital, or to restore the domination of society by unregulated market forces. Johanna Bockman's suggestion that Imre Nagy was a closet neo-liberal is an unsustainable and unfortunate historical revision as is the one that is in the process of resurrecting Stalin as the legitimate heir of Karl Marx along with the affinity-fraudster in charge of the Chinese Communist Party, who has installed himself in power for life in that country and serves as a role model for such Kleptocrats as Russia's Putin or Hungary's Orbán..[40]

Like its 1919 prototype, 1956 was a broadly embraced workers' rebellion against the seismic-plates of a world-system that generates tensions and manifests abusive behavior at its various poles.[41] It was the immortal spirit that moved both of these revolutions that sealed both revolution's fate. It had to be put back in the bottle and forgotten before it swept everyone away from Moscow, Peking, Washington or Berlin. As Tamás Krausz observes: "The Hungarian experience had proved that the workers' councils were able to manage the processes of production, they were able to systematically build up and begin to introduce a socialist-communal system of self-management, but the local experience under the given political conditions could not survive".[42]

Nothing scared the Bolshevik rulers of Hungary more between 1957 and 1990 than references to 1956 as a social revolution. They slandered it for 33 years as a counterrevolution. They only changed their tune when Gorbachev pulled the ladder out from under their feet. Nothing scares the current fortune-hunters in charge of Hungary more than talk of 1919 or 1956 as working class rebellions that are driven by the same spirit. It is fear and trembling that forces them to slander the working-class heroes of 1919 as "Red Terrorists". It is this fear that compelled

Viktor Orbán to move the monument honouring the memory of the man who embraced the workers' councils of '56 to a spot far away from Hungary's Parliament just before the centennial of the 1919 Revolution and to replace it with one from the Horthy era that honors the victims of the 1919 "Red Terrorists". It is this fear that forces Orbán's scribes to focus on those "Budapest Kids" (Pesti Srácok) rather than on the working men and women of Hungary, as the real heroes of 1956.

The Kádár Era: 1957–1990

The Chinese comrades were adamant in pressuring their colleagues in the Kremlin in October 1956: "You must kill the chicken to scare the monkey" that began to run free on one of the Bolsheviks' strategic properties. With Soviet tanks at his back, János Kádár, the Kremlin's newest "pinch-hitter" in Budapest, faithfully followed his masters' instructions.[43] Once the "monkey" was taken care of, Kádár pulled out the carrots given to him by Moscow.

There are many books on the Kádár era written by both domestic and foreign observers, and from divergent points of view.[44] They all talk of a kinder, gentler Bolshevik rule after Hungary's workers were put in their place. Whether it was from a personal or a broader systemic fear, the Kremlin's change of course is responsible for the emergence of a more liberal form of colonial governance in Hungary from 1962 onwards. It would have its own brand name: *"Gulyás Communism"* (GC).

This "rebranding" of one-party rule, however, did not fundamentally alter the Bolshevik affinity fraud in Hungary. To return to the analogy introduced in our preface, and leave the Maoist fairy tale behind, the aim of this new "socialist" chapter was the same as that of the previous one. It sought to return Sleeping Beauty to her slumber and get her to play "nice" with the Bolshevik patriarchy. To use Gramsci's language, it constricted somewhat the hegemony of the coercive state, decentralized some of its decision-making prerogatives to non-state actors while retaining the monopolistic use of coercion. In Poulantzas' terms, the Bolsheviks' state devoted a bit more attention to its legitimation, a bit less to its accumulation function without giving up the leading role of the party it put in place to manage its affairs. Instead of proclaiming that "whoever is not with us is against us", Kádár Bolsheviks proclaimed that "whoever is not against us is with us". As long as Sleeping Beauty put on a nice face, she would not be treated roughly.

GC reduced the "suction", the rigidity of the command economy. It allowed a greater share of the country's productive capacities to be devoted to the production and distribution of consumer goods. It permitted market forces to govern a limited subset of economic transactions especially in the countryside [45] and allowed those who wanted to make more money than the rest, to be able to do so through various after-hour entrepreneurial schemes of their own. Last but not least, it gave increased opportunities to the inhabitants of the blind alley to go "bumming for nylons and cigarettes in the American Zone"[46] as long they kept their mouths shut, and were willing to snitch on each other or on the people they met on the outside. GC added "Hungarian spices" to the Kremlin's stew in order to make it not only more palatable but more *addictive*.[47]

Bill Lomax, the Left-wing scholar who kept the keenest eye on Hungary's workers' councils in '56, is perhaps the most credible outsider to tell us what life was like inside the Soviet Empire's "happiest barrack":

> Hungary today has travelled far from the Stalinist state it was before 1956... it is no longer a totalitarian society... it is (however) still a police state of arbitrary rule...The Kádár regime presents its human face to those who please it. The opportunist, the careerist, the conformist and the coward has now learned how best to work the system, how to gain the benefits and privileges that the regime is prepared to hand down to those prepared to play the game according to its rules... But those who are not prepared to abandon their self-respect, their personal integrity and moral values, or their solidarity with their fellow men and women, those who seek to lead a life of their own making and deny the conduct of self-alienation demanded by the state, or those whom for whatever reason of its own choosing the regime decides not to smile upon, they can be denied all rights and find themselves faced with the total and arbitrary powers of the monolithic police state.[48]

Bill Lomax was the first to publicly reveal that which Ilona Duczynska preferred to keep to herself because she did not want to endanger her leverage with the counterrevolutionary leadership that ran Hungary until 1990. "Less widely known is that Ilona Duczynska, a lifelong socialist revolutionary, served as a moving inspiration and acted in many ways as a founding member of the Hungarian democratic opposition".[49] No one would describe better from the inside what it was like to be an exploited worker in a workers' state than one of Ilona Duczynska's "political grandsons" Miklós Haraszti.[50] It was Ilona's covert operation with two of her female "comrades", Júlia Rajk and Katalin Károlyi, that stopped the Hungarian Bolshevik state from incarcerating the Jerusalem born Haraszti for revealing to the world the abysmal working conditions inside the much vaunted Red Star tractor factory of Csepel, the home base of both the 1919 and the 1956 social revolutions. Haraszti was given a suspended sentence and was banned from publishing or lecturing in Hungary until the final days of the Kádár regime in 1990.[51]

The Third Movement: 1990–2010[52]

By 1990 and after all the indecent abuses they had to put up with for generations, Hungary's working men and women would no longer have the taste for yet another beating: besides, most of the files in their memory banks about 1919 and 1956 were deleted by their information managers. All they knew for certain was that this time around they would rather let their parliamentary representatives rush to the center of the political stage and deliver on their promises rather than attempt to take matters into their own hands.

There was a consensus throughout the territories of the former Soviet Empire that was constantly reinforced by the Western "shock-therapists" who descended upon them like a swarm of locust: whoever is fastest at installing the structures of universal capitalism on their territory will be the first recipient of the prosperity the "American Zone" has to offer. During this "structural transformation of the public sphere"[53], hardly anyone seemed to be aware of the fact that speed kills, that the structures of capitalism are congenitally hostile to the advances of democracy, and to the interests of the 99%. How did Hungary's newly formed political parties respond to this "new wave"?

It should not have come as a surprise to anyone, that after 40 years of Bolshevik rule, Hungary's long dormant Conservative political forces would not be interested in leading a revolution aimed at returning Hungary's working men and women to the center stage of history.

Hungary's ruling Communist Party took its cues, as always, not from the working men and women of Hungary but from its global headquarters in Moscow. Like Gorbachev, they also put on a new "business suit" and repositioned themselves by dropping their key constituents. They changed their party's name from the Hungarian Socialist Workers Party (HSWP) to the Hungarian Socialist Party (HSP). Instead of the hammer and the sickle the Party's emblem became the tulip.[54] They reinterpreted socialism as an instrument for the privatisation of public assets and gave free market forces a leading role in the transition from the blind-alley onto the global superhighway of universal capitalism. By rehabilitating a handful of their former victims, including Imre Nagy, by mastering the language of Western Liberalism or of Conservatism, by embellishing their narrative with references to the "blessings of God", "Western values", "Western civilization", "the rule of law", and "free markets", (along with providing some generous subsidies to the official Christian churches as a sign of their *good faith*), the former Bolsheviks had little to fear.[55] Many of them would quickly become multi-millionaires even before the 1990 elections, by simply helping themselves directly to the contents of the "safe" and the public assets that were up for grabs. Those that missed out during the first round of "spontaneous privatization" would be rewarded under Joseph Antall's conservative rule. Some of Antall's own family members and conservative friends didn't do so badly either.

Representation of the working classes was a mute-point for the two recently formed liberal parties—the Alliance of Free Democrats (SZDSZ) and its smaller look alike, the Alliance of Young Democrats (Fidesz). In their minds, the HSWP's *"Gulyás Communism"* made mincemeat of the proletariat. For János Kis,[56] and György Bence,[57] the recognized leaders of post-Stalinist liberalism in Hungary, the working class as such was no longer worth paying much attention to. In their view. It was not only impossible to operationalize this cohort, it could not be counted on to play a coherent role in the societal changes to come.[58] They decided to let Sleeping Beauty lie rather than waken her. (Little did they know that she was aware of their every move.)

Rather than putting my words into their mouths, I've chosen to let the leaders of Hungary's largest liberal party, the SZDSZ, lay out in a series of sound-bites their agenda for the future of post-Communist Hungary, which will explain why I consider them, along with the other political parties, key players in the post-1919 counterrevolutionary rhapsody:

Our masses, consisting of millions of poorly educated people constitute a great barrier to the growth of economic efficiency. Their members are unsuitable for efficient work and act as a brake on the needed structural transformations… Workers self-management as the dominant form of ownership is out of the question for us… While there may be some participation by local councils in the new, restructured enterprises, this is not an ideal solution because these non-profit driven organizations will always try to avoid risk… We must support only those interventions that are driven by profit considerations and oppose all those who do not make this their priority… The modern market economies have overcome their earlier tendencies to generate crises… The market has become civilized… It has become increasingly effective at protecting our natural environment... We must follow its latest directions now... We simply do not know of a third way ahead… It's unrealistic to expect our country to be able to apply the tough stance of Sweden or even our neighbour Austria against capital, or come anywhere near the application of their welfare policies… Our only hope is to privatize and expand the role of foreign capital in our economy... The establishment of market control over public expenditure is of the utmost urgency… The goal of our economic policy must be the expansion and protection of the market… Our aim is to protect and promote the free movement of capital and the establishment of those structures that provide for this and for a diversified capital market… We are aware of some of the deleterious effects of multinational corporate penetration, but we must not place any barriers against it because this may hinder our ability to catch up with the West and will leave us stranded as a third world country... All non-market interventions merely hinder the structural transformation of our economy... We are convinced that our adult population is able to look after itself if they are not hindered in their efforts by artificial state interventions.[59]

The leaders of the SZDSZ were blind even to the desires of their own rank and file members as an early internal poll would plainly reveal to those who were not blinded by their rhetoric.[60] In sharp contrast to the positions put forward in the aforementioned "Blue Book", over three quarters of the Party's rank-and-file stated in a 1991 survey that their leaders should follow a hybrid political-economic path into the future rather than follow blindly and to the letter, the "prescriptions of the West".[61] Only 12% of the party membership supported the idealized "liberal" prescription [62] and these came from the most affluent strata of its membership.[63] Even 30 years later, it is painful to be reminded of the blindness of the SZDSZ leadership to the wishes of its members, as expressed by the following sentence from the aforementioned survey: "The consistently liberal political-economic option is the least popular option for our members... It seems like it will take a long time for people to accept and adapt their minds to the negative effects market forces have upon their lives".[64]

Laying the blame for the failure of the post-Communist transition to Democracy in Hungary on the shoulders of that country's liberals alone would be as foolish as blaming the Bolsheviks alone for the collapse of the 1919 Republic of Councils. We need to briefly outline the ideological and criminal cross-currents that swept this third, post-1919 wave along its socially destructive path.

That this country of less than 9 million people would send candidates from 58 different political parties into its first democratically run national elections in 1990 [65] should have set off alarm bells immediately about the political wisdom of the "Founding Fathers" of this new democracy.[66] After the votes were tallied in 1990, three Conservative parties—the Hungarian Democratic Forum (MDF), the Independent Smallholder's Party (FKgP) and the Christian Democratic People's Party (KDNP) would form a majority coalition government, with MDF Party leader József Antall as Prime Minister. It was the job of these politically untested Conservative rookies to apply the cure-all everyone had pinned such high hopes on in Hungary after they stumbled into sunlight from the Bolsheviks' blind-alley.

It didn't take long to demonstrate not only how ill-prepared Hungary's born-again Conservatives were to navigate the uncharted waters that lay ahead but what utter disdain they had for Hungary's working men and women. Under their watch, full employment was quickly followed by double digit unemployment. Price stability was replaced by galloping inflation. A secure social safety net suddenly had giant holes in it, through which millions tumbled downwards into the unknown, and no one more deeply than Hungary's own almost one million strong visible minority, the Roma. Foreign investors poured into the country, chasing for new markets and cheaper sources of profit, and were buying up everything in sight thrown their way by the country's hapless state administration. Everyone took their cut where they could and remained utterly oblivious to the fact that privately owned corporations, and especially the foreign multinationals, do not generate profit by hiring more workers per unit of output, but by reducing their unit labour costs, by increasing productivity through the substitution of technology for labour, and by practicing transfer pricing to suck out the profits and leave only crumbs behind for the locals.[67] The dream that privatization and a market economy would improve the lot of the ordinary Hungarian citizen, quickly turned into a nightmare.

After giving the Conservative forces the first chance to improve their lives, Hungarians quickly gave two thirds of the seats in the 1994 parliamentary elections to those who governed them during the previous 40 years and brought the country to the brink. Though the Hungarian Socialist Party (the MSZP) won a super-majority in Parliament in 1994, its leader Gyula Horn, was hesitant to take sole responsibility for the drastic acts demanded by the newly triumphant neo-liberal creed.[68] The ex-Bolshevik turned to the largest liberal party, the SZDSZ, and talked them into carrying the can for his party. Desperately hungry for power and eager to implement the platform outlined in their aforementioned "Blue Book", the liberals swallowed the socialist's bait, hook line and sinker.[69]

The Socialist-Liberal coalition partnership wasted very little time. In 1995 they introduced the most restrictive austerity program ever seen by anyone in Hungary.[70] Instead of reaching for the recipe-book that produced a strong and decades long economic recovery for labour and the wage earning classes in Europe after WWII, instead of taking a page from the practices of the Scandinavians, or the Austrians, Hungary's Socialist-Liberal leaders opted to follow the advice of those who shredded Breton Woods and "liberated" capital, so it could freely perform its grossly indecent acts against wage earners world-wide as documented by Thomas Piketty,[71] or as summarized by Kari Polanyi-Levitt in the following passage:

Since the demise of the Bretton Woods financial order in 1971, capital has been progressively freed from discipline and oversight both in North America and Europe… Of all the aspects of globalization, the liberation of capital from regulatory constraint or supervision has had the most profound consequences…The objective of the neo-liberal counterrevolution was to restore the discipline of capital over labour, and the principal means of achieving it were deregulation, liberalization, privatization and explicit attacks on trade unions... Financialization assumed unimaginable proportions, the estimated value of total derivatives in 2007 was $600 trillion, according to the United Nations—964% of world GDP...Grotesque fortunes were made in this gilded age of financial prosperity. Asset inflation in real estate and the stock market gave the illusion of ever-increasing wealth encouraging ever more risky financial investment and ever more debt financed consumption while real median wages and salaries did not increase in the thirty years from 1980… Financial markets have acquired an effective veto over government policy. Markets rule. Democracy is in suspense in the heartlands of capitalism.[72]

The public rejection of the Socialist-Liberal austerity package was swift and it served as a wake-up call for the junior liberal partner of the SZDSZ—Viktor Orbán's Fidesz. While the latter retained its membership in the Liberal International after the introduction of the "Bokros Package", Orbán began to concoct a new "right-wing bait" to distance himself from the "left-liberal party-poopers".[73] The electorate took the bait in 1998 and gave the young Liberals and two right-wing conservative parties—the Independent Smallholders and a remnant of the MDF—the right to form a coalition government that year. By 2002 they too were sent packing.[74]

In 2002, Hungarian voters passed the ball back to the Socialist-Liberal coalition in the hope that they may have learned something from their earlier mistakes. It quickly became clear that they did not. They merely deepened the country's indebtedness and diminished her ability to brace herself against the approaching hurricane—the global financial crisis of 2007–8. After 2002, and with increasing fury, party-politics in Hungary rapidly degenerated into a corrupt slugfest. The world of business and politics became co-dependent, and created a new system which Hungarian political scientist, András Bozóki would classify as a "partocracy".[75] The defining attribute of this system is that it burns up everything that's needed for the survival of justice, equality for all under the law, or for an ecologically sustainable path to development.

Buoyed on the one hand by the hopes that Hungary's entry into the EU in 2004 would bring about an upturn in the debt-financed Hungarian economy, and on the other, by the emergence of a confident, articulate new Socialist leader—Ferenc Gyurcsány—the Socialist-Liberal alliance narrowly defeated Fidesz for an unheard of second governing term in the spring 2006 national elections. During the summer and prior to the fall 2006 session of Parliament, Gyurcsány called for a closed-door retreat with his newly elected parliamentary deputies, to outline his upcoming legislative agenda. In a passionate and brutally honest confrontation with some of the colleagues he inherited from the Kádár era and from his predecessors (Horn and Medgyessy), Gyurcsány declared that, he is done with lying to the public on their behalf, and solely for the sake of returning them to office so they can carry on as before. If they want him to carry their bucket, they should find a new water-boy. He sealed his own fate by announcing that he wanted to bring an end to Hungary's 100 year-long counterrevolutionary rhapsody.[76] Given Bozóki's earlier assessment, the end-game was predictable.

Some of Gyurcsány's disgruntled colleagues leaked the confidential text of the newly elected PM's speech to his nemesis, Viktor Orbán. The latter kept quiet about it while he laid his plans for the orchestration of a "national outrage" in the fall before the opening of Parliament. Once all the pieces were in place for bringing down the newly elected government, Orbán released selective and out of context parts of Gyurcsány's secret speech to the public—especially the one in which the PM talks of lying night and day to the "god-forsaken public" in order to mislead it and to re-elect his hapless colleagues. Orbán called for a boycott of Parliament, issued an ultimatum to the government to resign, and sent his troops out into the streets. They declared war on mainstream media, invaded the headquarters of the National Broadcaster by overwhelming a small police contingent sent out to defend it, ransacked its offices and nearly burnt the building down to the ground. Riots, bloody street-battles between the police and angry mobs became a weekly occurrence in the Hungarian capital. Parliament had to be barricaded as leaders of the protests promised to hang Jews, liberals, and socialists from the lamp-posts. The city was literally turned upside down on October 23, 2006, the 50th anniversary of the 1956 revolution. Police violence followed suit as it always does under such circumstances.[77] After the failure of the October riots to dislodge the legally elected government, Orbán opted to pursue a protracted trench warfare against the government that increasingly paralyzed Hungary's decision-making arena and at a time when the country could least afford it.

At the end of 2006, when Hungary's democracy was at its pivotal point, I sent an opinion piece from my outpost in Budapest to the *Los Angeles Times* which contained, among others, the following prognostication:

> The odds of survival for Hungary's hard-won constitutional democracy are only about 50–50. These will quickly turn for the worse if the European Parliament's conservative political establishment continues to lend public support to Hungary's rogue democrat, Viktor Orbán… The endorsement of Orbán's political strategy by Wilfried Martens, leader of the European People's Party, has given considerable encouragement to Orbán's reckless

followers. This was a grave mistake... If the ghost of Hungary's anti-democratic past is allowed to rise again, the democracy of not just Hungary, but all of Europe, will be in peril.[78]

On hindsight, I overestimated the survival chances of Hungary's fragile, post-Communist democracy.

The Finalé: 2010–?

In April 2010, and after two decades of fruitless waiting for a social-liberal Godot, Hungary's working men and women finally succumbed to "the structures of magic", the affinity-fraud concocted by Orbán and his American spin-doctors. This is how Orbán summarized the score for his finalé:

> In my head, what one should do is make a deal with the country's top 8–10 businessmen... no need for more than that. One should develop good personal contacts with these men, bring them into the Prime Minister's tent by enhancing their competitive market advantages... This is what we must do now. After we have achieved this, the business community will take care of the rest.[79]

Our aim with this finalé, as with the earlier movements of Hungary's 100 year-long counterrevolutionary rhapsody is to highlight its connection to the focus of this book: Hungary's long-forgotten social revolution of 1919 and the heroic efforts of Hungary's working men and women to move to the center stage of their country's political arena. This section does not intend to reveal the full score and will concentrate only on those measures that purposefully restrict Hungary's working men and women from the path of justice, equality before the law, and their right to construct a habitat for themselves that is ecologically sustainable. These measures will show that like his role model, Nicholas Horthy in 1919, Orbán also took Hungary's working men and women out of the fast lane when he came to power in 2010. Instead of putting them first, he put them last. Instead of enhancing their competitive edge in the "new digital economy", [80] instead of making them smarter than the rest, instead of preparing them to survive and thrive in the age of artificial intelligence, instead of using Europe's massive subsidies for the construction of ecologically sustainable communities for his subjects,[81] Orbán has robbed Hungary's working men and women of their birthright in order to fatten himself and his oligarchs. Instead of pushing Hungary's working men and women towards the center of that country's political stage, he pushed them to the periphery with an elaborately constructed disinformation campaign that leaves them voiceless and defenseless as pacified sources of cheap labour for the fortune hunters of universal capitalism.[82] Here is his public record.

Worsening Living Conditions for Labour

\The EU's 2020 country report on Hungary, based on official and empirically verifiable data, does not mince words: "The proportion of the population experiencing difficult living conditions in Hungary is among the highest in the EU". [83] According to the figures provided by the European Union's statistical office, *Eurostat*, Actual Individual Consumption[84] in Hungary under Orbán has fallen second to last place in the EU.[85] The conclusions of the economist Annamária Artner are empirically verifiable: "Hungarian employees belong to those who work the most in the European Union and their relative position has worsened in the last decade".[86]

Low Wages and high taxes

The OECD's figures show, that although average wages in Hungary increased substantially in 2017 because of labour shortages caused by the flight of close to a million workers to parts of the world where they are better treated, average wage levels of Hungary's workers were still 2nd from the bottom among OECD members.[87] As far as taxes on those wages, the Orbán government's bite was the second biggest among members of the EU at the end of 2015.[88] By now, that lean on the wages of working men and women has become the heaviest in Europe, while the lean on corporate profits is the lightest on the continent.

Orbán's disinformation specialists also hide from the public's view the fact that this regime takes the biggest bite in Europe out of those workers' pay-checks who are on minimum wages.[89] Consumption tax, or VAT levels in Hungary are higher than anywhere else on the planet. These exacerbate the hardship on the country's underpaid, over-taxed workers. According to OECD and EU figures, direct and indirect taxes take a bigger bite out of the incomes of Hungarian workers than anywhere in Europe, and this is especially true in the case of those who are at the lowest end of the income scale.

To add insult to injury, *Eurostat* figures show that Hungarian workers faced the sharpest increases in their health care costs in all of Europe along with the sharpest increases in the cost of public utilities during the past decade (the price of public housing, water, electricity, gas, and other fuels).[90]

Exploitation of the Working Poor

According to *Eurostat's* latest comparative figures on this subject,[91] Hungary registered the steepest rise in the number of its working poor in all of Europe under Viktor Orbán's leadership between 2010 and 2017.

Curtailment of Workers' Rights

Evidence for the drastic curtailment of workers' rights in Hungary has steadily mounted under Orbán's rule. A series of legislative acts, the so-called "Slave Laws" have prompted massive public demonstrations in Hungary in 2018–19, because they favour the fortune hunters at the expense of those who can least afford it. The vulnerability of those that matter is clearly revealed by János Kolló, research director of the Institute of Economics at the Hungarian Academy of Sciences: "There are hundreds of thousands of workers in our country who are not in a position to say no".[92] Instead of quoting foreign sources, or academics, perhaps it's best to turn this time to the leaders of Hungary's labour movement. László Kordás, the President of the Hungarian Trade Union Confederation (MASZSZ) summed up Orbán's measures in the following manner: "In Hungary, we carry the largest burden on our back and, in return, we get the lowest wage in Europe".[93] The spokesperson for the Association took a broader, historical view: "The government is busy eliminating all of the rights Hungary's workers have achieved during the past 200 years".[94]

Arrested social mobility, income inequality

Poverty figures have become more difficult to deal with in Hungary after the Orbán government halted their publication for a while because they were so alarming. It finally changed the poverty index, so it would provide a better view.[95] According to the OECD, social mobility under the Orbán government has become the worst among its members.[96] The data on Hungary's performance on income inequality doesn't lie. As expressed by the Gini-index "Only Bulgaria has shown a larger increase in income inequality in all of Europe".[97]

The assault on the elderly

The neglect and disdain shown towards the elderly by the Orbán regime is even more disgusting than its treatment of the working poor because of the utter helplessness of the victims.[98] The OECD's findings and a study by a group of researchers under John Rowe at Columbia University have demonstrated that Hungary had the worst record on elderly care among the (then) 28 member states of the European Union. Under Orbán, Hungary has become the least prepared EU member to deal with the challenges stemming from the increasing share of elderly in the country's demographic mix.[99]

The neglect of public healthcare

The neglect of the physical and mental well-being of the country's less fortunate citizens is as true of the Orbán regime as it was of its role model, the post-1919 administration of Admiral Nicholas Horthy. Hungary under Orbán is the only country in Europe where public expenditures on public health-care as a share of the GDP *decreases* rather than increases over time.[100] The kleptocracy spends more on propaganda than on preserving the health of its hard-working citizens.[101]

The assault on public education

Non-partisan and empirically verifiable studies also document the growing gap between Hungary and the rest of Europe in the provision of quality public education for ordinary citizens and identify Hungary's broken public education system as the principal cause of its inability to live without hand-outs from Europe's hard-pressed taxpayers.[102] The Orbán government's answer to this crisis is to distract the working classes' attention and turn its anger onto artificially concocted scapegoats, discredit those who speak truth to power, and to accelerate the welfare of its corporate cronies by giving them Hungary's public educational institutions to play with. The give-away of Hungary's public education system to private corporations not only diminishes the access to quality education by the children of Hungary's underpaid workers, but submerges the pursuit of critical knowledge to corporate interests. Under the Orbán government's destructive public education policies Hungary has now the lowest share of its population in all of Europe who are pursuing a higher degree (a college or university diploma).[103] Under Orbán's rule, Hungary became the country that has the fewest number of its citizens being able to speak a second language in all of Europe.[104] As one observer noted:

> What's happening with the education of our young people has no parallel in Europe… our government's practices are in total opposition to the European trends and this appears to be accelerating rather than slowing down. In the countries next door to us, countries who are our competitors, the ratio of highly qualified young graduates has not diminished but surpassed the European average… In our case, and parallel with this deplorable trend, it has become even harder for young people from the less developed, poorer parts of the country to have access to a higher degree.[105]

The Orbán regime uses the EU's Money to Increase its Assault on working men and women during the Covid Pandemic

The systematic exploitation of working men and women, and of their children along with the elderly did not diminish but increase as the Covid-19 pandemic hit the country's shores in 2020. After an analysis of the Orbán government's Covid 'rescue package' one of Hungary's leading research economists, Mária-Zita Petschnig concluded that "The government is out to rescue itself and its friends rather than the ordinary citizens of Hungary … In order to preserve its power, it decided to gamble away the lives of those millions who are least able to resist, those who have been most severely affected by this pandemic".[106]

Overall Economic Performance

According to Orbán's tightly controlled media, and his government's "communicators", Hungary's working men and women have never had it as good as they do now. We're told that Hungary had become a "Little Tiger" under Orbán's grooming, that she is now the envy of everyone in Europe. This lie is about as close to reality as Donald Trump's claim that he ended the Covid-19 pandemic during the summer of 2020 and scored an overwhelming victory in the 2020 Presidential elections in November that year. As a former advisor of Orbán and one of Hungary's most respected conservative economist, László Csaba, argues: "It is empirically verifiable, that along virtually the entire axis of key economic indicators, we have fallen behind our competitors in Europe under Orbán's rule. We are not only not getting ahead in the rankings, but falling further behind".[107] The country's best non-partisan economists agree—without massive subsidies from Brussels, totalling more than 90% of the country's annual public investments on economic development, the country would be bankrupt.[108]

The Flight of Labour from Hungary

The flight of hundreds of thousands of able-bodied working men and women from Hungary is not a new phenomenon. The magnitude of the exodus since Orbán came to power is, however, unprecedented and is the consequence of the brutality that we have outlined above. Close to one-million workers—roughly 15% of the able-bodied 21–50-year-old cohort—left Hungary since the start of Orbán's *finalé*.[109] This is the largest per capita exodus of workers among any European nation, and is the biggest exodus of able-bodied workers from Hungary during the past 100 years.[110]

The Promotion of Racial Hatred and the Demonization of Refugees

The harsh measures taken against non-white, non-Christian minorities, immigrants and refugee claimants in Hungary under Orbán are well known throughout the world. What is largely unknown is that these measures are the consciously chosen supporting beams of the anti-labour legislation we have listed above. The two policy clusters are Siamese twins. Not only are they virtually inseparable from each other, they are virtually inseparable from the public anger-management formula of the man who put an end to the workers', peasants' and soldiers' councils that were the heart and soul of the 1919 Hungarian Republic of Councils. Then as now, hate mongering is the consciously chosen instrument for shifting the attention of the betrayed, brutalized working people of Hungary from the real source of their pain and anger onto ones that are totally artificial.[111]

Rather than dousing the flames of prejudice and protecting those who are the targets of various forms of hatred in Hungary, Orbán's entire political strategy has been built upon using those forces to his political advantage and in order to cover his exploitation of Hungary's working men and women. In 2011 the European Council's Advisory Committee on the Framework Convention for the Protection of National Minorities (FCNM) reported that "there is an alarming increase in violence towards the Roma minority, who have been victims of displays of intolerance insults and racist acts".[112] Amnesty International and the European Roma Rights Centre also added their voices criticizing the Hungarian authorities for their "lack of procedures for investigating racially motivated crimes".[113] The Council of Europe's February 2012 report gave a damning assessment of the widespread use of "anti-Roma hate speech by public figures and the lack of any strong official condemnation of such speech in Hungary".[114] Numerous reputable studies, including those by the Anti-Defamation League in 2012[115] or the Simon Wiesenthal Institute,[116] show that it was under the Orbán regime that anti-Jewish hatred accelerated most rapidly in all of Europe. All of these reports showed that Hungary under Viktor Orbán moved to the top in Europe in the public manifestation of racist prejudices and the country's two most prominent ethnic minorities, the Jews and the Roma, bore the brunt of the pain emanating from this escalation in racial prejudice and violence.[117]

The demonization of Muslim refugees in Hungary emerges hand in hand with the worsening socio-economic conditions of Hungary's labouring classes after Orbán begins his second term in office in 2014–2015 and is carried aloft by the sudden increase in the number of people fleeing towards Europe from the wars, the hunger and the ravages of climate change in the Middle East and Africa. This is how Hungary's Civil Liberties Union (TASZ) and a dozen other civil-organizations assess their EU funded government's response to this global crisis: "Instead of informing people, the government seeks to eliminate the possibility of free citizens making rational, fact-based decisions… It is inciting hatred against refugees that will further weaken the already shattered social solidarity in our country, which is incompatible with the concept of human rights".[118]

Two of Hungary's young social scientists, Ákos Huszár and Viktor Berger reached a similar conclusion in 2020 after a thorough analysis of all the available data: "In order to further its political ambitions, this regime uses a variety of policy tools for fomenting fear and transforming that fear into hatred against various publicly created enemies (the homeless, the unemployed, drug addicts, the poor, various ethnic, religious or racial minorities, migrants, etc)… By 2016 Hungary registers the highest levels of hatred against immigrants in all of Europe (64%), our nearest competitor, Russia comes in at 40%… It is clearly visible from the data that while the hatred of immigrants has become the majority view of the middle and upper middle classes in Hungary, it peaks within the ranks of the unskilled and skilled labouring classes... This fully conscious and purposeful policy approach has had a devastating effect on social solidarity in Hungary".[119]

Global Capitalism's Response to Orbán's Finalé

Orbán's anti-labour stance is as warmly endorsed by Wall Street today as the one pursued by Nicholas Horthy after he told Hungary's workers where to get off in 1919. We have spoken of the American "brains" behind Orbán's 2010 "home run" and of his embrace of the American designed political language of cyber-capitalism. Trump and his top political strategists were highly appreciative of Orbán's assistance during the real-estate mogul's race to the White House in 2016.[120] The first trip abroad by the operative head of the Trump Campaign's National Security and Foreign Affairs Committee, J.D. Gordon, was to Budapest even before Trump was sworn in as President. He openly declared in the Hungarian capital that the President Elect will become Orbán's best friend in the West.[121] The rest is history.

Germany's *"Ostpolitik"* in 2020 is as supportive of the current Hungarian autocrat as Trump's or as Hitler's or Mussolini 's were of Nicholas Horthy after the latter put Hungary's working men and women at work in the service of Fascism's military industrial complex. The German Chancellor is Orbán's ace in the hole within the EU. Here is what she thinks of his performance: "The Orbán government is doing an excellent job with the European Union's cohesion and structural funds... Our two countries are on a common path together. Our economies have become tightly interlinked". [122] It is Orbán's willingness to allow Germany's fortune hunters get a 'good bang for their buck' in Hungary that makes Angela look the other way. It is Orbán's embrace of universal capitalism's pleasure principle that enables him to bond with not only Angela or Donald but to reach across the aisles and gain endorsement for his rape of Hungary's "Sleeping Beauty" by the fortune hunters of Russia, China, Turkey, Saudi Arabia, Israel, Brazil, and elsewhere.

After numerous futile attempts over the past decade, first in 2012[123] then in 2015,[124] the European Parliament issued its first "stern warning" to the Orbán government in May 2017.[125] It raised the ante significantly on September 12, 2018. On that day, it passed a new motion (448 votes in favour, 197 against and 48 abstentions) that triggered Article 7(1) of the European Treaty by alleging that the Hungarian government had breached the terms of its treaty obligations by curbing, among others, fair electoral practices, freedom of expression, freedom of the press, attacking civil organizations, undermining judicial independence, engaging in corrupt practices, and limiting the rights of minorities and migrants.[126] This was an unprecedented step taken by the EU Parliament against a member state since the founding of this organization. The motion also made it clear that if the warning is not heeded, the EU could reach for Article 7(2) that calls for the imposition of sanctions and the suspension of Hungary's voting rights in the EU. What has the EU done since 2018 to uphold its own rules, and the trust placed in its institutions by those who look towards it as their last line of defense against those who abuse them? Nothing of substance.

The last time the Hungarian state pulled the wool over the eyes of her working classes via a government coordinated hate campaign against immigrants and minorities she was an ally of Nazi Germany. Today, paradoxically, she can get away with it as a member of an international organization—the European Union—that is expressly mandated to protect Europe's citizens from such gross abuses.

We conclude this review of Viktor Orbán's finalé with two of the clearest "overhead" shots of the wasteland it produced.[127] The first was taken by a former member of the Hungarian Academy of Sciences, a philosopher of religion, György Gábor, an early target of the Orbán regime's decade long war on those who dare to speak truth to power:

> What is the worst, most destructive impact of this last performance? It's not the theft of just about everything they could lay their hands on. We've seen that before. With time everything is replaceable... It's not the sellout of the country to foreign interests, or the *carte blanche* given to the secret services of Russia. We've come back from such betrayals... The greatest, most harmful impact of this last performance is on the minds of our citizens. That cannot be repaired easily, its impact is *longue durée*... The scar will require generations to heal... The new *numerus clausus no* longer targets the Jews alone but anyone and everyone who thinks... It has left us saddled with collaborators, enablers for whom everything is for sale, even our souls are treated as commodities.[128]

The second "overhead" is by another multidisciplinary scholar, the political ecologist András Lányi and was taken shortly before this book went to print.

> We are now in the most dangerous period of our modern history. Our Prime Minister does not understand the challenges of the twenty-first century, he has nothing to say about them. He is fighting the battles of the 20th century to this day. He wants to resurrect the same public spirit of hatred, the same political culture that characterized official Hungary in the Horthy era. Everything he touches is a reflection of the injustices of the

past—from the design of our public squares to the design of the national curriculum. All of it rests on the kind of smug self-delusion, hate filled and misleading rhetoric that we know from a different era and which some of our more charitable contemporaries register as an inevitable consequence of the trauma of 1919 and Trianon. There is no mistaking it: the smell of civil war is in the air today.[129]

Epilogue

What can be learned from that long-forgotten revolution of 1919 and the counterrevolutionary rhapsody that followed it in order to prevent a destructive, violent civil war from becoming the only alternative for those who feel hopelessly exploited, violated, angry, and betrayed by governments that promise but never deliver them justice, equal rights under the law and an ecologically sustainable communal well-being? What are the lessons of the 1919 Republic of Councils that may not only help us to avoid some of its mistakes today but help working men and women all over the world to follow the path of righteousness towards an ecologically sustainable future for themselves, and for their neighbours?

The first lesson from the 1919 Hungarian Republic of Councils and of the counterrevolutionary rhapsody that followed it is that historical changes in one country cannot be divorced from their global context. We began this book by showing that the movement of working men and women towards the central stage of history from the 19th century onwards is a global phenomenon fueled by a fire that cannot be permanently extinguished because its supply of oxygen has always been guaranteed by the fire fighters who are sent out to extinguish them. It's not the theoreticians of socialism but the practitioners of universal capitalism that cause these fiery eruptions. The 1919 Hungarian Republic of Councils was not a failure of socialism but of capitalism. This wisdom is the departure point for any resolution of the recurring crises in Hungary and in other parts of universal capitalism's vast holdings. It is also the departure point from the portrait of that post-modern *aporia* by Baudrillard that I placed rather strategically next to the opening of Hungary's 100 year-long counterrevolutionary rhapsody. We can, in fact draw some consequences from the post-Communist "events" of Eastern Europe that have left "a strange aftertaste of something that has already happened before, something unfolding retrospectively".

The past century saw electoral as well as violent attempts by Hungary's common people to reclaim the central stage of their political arena only to see the hoped-for changes evaporate before their eyes like a mirage. The globalization of cyber capitalism, the universalization of its deceptive political language, the arrival of artificial intelligence, the emergence of new techniques for the manipulation of information as instruments of domination by the 1% are compounding the difficulties of the 99% everywhere. Overturning this domination is becoming increasingly difficult not only via the ballot box, but through any kind of revolutionary change—violent or peaceful. Decades of investments by the fortune hunters of the world into "Manufacturing of Consent",[130] into new, post-Machiavellian techniques for destroying the ordinary citizen's abilities to distinguish fact from fiction, illusion from reality, right from wrong is making it not only increasingly difficult for the oppressed to rise but to stay on the path of righteousness once they succeed in breaking the chains that bind them. Polanyi's warnings about the rise of fascist power-plants throughout the world with the help of hundreds of millions of ill-informed but enthusiastic working men and women looms large on the global horizon again. Looking at the faces of the working men and women who laid siege to the US Capitol on January 6, 2021 at the behest of a fraudulent fortune hunter, who gave America's 1% its biggest tax break at the expense of those who could least afford it brings us face to face with this reality.

Notwithstanding the odds that work against them, workable breakout strategies are within the sight of humanity even on the eve of its destruction. There is universal agreement by now about the meaning of justice, constitutionalism, the rule of law, and the parameters of ecological sustainability. All we're missing now is the commitment to "walk the talk".

The new communications technologies that have given a communicative edge to the 1% throughout the world, and nowhere more so than China, and have accelerated their ability to pull the wool over the eyes of the vulnerable "masses" are also available to the 99% at virtually no cost today. The ill-informed, the oppressed can recover their eyesight with the aid of the very technology that blinded them.[131]

The 1%'s initial edge can be overcome through appropriately organized local, national and international coalitions committed to *communicative action* on behalf of the 99%.[132] Those actions should not be undertaken or evaluated according to their conformity to various ideological labels from the past that divide even their followers and are utterly meaningless to a family living on welfare (e.g.: labels such as socialism, liberalism, conservatism, etc.), but on the basis of their ability to restore the sight of those that matter at local, national and international levels. A new, commonly shared universal language that responds to and resonates with the spontaneous, indestructible spirit and desire of 'the common people' for social justice, equality under the law, and ecologically sustainable communal life is the only force that can put an end to the false, destructive, and infectious counterrevolutionary rhapsody we have described above.

At its most luminous, brightest moment, the 1919 social revolution in Hungary came as close to a national consensus and as far from being a *coup* as one could imagine. There was no fighting in the streets when the news broke out that Hungary's workers', peasants' and soldiers' councils had moved to the center of their country's political arena. The number of the casualties of this social tsunami during its first three weeks were less than the number of lives lost in road accidents on average weekend. Nothing captures more clearly the tenor of this heroic 1919 revolution than the fact that the person who lit its fuse was not an illiterate or violent man with a bent back and hardened hands, but a five-feet tall, 20 year old Hungarian "gentry-girl", an engineering student and her fellows, who linked arms with the country's coal miners, factory workers, landless agricultural labourers and pledged to fight for the rights of working men and women to live at peace with their neighbors, and for their right to play a central role in deciding who gets what, when and how in their local, regional and national communities. What made Hungary's 1919 social revolution so unusual and so frightening to the powerful was its spontaneity, its embrace of altruism, its rejection of the virtues of selfishness, it's willingness to sacrifice all for one.

The days are long gone, when intellectuals, university students, poets, artists and office workers marched arm in arm with factory workers, agricultural labourers and the poor, to reclaim the center stage of their country's polity from their exploiters: the fortune-hunters, the 1%, the self-appointed Bolshevik vanguards, the affinity-fraud practitioners who rely on the State to destroy humanity's ability to distinguish illusion from reality. Salvation for the wilfully misinformed, exploited and abused workers of the world may no longer require the use of the same instruments of self-governance and liberation as the ones used a century earlier in Budapest. It will, require, however, that we embrace that spirit which put aside class, religious, ethnic, and gender differences, moved time and time again, from the periphery to the center, from the bottom to the top, to free that "sleeping beauty" within us that refuses to die, to submit - either to the "unconscious masochism" implanted in our minds or to the one that openly abuses and degrades us when we are gagged and our hands are tied behind our backs. The score for the termination of Hungary's 100-year counterrevolutionary rhapsody has been written. It's only the performance that's awaiting.

NOTES

1   The theory of "secret attachments" originates with Edmund Bergler (1989–1962), an Austrian colleague of Sigmund Freud, who fled to the Unites States in 1937 to escape the clutches of Austro-Fascism. Bergler's theory, based on decades of clinical analysis provides a cogent explanation for much of humanity's self-destructive behavior and differs from the one offered by that flamboyant Slovenian thinker, Slavoj Zizek (1949—), who as we know, is not secretly, but openly attached to another Freudian, Jacques Lacan (1901–1981). See: Slavoj Zizek, *Less than Nothing: Hegel and the Shadow of Dialectical Materialism* (London: Verso, 2012). and his *Living in the End Times* (London: Verso, 2010). For the concept of "the universality of unconscious masochism" see: Edmund Bergler, *Principles of Self-Damage* (New York, The Philosophical Library, 1958). For my own brief, Berglerian analysis of this type of behavior, as manifested by a founder and leading

publicist of Hungary's ruling political party (the Fidesz), please see, András B. Göllner, "Bayer: A polgári fájdalomcsillapító" (Bayer: Hungary's Christian-Nationalist Pain-Killer) Budapest, *Magyar Hírlap*, (October 5, 2002).

2   István Bibó (1911–1979) was the leading Hungarian political theorist of the 20th century who recognized the role social-psychological factors play in history. After 1948, at the age of 37, he was "mothballed" by Hungary's Bolsheviks, only to emerge out of nowhere as Minister of State in the revolutionary government of Imre Nagy in 1956. Unlike the rest of his colleagues, Bibó did not flee for his life when the Soviet troops invaded Budapest on November 4, 1956, but stayed in his Parliamentary office, composing, among others, his unforgettable proclamation "For Freedom and Truth", and waited to be arrested. A surprised officer of the Soviet military detachment found him at his desk as they swept through the Parliament building. The prosecutor asked for the death-sentence, but Bibó was only given life imprisonment for defending freedom and truth with his pen. He was eventually released from prison with hundreds of other political prisoners after the 1963 amnesties. He was banned forever from teaching and publishing any of his writings. He died more or less in obscurity in 1979 after retiring from his low-level job in the library of Hungary's Central Statistical Office.

3   As far as I know (meaning, I could be wrong), mine is the first English translation of a part of this 1948 essay by Bibó: *"Eltorzult Magyar alkat, zsákutcás Magyar történelem"* (Hungary's Distorted Character, the Blind Alleys of her Past), in István Bibó. *Válogatott tanulmányok* (Selected Essays) (Budapest: Corvina, 2004), 123–151.

4   While the Soviet tanks rolled into Budapest and surrounded his office in November 1956, Bibó drafted another memorandum that became the central agenda item at the founding Congress of the Workers' Council of Greater Budapest on November 16, 1956. In a follow up, he made his position even clearer: *"In Hungary, the revolutionary forces were and are united in favor of the cause of socialism, as well as their ability to defend the achievements of socialism and maintain the internal order of the country against all attempts at the restoration of capitalism".* (István Bibó. Declaration of December 8, 1956) This single sentence provides the best argument for why the Generals of Universal Capitalism in Washington did not rush in to rescue the Hungarian Revolution from "The Evil Empire" of Socialism. The CIA knew better than anyone, what was going on in Hungary in 1956. The leaders of NATO knew fully well, this was not a heroic struggle to restore free markets and capitalism. What saved Bibó's life was an utterly fateful decision on his part. On his way home from his parliamentary office, he dropped off a copy of his memo with India's high-profile Ambassador to Hungary, Krishna Menon, a trusted comrade of Nehru, the Indian PM. Nehru was a key element of the Kremlin's strategic affinity fraud towards the non-aligned nations of the world. Nehru's intervention with Khrushchev did the trick. For details about India's involvement in the '56 uprising see: Surjit Mansingh, "India and the Hungarian Revolution," *India Quarterly* 21, no 2, (1965), 138–155.

5   The leader of this dismissal was Gáspár, Miklós Tamás a founding member of the Hungarian liberal party, the SZDSZ, and a member of the first freely elected Parliament between 1990–1994 (See: "Búcsú a baloldaltól"(Farewell to the Left). *Kritika*. (December, 1989). This once "liberal-neo-conservative" thinker has become by now one of the leading voices of the Hungarian Left.

6   István Bibó. "A Magyar demokrácia válsága" (The Crisis of Hungarian Democracy). *Valóság*. October-December 1945.

7   Tyrus Miller. "The Phantom of Liberty: György Lukács and the Culture of 'People's Democracy' in György Lukács. *The Culture of People's Democracy: Hungarian Essays on Literature, Art and Democratic Transition, 1945–1948*. (Edited and translated by Tyrus Miller) (New York: BRILL. 2013), xxi

8   It was not Horthy's Army, but the French backed Romanian army that forced Kun and his comrades to run for their lives. The Romanian army was particularly ruthless in looting the capital and the surrounding countryside of its last morsels of food, fuel, and movable items.

9   Horthy's National Army was put together with the help of the French, who played an instrumental role not only in the dismemberment of Hungary but in the rape of Indochina, North Africa, and parts of the Middle East during the 20th century. Tens of millions of Kurds, to say nothing of the Palestinians, have them and the British to thank for not having a homeland after the break-up of the Ottoman Empire in 1917.

10   For an early report on the gruesomeness of the "White Terror" instituted under Horthy's administration please consult Oscar Jászi, *The Revolution and Counterrevolution in Hungary*.

Op.cit., 153–177. The most recent scholarly account in English is by Béla Bodó. *The White Terror: Anti-Semitic and Political Violence in Hungary, 1919–1921* (London: Routledge, 2019).

11   On the falsification of the historical record, please turn to our discussion of "Red Terror" in Chapter 5. One of the leading, anti-Semitic members of this historical chorus today is Ernő Raffay, who runs a small, government funded cottage industry built on lies, conspiracy theories and hatred of Jews inside Hungary and within the global Hungarian diaspora. Raffay received one of the highest state awards from the Orbán government in 2020 (please note the date) for his falsification of the events surrounding the 1919 Republic of Councils and for his depiction of "the Jew" as congenitaly hostile towards Hungary's Christian national identity.

12   For example, Jakab Weltner. *Forradalom, bolsevizmus, emigráció* (Revolution, Bolshevism, Emigration) (Budapest: Weltner, 1929).

13   Tamás Krausz. "The Hungarian Workers' Councils of 1956". *Workers Liberty*, (October 31, 2006).

14   L. D. Schweng. *Political, Social and Economic Developments in Postwar Hungary* (manuscript), National Planning Association, (Washington, D.C., 1950), 7 8.

15   See Ivan T. Berend and György Ránki. *Economic Development in East-Central Europe in the 19th and 20th Centuries* (New York: Columbia University Press, 1973).

16   See Imre Kovacs, *A néma forradalom* [The Silent Revolution] (Budapest:1938). Or Mátyás Matolcsy, *Mezőgazdasági munkanelküliség Magyarországon* [Agricultural Unemployment in Hungary] (Budapest: 1933). The classic sociography of the Hungarian peasantry's brutalization under the Horthy regime's counterrevolution is by Gyula Illyés, *Puszták népe* (People of the Plains) (Budapest: 1936). For the English translation see: *People of the Puszta*, Translation and afterword by G.F. Cushing, (London: Chatto and Windus 1967).

17   For a comparison of the 1938 Munich agreement and Donald Trump's "done deal" with the North Korean leader in Singapore 80 years later; see András B. Göllner, "The Spectre of Munich 1938 Hangs Over Singapore," *Social Europe*, (June 18, 2018).

18   For a first-hand account of this mass murder please see, Zvi Zelikovits. *The First to the Slaughter, at Orania Ukraine. 26, August, 1941.* (Translated from the Hebrew, by Marc Zell. Rana'na. Docostory. 2005.) I am grateful to my friend, the filmmaker András Szirtes for sending me his father's account of his fruitless efforts to unmask the cover up that exists in official circles in Hungary to this day about this mass-murder. See: Zoltán Szirtes ed., *Temetetlen Halottaink: 1941 Kőrösmező. Kamenyec-Podolszk* (Our Unburied Dead) (Budapest, Kopint-Datorg, 1996). The definitive work on Hungary's role in the Holocaust is: Randolph L. Braham. *A népírtás politikája: A holokauszt Magyarországon* (The Policy of Genocide: The Holocaust in Hungary), I & II. 3rd ed., (Budapest: Park Kiadó, 2015). Braham discusses the Kamanets-Podolski massacre in Vol I of his work on pp. 231–240 as well as in person with me in New York two years before his passing.

19   For two recent in-depth analyses of this horrific military campaign see Péter Szabó. *Don-kanyar* (At the River Don). Budapest. Zrínyi Kiadó, 1994 and Tamás Krausz, Éva Varga eds. *A magyar megszálló csapatok a Szovjetunióban. Levéltári dokumentumok 1941–1947* (The Hungarian Occupation Forces in the Soviet Union. Archival Documents 1941–1947) Budapest. L'Harmattan. 2013)

20   One of these was Antal Szerb (1901–1945), a great literary scholar, the author of one of the greatest works of 20th century European literature—*Journey by Moonlight* (First published in Hungarian in 1937). For an English version see New York. New York Review of Books Publishers. 2014). Szerb was beaten to death with a shovel, his body dumped into a ditch by the side of the road after he became too weak to pull his weight. The gentle poet, Miklós Radnóti (1909–1944) was shot under similar circumstances and left by the roadside. For a comprehensive collection of his works in Hungarian and English see: Miklós Radnóti, *The Complete Poetry in Hungarian and English* (Jefferson, NC: McFarland & Company, 2014). Also: *Death Blows Overhead: The Last Transports from Hungary, November, 1944.* European Holocaust Research Infrastructure (EHRI).

21   For a discussion see: <http://www.nytimes.com/2014/10/27/us/in-cold-war-us-spy-agencies-used-1000-nazis.html?emc=eta1&_r=0>.

22   One of the highest-ranking members of these former pro-Nazi officers is Vitéz Gyula Detre, the man who was personal bodyguard and head of military security for Hungary's Führer. The latter was executed as a war criminal at the end of WWII. Detre managed to flee Germany and slip into Canada by hiding his true identity. Posing as one of Canada's fiercest anti-Communist warriors, the RCMP recruited him as a stool pigeon at the height of the Cold War to keep tabs on

"Commies" in Montréal's sizeable Hungarian community. Detre ran the Montréal Hungarian Community for half a century the way Mayor Richard J. Daley ran Chicago for the Democrats. I recall my mother's fears of this man when I was a child growing up in Montréal, and her admonishments to my father to keep his mouth shut about politics when he goes to church, where Detre was God. This bodyguard to Hungary's Nazi butcher, just missed getting the Order of Canada by a whisker. Detre, lived to be 103 and passed in 2021. He is the highest decorated lieutenants of the autocratic Orbán regime in Canada today. He lived just down the street from me. I knew him well. The English version of his autobiography is publicly available on the internet: <http://www.magtudin.org/Detre_Gyula_History_First_Hand.pdf>.

23 Karl Polanyi, "Universal Capitalism or Regional Planning?" *The London Quarterly of World Affairs* 10, no 3. (1945).

24 See Ungváry Krisztián. *Budapest ostroma* (The Siege of Budapest) (Budapest: Corvina, 2016).

25 My own father was arrested twice by the Soviet military patrols as he was scavenging for food to feed his starving family in Budapest during the last days of the war. He managed to escape both times from the holding centers where they were assembling the innocent for a one-way trip to the Gulag.

26 For the text of the Armistice Agreement signed between Hungary and the Allies on January 20, 1945; see William Juhasz, ed., *Hungarian Social Science Reader: 1945–1963* (Munich: Aurora Editions, 1965), 1-6.

27 See Béla Balázs, *Népmozgalmak és nemzeti bizottságok: 1945-46* [Popular Movements and National Committees: 1945–1946] (Budapest: Kossuth Könyvkiadó, 1961); and Károly Jenei, *Az iizemi bizottságok a munkáshatalomért* [The Factory Committees in the Struggle for Workers' Power: 1944- 1948] (Budapest: Táncsics, 1966).

28 András B. Göllner. "The Foundations of Soviet Domination and Communist Political Power in Hungary: 1945–1950" in *The Canadian-American Review of Hungarian Studies*. Vol III. No 2. 1976. This paper was based on the data I gathered during my doctoral studies at the London School of Economics during the early 1970s. As László Borhi rightly points out, this 1976 article was the first and only one until the late 1990s, to examine in a comprehensive fashion the early *economic instrumentality* of the colonial penetration of Hungary's prostrate, post-war body politic by the Union of Soviet Socialist Republics. See: László Borhi , *The Merchants of the Kremlin: the Economic Roots of Soviet Expansion in Hungary* (Washington, D.C.: Cold War International History Project, Woodrow Wilson International Center of Scholars, 2000), 5-6, or his follow up publication, *Hungary in the Cold War: 1945–1956* (Budapest: Central European University Press, 2004), 48.

29 Iván T. Berend, George Ránki and a new school of Hungarian economic historians during the Kádár era brought in a breath of fresh air to the construction site, but they could only partially alter the one-dimensional pre-1956 Stalinist narrative about the economic basis of the post-war Bolshevik power grab in Hungary. (See: Iván T. Berend. *A Szocialista gazdaság fejlődése Magyarországon: 1945–1968.* (The Development of the Socialist Economy in Hungary Between 1945–1968) (Budapest: Kossuth Könyvkiadó, 1974).

30 Ivan T. Berend and György Ránki, *A magyar gazdaság száz éve* [A Hundred Years of Hungary's Economy], Kossuth Könyvkiadó, (Budapest: 1972), 211–212.

31 Small, "mom and pop" businesses would gradually follow the same fate over the next year.

32 On the forms of this control, see Monthly Bulletin of the National Bank of Hungary, New Series, Fourth Year, no. 5 & 6, (May-June, 1948), 144.

33 Mátyás Rákosi, addressing the workers of Csepel, February 4, 1948, in, *A fordulat éve*, op.cit p. 411.

34 Csepel had a long tradition of being the center of radical trade unionism in Hungary. This was the base of the 1918–19 revolution as well as the one in 1956.

35 Béla A. Balassa. *Collectivization in Hungarian Agriculture.* American Journal of Agricultural Economics 42, no. 1, 1960).

36 Bibó gives us the best description of the spirit of this 2nd social revolution. He spoke about it privately with the historian Tibor Huszár, who published his words after Bibó's death and when it was no longer dangerous to do so. See: Tibor Huszár, *Bibó István: Beszélgetések* (István Bibó: Conversations) (Budapest: Magyar Krónika, 1989), 160–161. For my own discussion of the spirit that moved Bibó see: András B. Göllner. " '56 Közszelleme". (The Public Spirit of '56) *Magyar Hírlap*, (Október 24, 2002).

37 I have spoken of this lie in my *Preface*. Lajos Csoma did so in much greater detail in Chapter 3 of this book.

38 See: Bill Lomax, *Hungary 1956*. (London: Allison & Busby, 1976). And István Kemény and Bill Lomax eds., *Magyar munkástanácsok 1956-ban. Dokumentumok* (Hungarian workers' councils in 1956: Documents). *Magyar Füzetek*, Paris, (1986). Also: Mike Haynes, "Hungary: Workers' Councils Against Russian Tanks" *International Socialism* (Autumn, 2006).

39 See: Tamás Krausz, "The Hungarian Workers' Councils of 1956" *Workers' Liberty* (Oct 31, 2006).

40 Johanna Bockman. *Markets in the Name of Socialism: The Left-Wing Origins of Neoliberalism* (Stanford, CA: Stanford University Press, 2011). For a more outspoken recent attempt at reinserting the Stalinist affinity-fraud into the Marxist tradition (the fraud that according to Ilona Duczynska and Polanyi himself produced the '56 Hungarian uprising) please consult the September 2021 Manifesto of the International Manifesto Group, headed by Radhika Desai and her husband, Alan Freeman at the University of Manitoba.

41 This is why '56 brought Ilona Duczynska and Karl Polanyi to their feet. See Gareth Dale (ed)., "Letter to Istvan Meszaros from Karl Polanyi and Ilona Duczynska, 30 March 1961". In *Karl Polanyi: The Hungarian Writings* (Manchester: Manchester University Press, 2016), 232–236. See also András B. Göllner, *Ilona: Portrait of a Rebel* (Forthcoming, 2022).

42 Tamás Krausz, "The Hungarian Workers' Councils of 1956" *Workers' Liberty* (Oct 31, 2006).

43 200,000 people fled Hungary after the Soviet tanks rolled in and occupied Budapest on November 4, 1956. Of those who stayed behind, 20,000 were imprisoned, more than a thousand were executed. Imre Nagy was executed with 4 of his comrades following a secret trial on June 16, 1958.

44 For a small sample see: Andrew Felkay. *Hungary and the USSR, 1956–1988: Kádár's Political Leadership*. (Greenwood Press, 1989); Rudolf Tökés. *Hungary's Negotiated Revolution: Economic Reforms, Social Change, and Political Succession, 1957–1990*. (Cambridge: Cambridge University Press, 1996); Roger Gough. *A Good Comrade: János Kádár, Communism and Hungary*. (Bloomsbury Academic Press, 2006); Kopátsy Sándor. *Kádár és kora* (Kádár and his Era) (Budapest. Belvárosi könyvkiadó, 2005).

45 For a sympathetic look at this conversation see: Chris Hann. *Repatriating Polanyi* (Budapest, Central European University Press, 2019).

46 For the musical score listen to the Rolling Stones, *Down in the Hole*. <https://www.youtube.com/watch?v=2DeDh1T_KYo>.

47 For a view of "Gulyás Communism" by those philosophers who belonged to the George Lukács led "Budapest School" of philosophy see: Ferenc Fehér. "Kádárism as the Model State of Khruschevism', *Telos*, St. Louis, No. 47, Summer 1979 and Mihály Vajda. "Is Kádárism an Alternative? 'in Mihály Vajda, *The State and Socialism*. (London. Allison & Busby, 1981); András Hegedüs et al. *The Humanisation of Socialism: The Writings of the Budapest School*. (London. Allison and Busby. 1976). For a survey of the economic reform initiatives of the Kádár era see: William F. Robinson, *The Pattern of Reform in Hungary: A Political, Economic and Cultural Analysis* (New York, NY: Praeger, 1973).

48 Bill Lomax. '25 Years Later-New Light on 1956', *The Socialist Register: Labour Focus on Eastern Europe* 5, no. 3, (Summer 1982). This matches fully the account of this period provided by a "political grandson" of Ilona Duczynska, my late friend, László Rajk Jr. *A tér tágassága* (The Expansiveness of Space). (Budapest, Magvető, 2019), op.cit,. 60, 90.

49 Bill Lomax. Ibid. p. 96 and Bill Lomax, 'Hungary 1977–1982: The Rise of the Democratic Opposition', in *The Socialist Register: Labour Focus on Eastern Europe* 5, no. 3, (Summer 1982). For Rajk's views of Duczynska's support of the anti-Kádár opposition see, László Rajk Jr. *A tér tágassága* (The Expansiveness of Space). Op. cit., 60 & 69 and my own forthcoming book on Duczynska that contains a lengthy interview with Rajk.

50 Miklós Haraszti, *A Worker in a Workers' State* (London: Penguin Books, 1977).

51 The first time that Haraszti was able to address a university class in Hungary after he was banned from doing so came when I took a group of 37 students from Concordia University in Montréal for a summer course to Budapest in 1987. The professors who addressed my students over a two-week period were hand-picked by Kádár's state officials. During our last weekend of unplanned free time to come and go, I rented a bus, put my students on it, gave our official hosts the slip and headed down to the town of Siófok next to Lake Balaton, where Admiral Nicholas Horthy's forces

swarmed prior to descending on Budapest in November 1919. I asked two of Ilona Duczynska's "political grandsons"—the late László Rajk and Miklós Haraszti—to meet us in this small town and reveal for us the affinity fraud that masquerades under the label of Socialism in Hungary. This time around it was not Horthy's troops, but Kádár's secret service men who were swarming in the streets of this small resort community. Ilona Duczynska would have greatly appreciated this clandestine maneuver orchestrated by three of her political grandchildren.

52   I should remind readers at the outset of this third movement that I moved back to Budapest from Montréal in 1990, initially for a two-year term, in order to help my fellow citizens, find the path out of the blind alley that I've described earlier. The two years turned into 20. During this 20-year period I had an opportunity to interact, one way or another with every single one of the country's prime ministers, many of the country's top political-economic decision-makers along with thousands of ordinary citizens in the cities, towns and villages of Hungary. My familiarity with this third movement does not come from academic books but from firsthand, on-the-ground engagement in "Communicative action".

53   The phrase is consciously borrowed from Jürgen Habermas, *the Structural Transformation of the Public Sphere:* (Cambridge: MIT Press, 1991)

54   A small rump of die-hard Bolsheviks under Moscow trained Gyula Thürmer would stick to the old path, and persist with the HSWP's affinity-fraud under a new name: *The Hungarian Workers Party* (HWP). They kept the word "workers" in their name but dropped that problematic "socialist" word from their logo.

55   Kádár's last minister of Justice (sic), Kálmán Kulcsár became the first democratically elected conservative government's ambassador to Canada in 1990 under circumstances that made my stomach turn at the time. Kulcsár's cabinet secretary during the last years of the Kádár era, Attila Tárkány-Szűcs, a close friend of Antall's eldest son was put in charge of privatizing significant chunks of Hungary's public assets.

56   The SZDSZ, led by philosopher János Kis (1943-) was the best organized and strongest of the two liberal political parties going into the first free elections in 1990.

57   The philosopher György Bence (1941–2006) would part ways with the SZDSZ, even before the 1990 elections largely because of a personal conflict with János Kis. He threw his weight behind the smaller liberal party, Fidesz, that was founded by a young Bolshevik undergrad, Viktor Orbán, and his dormitory buddies at Bibó College. They saw the writing on the wall earlier than their elders in the Hungarian Socialist Workers' Party and chose the neo-liberal dictionary as their passport to political power. Bence would remain an informal adviser of Orbán until his passing in 2006.

58   György Bence and János Kis, 'On Being a Marxist: A Hungarian View', in *The Socialist Register 1980*, (London, Merlin Press, 1980). Additional views: Bill Lomax".25 Years Later-New Light on 1956". *Labour Focus on Eastern Europe* 5, no. 3, (Summer, 1982). See also Mihály Vajda, 'The End of Reformist Thought,' *The State and Socialism* (London: Allison & Busby, 1981). And Gabriel Becker, 'The Left in Hungary,' *Critique* Glasgow, no. 9, (1978).

59   I have chosen and translated these soundbites from the Alliance of Free Democrat's "Blue Book" —a document compiled by the Party's core group of economic thinkers. See: *A Rendszerváltás Programja*, (The Program for Systemic Change) (Budapest: The Alliance of Free Democrats, 1989), 41-63. This blueprint was subsequently endorsed by the Party's founding congress of March 19- April 16, 1989. To be fair: the authors of this neo-liberal road map did not use it to enrich themselves at the public's expense. The ones I came to know closely, including János Kis, Bálint Magyar, Attila Sós-Károly, Márton Tardos, Béla Greskovits, Tamás Bauer have all led frugal, modest lifestyle in and out of office. Many have shifted their positons since, some may even be embarrassed by what they stood for once. These passages should not be treated as evidence for willful malice, an inclination towards corruption or greed but evidence for how 45 years inside the Bolshevik's "blind alley" can produce just as much ignorance and insensitivity to the plight of working men and women as the pursuit of a doctorate in Economics at the University of Chicago under the supervision of Nobel Laureate Milton Friedman.

60   Through its Institute of Political Studies, the Party mandated the well-known sociologist, Mária Vásárhelyi to conduct this sounding of the membership in 1991. The results of this internal survey were published in combination with the results of a larger national survey of the public, and a smaller one focusing on the Budapest population. These last two surveys were conducted by Médian Kft. See: *Hol tart a szabad gondolat?* (Where is Free Thought Today?) Budapest. The Foundation for the Institute of Political Studies. 1991.

61 *Ibid*, p. 78

62 *Ibid*., p.76

63 *Ibid*., p. 76

64 *Ibid*., p.71

65 Of the 58 parties "only" 12 were able to field candidates in every single one of the country's 386 ridings

66 The country's new 1989 Constitution was as unconstitutional as the one put in place after Orbán came to power in 2011. The National Round Table Agreement of September 1989 that produced the constitution of this third movement was drafted behind closed doors by a group of self-appointed, non-elected *men* (emph. ABG) who simply banned the participation of Hungary's Labour Organizations and Social Movements from the constitutional process. As Rudolf Tökés would rightly observe, "Their institutional blueprint for the new house of democracy made no provisions for the care and feeding of its inhabitants". (Rudolph Tökés. "Political Transition and Social Transformation in Hungary" Fundació CIDOB. 1996. p. 87

67 The first to systematically expose this destructive behavior in the case of Canada was none other than the daughter of Ilona Duczynska and Karl Polanyi. (See: Kari Polanyi Levitt. *Silent Surrender*. (First published in 1970) Revised Edition McGill-Queens University Press, 2002.)

68 A reflex not at all unlike the one that seized the Hungarian Social Democratic Party leadership during the evening of March 20, 1919 when the President, Count Mihály Károly, unexpectedly asked them to take charge of the government. Instead of taking the country towards socialism on their own, they sucked the much weaker Bolsheviks into the project and as we have seen in earlier parts of this book, blamed the latter for their collective failures.

69 For an honest insider's account of the struggle within the ranks of the SZDSZ to accept or reject the Socialist Party's dangerously "irresistible" invitation please see: Ripp Zoltán. *Szabad Demokraták: Történeti vázlat a Szabad Demokraták Szövetségének politikájáról (1988–1994)* (Free Democrats: Historical Sketches of the Alliance of Free Democrat's Politics and Policies: 1988-1994) (Budapest. Napvilág Kiadó. 1995). 189–201. I cannot recall why some members on that Party's executive chose to give me that book as a birthday present in 1995 but I am happy to have been able to return to it at my "hideout" in Montréal's Little Italy in 2021 and to refresh my memory of their shortcomings. I'm also grateful to my friend Bálint Magyar, the editor of the Blue Book for taking a call from me in Budapest to discuss all of this in person while I was preparuing this chapter.

70 This initiative, popularly known as "The Bokros Package" was named after the Horn government's newly appointed Minister of Finance, Lajos Bokros, who spent the years prior to joining the Socialist Party led coalition government as President of GE Capital's newly acquired bank in Hungary, the Budapest Bank. After he left his post as Hungary's MF (sic), Bokros joined the World Bank, then hooked up with a conservative fringe party in Hungary that provided him with a seat in the EU Parliament and very handsome compensation for years. He is the head of his own little party today and teaches economics at the Central European University.

71 Thomas Piketty. *Capital in the 21st Century*. Op.cit and *Capital and Ideology*. (Boston: Harvard University Press. 2020).

72 Kari Polanyi-Levitt, *From the Great Transformation to the Great Financialization*. (Halifax/Winnipeg. Fernwood Publications. 2013). 164-67.

73 Like many others, I too was taken in by Orbán's "linguistic turn" in the late 1980s and became supportive of his efforts when I moved back to Budapest in 1990. I organized the Montréal leg of Orbán's first visit to Canada in February 1994 (he was accompanied on this trip by József Szájer, and László Urbán). It was after Orbán and Szájer addressed my students at Concordia University and I joined them on the back seat of a black stretched limo put at their disposal by the leading financiers on Bay Street, and drinking some of the champaigne that was flowing freely as we drove to ur next venue, that I recognized Orbán's and Szájer's secret attachment to making it on other people's money, their willingness to climb to the top on the back of those who could least afford it. László Urbán, the third man on this Fidesz delegation would reach the same conclusion a bit later on.

74 I warned of this eventuality while Orbán was in power in an article that appeared in Hungary's largest daily. (See: András B. Göllner. "Titokzatos kötődések" (Secret attachments) *Népszabadság*.

Budapest. February 3, 2001.) From that moment on—the moment when I began speaking truth to power publicly in Hungary—I was subjected to years of legal and police harassment and death threats by Orbán's followers. I stopped commuting between Montréal and Budapest just before Orbán came to power the second time around in 2010 and have not been back since.

75 See András Bozóki. *"Façade Pluralism in Semi-Democracies: The Case of Hungary"*. A paper presented to the IPSA World Congress, Montréal, Canada. July 24, 2014. Before 1990, Bozóki was an advisor of Orbán but broke with him after it became clear to him as well what the Fidesz leader was up to. Between 2003 and 2004 Bozóki and I served briefly on a small team of advisors to the newly appointed Minister of Equal Opportunities, Katalin Lévai until she was stripped of her posting because she took her role too seriously. Bozoki would go on to serve as Minister of Culture in the first Gyurcsány government between 2005 and 2006 before returning to his academic calling at Central European University. Lévai became a fiction writer.

76 A full text of Gyurcsány's speech can be read here: A Teljes Balatonöszödi beszéd szövege (the Full text of the Speech at Balatonőszöd) NOL.hu. May 26, 2007. The audio of this historic and impromptu address can be heard here: <https://www.youtube.com/watch?v=SQkl8701JfE>.

77 Donald Trump's coup attempt in Washington DC on January 6, 2021, was a virtual carbon-copy of Orbán's theatrical performance in Budapest in the fall of 2006. No wonder Steve Bannon, Trump's 2016 campaign strategist would refer to Orbán as "Trump before Trump". Both depend on a score written by the late Arthur J. Finkelstein, one of the earliest and perhaps most masterful Republican Party practitioners of cyber-capitalism's post-modern political language.

78 András B. Göllner. "Hungary's Anti-Democratic Revolution" *Los Angeles Times*. October 7, 2006.

79 Quoted by Orbán's biographer and former ally, József Debreczeni in *Arcmás* (The Other Face). (Budapest: Noran Libro. 2009), 107–108. Attila Antal provides an excellent recent synthesis of Capitalism and Autocracy in Hungary under Orbán in: Antal, Attila. *The Rise of Hungarian Populism: State Autocracy and the Orbán Regime*. (London: Emerald Publishing, 2019).

80 The EU's 2020 country report on Hungary shows that the Orbán government has perhaps the worst record in all of Europe in promoting the use of productivity-enhancing digital technologies in the production and distribution of goods and services for domestic and international markets. (European Commission. *2020 Country Report for Hungary*. Brussels. February 26, 2020).

81 European Commission. Eurostat. *Renewable Energy Statistics: 2019*. For a Hungarian language review see: Péter Magyar. "Egyetlen ország van az EU-ban ahol stabilan csökken a zöld energia aránya" (Hungary is the only country in the EU Where the Share of Green Energy of Total Energy Consumption is Continuously Decreasing) *444.hu*. February 7, 2019. Hungary under Orbán became the "least green" among her neighbors, the so called V4 countries. She is the only country in all of Europe that does not actually have a stand-alone ministry of the environment. Only three other governments in the entire world share this distinction with Orbán's: Saudi Arabia, Tanzania and Somalia. (See: Gabriella Horn. "Magyarországon kiiktatták a környezetvédelmet, hogy ne akadályozza a gazdasági fejlődést" (In Hungary they Got Rid of Environmental Protection in Order to Stop its Hindrance of Economic Growth) *Átlátszó*. June 26, 2020.

82 For a journalistic snapshot, see: Zoltán Farkas. "A haveri kapitalizmus nyolc éve Magyarországon: 1.3 millió embert hagytak az út szélén" (8 Years of Crony-Capitalism in Hungary: They Left 1.3 million People at the side of the Road) Part I and II. *HVG.hu* March 8 and 9, 2018

83 European Commission. *2020 Country Report for Hungary*. Op.cit,

84 AIC is a measure of the material welfare of households.

85 The *Eurostat* figures are based on official purchasing power parities, and the latest GDP and population figures of the countries in question. See: *Consumption per capita in purchasing power standards in 2018* Eurostat. December 13, 2019.

86 See: Annamária Artner. "Workfare Society in Action—The Hungarian Labour Market and Social Conditions in European Comparison". *Romanian Journal of European Affairs*, Vol 20, No 1, June 2020. p. 114.

87 For a discussion of the Hungarian figures please see, Sarolta Székely, "Ime a friss adat: kiábrándítóan alacsony a magyarok fizetése" (Here are the newest figures: The Wages of Hungarians are Disappointingly Low). *Mfor.hu*. June 27, 2018. Artner. argues that Hungary will be shortly overtaken by last place Bulgaria.

88   See: "13 éves csúcson ragadt a magyar bérek adóterhelése" (The tax-bite on wages is stuck at a 13 Year High) *mfor.hu*. March 16, 2015 and "Elképesztően sokat vesz el az állam a munkánk után kapott bérből" (The State takes an Incredible Amount Away from the Wages Paid for our Work). *444.hu*. April 12, 2016; And, "Az OECD Riport: A Fidesz rommá adóztatja a magyar családokat "(OECD Report: The Destructive Effect on Hungarian Families of the Fidesz Imposed Taxes). *Zoom.hu*. May 8, 2018.

89   "Magyarországon kell adózni a legtöbbet a minimálbér után" (Hungary has the highest taxes on Minimum Wage) http://rtl.hu/rtlklub/hirek/magyarorszagon-kell-a-legtobbet-adozni-a-minimalber-utan

90   For a discussion see: Csaba Csernátony. "Durva drágulás a Magyar rezsidíjjaknál és az egészségügyben" (Rough Price Increases For Rents, Public Utilities and Healthcare) *Napi.hu*. July 4, 2018.

91   See: *The Working Poor*. European Foundation for the Improvement of Working and Living Conditions. Brussels. June 4, 2020.

92   Kolló was quoted by Palko Karasz and Patrick Kingsley in the *New York Times* "What is Hungary's Slave Law" December 22, 2018.

93   Quoted by Germany's public broadcaster, on December 8, 2018. See: <https://www.dw.com/en/hungarian-workers-protest-slave-law-overtime-rules/a-46649065>.

94   Quoted by Gergely Kiss. *Napi.hu* April 14, 2020

95   See: *Sikerpropaganda módszertani váltással*. (Success Propaganda with Methodological Change). *Hvg.hu*. January 31, 2016.

96   According to the OECD, it will take 200 years on average for a member of the lower class in Hungary to move up into the Middle Class. See: OECD. *A Broken Social Elevator? How to Promote Social Mobility*. June 15, 2018. See also, Bence Stubnya. "Kasztosodik a magyar társadalom és ennek mind mi isszuk a levét". (Hungarian Society is being Broken into Casts and We're all Suffering from its Aftertaste) *g7.hu*. November 3, 2019

97   Annamária Artner. *Op.cit.* 121

98   See: Márton Gera. "A Fidesz az út szélén hagyja a hátrányos helyzetű gyerekeket és még a kitörési lehetőségeket is elzárja előlük" (Disadvantaged children are left at the roadside by Fidesz, and are denied the opportunity to break out of their entrapment) *Magyar Narancs* (May 7, 2018).

99   For a good discussion of the various studies see Zoltán Lakner, "Biztosan őrizzük az európai utolsó helyet az idősellátásban" (We Are Securely Holding Down Last Place in Europe in the Care for our Elderly). *168 Óra*. (February 27, 2019). See also "Nem sok jó vár a magyar idősekre" [Not much good ahead for Hungary's elderly], *Infóvilág*. September 5, 2018.

100 For Hungary's leading scholars on this policy area, see: Éva Orosz and Zsófia Kollányi. *Egészségi állapot, egészség-egyenlőtlenségek nemzetközi összehasonlításban* (Hungarians' Health, Health-Inequality in International Comparison). Pdf Manuscript. Budapest. 2017. <https://www.tarki.hu/hu/publications/SR/2016/16orosz.pdf>. Or "Az egészségügyre fordított GDP-arányos kiadások csökkentek 2010-hez képest" (Public Expenditures on Public Health as a Share of GDP Have Declined Since 2010). *Zoom hu*, (October 2, 2018).

101 For a brief discussion of these numbers see: Zalán Zubor. "Több pénz jutott a propagandára mint az egészségügy fejlesztésére" (More Money was Spent on Propaganda than the Development of Public Health-care). *Hírtv.hu*, (October 27, 2017).

102 E.g., "Education at a Glance" Annual Reports of the OECD between 2016 and 2020. Paris. OECD Publishing. For a brief discussion of the most recent initiatives of the Orbán government to "privatize" public education and hinder the opportunities of the less fortunate to public education see: Kitti Fődi. "Adományokból próbálják átvészelni a tanévet az állami támogatás nélkül maradt iskolák" (After the Withdrawal of Public Funds, Schools Must Turn to Private Donations to Survive) *444, hu*, (September 1, 2020). On the neglect of vocational education see: Dóra Onódy-Molnár. "Siralmas állapot—összeomlott a magyar szakképzés" (Dreadful Conditions—The Collapse of Vocational Training in Hungary) *168 Óra* (June 10, 2019).

103 Anita Rigó. " Azt senki sem köszöni majd meg amit az oktatással tett ez a kormámy" (No One Will Thank this Government for what it Did with Our Public Education System) *g7.hu*, (March 21,

2018). And "Szinte példátlan az EU-ban ami a fiatal magyar diplomásokkal történik" (The Treatment of Young Hungarian University Graduates is Unprecedented in the EU). *G7.hu*, (September 9, 2018); Katalin Erdélyi and Attila Bátorfy. "Durván csökken a felsőoktatási hallgatók száma Magyarországon 2005 óta" (The Number of Students Seeking post-Secondary Education in Hungary is Drastically Falling) *Átlátszó* (November 11, 2018).

104 According to *Education First* and *Eurostat* only 37% of Hungary's adult population speaks another language, which is the lowest figure for an EU member state. Among those who speak English as a second language the proficiency rate is, however, very good. The source of the problem is not a lack of skills, but the government's restrictive educational policies that limit the ability of her citizens to excel. For a discussion, see: *168 Óra*. September 15, 2018.

105 Anita Rigó. *G7.hu*, September 9, 2018, op.cit

106 Zita Mária Petschnig. "Valami nem stimmel, valami nagyon nem stimmel". (Something is wrong here, something is really wrong) *Hírklikk.hu*, (April 14, 2020).

107 Interview with László Csaba in *Qubit* (November 4, 2019).

108 See Balázs Szentkirályi's interview with conservative economist László Urbán. "Ha a pénzcsapot elzárják, Orbán megbukhat" (If they shut the flow of EU subsidies, Orbán Could be Out). *Index* (April 4, 2017).

109 OECD. *2018 International Migration Outlook* (June 20, 2018). For a Hungarian discussion see: Károly Beke, Sokkoló számok: közel egy millió magyar vándorolhatott már ki" (Shocking Numbers: Close to a Million Hungarians May Have Emigrated Already). *Portfolió.hu*, (June 18, 2018).

110 See: "A magyar diákok két-harmada kivándorlást tervez" (Two thirds of Hungary's students are planning to emigrate). *Napi.hu*. January 13, 2016. For another survey see: A magyar fiatalok a legboldogtalanabbak a térségben" (Hungary's young are the unhappiest in the region) *444.hu*, (April 2, 2016).

111 As we have stated earlier, Horthy's government passed the world's first anti-Jewish laws of the 20th century. Orbán's was the first EU member state to criminalize and demonize migrants in the 21st century.

112 FCNM 3rd Report. Council of Europe. Brussels. September 17, 2010.

113 ibid., 71-72

114 See: Council of Europe, *Human Rights of Roma and Travellers in Europe* (February 2012), 42

115 ADL. *Attitudes Towards Jews in 10 European Countries*, March 2012.

116 Simon Wiesenthal Institute. *European Extremist Movements*, June 2012.

117 It was this phenomenon that compelled Nobel Laureate Elie Wiezel and the late Randolph L. Braham to return all of their state honours to the Orbán Government It was for their important manifestation of solidarity with Hungary's exploited that I dedicated my piece to these Holocaust survivors (ABG, *Orbán and the Jews*. op cit.)

118 For the full text please click on the following URL: <https://www.helsinki.hu/ez-a-mi-orszagunk-ervenytelenitsd-a-nepszavazast/>.

119 Huszár Ákos and Berger Viktor. "Az új középosztály?" (The New Middle Class?) *in Politikatudományi Szemle*. (Political Science Review of the Hungarian Academy of Science) XXIX, no. 2, (2020), 71-99. For additional evidence see: Péter Krekó, Bulcsú Hunyady and Patrick Szicherle. *Anti-Muslim populism in Hungary: From the margins to the mainstream* (Washington, DC., Brookings Institute, July 24, 2019). For an earlier assessment see: Attila Juhász, Bulcsú Hunyadi, and Edit Zgut, *Focus on Hungary: Refugees, Asylum and Migration* (Berlin: Heinrich Böll Stiftung, 2015). By 2021, Krekó, one of Hungary's top social scientists has become the target of a vicious government coordinated hate campaign. As this book was going to press Kreko's personal safety was increasingly in jeopardy.

120 As reported by Lily Bayer in the *Budapest Beacon* on December 18, 2016, after she interviewed J.D. Gordon in Budapest.

121 His exact words were "We very much admire and respect Prime Minister Orbán and what he is doing to make Hungary great again.,. Donald Trump deeply admires Mr. Orbán... He and Mr. Orbán will become good friends". Christian Keszthelyi. "Trump Adviser: Orbán Aims to "Make Hungary Great Again" *Budapest Business Journal*. December 2, 2016.

122 See "Közös úton jár Németország és Magyarország" (Germany and Hungary are on a Common Path). *Híradó.hu*. February 20, 2020. See also "Dícséret Merkeltől" (Praise from Merkel). *Demokrata*. August 30, 2019.

123 On July 3, 2013, the European Parliament adopted the findings of the Tavares Report by a vote of 370 to 249 with 82 abstentions.

124 In 2015, the European Parliament passed two additional resolutions, in June and December, condemning the Orbán government's breach of the EU covenant.

125 European Parliament resolution of 17 May 2017 on the situation in Hungary. <https://www.europarl.europa.eu/doceo/document/TA-8-2017-0216_EN.html>.

126 The basis of the September resolution was a new report by the EU Parliament's Committee on Civil Liberties, Justice and Home Affairs headed by Judith Sargentini, which submitted the results of its more than a year-long investigation on April 7, 2018 <https://www.europarl.europa.eu/doceo/document/A-8-2018-0250_EN.html>. For the text of the EU Parliament's September resolution see: European Parliament resolution of 12 September 2018 on a proposal calling on the Council to determine, pursuant to Article 7(1) of the Treaty on European Union, the existence of a clear risk of a serious breach by Hungary of the values on which the Union is founded. *Official Journal of the European Union* or on-line: <https://www.europarl.europa.eu/doceo/document/TA-8-2018-0340_EN.html#title1>.

127 I selected these shots because they were taken by reputable scholars who share the "prism" or filter of István Bibó that I revealed at the beginning of this chapter and because they use the universal moral compass that guided our exploration of the public policy universe of the 1919 Republic of Councils in chapter 4 of this book.

128 These words from György Gábor's Facebook page were reprinted in *Civil Hetes*. February 8, 2019, and were translated from that text into English by the editor of this book.

129 Lányi András, "Történelmünk legveszedelmesebb pillanatait éljük." (We are Living Under the Most Dangerous Moments of Our History) (trans. ABG), *Válasz* (April 3, 2020). For a similar assessment, a year later see the Sociologist Mária Vásárhelyi's most recent blog posting on her Facebook page, "Haza a mélyben" (Our Homeland in the Deep). February 17, 2021.

130 See: Edward S. Herman and Noam Chomsky, *Manufacturing Consent* (New York, NY: Pantheon Books, 1988) and Jane Mayer. *Dark Money*, op cit; Also Nicole Hemmer. *Messengers of the Right: Conservative Media and the Transformation of American Politics*. Philadelphia. University of Pennsylvania Press. 2016. Brian Rosenwald, *Talk Radio America: How an Industry took Over a Political Party that Took Over the United States* (Cambridge, MA: Harvard UP, 2019).

131 While I disagree with many of Paul Mason's conclusions in his book, *Post Capitalism*. Op.cit, he is right in observing that the reduction of the marginal cost of information to zero will have a profound impact on our lives in the future and on how we decide who gets what, when and how in our communities.

132 I borrow the term from Jürgen Habermas (but use it in a more focused, narrowly targeted fashion that brings me closer to Michel Foucault and the approach that he so ably outlined shortly before his passing, in a series of lectures in San Francisco on *Parrhesia* (this is an ancient Greek term in reference to the obligation to speak the truth for the common good, even at personal risk). (See: M. Foucault. *On Fearless Speech*. Op.cit.) For a good discussion of the harmony between Foucault and Habermas, see: Bent Flyvbjerg, *Ideal Theory, Real Rationality: Habermas Versus Foucault and Nietzsche*. Paper for the Political Studies Association's 50th Annual Conference, *The Challenges for Democracy in the 21st Century*, London School of Economics and Political Science, 10–13 April 2000.

And 1956: Coda

Dimitrios Roussopoulos

IS HUMAN HISTORY a series of sorrows? An unending saga of slaughterhouse crimes and ass licking opportunism? A more careful review of social history informs us that is not the case. I am listening to Shostakovich's 11th Symphony, 'The Year 1905', the second movement, "The 9th of January". What am I learning intellectually and subjectively?

The seemingly fatalistic mould of cruel servitude can be shattered, as happened more than 2,700 years ago when Greeks living on the south-eastern fringes of what became Europe laid claim to a creation that now ranks in historical importance with the wheel, the printing press, the steam engine, and the cloning of stem cells. Born of resistance to authoritarian privileges and tyranny, their claimed creation slipped into human history. Only in time did it ring loud and clear. It caused unease among the upper class and was condemned as bringing chaos to the social order. It seemed simply to be part of the cycle of history's ups and downs. Few predicted its universal and lasting appeal. The creation was soon to be remarked as different. It was to enthral millions and to arouse emotions on a world scale, as it required humans to look at themselves afresh, to arrange their daily lives differently, and to openly embrace community in urban spaces sidestepping tribalism. The creation was a potent force driving the imagination as to the possible, which is still with us today, and in many places heretofore closed to radical social change. The Greeks called their creation *demokratia*—it was assembly democracy, or direct democracy.

Often scoffed at as wishful thinking, and mocked by intellectuals and politicians, the fact is that assembly democracy is a regular feature of the human condition, as in Hungary in 1919, and significantly again in Hungary in 1956. We learn from one on the spot observer that the Hungarian revolution of the councils showed "ordinary working men and woman taking their affairs into their own hands and manage them without a special caste of officials".

On October 22, 1956, Hungarian students compiled a list of sixteen demands, containing key policy changes. Following an anti-Russian protest march through

Budapest the next day, the students entered the main radio station with the aim to read their demands on air. They were detained, and when a large crowd gathered around the radio station demanding their release, the State police fired on the unarmed people, setting off the revolution.

On October 26th, the newly formed National Council of Free Trade Unions published its revolutionary programme. This programme in the form of a multi-dimensional resolution was very bold as it gathered together the demands put together by Workers' Councils from throughout the country. The programme included seven political demands and intentions, and eight economic demands. The new federation was shorn of bureaucrats and elected democratically based on workers councils and their demands, pronounced features of the October 1956 social revolution. The response throughout society was people rearranging their daily lives in their thirst for assembly democracy.

The network of councils which sprang up was the biggest single gain of the Hungarian revolution. This was its greatest achievement and has immortalised its activists. By the end of October, the councils were, in fact, the government of the country. This monumental accomplishment was lost to so many at the time outside Hungary, including to a large portion of the "Left". The entire "State communist" hierarchy and its political parties everywhere unanimously supported the Russian invasion. A chill ran through these bureaucrats when it became known that Russian soldiers were handing over weapons to Hungarian revolutionaries and, in some cases, were actually joining their ranks.

The academics and intellectuals who subsequently rushed to publish their writings on what happened and why rarely concluded that only when the 99% move boldly into the welcoming arms of radical democracy can our actual desperate situation and its many ugly features begin to be cured.

INDEX

Adam, Christopher 184
Adler, Friedrich 179
Adler, Viktor 179
Ady, Endre 194
Ágoston, Péter 155
Akerlof, George 29
al Assad Bashar 145
Anderson, Kevin B. 29
Anka, László 150
Antall, József 218
Apor, Péter 64
Aranyossi, Magda xvi, 157-178
Aranyossi, Pál 159, 162, 164
Arcary, Valério 5, 6, 27, 28
Arendt, Hannah 22, 31
Aristotle 26, 120, 121, 124, 143-144
Artner, Annamária 28, 223, 239, 240

Babits, Mihály 154
Bak, János M 144
Balabanoff, Angelica 1, 2, 17-19, 22, 25, 27,
    30, 31, 54, 55, 156
Balassa, Béla A. 235
Balázs, Béla 235, 241
Bandl, Ferenc 154
Bannon, Steve 7, 8, 28, 239
Barr, James 145
Barth, Emil 83
Bartha, Albert 50, 66
Bartha, Eszter xv
Basile, Giambattista xx, xxv
Bátorfy, Attila 241
Batthány, Ervin 25, 143
Baudrillard, Jean 204, 230

Bauer, Otto xvii, 180, 181
Bauer Tamás 237
Bayer, Lily 241
Bayer, Zsolt 233
Bebel, August 141, 148, 154
Becker, Gabriel 237
Bence, János 194
Bence, György 217, 237
Berend Ivan T 211, 234, 235
Berger, Viktor 227, 241
Bergler, Edmund 232
Berinkey, Dénes 53, 59, 104, 149
Berkman, Alexander xviii, 19, 30
Bernstein, Edouard 37
Bethlen, István 192
Bezos, Jeff 15, 28
Bibó, István 148, 205, 207, 233, 235, 237, 242
Biden, Joe 20
Bihari, Péter 65
Bingham, Tom 146
Bíró, Dezső 155
Biró, Mihály 35
Black Elk 145, 149
Bockman, Johanna 213, 236
Bodó, Béla 234
Bödők, Gergely 147, 150, 151
Böhm, Vilmos 109, 138-140, 152
Bokányi, Dezső 42, 97, 100, 109
Bokros, Lajos 220, 238
Borgos, Anna 152
Borhi, László 235
Borsányi, György 56, 65, 66
Botz Gerhard 164
Bozóki, András xvi, 143, 220-221, 239

Braham, Randolph 234, 241
Brecht, Arnold 80, 90, 91
Broué, Pierre 88-91
Brus. Wlodzimierz xiv
Bucsin, Béla 193, 202
Buffett, Warren 15
Bukharin, Nikolai 30
Burger, Anne 201
Bús, László Fekete 66, 250

Carnoy, Martin 143
Carville, James xxiv, 28
Charles IV, King of Hungary xxii, xxv, 40,
    42, 45, 47
Chlepko, Ede 154
Chomsky, Noam 27, 30, 149, 242
Clemenceau, Georges 145, 149
Clinton, Bill xxiv, 28
Clinton, Hillary 150
Coggiola, Osvaldo 29
Cohen, Adolf 75
Cohen, Leonard 156
Cohen, Ronald 143, 144
Cohn, Roy 209
Constantin, the Emperor 145
Craig, Nelson R 27
Csaba, László 226, 240, 241
Csernátony, Csaba 240
Cserny. József 138-141, 149, 153-155
Csikszentmihályi, Mihály 28
Csoma, Lajos 92, 117, 119, 128, 132, 152, 156, 236
Csunderlik, Péter xxii, 3, 30, 32, 64, 65, 67,
    128, 142
Czeferner, Dóra xv

Dafoe, John W. 187
Dale, Gareth 64, 236
Däumig, Ernst 70, 83, 87, 88, 91
Deák, István 65
Debreczeni, József 239
Derrida, Jacques 248
Desai, Radhika 31, 236
Detre, Gyula 195, 234, 235
Deutsch, Julius 180
Dietz, Károly 66, 248

Disney, Walt xxv
Dostoevsky, Fyodor 67
Dreisziger, Nándor 201
Duczynska, Ilona x, xii, xiii, xv-xix, 2, 18,
    26-28, 30, 42, 43, 56, 57, 64, 97, 98, 101, 105,
    143, 148, 151, 154-157, 177, 180, 183, 197, 202,
    209, 215, 236-238
Dye, Thomas R 146
Dzerzhinsky, Felix 154

Ebert, Friedrich 59, 68, 70, 77, 81-85
Egry, Gábor 67
Eichmann, Adolf 208
Engels, Friedrich 23, 37, 69
Epkenhans, Michael 89, 90
Erdélyi, Katalin 241
Erdogan, Recep Tayyip 145
Erdős, Patrik András 136, 153
Erényi, Tibor 64, 164
Etzioni, Amitai 146

Fanon, Franz 13, 29
Farkas, Zoltán 239
Fehér, Ferenc 236
Felkay, Andrew 236
Ferguson, Niall xxv
Ferenczi, Sándor 152
Ferro, Marc 88, 90
Fitzgerald, Edward Peter 145
Flyvbjerg, Bent 242
Fődi, Kitti 240
Foucault, Michel 4, 27, 242
Fowkes, Ben 91
Franz Joseph I, the Emperor 40, 183
Franz Ferdinand, the Archduke xxv
Freud, Sigmund 152, 232
Friedman, Milton 11, 237
Fuchs, Christian 27

Gábor, György 229
Garami,Ernő 38, 39, 48, 49, 60, 65, 66, 103
Garbai, Sándor 62, 129, 131, 151, 154
Gárdos, Mariska 38, 65
Gates, Bill 15
Geary, Dick 27
Gellért, Ádám 150, 151

George, Lloyd 145, 149
Gera, Eleonóra xv
Gera, Márton 240
Gerber, John P. 147
Gerő, András 65
Gerschenkron, Alexander 182
Gimes, Miklós 153
Gimes, Judit 153
Gioielli, Emily xv
Godot 222
Goldman, Emma xviii, 17, 19, 30, 156
Gollner, Adam Leith xviii, 150
Göllner, András B. xix, xx, 1, 18, 27, 29, 36, 42, 120, 146, 155, 157, 166, 202, 204, 233-236, 238, 239
Gomez, Ana xvii
Gordon, J. D. 228, 241
Gough, Roger 236
Gramsci, Antonio 146, 214
Gratz, Gusztáv 118, 150
Greenhouse, Steven 30
Greskovits, Béla 237
Grossman, Henryk 27
Guthrie, W. K. C. xxiv
Grimm Brothers xx, xxv
Gyurcsány, Ferenc 220, 221, 239

Haase, Hugo 85
Habermas, Jürgen 143, 237, 242
Hadik, János 45, 47
Haffner, Sebastian L 67
Hajdú, Lilly 152, 153
Hajdú, Tibor 64-67, 100, 104, 116-119
Halász, Pál 153
Haley, Nikki 8, 9, 10, 15, 28
Halsall, Paul 149
Hamburger, Jenő 129
Hanák, Péter 65
Hanebrink l. Paul 67
Hann, Chris 236
Harari. Yuval Noah 143
Haraszti, Miklós xiii, xiv, xix, 215, 236, 237
Harman, Chris 14, 29
Harmstone Rakowska Teresa viii
Hatos, Pál 65, 152

Haubrich József 139, 153
Hayek, Friedrich 29, 181
Hedges, Chris 30
Hegedűs, András 236
Held, David 143
Held, Joseph 65
Helfert, Veronika xv
Hemmer, Nicole 242
Hevesi, Gyula 106, 113, 114, 117-119
Hitler, Adolph 20, 195, 200, 208
Hobsbawm, Eric J. xxii, xviii, 29, 93, 117
Hochschild, Adam 29
Hoffrogge, Ralf 89-91
Holst, Henriette Roland 2
Horn, Gabriella 239
Horn, Gyula 219, 221, 238
Horthy, Nicholas 19, 33, 36, 50, 64, 132, 138, 150, 151, 153, 155, 180, 184, 185, 189, 190, 191, 192, 194, 195, 198, 200, 203, 206, 207, 208, 209, 210, 211, 212, 214, 222, 224, 228, 229, 234
Howlett, Michael 146
Hubbard, Ben 29
Hudis, Peter 29
Hunyady, Bulcsú 241
Huszár, Ákos 227, 241

Illyés, Gyula 234
Ingraham, Laura 10
Innes, Harold A. 211, 234, 235
István, the King (St Stephen) 122, 144

Jablonczay, Tímea xv
Jancsik, Ferenc 153
János, Andrew C. 31, 148
Jászai, Samu 109, 119
Jászi, Oszkár xxv, 40, 44, 46, 47, 61, 65, 66, 118, 132, 141, 149, 152, 156, 180, 233
Jedwab, Jack 201
Jenei, Károly 235
Jennings, Francis 29
Jesus Christ xxii, 144, 145
Juhász, Attila 241
Juhász Nagy, Sándor 104

Kádár, János 153, 154, 200, 201, 213-215, 221, 235-237

Kádár, Zsuzsanna B. xv

Kaes, Anton 91

Kaldor, Nicholas xiv

Kant, Emanuel xxii

Kaplan, Fanny 17, 19, 54

Karasz, Palko 240

Károlyi, Mihály 37, 43, 44, 47-53, 55, 58-61, 64-67, 99, 101-106, 117, 127, 137, 138, 142, 149, 154, 155, 215

Kassák, Lajos 128

Kautsky, Karl 37, 156, 256

Kávássy, Sándor 118

Kelen Jolán 57, 105

Kelen, József 57, 105, 154

Kemény, István 236

Kende, János 118

Kenez, Peter 25, 31, 130, 148

Kenyeres, Ágnes 164

Kéri, Pál 60

Keszthelyi, Christian 241

Kets, Gaard 88

Keynes, John, Maynard 6, 12

Khashoggi, Jamal 149

Kingsley, Patrick 240

Király. Albert 109

Kirsch, Noah 29

Kis, János 217, 237

Kiss, Gergely 240

Kóbor, Tamás 35, 64

Kolasky, John 201

Kollányi, Zsófia 240

Kolló, János 224, 240

Konok, Péter 154

Konrád, György 260

Kopátsy Sándor 236

Kordan, Bohdan 201

Kordás, László 224

Korvin, Ottó 56, 57, 67, 138, 140, 154

Kossuth, Lajos 195

Kovács, Imre 234

Kövér, László 140, 155

Kövess, Lajos 189

Kozák, Péter 164

Krausz, Tamás 206, 213, 234, 236

Krekó, Péter 241

Kropotkin, Peter 143, 154

Kuhn, Gabriel 88, 90, 91

Kuhn, Thomas xxv

Kulcsár, Kálmán 237

Kun, Béla xii, 18, 19, 24-26, 30, 47, 54-62, 64, 66, 67, 86, 105, 113, 114, 128-130, 134, 142, 147, 148, 151, 152, 154, 155, 206, 212, 233

Kunfi Zsigmond 38, 48, 61, 97, 109, 206

Kuttner, Robert 7, 28, 29

Lacan, Jacques 232

Lademacher, Horst 27

Lafont, Maria 27

Lakner, Zoltán 240

Lakoff, George 30

Landler, Ernő 152, 153

Landler, Jenő 135, 152

Lányi, András 66, 67, 229, 242

Lassalle, Ferdinand 37

Lasswell, Harold 121, 143, 255

László, Péter 145

Lászlófi, Viola 136

Lavallée, Marie Josée xvi, xvii, 5, 68

Lehman Brothers 14, 29

Lékai, István 135, 147

Lengyel, József 58, 67, 153, 154

Lenin, V.I. xxiv, 2, 7, 17, 19, 22, 26-28, 30, 31, 37, 54, 55, 57, 61, 62, 66, 69, 78, 87, 90, 116, 128-131, 135, 140, 143, 147, 148, 151, 152, 154, 156, 166, 192, 206, 212

King Leopold of Begium 13, 29

Leonnig, Carol xiv

Levitt, Tom x, xviii

Lévai, Katalin 239

Liebknecht Karl 2, 37, 68, 71, 72, 78, 80-83, 86, 87, 89-91

Lipton, Charles 201

Litván, György 64, 65

Lomax, Bill xix, 201, 215, 236, 237

Lord, Carnes 143

Louis XIV 123

Löwy, Michael 148

Luban, Ottokar 147, 156

Lukachich Géza 45-47, 66

Lukács, György 19, 25, 30, 35, 37, 57, 105, 130, 148, 152, 154, 156, 206, 233, 236

Lukashenko, Alexander 150

Luxemburg, Rosa   2, 17, 18, 25, 28, 30, 72, 81, 84-87, 89, 91, 116, 130, 141, 147, 148, 152, 154, 156, 207

Machiavelli, Niccolo   123
MacMillan Margaret   xxiv, xxv, 148
Madzsar, József   152, 153
Magyar, Bálint   237, 238
Magyar, Péter   239
Mansingh, Surjit   233
Mánuel, Sári   175
Mao Tse tung   10
Márai, Sándor   35
Martens, Wilfried   221
Marx, Karl   xxiv, 2, 3, 6, 7, 20, 23, 27, 68, 69, 155, 179, 181, 206, 213
Mary, the Virgin   144, 145
Mason, Paul   27, 242
Matlekovits, Sándor   118, 119
Matolcsy, Mátyás   234
Maximilian, the Prince   82
Mayakovsky, The Poet   3
Mayer, Jane   xxiv, 28, 29, 242
Mazzocchi, Paul   88, 89
McAdams, James   89
McCarthy, Joe   209
McLuhan, Marshall   21, 30
McRobbie, Kenneth   151
Medgyessy, Péter   221
Meiksins Wood, Ellen   23, 31
Melegh, Attila   xvi
Mendell, Margie   xvii
Mengele, the angel of death   209
Menon, Krishna   233
Mentzer, Berta   175
Mérei, Gyula   66
Merkel, Angela   242
Mészáros, István   257
Mett, Ida   19
Miklós, Gáspár, Tamás   Xxv, 233
Miley, Jeffrey Thomas   xviii, 27, 31, 145
Miljan, Lydia   146
Miller, Tyrus   205, 233
Mink, András   xviii
Mises, Ludwig von   29, 182
Morlino, Leonard   146

Müller, Richard   75, 78, 83, 87, 89, 91
Müller B. Tamás   150, 151, 258
Münnich, Ferenc   54, 56, 67
Mussolini, Benito   20, 200, 208, 228

Nádas, Péter   xvi, 159-165
Nagy, Imre   153, 213, 216, 233, 236
Nagy, Zsófia   136
Nagy, Zsuzsa   175
Nánássy, György   56, 67
Nehru, Jawaharlal   205, 233
Neihard John G   145
Nemes, Gusztáv   190, 202
Noske, Gustav   59, 70, 80, 81, 86, 90

Öcalan, Abdullah   xviii, 2
Olzak, Susan   186, 201
Onódy-Molnár, Dóra   240
Orbán, Viktor   xvi, 16, 20, 29, 122, 144, 150, 151, 155, 159, 213, 214, 220-229, 234, 235, 237-242
Ormos, Mária   149
Orosz, Éva   240
Orpheus   xx, xxiv
Orwell, George   xxii, 16
Otto III, the Bavarian   144
Overy, Richard   91

Pannekoek, Anton   25, 130, 141, 147, 148, 154
Pastor, Peter   66, 149
Patrias, Carmela   201, 202
Paxton, Robert O.   28
Pearlstein, Steven   31
Pelosi, Nancy   20
Pepper, John   155, 260
Péteri, György   116, 118, 119
Pető, Andrea   xv
Petőfi, Sándor   195
Petschnig, Mária-Zita   225, 241
Piketty, Thomas   28, 219, 238
Pikler, Gyula   152
Pogány, József   101, 109, 135, 138, 139, 152, 155
Pók, Attila   65
Polanyi, Karl   x, xiii, 2, 7, 23, 28, 29, 64, 97, 143, 144, 179, 180, 182, 209, 235, 236, 238, 266
Polanyi-Levitt, Kari   xvi, xvii, 64, 152, 219, 238
Pór Ernő   30, 54, 105

Poulantzas, Nicos 146, 214
Priestland, David 88, 89
Princip, Gavrilo xxv
Pulszky, Ágost 152
Puskás, Julianna 65, 260
Putin, Vladimir 145, 150, 213

Radek, Karl 17, 30
Radnóti, Miklós 234
Rajk, László Sr. xviii
Rajk, László Jr. xii, xiii, 148, 236, 237
Rákos, Ferenc 137, 138, 153, 154
Rákosi, Mátyás 86, 144, 152-154, 163, 198-200, 202, 203, 212, 235
Rand, Ayn 142
Ránki, György 211, 234, 235, 246
Raska, Jan 201
Rawls, John 143
Reisman, George 142
Riddell, John 90, 91
Rigó, Anita 240, 241
Ripp, Zoltán 238
Roberts, Michael 29
Robespierre, Maximilien 149
Robinson, William F. 236
Romney, Mitt 10
Romsics, Ignác 65, 151
Rónai, Zoltán 129, 135, 152, 153
Rosenfeld, Gavriel D. 91
Rosenwald, Brian 242
Roussopoulos, Dimitrios x, xi, xv, 243
Rowe, John 224
Rucker, Philip xxiv
Rudas, László 25, 130, 147, 148, 156

Sakmyster, Thomas 155
Salazar, Antonio 20
Salée, Daniel xvii, 265
Sallai, Imre 138, 154
Salman, Mohammed bin 15, 29, 149, 150
Sanders, Bernie 20
Sántha, Pál 202
Sargentini, Judith 242
Sarlós, Béla 153, 260
Schafranek, Hans 164

Schapiro, Leonard xiv, xv
Scheidemann, Philipp 68, 71, 82, 85, 91
Schlett, István 65
Schumer, Chuck 20
Schumpeter Joseph A. 13, 29
Seery, John E. 148, 260
Seidler, Ernő 56, 153
Sen, Amartya 143
Serge, Victor 7, 17, 28
Simor, András 67
Sinkó, Ervin 58, 67
Sipos, Mihály 196
Sleeping Beauty x, xx, xxi, xxiv, xxv, 211, 214, 217, 228, 232
Slottman, William B. 31, 148, 253
Smith, Adam 13, 15
Smith, Stephen A. 91
Somogy, Zoltán 150
Sós-Károly, Attila 237
Spence, Michael 29
Sperber, Jonathan 89
Stalin, Joseph xviii, 17-20, 30, 34, 116, 144, 155, 166, 213
Stephenson, Scott 89-91
Stiglitz, Robert 29
Stolpa Józsefné 178
Street, Paul 27
Stubnya, Bence 240
Sugár, Tivadar 43, 47, 56, 97, 101, 178
Sükösd, Miklós 143, 247
Suzanne 156
Sykes and Picot 145, 250
Sylvester II, the Pope 144
Szabó, András 153
Szabó, Dezső 35
Szabó, Ervin xiii, 26, 42, 57, 97, 143, 151
Szabó, Péter 234
Szájer, József 144, 238
Szálasi, Ferenc 195, 208
Szalatnay, Mark 188
Szamuely, Tibor 18, 30, 105, 130, 138-141, 148, 149, 153-155
Szapor, Judit xv, xix, 65
Székely, Sarolta 239
Szentágotai, József 194, 202

Szentkirályi, Balázs 241
Szerb, Antal 234
Szicherle, Patrick 241
Szilágyi, Dezső 67
Szirtes, András 234
Szirtes, Zoltán 234
Szőke, István 190, 196
Szőts, Zoltán 151, 153

Tambakaki, Paulina 147
Táncsics, Mihály 195, 235
Tardos, Márton 237
Tarján, Tamás M. 153, 154, 262
Tárkány-Szűcs Attila 237
Tarr Márkus Judith 148
Tarr, Zoltán 148
Tilly, Charles 5, 27, 143
Tisza, István xii, 41, 42, 44, 47, 48, 65, 168
Tito, Josip Broz 144
Tőkés, Rudolf L. 64, 67, 129, 147, 236, 238
Tömöry, Márta 27
Tormay, Cecile 150, 178
Tóth, Árpád 3, 27, 35, 36
Trádler, Henrietta 136
Trotsky, Leon 2, 5, 17, 27, 90, 149
Trump, Donald J. xxiv, 9, 15, 20-22, 27, 28, 30, 129, 145, 150, 228, 239, 241

Urbán, László 238, 241

Vajda, Mihály 236, 237
Vámbéry, Rusztem 152
Vántus, Károly 62
Varela, Raquel xxi, 1
Varga, Jenő 104, 113, 115
Varga, Lajos 118
Váry, Albert 150
Vásárhelyi, Mária 237
Vermes, Gábor 65
Vincent, Andrew 143
Vincze Edit S. 64
Vix, Ferdinand 149
Völgyes, Iván 65
Vrousalis, Nicholas 91
Wallerstein. Emanuel 146

Weber, Max 121, 122, 143, 148
Weitz, Eric D. 89, 91
Weltner, Jakab 147, 234
Wiezel, Elie 241
Wiles, Peter J. xiv
Wilhelm II, the Emperor 37, 68
Wilkie, Richard W. 31
Will, George F. 28
Wilson, Woodrow 145, 149, 235
Winkler, Heinrich 89
Winter, Károly 199
Wolfe, Bertram D. 31, 156
Wolff, Michael 28
Wolfreys, Jim 22, 23, 31

Yates, Halsey E. 149

Zelikovits, Zvi 234
Zetkin, Clara 2, 164
Zgut, Edit 241
Zimmermann, Susan xv, xvi, 157, 164-166
Zizek, Slavoj 232
Zuboff Shoshana 29
Zubor, Zalán 240

SELECTED BIBLIOGRAPHY

Aczél, Tamás and Mérai, Tibor. *The Revolt of the Mind. A Case History of Intellectual Resistance Behind the Iron Curtain*. New York: Praeger 1959.

Adorno, Theodore W, and Horkheimer, Max. *The Dialectics of the Enlightenment*. Stanford: Stanford UP. 2002.

Ambrus Béla: *A Magyarországi Tanácsköztársaság pénzrendszere*. (The Financial System of the Hungarian Republic of Councils) Budapest, 1979,

Anderson, Harriet. *Utopian Feminism: Women's Movements in fin-de-siècle Vienna*. New Haven. Yale University Press. 1992.

Andics, Erzsébet: *Demokrácia és szocializmus 1918-1919-ben* (Democracy and Socialism: 1918-1919). Budapest, 1948.

Anka. László. "A Vörösterror Magyarországon" (The Red Terror in Hungary). Budapest. *Magyar Hirlap*. August 1, 2019.

Antal, Attila. *The Rise of Hungarian Populism: State Autocracy and the Orbán Regime*. London: Emerald Publishing, 2019

Antal, Attila: "Towards European Direct Democracy: Recommndations on the European Citizens' Initiative" *Civil Szemle*. Vol 22, No 1, 2010

Apor, Péter. *Fabricating Authenticity in Soviet Hungary: The Afterlife of the First Hungarian Soviet Republic in the Age of State Socialism*. London: Anthem Press, 2015.

Aranyossi, Magda. *Az én régi, elsüllyedt világom. Nádas Péter* széljegyzeteivel [My old, drowned world. With annotatons by Péter Nádas). Budapest: Jelenkor Kiadó, 2018.

Aranyossi, Magda. *Rendszertelen önéletrajz* (Unorderly autobiography). Budapest: Kossuth Könyvkiadó, 1978.

Aranyossi, Magda. *Lázadó asszonyok: A magyar nőmunkásmozgalom története 1867– 1919 [Rebellious women: The history of the Hungarian woman workers' movement 1867–1919]*. Budapest: Kossuth Könyvkiadó, 1963.

Arcary. Valerió. *O Martelo da História* (The Hammer of History). Sundermann: 2016

Arendt, Hannah. *On The Origins of Totalitarianism*. Mariner Books, 2001.

Arrighi, Giovanni. *Adam Smith in Beijing*. London: Verso, 2009.

Azzelini, Dario (ed). *An Alternative Labour History: Worker Control and Workplace Democracy*. London: Zed Books Ltd. 2015.

Balabanoff, Angelica. *My Life as a Rebel*. NY: Harper & Brothers, 1938.

Balabanoff Angelica. *Impressions of Lenin*. Ann Aarbor: University of Michigan Press, 1964.

Balassa A. Bela." Collectivization in Hungarian Agriculture". *American Journal of Agricultural Economics*. Vol 42. No. 1. 1960 .

Balázs, Béla. *A látható ember* (The Visible Man). Budapest: Palatinus. 2005 .

Balázs, Béla. *Népmozgalmak és nemzeti bizottságok: 1945-46* (Popular Movements and National Committees: 1945-1946). Budapest: Kossuth Könyvkiadó, 1961.

Bandler, Richard and Grinder, John. *The Structure of Magic: The Book on Language and Therapy*. Palo Alto. Science and Behavior Books (Vol II).1976.

James Barr. *A Line in the Sand: Britain, France and the Struggle That Shaped the Middle East*. New York: Simon & Schuster, 2012.

Bayer, Zsolt. "Sajnos megint ugyan az a bűz".(Unfortunately it's the Same Stench Once Again) *Magyar Hírlap*. January 4, 2011

Bayer, Zsolt. *Hol a pofátlanság határa?* (Where is the Boundary of Shamelessness). Budapest: Kairosz. 2003.

Bayer, Zsolt. *Tűrhetetlen* Part 4. (Intolerable) *Magyar Idők*, July 14, 2017.

Becker, Gabriel. 'The Left in Hungary', *Critique*, Glasgow, No. 9, 1978.

Bentsur, Eytan. *Láng Európa szívében. Kun Béla hatalmának 133 napja* (A Flame in Europe's Heart: The 133 Days of Béla Kun's Rule). Budapest, 2010.

Beller, Steven. *Vienna and the Jews 1867–1938*. Cambridge: Cambridge UP,1989.

Bence, György and Kis, János. 'On Being a Marxist: A Hungarian View', in *The Socialist Register* . London, Merlin Press, 1980.

Berduc, Manuel. *Against Putschism: Paul Levi's Politics, The Comintern, and the Problem of European Revolution, 1918-1923*. Minneapolis: University of Minnesota Press. 2016.

Berend, Iván T and Ránki. György. *Economic Development in East-Central Europe in the 19th and 20th Centuries*. New York: Columbia University Press. 1973.

Bergler, Edmund. *Principles of Self Damage*. New York: The Philosophical Library, 1958.

Bibó, István: "Eltorzult Magyar alkat, zsákutcás Magyar történelem" (Hungary's Distorted Character, the Blind Alleys of her Past), in Bibó István. *Válogatott tanulmányok* (Selected Essays) Budapest: Corvina. 2004.

Bibó István. "A Magyar demokrácia válsága" (The Crisis of Hungarian Democracy). in Bibó, István. *Válogatott tanulmányok* (Selected Essays) Budapest: Corvina. 2004.

Bihari, Péter. *Lövészárkok a hátországban. Középosztály, zsidókérdés, antiszemitizmus az első világháború Magyarországán* (Trenches in the hinterland. Middle class, Jewish question, antisemitism in Hungary during World War I). Budapest: Napvilág. 2008.

Bockman, Johanna. *Markets in the Name of Socialism: The Left-Wing Origins of NeoLiberalism*. Stanford UP. 2011.

Bodó, Béla "The White Terror in Hungary, 1919-1921: The Social Worlds of Paramilitary Groups". *Austrian History Yearbook*. Vol. 42. 2011.

Borgos Anna. "Madzsarné Jászi Alice: A női testkultúra új útjain" (Alice Jászi: On the new paths of Female Body Culture). *Holmi*. May, 2013.

Borgos, Anna. "Elhárító mechanizmusok: Pszichoanalízis és politika találkozásai Hajdu Lilly életútjának tükrében" (Denial Mechanisms: The Encounters of Psychoanalysis and Politics on the Life-Path of Lilly Hajdú) *Thalassa*. Vol 20. No. 1. 2009.

Borhi, László. The *Merchants of the Kremlin: The Economic Roots of Soviet Expansion in Hungary*. Cold War International History Project, Working Paper Series, Vol. 28. Woodrow Wilson International Center of Scholars. 2000.

Borsányi, György. *The Life of a Communist Revolutionary: Béla Kun*. Boulder, Colo: Columbia University Press. 1993.

Borsányi, György. *Októbertől márciusig. Polgári demokrácia Magyarországon, 1918* (From October till March. Bourgeois democracy in Hungary, 1918). Budapest: Kossuth. 1988.

Borus Rózsa (ed). *A század nagy tanúi* (The Century's Great Wirnesses). Budapest: 1978.

Botar, Oliver A. I. "From Avant-Garde to Proletkult in Hungarian Emigre Politico-Cultural Journals: 1922-1924" in *Art and journals on the political front, 1910-1940*. Manuscript. 1997.

Bozóki, András and Sükösd, Miklós. *Anarchism in Hungary: Theory, History, Legacies* (originally published in Hungarian in 1994 as *Az anarchizmus elmélete és magyarországi története*). Translated from the Hungarian by Alan Renwick. New York: Columbia UP. 2005.

Bozóki, András. "Anarchista elméletek Magyarországon: Batthyány Ervin és Schmitt Jenő Henrik." (Anarchist Theories in Hungary: Ervin Batthyány and Jenő Henrik Schmitt). *Világosság*, No. 3. 1985.

Bozóki, András. *The Roundtable Talks of 1989: The Genesis of Hungarian Democracy*. Central European University Press, 2002.

Bozóki. András. "*Façade Pluralism in Semi-Democracies: The Case of Hungary*". A paper presented to the IPSA World Congress, Montréal, Canada. July 24, 2014.

Bödők Gergely. *Vörös és Fehér Terror Magyarországon: 1919-1921*(Red and White Terror in Hungary: 1919-1921). PhD Dissertation. Eszterházy Károly University. Department of History. 2018.

Bödők, Gergely. "Kegyelmes urak a Gyűjtőfogházban: A vörös terror fővárosi túszai" (Gentlemen in the Central Prison: The Hostages of the Red Terror in the Capital). *Múltunk*. No. 4. 2014.

Böhm Vilmos. *Két forradalom tüzében* (In the Cross-fire of Two Revolutions). Münich: Verlag für Kulturpolitik,1923.

Brie, Michael and Thomasberger, Claus (eds). *Karl Polanyi's Vision of a Socialist Transformation*. Montréal: Black Rose Books. 2018.

Broué, Pierre. *The German Revolution 1917-1923*. Chicago: Haymarket Books. 2006.

Broué, Pierre. *Histoire de l'Internationale communiste 1919-1943*, Paris, Fayard. 1997.

Burger, Anne. *The Communist Party of Canada During the Great Depression—Organizing and Class Consciousness*. Burnaby, BC: Simon Fraser University Press. 1980.

Carnoy. Martin. *The State and Political Theory*. Princeton: Princeton University Press, 1984.

Chomsky, Noam and Herman, Edward S. *Manufacturing Consent*. New York: Pantheon Books. 1988.

Cohen, Ronald and Service Elman R. (eds), *Origins of the State*. Philadelphia: Institute for the Study of Human Issues, 1978.

Collier, George A. *Basta! Land and the Zapatista Rebellion in Chiapas (3rd. ed.)*. Oakland, CA: Food First Books. 2008.

Conant, J. *A Poetics of Resistance: The Revolutionary Public Relations of the Zapatista Insurgency*. Oakland, CA: AK Press. 2010.

Congdon Lee. *Exile and Social Thought: Hungarian Intellectuals in Germany and Austria 1919-1933* Princeton UP. 1991.

Congdon, Lee. *Seeing Red: Hungarian Intellectuals in Exile and the Challenge of Communism*. DeKalb, IL: Northern Illinois University Press, 2001.

Conquest, Robert. *The Great Terror: A Reassessment*. 40thAnniversary edition. Oxford: Oxford UP. 2007.

Csunderlik, Péter. Variációk a "defaitizmusra": Az I. világháború és a Galilei Kör antimilitarista tevékenysége galileista memoárokban (Variations on Defeatism : WWI and the Anti-War Activities of the Galilei Circle from the Memoirs of the Participants). *Kommentár*, No 2. 2014.

Csunderlik, Péter. A „vörös farsangtól" a „vörös tatárjárásig." *A Tanácsköztársaság a korai Horthy-korszak pamflet- és visszaemlékezés-irodalmában* (From the 'red carnival' to the 'red invasion.' The Hungarian Soviet Republic in the pamphlet- and remembrance literature of the early Horthy Era). Budapest: Napvilág. 2019.

Csunderlik, Péter. *Radikálisok, szabadgondolkodók, ateisták. A Galilei Kör (1908–1919) története* (Radicals, freethinkers, atheists: The history of the Galilei Circle (1908–1919). Budapest: Napvilág. 2017.

Csunderlik, Péter. *Suhanó kísértetek. Hadszíntér és Hátország* (Scurrying Ghosts Behind the Lines). Budapest: Politikatörténeti Intézet. 2014.

Csunderlik, Péter. „*Tüdővészes diákok"*. *A galileisták képe Tormay Cécile Bujdosó könyvében"* (Tubercular students: The Image of the Galilei Circle's Students in the work of Cecile Tormay). *Kommentár* No. 3. 2012.

Csunderlik Péter, Egry Gábor, Fodor János, Emily Gioielli, Hajdu Tibor (eds). *Kérdések és válaszok. sorozat. 1918-1919-ről* (Questions and Answers on 1918-1919). Budapest: Napvilág. 2018, 2019.

Dale, Gareth. *Karl Polányi: A Life on the Left*. New York: Columbia UP. 2016

Dale, Gareth. *Karl Polanyi: The Hungarian Writings*. Manchester: Manchester UP, 2016.

Dalos, György. *Duczynska Ilona: A cselekvés szerelmese*. (Enraptured by Action.) Budapest: Kossuth kiadó. 1984.

Deleuze, Gilles and Félix Guattari. *Anti-Oedipus: Capitalism and Schitzophrenia*. London: Penguin Classics. 2009.

Demény, Pál: *A párt foglya voltam* (I was the Party's Prisoner). Budapest: Elte/MKKE.1988.

Derrida, Jacques. *Specters of Marx*. (trans. Peggy Kamuf) London: Routledge 1994.

Derrida, Jacques. *Positions*. London: The Althone Press, 1981.

Dietz, Károly. *Októbertől – augusztusig: Emlékirataim* (From October till August. My memoirs). Budapest: Rácz Vilmos Könyvkiadó. 1920.

Donáth, Ferenc. "István Bibó and the Fundamental Issue of Hungarian Democracy", in *The Socialist Register 1981*, London, Merlin Press, 1981.

Duczynska, Ilona. *Workers in Arms. The Austrian Shutzbund and the Civil War in Austria*. New York: Monthly Review Press. 1978.

Duczynska, Ilona and Horváth, Zoltán. *Polányi Károly és a Galilei Kör* (Karl Polanyi and the Galilei Circle) *Századok*, No. 1. 1971.

Duczynska Ilona, *Korán Reggel* (Early Morning) *Új Írás*. March. 1973.

Duczynska, Ilona. *A cselekvés boldogtalan szerelmese* (The Unhappy Lover of Action*). Valóság*. No 5. 1978.

Dye, Thomas R. *Understanding Public Policy*. Englewood Cliffs, NJ: Prentice Hall. 1972.

Erdély, Jenő. *Mit akarnak? Károlyi pártja, a szociáldemokraták, radikálisok, keresztény szocialisták, földművelők, bolsevikiek? Az összes magyar politikai pártok programmja és szervezete* (What do they want? The party of Károlyi, the social democrats, radicals, christian socialists, farmers, bolsheviks? A complete guide to the program and organization of Hungarian political parties). Budapest: Benkő Gyula Publisher. 1919.

Erényi, Tibor. *Szocializmus a századelőn:Tanulmányok a magyarországi munkásmozgalom történetéből* (Socialism at the beginning of the twentieth century. Essays on the history of the Hungarian labour movements, 1868–1898) Budapest: Kossuth Könyvkiadó. 1979.

Éber, Márk Áron. *A csepp: A félperifériás magyar társadalom osztályszerkezete* (The Drop: The Structure of Hingary's Semi-Peripheral Society). Budapest: Napvilág Kiadó. 2020.

Eckelt, Frank . *The Rise and Fall of the Béla Kun Regime in 1919*. New York: PhD Dissertation, New York University.*1965.*

Epkenhans, Michael. "'Red Sailors' and the Demise of the German Empire", in Bell, Christopher and Elleman, Bruce, eds., *Naval Mutinies of the Twentieth Century. An International Perspective*, London: Routledge 2003.

Erdős, András Patrik. „A Tanácsköztársaság alternatív büntetőpolitikája: A Budapesti Forradalmi Törvényszék Kísérleti Kriminológiai Osztályának működése (The Alternative Punitive Policies of the Republic of Councils: The Budapest Revolutionary Court's Department of Experimental Criminology). *Clio Műhelytanulmányok*. No. 3. 2018.

Eshelman, Nancy G. "Forging a Socialist Women's Movement: Angelica Balabanoff in Switzerland," in Betty Boyd Caroli, R.F. Harney, and Lydio F. Tomasi Eds., *The Italian Immigrant Woman in North America*. Toronto: Multicultural Historical Society of Ontario, 1978.

Fanon, Frantz. *The wretched of the earth*. Harmondsworth: Penguin. *1983.*

Farkas, József. Gondolatok a Tanácsköztársaság Irodalmáról II. (Thoughts About the Literature of the Commune). *Irodalomtörténeti Közlemények*. Vol. LXIII. No 3-4. 1959.

Farkas, József. *Értelmiség és forradalom: Kultúra, sajtó és irodalom a Magyar Tanácsköztársaságban* (Intellectuals and Revolution: Culture, Media and Literature in the Hungarian Republic of Councils). Budapest: 1984.

Fábry, *Ádám. The Political Economy of Hungary: From State Capitalism to Authoritarian Neoliberalism.* London: Pelgrave Pivot, 2019.

Fekete, László Bús. *Katona-forradalmárok* (Soldier revolutionists). Budapest: Phőnix, 1918.

Fehér, Ferenc. "Kádárism as the Model State of Khruschevism", *Telos,* St. Louis, No. 47, Summer 1979.

Felkay, Andrew. *Hungary and the USSR, 1956-1988: Kádár's Political Leadership.* Greenwood Press, 1989.

Fernbach, David. *In the Steps of Rosa Luxemburg: Selected Writings of Paul Levi.* Chicago: Haymarket Books. 2011

Ferro, Marc. *Des soviets au communisme bureaucratique,* Paris : Gallimard, 2nd ed. 2017

Fischer, Ruth. *Stalin and German Communism.* Cambridge, Mass: Harvard UP 1948.

Fitzgerald, Edward Peter. "France's Middle Eastern ambitions, the Sykes-Picot negotiations, and the oil fields of Mosul, 1915–1918". *Journal of Modern History.* Vol 66. No. 4. 1994.

Florence, Ronald. *Marx's Daughters: Eleanor Marx, Rosa Luxemburg, Angelica Balabanoff.* NY: Dial Press, 1975.

Flyvbjerg, Bent. *Ideal Theory, Real Rationality: Habermas Versus Foucault and Nietzsche.* Paper for the Political Studies Association's 50th Annual Conference, *The Challenges for Democracy in the 21st Century,* London School of Economics and Political Science, 10-13 April 2000.

Foucault, Michel. *Discourse and Truth: the Problematization of Parrhesia.* Digital Archive: Foucault.info, 1999.

Freidenreich, Harriet Pass. *Female, Jewish, and Educated: The Lives of Central European University Women.* Bloomington: Indiana University Press. 2002.

Frölich, Paul. *Rosa Luxemburg: Ideas in Action.* Chicago: Haymarket Books. 2010 (First published in German in 1928).

Garami, Ernő. *Forrongó Magyarország. Emlékezések és tanulságok* (Seething Hungary. Recollections and lessons). Budapest: Primusz. 1989 (First published in 1922).

Gábor Sándorné: *Ausztria és a magyarországi Tanácsköztársaság* (Austria and the Hungarian Republic of Councils). Budapest, 1969.

Gábor Sándorné–Hajdu Tibor–Szabó Gizella (ed.): *A magyar munkásmozgalom történetének válogatott dokumentumai. Hatodik kötet. A Magyar Tanácsköztársaság 1919. március 21.–1919. augusztus 1. Első rész. 1919. március 21. – 1919. június 11.* (Selected Documents of the Hungarian Labour Movement). Budapest: Kossuth. 1959.

Gárdonyi, Máté. *Az antiszemitizmus funkciója Prohászka Ottokár és Bangha Béla társadalomképében.* (The Role Played by Antisemitism in the Social Views of Ottokár Prohászka and Béla Bangha). Budapest: Holokauszt Emlékközpont. 2005.

Gárdos, Mariska. *Százarcú élet* (Hundred-faced life). Budapest: Szépirodalmi Könyvkiadó, 1975

Gáti. Charles. *Failed Illusion: Moscow, Washington Budapest and the Hungarian Revolt.* Woodrow Wilson Center Press. 2006.

Gáti. Charles. *Hungary and the Soviet Bloc.* Duke University Press. 1986.

Gellért, László. *Diákok a forradalomban. 1918-1919*. Budapest, 1969.

Gellért, Ádám.. "Temessétek élve a holttestek közé". (Burry them alive Between the Dead).*Index.hu*. August 13, 2019.

Gerber, John P. *Anton Pannekoek and the Socialism of Workers' Self Emancipation, 1873-1960*. Springer. 1990.

Gergely, Jenő: *A magyarországi forradalmak 1918-1919* (The Hungarian Revolutions). Budapest: 1991.

German, Jurij. *Történetek Drzezsinszkij életéből* (Stories from Dzerzhinsky's Life). (Trans: Rákos, Ferenc). Budapest: Új Magyar Könyvkiadó. 1949.

Gioielli, Emily R. *"White Misrule": Terror and Political Violence during Hungary's Long World War I, 1919-1924*. Budapest: PhD Dissertation. Central European University. 2015

Gluck, Mary. *Georg Lukacs and his Generation: 1900-1918*. Cambridge, Massachusetts: Harvard University Press. 1985.

Goldman, Emma, Alexander Berkman, *et al. 1917: The Revolution in Russia and its Aftermath*. Montréal: Black Rose Books. 2017.

Göllner, András B. "The Foundations of Soviet Domination and Communist Political Power in Hungary: 1945-1950" in *The Canadian-American Review of Hungarian Studies*. Vol III. No 2. 1976.

Göllner, András B. *The Politics of Hungary's New Economic Mechanism*. London: Phd Dissertation. The London School of Economics. 1978

Göllner, András B. *Social Change and Corporate Strategy*. Stamford. IAP. 1983.

Göllner, András B. "Portrait of an Abusive Relationship" *Journal of Parliamentary and Political Law*. Ottawa. Thomson Reuters. 2017.

Göllner András B. "Aporetika: A Demokratikus politikai diskurzus csődje Magyarországon" (Aporetics: The Bankruptcy of Democratic Political Discourse in Hungary). Budapest. *Élet és Irodalom* (Life and Literature). April 17, 2009.

Göllner András B. "A Fidesz Nyelve" (The Language of Fidesz). *Kanadai Magyar Hírlap*. April 24, 2015

Gough, Roger. *A Good Comrade: János Kádár, Communism and Hungary*. Bloomsbury Academic Press, 2006.

Gramsci.Antonio. *Prison Notebooks*. (Vol 1-3) New York: Columbia University Press. 2011.

Gratz, Gusztáv. *A Bolsevizmus Magyarországon* (Bolshevism in Hungary) (new ed) Budapest Méry Ratio, 2016.(First published in 1921).

Gratz, Gusztáv. *A forradalmak kora. Magyarország története 1918-1920*. (The Age of Revolutions: The History of Hungary 1918-1920) First Published in Budapest in 1935, Latest ed. Budapest . Akademiai Könyvkiadó, 1992.

Gruber, Helmut. 1991. *Red Vienna. Experiment in Working Class Culture, 1919-1934.*, Oxford University Press.

Gyarmati, György. *Államvédelem a Rákosi korszakban* (State Security in the Rákosi Era). Budapest. Történeti Hivatal. 2000.

Györe, Balázs *Barátaim, akik besúgóim is voltak* (My Friends Who Snitched on Me) Budapest. Kalligram. 2012.

Haas, György. *A szabadság tábornoka. Bartha Albert* (The general of freedom. Bartha Albert). Budapest, Kairosz. 2002.

Habermas, Jürgen. *Theory of Communicative Action, Volume One: Reason and the Rationalization of Society.* Boston: Beacon Press. 1984.

Habermas, Jürgen. *Theory of Communicative Action, Volume Two: Lifeworld and System: A Critique of Functionalist Reason. Boston: Beacon Press.*1987.

Habermas, Jürgen. *The Philosophical Discourse of modernity.* Cambridge, MA: MIT Press, 1987.,

Habermas, Jürgen. *Moral Consciousness and Communicative Action.* Cambridge Polity Press, 1990.

Habermas, Jürgen. *Between Facts and Norms.* Cambridge Polity Press, 1996.

Haffner, L. Sebastian. *Az elárult forradalom: Németország, 1918–19* (The betrayed Revolution: Germany, 1918–19), Budapest. Európa. 2007.

Hajdu, Tibor. *Tanácsok Magyarországon 1918–1919-ben* (Councils in Hungary in 1918–1919). Budapest, Kossuth), 1958.

Hajdu, Tibor. *A Magyarországi Tanácsköztársaság* (The Hungarian Soviet Republic). Budapest, Kossuth, 1969.

Hajdu. Tibor. "The Hungarian Soviet Republic". *Studia Historica.* Vol. 131. Academiae Scientiarum Hungaricae. Budapest, 1979.

Hajdu, Tibor. *Ki volt Károlyi Mihály?* (Who was Mihály Károlyi?). Budapest, Napvilág. 2012.

Hajnal, István. *Az újkor története* (The History of the Modern Age). Budapest. Magyar Szemle Társaság. 1936.

Halasi, Béla. "Szabó Ervin". *Szociálpolitikai Szemle,* 1918.

Halász, Pál. (ed). Tanulmányok a Magyar Tanácsköztársaság államáról és jogáról (Studies on the State and Legal System of the Republic of Councils) Budapest, 1955.

Hanebrink, l. Paul. *A Specter Haunting Europe. The Idea of Judeo-Bolshevism in Twentieth Century Europe.* Cambridge, Mass: Harvard University Press. 2018.

Harari, Yuval Noah. *Sapiens: A Brief History of Humankind.* New York: Signal Editions. 2016.

Haraszti, Miklós. *A Worker in a Workers' State.* New York: Universe Books, 1978.

Haraszti, Miklós. 'What is Marxism? ' in Frantisek Silnitsky, Larisa Silnitsky and Karl Reyman (ed.), *Communism and Eastern Europe,* Brighton: Harvester Press, 1979.

Haraszti Miklós. *A cenzúra esztétikája.* Budapest: AB Független kiadó 1986.

Haraszti, Miklós. *The Velvet Prison.* New York: Basic Books. 1987.

Hatos, Pál. *Az elátkozott köztársaság – Az 1918-as összeomlás és forradalom története* (The Damned Republic – The Story of the 1918 Collapse and Revolution). Budapest. Jaffa. 2018.

Hatos, Pál. *Rosszfiúk világforradalma: Az 1919-es Magyarországi Tanácsköztársaság története* (The World Revolution of the Bad Boys: The Story of the 1919 Hungarian Republic of Councils). Budapest. Jaffa. 2021.

Haynes. Mike "Hungary: Workers' Councils Against Russian Tanks" *International Socialism*. Autumn, 2006.

Hedges, Christopher. *Empire of Illusion: The End of Literacy and the Triumph of Spectacle*. Toronto: Alfred A. Knopf. 2009.

Held, David, *et al*, eds, *States and Societies*. Oxford. Basil Blackwell, 1985.

Hevesi, Gyula: *Szociális termelés. A Magyar Tanácsköztársaság iparpolitikája.* (Socialist Production: The Industrial Policy of the Hungarian Republic of Councils). Budapest, 1959.

Hevesi, Gyula: *Egy mérnök a forradalomban.* (An Engineer During the Revolution) Budapest: Európa.1959.

Hobsbawm, Eric. *The Age of Extremism*. London: Abacus Books. 1994.

Hochschild, Adam. *King Leopold's Ghost*. New York: Houghton Mifflin. 1999.

Hoffrogge, Ralf. *Working-Class Politics in the German Revolution: Richard Müller, the Revolutionary Shop Stewards and the Origins of the Council Movements*. Chicago, IL. Haymarket Books. 2015.

Holloway, John. *Change the World Without Taking Power*. London: Pluto, 2002.

Honeycutt, Karen. "Clara Zetkin: A left-wing socialist and feminist in Wilhelmian Germany," New York: Columbia University, 1975.

Howlett, M. Ramesh and A. Perl. *Studying Public Policy: Policy Cycles and Policy Subsystems*. 3rd Edition. London. Oxford University Press. 2009.

Hulse, James, W. *The Forming of the Communist International*. Stanford, CA: Stanford University Press. 1964.

Huszár, Ákos and Berger, Viktor. "Az új középosztály?" (The New Middle Class?) *in Politikatudományi Szemle*. (Political Science Review of the Hungarian Academy of Science) Vol. XXIX, no. 2, 2020.

Huszár Károly (ed). *A proletárdiktatúra Magyarországon. A bolsevista rémuralom hiteles története* (The Proletarian Dictatorship in Hungary: The Authenthic Story of the 1919 Bolshevik Reign of Terror) Budapest, 1920.

Huszár, Tibor. *Bibó István: Beszélgetések* (István Bibó: Conversations) Budapest. Magyar Krónika. 1989.

Illyés, Gyula. *Puszták népe* (People of the Plains) Budapest: 1936. For the English translation see: *People of the Puszta*, Translation and afterword by G.F. Cushing, London: Chatto and Windus. 1967.

Innis, Harold A. *The Bias of Communications*. Toronto: University of Toronto Press, 1951.

Janos, Andrew C. and Slottman, William (eds). *Revolution in Perspective: Essays on the Hungarian Soviet Republic of 1919*. Berkeley, CA: University of California Press, 1971.

Jászai, Samu. *A szakszervezetek föladatai a kommunista társadalomban.* (The Role of the Trade Unions in Communist Society) *Szakszervezeti Értesítő.* (Trade Union News) Vol XVI. No.7. May 31, 1919.

Jászi, Oscar. *Revolution and Counterrevolution in Hungary.* London: P.S. King and Sons Ltd. 1924.

Jenei, Károly. *Az iizemi bizottságok a munkáshatalomért* (The Factory Committees in the Struggle for Workers' Power: 1944- 1948). Budapest: Táncsics. 1966.

Kaes, Anton, Jay, Martin, and Dimendberg, Edward, eds., 1994. *The Weimar Republic Sourcebook,* Berkeley:University of California Press.

Kassák Lajos. *Levél Kun Bélához a művészet nevében.* (Letter to Béla Kun in the Name of Art) Budapest. *Ma.* Vol 4. No.7, 1919.

Kassák, Lajos. *Egy ember élete. Önéletrajz.* (Memoirs) Budapest. Magvető, 1983.

Katsiaficas, George. *The Subversion of Politics: European Autonomous Social Movements and the Decolonization of Everyday Life.* BRILL, 1997.

Katsiaficas, George. *The Global Imagination of 1968: Revolution and Counterrevolution.* PM Press, 2018.

Kautsky, Karl. *The Dictatorship of the Proletariat.* Ann Arbor, MI: University of Michigan, 1964. (First published in 1918).

Kautsky, Karl. *Terrorism and Communism: A Contribution to the Natural History of Revolution.* London: National Labour Press, 1921.

Károlyi, Mihály. *Hit illúziók nélkül.* (Faith Without Illusions) Budapest: Európa Könyvkiadó, 1982.

Károlyi, Mihály: *Egy egész világ ellen* (Against the Whole World). Münich: Verlag. 1922.

Kelen Jolán: *Eliramlik az élet* (Life Goes Fast). Budapest, 1976.

Kelen, Jolán: *Galilei-per a XX. Században* (The Galilei Trial in the 20th Century). Budapest, Kossuth. 1957.

Kemény István and Bill Lomax (eds). *Magyar munkástanácsok 1956-ban. Dokumentumok* (Hungarian workers' councils in 1956: Documents). *Magyar Füzetek,* Paris, 1986.

Kende János. *Forradalomról forradalomra. Az 1918-1919-es forradalmak Magyarországon* (From revolution to revolution: The revolutions of 1918-1919 in Hungary). Budapest., Gondolat, 1979.

Kende János. "Az önigazgatás kezdeményei a Tanácsköztársaságban" in. Krausz Tamás – Vértes Judit (eds) *A Magyarországi Tanácsköztársaság és a kelet-európai forradalmak.* Budapest, 2010.

Kets, Gaard, and Muldoon, James, "The "Forgotten" German Revolution: A Conceptual Map", in Kets, Gaard and Muldoon, James, (eds). *The German Revolution and Political Theory,* Cham (Switzerland): Palgrave Macmillan. 2019.

Kis, János 'Thoughts on the Immediate Future' in *Labour Focus on Eastern Europe,* Vol. 5, No. 5, Autumn 1982.

Kis, János (alias Marc Rakovski). *Towards an East European Marxism,* London: Allison & Busby,1978.

Knight, Amy. *Beria: Stalin's First Lieutenant.* Princeton University Press. 1995.

Kóbor, Tamás. *A bolsevismusról a bolsevismus alatt (About Bolshevism during Bolshevism).* Budapest: Franklin Társulat. 1919.

Kolnai, Aurél: *Politikai emlékiratok* (Politikai Memoirs). Budapest : Európa. 2005.

Konok, Péter. « Az erőszak kérdései 1919-1920-ban : Vörösterror-Fehérterror" (The Questions of Coecion in 1919-1920: Red and White Terror). *Múltunk.* No 3. 2010.

Konrád, György and Szelényi, Iván. *The Intellectuals on the Road to Class Power,* Brighton: Harvester Press, 1979.

Kopácsi, Sándor. *In the Name of the Working Class: The Inside Story of the Hungarian Revolution.* New York: Grove Press, 1987.

Kopátsy Sándor. *Kádár és kora* (Kádár and his Age). Budapest : CET Belvárosi könyvkiadó, 2005.

Krausz, Tamás – Vértes Judit (eds). *A Magyarországi Tanácsköztársaság és a kelet-európai forradalmak.* Budapest, 2010.

Krausz, Tamás. *Reconstructing Lenin: An Intellectal Biography.* New York: Monthly Review Press. 2015.

Krausz, Tamás. "The Hungarian Workers' Councils of 1956". *Workers Liberty.* October 31, 2006.

Krausz, Tamás and Varga, Éva (eds). *A magyar megszálló csapatok a Szovjetunióban. Levéltári dokumentumok 1941–1947* (The Hungarian Occupation Forces in the Soviet Union. Archival Documents 1941-1947) Budapest: L'Harmattan. 2013.

Kropotkin, Peter. *Mutual Aid: A Factor of Evolution.* London. Freedom Press. 2009.

Kruks, Sonia, Rapp, Rayna and Young, Marilyn B (eds). *Promissory Notes: Women in the Transition to Socialism.* New York: Monthly Review Press, 1989.

Kuhn, Gabriel (ed). *All Power to the Councils! A Documentary History of the German Revolution of 1918-1919,* Oakland: PM Press. 2012.

Kun, Béla. *A Magyar Tanácsköztársaságról. Válogatott beszédek és írások* (About the Hungarian Soviet Republic. Collected speeches and essays). Budapest: Kossuth. 1958.

Kun Béláné *Kun Béla.* Budapest : Magvető. 1969.

Lafleur, Ingrun. "Five Socialist Women: Traditionalist Conflicts and Socialist Visions in Austria, 1893–1934." In Marilyn J. Boxer & Jean H. Quataert, eds. *Socialist Women: European Socialist Feminism in the Nineteenth and Twentieth Centuries.* New York: 1978.

Lafont, Maria. *The Strange Comrade Balabanoff: The Life of a Communist Rebel.* McFarland Publishers. 2016.

Lampert, Evgeny. *Sons Against Fathers: Studies in Russian Radicalism and Revolution.* Oxford: Oxford University Press. 1965.

Lasky, Melvin J (ed). *The Hungarian Revolution,* London: Secker & Warburg,1957.

Lasswell, Harold D. *Politics: Who Gets What, When and How.* New York: Whittlesey House. 1936.

Lazitch, Branko and Drackovitch, Marko. *Lenin and the Comintern.* Vol I. Stanford: Stanford UP. 1972.

Lányi, Ernőné (ed.), *Nagy idők tanúi emlékeznek, 1918–1919* (Witnesses of great times remember, 1918–1919). Budapest. Kossuth. 1959.

László Péter. "The Holy Crown of Hungary, Visible and Invisible." *The Slavonic and East European Review*, Vol. 81, No. 3. 2003.

Lengyel, József. *From beginning to end.* (Translated from the Hungarian by Ilona Duczynska). London. Peter Owen 1966.

Lengyel, József. *Confrontation.* (Translated from the Hungariann by Ilona Duczynska) London, Peter Owen, 1973.

Lenin, V. I. *The Proletarian Revolution and the Renegade Kautsky* in *V.I. Lenin Collected Works: Volume 28, July 1918-March 1919.* Moscow: Progress Publishers, 1965.

Lenin, V.I. *The State and Revolution.* Penguin classics ed. 1993.

Liptai, Ervin. *A Magyar Tanácsköztársaság* (The Hungarian Republic of Councils). Budapest: Kossuth. 1965.

Litván, György and Varga, János F (eds) *Jászi Oszkár válogatott levelei* (Selected Letters of Oszkár Jászi) Budapest: Magvető. Budapest,1990.

Litván, György. *Szabó Ervin, a szocializmus moralistája.* Életrajz (Ervin Szabó: Socialism's Moralist. A Biography). Budapest: Századvég, 1993.

Litván, György. *A Twentieth-Century Prophet: Oszkár Jászi, 1875–1957.* Budapest, CEU Press. 2006.

Lomax, Bill. *Hungary 1956.* London: Allison & Busby, 1976.

Lomax, Bill. "A Chronology of Political and Intellectual Opposition under the Kádár Regime: 1956-1978". *Labour Focus on Eastern Europe*, Vol. 3, No. 3, July-August 1979.

Lomax, Bill. "25 Years Later-New Light on 1956", *Labour Focus on Eastern Europe,* Vol. 5, No. 3, Summer 1982.

Lomax, Bill. 'The Workers Councils of Greater Budapest', in *The Socialist Register 1976,* London, Merlin Press, 1976.

Löwy, Michael. "Lukács and Stalinism." *New Left Review.* May-June. 1975.

Luban, Ottokar. "Rosa Luxemburg's critique of Lenin's ultra-centralistic party concept and of the Bolshevik Revolution." *Critique,*Vol 40. No.3. 2012.

Lukács, György. *Political Writings,* (ed by Rodney Livingstone, trans by Michael McColgan). New York: Harper and Row. 1974.

Lukács. György. *History and Class Consciousness.* London:Merlin Press. 1967.

Lukács. György. *The Culture of People's Democracy: Hungarian Essays on Literature, Art and Democratic Transition, 1945–1948.* (Edited and translated by Tyrus Miller) New York: BRILL. 2013,

Luxemburg, Rosa. "Rebuilding the International" *Die Internationale.* Vol 1, No 1. 1915.

Luxemburg, Rosa. *Selected Political Writings.* New York: Monthly Review Press. 1971.

Luxemburg, Rosa. *Socialism or Barbarism?* London: Pluto Press. 2010.

MacMillan, Margaret. *The War that Ended Peace.* New York: Random House. 2014.

MacMillan. Margaret. *Paris 1919.* New York: Random House. 2001.

Magda, Imre and Szerényi Imre. *Budapest – Moszkva: Szovjet-Oroszország és a Magyarországi Tanácsköztársaság kapcsolatai táviratok tükrében. 1919. március 22 - augusztus 1* (Budapest- Moscow: The Relationship Between the Soviet Union and the Republic of Councils in the light of the telegrams between March 22 and August 1, 1919) Budapest, 1979.

Magda, Imre and Szűcs László (eds): *A Forradalmi Kormányzótanács jegyzőkönyvei. 1919* (The Minutes of the Revolutionary Governing Council) Budapest. 1986.

Mason, Paul.*Postcapitalism: A Guide to Our Future.* London: Alan Lane, 2015.

Matlekovits Sándor. *A Tanácsköztársaság közgazdasági politikája* (The Economic Policy of the Republic of Councils). *Közgazdasági Szemle.* No. 47 1920.

McAdams, James A., *Vanguard of the Revolution. The Global Idea of the Communist Party.* Princeton:Princeton University Press. 2017.

McDermott, Kevin; Agnew, Jeremy. *The Comintern. History of international Communism from Lenin to Stalin.* London: MacMillan. 1996.

McRobbie, Kenneth. "Ilona Duczynska Meets Ervin Szabó: The Making of a Revolutionary Personality – From Theory to Terrorism" *Hungarian Studies Review.* No 1-2, 2006.

McRobbie, Kenneth: "Education and the Revolutionary Personality: The Case of Ilona Duczynska," *Canadian Slavonic Papers* Vol 51, No. 4. 2009.

Martyn, Everett. *War and Revolution. The Hungarian Anarchist Movement in World War I and the Budapest Commune.* The Kate Sharpley Library. 2006.

Méray. Tibor.*Thirteen Days that Shook the Kremlin.* New York: Praeger 1959.

Mészáros, István. *Beyond Capital: Toward a Theory of Transition.* New York: Monthly Review Press. 1995

Mészáros, Károly. *Az őszirózsás forradalom és a Tanácsköztársaság parasztpolitikája* (The Chrysanthemum and the Council Revolutions Policies Towards the Peasants). Budapest, 1966.

Mérei, Gyula, *A magyar októberi forradalom és a polgári pártok* (The Hungarian October revolution and bourgeois parties), Budapest, Akadémiai Kiadó. 1969.

Mikonya, György. *A magyar anarchisták iskolaügyi és életreform törekvései* (The Life and Education Reform Efforts of the Hungarian Anarchists) in *Iskolakultúra*, Number 2. 2005

Miljan, Lydia. *Public Policy in Canada.* Oxford: Oxford University Press. 2012.

Miller, Tyrus. "The Phantom of Liberty: György Lukács and the Culture of 'People's Democracy' in György Lukács. *The Culture of People's Democracy: Hungarian Essays on Literature, Art and Democratic Transition, 1945-1948.* (Edited and translated by Tyrus Miller) New York: BRILL. 2013.

Miley, Thomas Jeffrey and Venturini, Frederico (eds). *Your Freedom and Mine.* Montréal. Black Rose Books. 2018.

Molnár János: *A Nagybudapesti Központi Munkástanács* (The Central Workers' Council of Greater Budapest). Budapest, Akadémiai Kiadó, 1969.

Mommen, André. *Stalin's Economist: The Economic Contributions of Jenö Varga.* London: Routledge. 2011.

Móricz, Zsigmond. *A földtörvény kis kátéja. Az 1919: XVIII. néptörvény magyarázata és utasítása a földmíves nép földhöz juttatásáról* (Small catechism of the land reform. An explanation and statement to the XVIII. People Act of 1919 about 'The land to the peasants). Budapest, *Néplap*. 1919.

Mullaney, Marie Marmo. *Revolutionary Women: Gender and the Socialist Revolutionary Role.* NY: Praeger, 1983.

Müller, Rolf: *Politikai rendőrség a Rákosi-korszakban* (The Political Police in the Rákosi Era). Budapest: Jaffa. 2012.

Müller, Rolf. *Az erőszak neve: Péter Gábor* (The Name of Coercion: Gábor Péter) *Budapest:* Jaffa. 2017.

Müller Rolf, Takács Tibor, Tulipán Éva.*Terror 1918-1919. Forradalmárok, ellenforradalmárok, megszállók.* (Revolutionaries, Counterrevolutionaries, Occupiers) Budapest. Jaffa. 2019.

Müller, Tamás B. *Vörös terror az Országházban: 1919.* (The Red Terror in Parliament: 1919.) Budapest. Office of the Hungarian Parliament. 2016.

Münnich, Ferenc: *A Magyar Tanácsköztársaságról* (On the Hungarian Republic of Councils). Budapest. 1969.

Münnich, Ferenc. *Viharos út (Stormy road).* Budapest. Kossuth. 1986.

Nagy, Imre. *On Communism: In Defense of the New Course.* London: Thames and Hudson, 1957.

Nagy, Sándor. *A Budapesti Forradalmi Törvényszék Iratai* (Documents of the Budapest Revolutionary Courts) Budapest Fővárosi Levéltár. *Hungaricana.hu.* 2019.

Nation, Craig, R. *War on War: Lenin, the Zimmerwald Left and the Origin of Communist Internationalism* Duke UP. 1989.

Nádas, Péter. *Világló részletek. Emléklapok egy elbeszélő életéből* (Luminous details. Memory sheets from the life of a storyteller) 2 volumes. Budapest: Jelenkor Kiadó, 2017.

Nánássy, György. *Miért léptem ki a magyarországi kommunista-pártból? A magyar kommunista-vezérek üzelmei* [*Why did I leave the Hungarian communist party? Dealings of Hungarian communist leaders*]. Budapest: 1919.

Negri, Antonio and Hardt, Michael. *Empire.* Boston. Harvard University Pres, 2000.

Negri, Antonio and Hardt, Michael. "Empire, Twenty Years On". *New Left Review.* Vol. 120. 2019.

Ormos Mária. "A Vix jegyzék" (The Vix Memorandum) in *Padovától Trianonig: 1918.1920* (From Padua to Trianon) 3rd Edition. Budapest. Kossuth. 2020.

Pastor, Peter (ed*). Revolution and Interventions in Hungary and its Neighbor States, 1918–1919,* Highland Lakes, N. J: Atlantic Studies on Society in Change.1988.

Pastor, Peter. *Hungary between Wilson and Lenin. The Hungarian Revolution of 1918–1919 and the Big Three. East European Quarterly,* 1976.

Pastor, Peter. "The Vix Mission in Hungary, 1918-1919: A Re-examination," *Slavic Review.* Vol. XXIX, No. 3. 1970.

Pastor, Peter. "Franco-Rumanian Intervention in Russia and the Vix Ultimatum: Background to Hungary's Loss of Transylvania." *Canadian American Review of Hungarian Studies.* 1974.

Patrias, Carmela. *Patriots and Proletarians: Politicizing Hungarian Immigrants in Interwar Canada.* Montréal: McGill-Queen's University Press, 1994.

Patrias, Carmela. *The Kanadai Magyar Újság and the Politics of the Hungarian Canadian Elite,* Toronto: Multicultural History Society of Ontario, November 1978.

Petőcz, György. *Csak a narancs volt: A Fidesz egy története.* (It was Only the Orange: A History of Fidesz) Budapest: Irodalom Kft. 2001.

Péteri György: *A Magyar Tanácsköztársaság ipariránitási rendszere* (The Management of Industry Under the 1919 Republic of Councils). Budapest: 1979.

Petrák, Katalin- Milei György (eds) *A Magyar Tanácsköztársaság művelődéspolitikája* (The Educational Policy of the Hungarian Republic of Councils). Budapest: 1959.

Piketty, Thomas. *Capital in the Twenty-First Century.* Cambridge, MA: Belknap Press. 2014

Piketty, Thomas.*Capital and Ideology.* Boston. Harvard University Press. 2020.

Pók, Attila: *A Tanácsköztársaság helye a magyar történelemben* (The Republic of Councils Place in Hungarian History) in *Such, György (ed) A Magyarországi Tanácslöztársaság* (The Hungarian Republic of Councils). Budapest: Parliamentary Publishing House. 2020.

Pók, Attila. *A haladás hitele: Progresszió, bűnbakok, összeesküvők* (The Credibility of Progress). Budapest: Akadémiai, 2010.

Pók, Attila. *A magyarországi radikális demokrata ideológia kialakulása. A „Huszadik Század" társadalomszemlélete (1900–1907)* (The development of Hungarian radical democratic ideology: The Social attitude of Journal, *Huszadik Század* (1900–1907). Budapest: Akadémiai Kiadó. 1990.

Polanyi, Karl. "Universal Capitalism or Regional Planning?" *The London Quarterly of World Affairs.* Vol. 10. No 3. 1945.

Polanyi, Karl. *The Great Transformation.* Boston: The Beacon Press. 1957 (1st published in 1944).

Polanyi, Karl. "Aristotle Discovers the Economy." in Karl Polanyi, Conrad M. Arensberg and Harry W. Pearson (eds). *Trade and Markets in the Early Empires.* Glencoe: The Free Press. 1957.

Polanyi-Levitt, Kari (ed.) *The Life and Work of Karl Polanyi; A Celebration.* Montréal: Black Rose Books. 1990.

Polanyi-Levitt, Kari and McRobbie, Kenneth (eds). *Karl Polanyi in Vienna.* Montréal: Black Rose Books. 2006.

Polanyi-Levitt, Kari. *From the Great Transformation to the Great Financialization.* Halifax/Winnipeg: Fernwood Publications. 2013.

Poulantzas. Nicos. *State, Power, Socialism.* New York: New Left Books. 1978.

Priestland, David, 2009. *The Red Flag. A History of Communism,* New York: Grove Press.

Prohászka Ottokár. *A Zsidókérdés Magyarországon* (The Jewish Question in Hungary) Budapest. 1920.

Puskás, Julianna. *From Hungary to the United States, 1880–1914.* Budapest: Akadémiai Kiadó. 1982.

Rabinbach, Anson. *The Crisis of Austrian Socialism: From Red Vienna to Civil War. 1927–1934.* Chicago, IL: University of Chicago Press. 1983.

Réti, László (ed). *A Magyar Tanácsköztársaság* (The Hungarian Republic of Councils). Budapest, 1949.

Révész, Tamás. „Nemzetőrök, polgárőrök, népőrök: A Károlyi kormány karhatalmi szervei" (National Guards, Public Guards, Peoples Guards: The Law Enforcement Organs of the Károlyi Government). Budapest: *Rubicon.* No. 3, 2015.

Riddell, John (editor and translator). *Workers of the World and Oppressed Peoples, Unite!: Proceedings and Documents of the Second Congress, 1920.* In two volumes. New York: Pathfinder Press, 1991.

Riddell, John. (ed). *The German Revolution and the Debate on Soviet Power. Documents: 1918-1919. Preparing the Founding Congress,* New York: Pathfinder. 1986

Ripp Zoltán. *Szabad Demokraták: Történeti vázlat a Szabad Demokraták Szövetségének politikájáról (1988-1994)* (On the Alliance of Free Democrats) Budapest: Napvilág Kiadó. 1995.

Ripp Zoltán: 1956. Forradalom és szabadságharc Magyarországon (1956. Revolution and fight for freedom in Hungary). Budapest, Korona Kiadó, 2002.

Robinson, William F. *The Pattern of Reform in Hungary: A Political, Economic and Cultural Analysis.* New York: Praeger. 1973.

Romsics, Ignác *Hungary in the Twentieth Century.* Budapest: Corvina–Osiris. 1999.

Rosenfeld, Gavriel D. «Monuments and the Politics of Memory: Commemorating Kurt Eisner and the Bavarian Revolutions of 1918-1919 in Postwar Munich», *Central European History,* Vol 30, No 2, 1997.

Rorty, Richard M. (ed). *The Linguistic Turn, Essays in Philosophical Method.* Chicago: University of Chicago Press.

Rudas, László. „Lényeg és Forma" (Essence and Form).*Internationale* May, 1919.

Sakmyster, Thomas. *A Communist Odyssey: The Life of József Pogány/John Pepper* New York: Central European University Press, 2012.

Salamon, Konrád. *Nemzeti önpusztítás 1918-1920* (National Self-Destruction: 1918-1920). Budapest: Korona Kiadó. 2001.

Sargent, Lydia, ed., *Women and Revolution: A Discussion of the Unhappy Marriage of Marxism and Feminism,* Boston 1981

Sarlós, Béla. *A Tanácsköztársaság forradalmi törvényszékei* (The Courts of the Republic of Councils). Budapest: 1961.

Seery, John E. "Marxism and Artwork: Weber and Lukács in Heidelberg. 1912-1914". *The Berkeley Journal of Sociology.* Vol 27. (Special Feminist Issue). 1982.

Sen. Amartya.*The Idea of Justice.* London: Penguin Books. 2010.

Simon, Gyula. *Tanulmányok a Magyar Tanácsköztársaság nevelésügyének köréből* (Studies on the Educational Issues of the Hungarian Republic of Councils). Budapest: 1969.

Simor, András *Így élt Korvin Ottó* (The Life of Ottó Korvin). Budapest: Móra Könyvkiadó. 1977.

Sinkó, Ervin. *Szemben a bíróval* (Face to face with the judge). Budapest: Magvető Kiadó.1983.

Sinkó, Ervin: *Optimisták* (Optimists) Newest ed. Budapest: Noran Libro. 2010.

Sisa Miklós. "A tömeg lelke" (The Soul of the Masses) *Huszadik Század*. August 1916

Sisa Miklós. "A Bolsevizmus Budapestre érkezett." (Bolshevism has Arrived to Budapest) *Szabadgondolat* (Free Thought). 2019. March 1.

Slaughter, Jane. "Humanism versus Feminism in the Socialist Movement: The Life of Angelica Balabanoff," in *European Women on the Left*. Edited by Jane Slaughter and Robert Kern. Westport, CT: Greenwood Press, 1981.

Somogy. Zoltán. *A rémuralom napjaiból – Túszok és egyéb történetek* (The Days of the Reign of Terror: Hostages and other Events). Budapest: Pátria Irodalmi Vállalat és Nyomdai Részvénytársaság, 1922.

Stadler, Friedrich. *The Vienna Circle*. Springer-Verlag, Vienna. 2015.

Stephenson, Scott. *The Final Battle. Soldiers of the Western Front and the German Revolution of 1918*, Cambridge: Cambridge University Press. 2009.

Such, György (ed). *A Magyarországi Tanácslöztársaság* (The Hungarian Republic of Councils). Budapest:The Parliamentary Publishing House. 2020.

Szabó. András. "A Magyar Tanácsköztársaság büntetőjogának fő kérdései" (Key Aspects of the Republic of Councils' Criminal Code) in Pál Halász (ed). Tanulmányok a Magyar Tanácsköztársaság államáról és jogáról (Studies on the State and Legal System of the Republic of Councils) Budapest: 1955.

Szabó, Viktor. *A Magyarországi Tanácsköztársaság propagandája*. (The Propaganda of the Hungarian Republic of Councils) PhD Dissertation submitted to the Doctoral Sudies Program in History of the Károly Eszterházy College. Eger, Hungary. 2016.

Szapor, Judith. *Hungarian Women's Activism in the Wake of the First World War: From Rights to Revanche*. London: Bloomsbury Publishing. 2017.

Szapor, Judit. *A világhírű Polányiak: Egy elfelejtett család regényes története.* (The World Famous Polanyis: A Forgotten Family's Story). Budapest: Aura. 2017

Szemere, Vera: *Az agrárkérdés 1918-1919-ben.* Budapest: 1963.

Szirtes, Zoltán. *Tememetetlen Hallotaink* 1941 Kőrösmező – Kamanyec Podolszk. (Our Unburried Dead). Budapest: Váltóház Kft 1996.

Szőts. Zoltán "Mennyiben következett Bolshevik ideológiából a Vörös Terror" (To What Extent was the Red Terror the result of Bolshevik Ideology). Budapest: *ujkor.hu*. Nov 7, 2019.

Szőts, Zoltán. „A Tanácsköztársaság alternatív büntető politikája" (The Alternative Punitive Policies of the Republic of Councils) In *Újkor.hu*, June 14, 2019.

Tamás, Gáspár Miklós. *Észrevételek a kommünről* (Remarks on the 1919 Commune) in Krausz Tamás – Vértes Judit. *A Magyarországi Tanácsköztársaság és a kelet-európai forradalmak.* Budapest, 2010.

Tamás, Gáspár Miklós. *Másvilág: Politikai esszék* (Other World: Political Essays) Budapest: Új Mandátum. 1994.

Tambakaki, Paulina. "Why spontaneity matters: Rosa Luxemburg and democracies of grief." *Philosophy and Social Criticism.* Vol 47. No 1. 2021.

Tarján Tamás M. „Puccskisérlet a Ludovikán" *Rubicon.* June, 2019.

Tarr, Zoltán. "A Note on Weber and Lukács." *Socialism, Revolution, and Ethics* September, 1989.

Tilly, Charles. *Coercion, Capital, and European States.* New York: Wiley and Blackwell, 1993.

Tokody Gyula. *Németország és a magyarországi Tanácsköztársaság* (Germany and the Hungarian Republic of Councils). Budapest: 1980.

Tormay, Cecile. *Bujdosó Könyv* (An Outlaw's Diary). Budapest, Pallas, 1920.

Tóth, Eszter Zsófia. *A Csepel Vas- és Fémművek munkástanácsainak története és a munkástanács emlékezete* (The history of the workers' councils of Csepel Iron and Metal Works and the memory of the workers' council). Budapest: Manuscript, 2006.

Tóth, Eszter Zsófia. *Kádár Lányai: Nők a szocialista időszakban* (The Daughters of Kádár: Women in Socialist Hungary). Budapest: Nyitott könyvműhely. 2010.

Tóth, Eszter Zsófia and Murai András. *Sex és Szocializmus* (Sex and Socialism). Budapest: Libri. 2014.

Tőkés, Rudolf. *Béla Kun and the Hungarian Soviet Republic: The Origins and Role of the Communist Party of Hungary in the Revolutions of 1918–1919.* New York: F.A. Praeger, 1967.

Tőkés, Rudolf. "Political Transition and Social Transformation in Hungary." CIDOB. Affers Internationals. No. 34-35, 1996.

Tőkés, Rudolf. *Hungary's Negotiated Revolution: Economic Reforms, Social Change, and Political Succession, 1957-1990.* Cambridge: Cambridge University Press, 1996.

Tömöry, Márta. *Új vizeken járok (A Galilei Kör története).* (History of the Galilei Circle). Budapest: Gondolat. 1960.

Tömöry Márta. "Duczynska Ilona feljegyzései az 1918-as januári sztrájk előzményeiről." (The Notes of Ilona Duczynska on the Background of the 1918 General Strike). *Történelmi Szemle.* No 1-2. 1958.Vajda, Mihály. *The State and Socialism.* London: Allison & Busby, 1981.

Varela, Raquel. *A People's History of Europe: From WWI to Today.* London: Pluto. 2021

Varga Lajos: *Kényszerpályáról tévútra. Szociáldemokraták a Tanácsköztársaságban* (The Social Democrats in the Republic of Councils). Budapest: Napvilág Kiadó. 2019.

Varga Lajos: *A szocializálás illúziói és buktatói a proletárdiktatúra első, békés-békétlen hónapjában* (The Illusions of Socialization During the Hungarian Republic of Councils). *Múltunk* No. 4. 2015

Varga, Lajos. *Háború, forradalom, szociáldemokrácia Magyarországon, 1914. július–1919. március* [War, revolution, social democracy in Hungary, July 1914–March, 1919], Budapest: Napvilág., 2010.

Váry, Albert. *A vörös uralom áldozatai Magyarországon* (The Victims of the Reds in Hungary) 3rd Hungarian ed. Budapest, Szegedi nyomda, 1993.

Váry, Albert. *A forradalmak kora. Magyarország története 1918–1920* (The Age of Revolution: Hungary's History, 1918-1920) Budapest: Magyar Szemle Társaság, 1935.

Vermes, Gábor. *The Liberal Vision and Conservative Statecraft of a Magyar Nationalist.* New York: Columbia University Press. 1985.

Vezér, Erzsébet: „Duczynska Ilona" *Élet és Irodalom.* May 6, 1978.

Vértes, György (ed). *A Magyar Tanácsköztársaság kiadványai és az első kommunista kiadványok.* Bibliográfia. Országgyűlési Könyvtár, Budapest, 1958.

Vincze, Edit S. *Az útkeresés évtizedei. Tanulmányok a magyarországi munkásmozgalom történetéből, 1868–1898* [Decades of pathfinding. Essays from the history of the Hungarian labour movements, 1868–1898]. Budapest: Gondolat Könyvkiadó.1977.

Völgyes, Iván (ed). *Hungary in Revolution, 1918-19.* Nine Essays. Lincoln: Nebraska UP. 1971

Uraszov Vlagyimir. "Az orosz forradalmárok segítenek" (The Russian Revolutionaries Will Help) in Lányi, Sarolta (ed). *Nagy idők tanúi emlékeznek(1918–1919)* (The Winesses Remember) Budapest: Kossuth. 1958.

Vrousalis, Nicholas, "Revolutionary Principles and Strategy in the November Revolution: The Case of the USPD", in Kets, Gaard and Muldoon, James, (eds)., *The German Revolution and Political Theory*, Cham (Switzerland), Palgrave Macmillan.2019

Walker, Barrington. *The History of Immigration and Racism in Canada.* Toronto: Canadian Scholars Press, 2008.

Wallerstein. Immanuel. *The Modern World-System*, New York: Academic Press, 1974

Wallerstein. Immanuel. *World Systems Analysis.* Duke University Press. 2004.

Waters, Elizabeth. "In the Shadow of the Comintern: The Communist Women's Movement, 1920-43", in Sonia Kruks, Rayna Rapp, and Marilyn B. Young (eds.), *Promissory Notes: Women in the Transition to Socialism.* New York: Monthly Review Press, 1989.

Weber. Max. *Politics as a Vocation.* New York: Fortress Press, 1965.

Weitz, Eric D. *Creating German Communism, 1890-1990. From Popular Protest to Socialist State*, Princeton: Princeton University Press. 1997.

Zimmermann, Susan. "In and Out of the Cage: Women's and Gender History Written in Hungary in the State-Socialist Period", *Aspasia* 8, No. 1. 2014.

Zimmermann, Susan. *Frauenpolitik und Mannergeverkschaft* (Women's Politics and Men's Trade Unionism: International Gender Politics, Female IFTU Trade Unionists and the Workers' and Women's Movements of the Interwar Period). Vienna. Löcker Verlag. 2021.

Christopher Adam is a Canadian historian (PhD, University of Ottawa). His research focuses on the history of the Hungarian diaspora in Canada. He is Vice President of the Hungarian Studies Association of Canada and a Board Member of the Canada Hungary Educational Foundation. A prolific writer and editor, Dr. Adam is the founding editor and publisher of the largest Hungarian language on-line newspaper — *Kanadai Magyar Hírlap* (Canadian Hungarian News) and also edits, publishes and writes in *The Hungarian Free Press*. He is a frequent speaker and commentator at national and international conferences on the subjects of his expertise.

Magda Aranyossi (1896–1977) joined the Budapest based Galileo Circle of progressive students in 1917 (at the same time as Ilona Duczynska). As a supporter and participant of the 1919 Commune she was forced to emigrate after its collapse. She lived in exile in various European cities as a journalist and activist and was one of the founders in 1934 of the Women's World Committee Against War and Fascism. In 1941, at the height of World War II, she returned to Hungary with her husband to join the underground resistance movement against fascism. After the liberation of Hungary from the Nazis, she became one of the founders of the Hungarian Democratic Women's Association. Aranyossi was a long-term research employee of the Institute of Party History in Budapest and became a pioneering researcher and chronicler of the history of the Hungarian women's movement.

Lajos Csoma is a Hungarian historian (PhD, Loránd Eötvös University, Budapest). His area of expertise is the Hungarian workers' movement of the early 20th century and the Councils that played a prominent role in the 1918–1919 revolutionary period. His essays have appeared in numerous Hungarian language scholarly journals, and he is a frequent speaker at scholarly conferences.

Péter Csunderlik is a Hungarian historian (PhD, Loránd Eötvös University, Budapest). He is an Assistant Professor at Loránd Eötvös University and Research

Fellow of the Institute of Political History in Budapest. His area of expertise is the social history of 19–20th century Europe, focusing on the history of the Austro-Hungarian Monarchy (1871–1919), the intellectual life of the *fin de siècle* era, and left-wing radical movements of the period. He is recognized as one of the leading new historians on the events of 1918–1919. He has written extensively on the subject of his specialization in Hungarian scholarly journals as well as in the mass and social media, including *Radikálisok, szabadgondolkodók, ateisták. A Galilei Kör (1908–1919) története* (Radicals, freethinkers, atheists: The history of the Galilei Circle (1908–1919). Budapest: Napvilág. 2017..

András B. Göllner is a Hungarian born Canadian political economist (PhD, The London School of Economics). One of the Founders of Concordia University's School of Community and Public Affairs, he is now an Emeritus Associate Professor of Political Science at Concordia and an active civil-rights advocate. He was the Founder of the Montréal based civil-rights advocacy group, the Canadian-Hungarian Democratic Charter in 2011. Dr. Göllner is the author/editor of five books, including *Social Change and Corporate Strategy* (1983), *Canada Under Mulroney* (with Daniel Salée, 1988), and his forthcoming biography, *Ilona: Portrait of a Rebel* (2022). His shorter writings have appeared in numerous scholarly journals in Europe and North America, including *Hungarian Cultural Studies, The Journal of Parliamentary Law and Politics, The Canadian-American Review of Hungarian Studies,* as well as on mass and on-line media surfaces including, *The Los Angeles Times, The Huffington Post, The National Post, Social Europe, Élet és Irodalom* (Life and Literature) to mention but a few. His current research focuses on the political language of cyber-capitalism.

Marie-Josée Lavallée is a Quebecoise historian and political philosopher (PhD, Université de Montréal) who teaches in the Department of History of the Université de Montréal. Among her most recent publications is a book on Hannah Arendt, *Lire Platon avec Hannah Arendt: Pensée, politique, totalitarisme* (PUM, 2018) and a chapter "October and the Prospects for Revolution. The Views of Arendt, Adorno, and Marcuse", in *The Russian Revolution as Ideal and Practice: Failures, Legacies, and the Future of Revolution* (Palgrave Macmillan, 2019). She's currently writing a book on the political and intellectual history of the Austrian revolution and preparing a collective volume on Western imperialism. The history, theory, and practices of democracy is the central thrust of her work.

Kari Polanyi-Levitt is a Canadian economist (a graduate of The London School of Economics and the University of Toronto) and is now Emerita Professor of Economics at McGill University. Born in Austria and emigrating to Canada after

WWII, Professor Polanyi-Levitt is the author of numerous books and scholarly publications recognized worldwide for their substantive contribution to political economy and our understanding of the dynamics of economic development. She is a founding member of the Canadian Association for International Development (CASID) and the honorary president of the Karl Polanyi Institute of Political Economy at Concordia University. She is a recipient of an honorary doctorate from the University of the West Indies (2008), the J. K. Galbraith Prize from the Progressive Economics Forum of Canada (2008), the Ifigenia Martinez award from the National University of Mexico (2017), and the Order of Canada (2014).

Dimitrios Roussopoulos is an economist by education but a political activist in daily life and an active ecologist. He lives and works in Montréal but enjoys a world-wide reputation as a writer, editor, publisher—most of his fifteen English-language books have been translated into other languages. He is the Founder of the internationally acclaimed Left-Wing publishing house, Black Rose Books. He is frequently invited to speak at international conferences on his areas of expertise.

Raquel Varela is a Portuguese Historian (PhD, in Political and Institutional History from ISCTE—the University Institute of Lisbon). She teaches at the Institute of Contemporary History at the New University of Lisbon and conducts research at the International Institute of Social History, Amsterdam. Dr. Varela is the founder of the Global Labor Studies Network (New Delhi, India) and serves as Deputy Coordinator of the Labor Studies Network of Portugal. She is the President of the International Strikes and Social Conflicts Association, a network of 35 institutions from Northern and Southern Europe, the USA, and Latin America. She has published numerous highly acclaimed books, including *People's History in the Portuguese Revolution 1974- 1975* (2014) and *A People's History of Europe: From WWI to Today* (2021). Several of her books have been translated into German, English and French. She has also published over 60 articles in peer reviewed journals. She is executive editor of *Critique,* Journal of Socialist Studies (Uni. Glasgow, Scopus 4) and *Workers of the World* (IASSC).

Susan Zimmermann is a university professor at Central European University (Budapest & Vienna) in its Departments of History and Gender Studies. Zimmermann's research brings a critical perspective on the past and present of global inequalities and the unequal international division of labour, as they inform key themes in modern history and interdisciplinary studies. Her current work, within a project funded by the European Research Council focuses on the history of women trade unionists in various political systems in 20th century Europe. Professor Zimmermann is a Founding Member of *The European Labour History*

Network. She is President of *The International Conference of Labour and Social History (ITH)*, since 2014 and a Board Member of *The International Federation for Research into Women's History*, since 2015. She won the *Käthe Leichter Award* in 2000 and is the recipient of many other academic distinctions. She is the author/editor/co-editor of numerous books, most recently: *Frauenpolitik und Mannergeverkschaft* (Women's Politics and Men's Trade Unionism: International Gender Politics, Female IFTU Trade Unionists and the Workers' and Women's Movements of the Interwar Period). (Vienna. Löcker Verlag. 2021) Her articles appeared in such well respected journals as *The International History Review* or *The Journal of Women's History*, to name just two.

Also from Black Rose Books

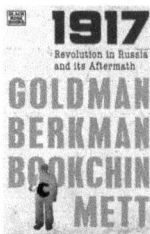

1917: Revolution in Russia and its Aftermath
Emma Goldman, Alexander Berkman, Ida Mett
and Murray Bookchin
Paperback: 978-1-55164-662-6
Hardcover: 978-1-55164-664-0
eBook: 978-1-55164-666-4

1968: On the Edge of World Revolution
Philipp Gassert and Martin Klimke ,eds.
Paperback: 978-1-55164-645-9
Hardcover: 978-1-55164-647-3
eBook: 978-1-55164-649-7

*Your Freedom and Mine: Abdullah Ocalan and
the Kurdish Question in Erdogan's Turkey*
Jeffrey Miley, Federico Venturini, eds.
Paperback: 978-1-55164-668-8
Hardcover: 978-1-55164-670-1
eBook: 978-1-55164-672-5

*Pioneers of Ecological Humanism:
Mumford, Dubos and Bookchin*
Brian Morris
Paperback: 978-1-55164-607-7
Hardcover: 978-1-55164-609-1
eBook: 978-1-55164-611-4

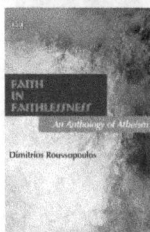

Faith in Faithlessness: An Anthology of Atheism
Dimitri Roussopoulos, ed.
Paperback: 978-1-55164-312-0
Hardcover: 978-1-55164-313-7
eBook: 978-1-55164-626-8

*Enlightenment and Ecology: The Legacy of
Murray Bookchin in the 21st Century*
Yavor Tarinski, ed.
Paperback: 978-1-55164-709-8
Hardcover: 978-1-55164-711-1
eBook: 978-1-55164-713-5

CPSIA information can be obtained
at www.ICGtesting.com
Printed in the USA
JSHW040952110922
30304JS00001B/34

9 781551 647173